MW01284260

Infor

Most social scientists associate politics nearly exclusively with the state. But political agendas are set and achieved in Asian countries as much by "informal politics" as by formal politics conducted within the parameters of institutional, authoritative, and legal structures. Some of the terms associated with informal politics – cronyism, factionalism, *guanxi* (in China) – have negative connotations in a Western context. But the term also includes more publicly accepted forms, such as grassroots activism and other activities that are political but not governed by the general, impersonal rules and procedures set by formal authorities. The authors of *Informal Politics in East Asia* argue that political interaction within the informal dimension (behind-the-scenes politics) is at least as common and influential, although not always as transparent or coherent, as formal politics, and that this understudied category of social interaction merits more serious and methodical attention from social scientists.

This book is a pioneering effort to delineate the various forms of informal politics within different East Asian political cultures and to develop some common theoretical principles for understanding how they work. Featured here are contributions by political scientists specializing in the regions of China, Taiwan, Japan, the Korean peninsula, and Vietnam. The common thread across these political cultures is a Confucian legacy that emphasizes personal relationships and reciprocity. The authors apply to this dynamic region the classic core questions of politics: Who gets what, when, how, and at whose expense?

Lowell Dittmer is Professor of Political Science at the University of California, Berkeley.

Haruhiro Fukui is Professor Emeritus of Political Science at the University of California, Santa Barbara.

Peter N. S. Lee is Professor of Political Science in the Department of Government and Public Administration at The Chinese University of Hong Kong.

INFORMAL POLITICS IN EAST ASIA

Edited by
LOWELL DITTMER
University of California, Berkeley

HARUHIRO FUKUI
University of California, Santa Barbara

PETER N. S. LEE
*The Chinese University
of Hong Kong*

CAMBRIDGE
UNIVERSITY PRESS

PUBLISHED BY THE PRESS SYNDICATE OF THE UNIVERSITY OF CAMBRIDGE
The Pitt Building, Trumpington Street, Cambridge, United Kingdom

CAMBRIDGE UNIVERSITY PRESS
The Edinburgh Building, Cambridge CB2 2RU, UK   http://www.cup.cam.ac.uk
40 West 20th Street, New York, NY 10011-4211, USA   http://www.cup.org
10 Stamford Road, Oakleigh, Melbourne 3166, Australia
Ruiz de Alarcón 13, 28014 Madrid, Spain

First published 2000

Printed in the United States of America

Typeface Garamond 3 11/13 pt.   *System* QuarkXPress [BTS]

A catalog record for this book is available from the British Library.

Library of Congress Cataloging-in-Publication Data
Informal politics in East Asia / edited by Lowell Dittmer, Haruhiro
Fukui, Peter N.S. Lee.
    p.   cm.
    Includes index.
    ISBN 0-521-64232-9 (hb.). — ISBN 0-521-64538-7 (pb.)
    1. Political culture—East Asia.   2. East Asia—Politics and
government.   I. Dittmer, Lowell.   II. Fukui, Haruhiro, 1935–   .
III. Lee, Peter N.S., 1940–   .
JQ1499.A58I54   2000
306.2'095—dc21   99-40245
                                                                          CIP

ISBN 0521 64232 9 hardback
ISBN 0521 64538 7 paperback

CONTENTS

PREFACE

This edited volume represents the homecoming of a scholarly odyssey lasting more than a decade and spanning 10,000 miles from one side of the Pacific to the other. We now find that our intellectual debts are so heavy and our creditors so numerous that we could not possibly repay or even mention them all.[1] In terms of intellectual origins the book represents a confluence of at least two currents: In the study of Japanese politics, it can be traced to Haruhiro Fukui's pioneering interest in the gaps between formal rules and actual political behavior, resulting for example in his attempt to explain the "consistent inconsistencies" between the theoretically expected and the actual results of every change in Japanese electoral laws since the late nineteenth century.[2] In the study of Chinese politics, although seasoned China-watchers have had an intuitive grasp of informal politics for some time, its methodologically self-conscious analysis dates from a debate between Andrew Nathan and Tang Tsou in the pages of the *American Political Science Review* and the subsequent intellectual fermentation of Tsou's teachings among his students (including Lowell Dittmer, Joseph Fewsmith, Peter Lee, and Ben Ostrov).[3] These two currents converged in the Santa Barbara–based research project, "Informal Politics in East Asia," codirected by Fukui and Dittmer and generously endowed with two-year funding (1991–1993) by the Pacific Rim Research Program of the University of California.[4] This enabled us to put together a research team consisting initially of recruits from the UC campuses and later cross-fertilized by other interested scholars. Though fluctuating in membership with changes in academic schedules and research interests,

1 In addition to those named below, we wish to thank Naomi Chazan, Susan McEachern, and Guoliang Zhang for their most useful contributions to this project.
2 Haruhiro Fukui, "Electoral laws and the Japanese party system," in Gail Lee Bernstein and Haruhiro Fukui, eds., *Japan and the World: Essays in Japanese History and Politics* (New York: St. Martin's Press, 1988), pp. 119–143.
3 A fuller account is provided in Dittmer, this volume, Chapter 2.
4 We are particularly indebted to Martha Kendall Winnacker, who was the Program Officer at the time.

this team covered not only the relevant theoretical perspectives, but the major representative East Asian political systems, making our project genuinely comparative and cross-cultural.

The book stems from but is by no means limited to a series of panels on informal politics at the annual meetings of the African Studies Association, the American Political Science Association, the Association of Asian Studies, and an international symposium in Hong Kong, held in 1989, 1990, 1992, and 1993. The panel on informal politics in Africa and Asia in 1989 was organized with the help of Professors Victor T. LeVine and Rene Lamarchand, and it also included presentations by Kelley Kun-mi Hwang and Ruth Iyob (UC Santa Barbara), and Haruhiro Fukui and Shigeko N. Fukai. The 1990 panel at the APSA meeting included papers on informal politics in China by Lowell Dittmer and Yu-shan Wu (Taiwan National University), on Korea by Hwang, and on Japan by Fukui and Fukai. The panel, "Informal Politics of Leadership Recruitment in East Asia," organized for the 1992 AAS Annual Meeting, included papers on China by Dittmer, on Korea by Soohyon Chon, on Japan by Fukui and Fukai, and on Taiwan by Tun-jen Cheng, with Fukui doubling as chair and Brian Woodall (UC Irvine, later Harvard) serving as discussant. A few months later, several members of the team attended a symposium on informal politics in East Asia organized by Peter Lee at the Chinese University of Hong Kong. Cosponsored by the UC-based project and the China Reform and Development Programme of the Hong Kong Institute of Asian-Pacific Studies, the symposium heard papers by Chon, Dittmer, Fukui and Fukai, and Hwang from the UC side, and by Lee, M. C. Lo, Benjamin Ostrov, and King Tsao from CUHK; serving as discussants were Yasheng Huang (University of Michigan, now Harvard Business School), Chien Chiao (Institute of Ethnology, Academica Sinica), Elizabeth Heiman (UC Santa Barbara), Janet Landa (York University), Byron Weng and Chinan Chen (CUHK), and Yih-jiun Liu (Academica Sinica's Sun Yat-sen Institute for Social Science and Philosophy). In 1993, a second (tandem) panel was organized for the AAS Annual Meeting on "Informal Politics and Economic Development" in communist and noncommunist systems, which included papers by Ying-mao Kau (Brown University), Guoliang Zhang (UC Berkeley), Woodall, Chon, and Dittmer; serving as discussants were Brantly Womack (University of Virginia) and T. J. Cheng.

The next three years were devoted to revisions and compilation for publication of a selection of the outstanding papers from this series of conferences as augmented by contributions solicited from distinguished scholars whose interests coincided. Three of the papers appeared in quite different forms in a special edition of *Asian Survey* in March 1996, to which Robert Scalapino (UC Berkeley) wrote a succinct but lucid introduction. All benefit from numerous critical commentaries, both anonymous and solicited, and from seminars and informal conversations with colleagues.

The book thus marks the culmination of a research project launched a decade ago but hopefully not the end of the investigation of informal politics, with its potentially far-reaching implications. Needless to say, none of the individuals or organizations mentioned above is to blame for any flaws to be found in the book; for these, the editors and contributors accept full responsibility.

Lowell Dittmer, Haruhiro Fukui, and Peter N. S. Lee

CONTRIBUTORS

T. J. Cheng is Professor of Government and Chair of the East Asian Studies Committee at the College of William and Mary.

Soohyun Chon, former Assistant Professor in the Department of Geography and Geology at Victoria University of Wellington, New Zealand, and Fellow of the Center for Korean Studies at the University of California in Berkeley, is an independent scholar.

T. C. Chou is Professor of Economics at the National Chung-hsing University, Taiwan.

Lowell Dittmer is Professor of Political Science at the University of California, Berkeley.

Joseph Fewsmith is Associate Professor of International Relations at Boston University.

Shigeko N. Fukai is Professor of the Law Faculty at Okayama University, Japan.

Haruhiro Fukui is Professor Emeritus of Political Science at the University of California, Santa Barbara.

Samuel S. Kim is Adjunct Professor of Political Science and Senior Research Associate at the East Asian Institute, Columbia University.

Peter Nan-shong Lee is Professor of Political Science in the Department of Government and Public Administration at The Chinese University of Hong Kong.

Benjamin C. Ostrov is Associate Professor in the Department of Government and Public Administration at the Chinese University of Hong Kong.

Douglas Pike is Adjunct Professor of History and Director of Research at the Vietnam Center, Texas Tech University.

Lu Xiaobo is Assistant Professor of Political Science at Barnard College and Fellow of the East Asian Institute at Columbia University.

Chung-fang Yang is Associate Professor in the Department of Psychology at Hong Kong University.

INTRODUCTION:
ON THE SIGNIFICANCE OF
INFORMAL POLITICS

HARUHIRO FUKUI

A PERSPECTIVE, DEFINITIONS, AND EXAMPLES

Politics is, in Harold Lasswell's elegantly spare definition, "Who gets what, when, how."[1] At the expense of its elegance of parsimony, we might embellish it a little as: "Who gets what, when, how, and at whose expense." The last phrase is added to make it explicit that politics is concerned with the distribution not only of the benefits derived from the use or consumption of goods and services, but also the costs required for their production and supply. The "what" here is to be understood as primarily a public, as opposed to private, good or service. Since, however, who gets a public good or service, how, and at whose expense critically affects who gets a private good or service, how, and at whose expense, we would leave the "what" in Lasswell's original formulation alone.

We adopt this broad and open-ended definition of politics rather than David Easton's well known but more restrictive definition: "authoritative allocation of values."[2]

As we will attempt to explain in this introduction and the chapters that follow, we believe, for both ontological and epistemological reasons, that any allocation of the costs and benefits of the production, distribution, and consumption of public goods and services – whether authoritative or questionable, legitimate or illegitimate, legal or illegal, overt or covert – is fundamentally political and therefore a proper subject for investigation by the political scientist. As we shall see, insistence on the authoritativeness of a political allocation would lead to a narrowly state-centric view of politics and limit the scope of our investigation unnecessarily and unjustifiably narrowly, leaving many of the most interesting and important issues of real-world politics outside of that scope. As another author notes, "Politics is everywhere, and not just in the hands of governments."[3]

1 Harold D. Lasswell, *Politics: Who Gets What, When, How* (New York: McGraw-Hill, 1936).
2 David Easton, *The Political System* (New York: Knopf, 1953), p. 129.
3 Ken Booth, "75 years on: Rewriting the subject's past – reinventing its future," in Steve Smith, Ken Booth, and Marysia Zalewski, eds., *International Theory: Positivism & Beyond* (Cambridge: Cambridge University Press, 1996), p. 337.

By comparison, our broader definition leads us to pay attention to the diverse and complex ways in which politics occurs in a variety of social organizations and groups in addition to the state. Such organizations include "labor unions, churches and sects, professional societies, business and trade associations, fraternal organizations, recreational clubs, civic service associations, political parties, social welfare councils, communes and other 'collectivist' organizations," as David Knoke suggests, or "state, empire, leopard-skin chief, moiety elder, etc.," as a contributor to an international encyclopedia of sociology put it.[4] We also believe, as we will argue later, that excessive emphasis on and preoccupation with the "authoritative" character of a political allocation would lead to false and misleading distinctions between state-level politics on the one hand and both infrastate-level (domestic) and suprastate-level (international) politics on the other. It is our view that politics is politics, driven by a common logic and dynamics and falling in similar and comparable, if not identical, forms and patterns at all three levels.

The "who, when, and how" of politics are determined not simply by the balance of power obtaining between actors, whether individuals or organizations, but also, and often more effectively, by an existing set or sets of rules. A rule is, by definition, a prescription for some types or forms of behavior and proscription against others. An internally coherent set of rules applicable to a large but specific and bounded functional area – such as economy, religion, and education, or a large segment of such an area, such as banking, priesthood, and higher education – is called an *institution*. There are thus economic, religious, and educational institutions, and so there are also banking, ecclesiastical, and higher educational institutions. Politics, too, is governed by a variety of political institutions, such as constitutional, legislative, administrative, judicial, electoral, party, interest group, and so on. Within an effectively institutionalized area, a political actor may defy or ignore a relevant institution at his or her own peril. To survive, not to mention thrive, within a given institutional setting, an actor had better abide by and adapt to its rules.

Some rules and institutions are deliberately created by an established authority – either a king, emperor, "leopard-skin chief, moiety elder," or a popularly elected president or parliament – to apply, at least in principle, to all actors in the relevant area or areas. Such rules and institutions are explicit, definite, and usually written. We define the kind of politics that is governed by such rules and institutions as *formal*. Just as often, however, rules and institutions are not deliberately created by an established authority, but

4 David Knoke, "The political economies of association," *Research in Political Sociology: A Research Annual*, vol. 1, p. 212; Michael Mann, ed., *The International Encyclopedia of Sociology* (New York: Continuum Publishing Company, 1984), p. 290.

instead they simply evolve as "conventions and codes of behavior."[5] Politics governed by such informal rules and institutions is what is meant here by *informal* politics. This is the kind of politics described by Douglas Pike in his chapter on Vietnam as "interpersonal activities stemming from a tacitly accepted, but unenunciated, matrix of political attitudes exisitng outside the framework of legal government, constitutions, bureaucratic constructs and similar institutions."

Formal politics is unquestionably very important. Decisions made and actions taken by recognized authorities tend to be not only very visible and easily known to most members of the organization concerned, but they are also effectively enforceable. Moreover, such politics also tend to become well institutionalized and impersonal, with set rules and procedures applied consistently across issues and actors. This type of politics is widely known and applauded as one under "the rule of law." The Civil Rights Act passed by the U.S. Congress in 1964 dramatically changed the allocation of educational and employment opportunities available to American blacks, as compared to whites. The Equal Employment Opportunities Act passed by the Japanese Diet (parliament) in 1985 had considerably less dramatic but nonetheless very significant impacts on the allocation of employment and promotion opportunities for Japanese women, as compared to Japanese men. A formal decision made by a labor union's executives for or against striking a company may critically affect the allocation of profits or losses between the company's management, stockholders, and employees, as may a decision by the management for or against negotiating a compromise with the union.

Without underestimating, much less denying, the obvious importance of formal politics in the lives of both individuals and organizations, however, we argue that informal politics that is not governed by general and impersonal rules and procedures set by formal authorities is no less important. Often equated with the "rule of man," as opposed to the "rule of law," this type of politics is nearly universally suspect and often condemned as arbitrary, unfair, or corrupt. Besides, the workings of such politics tend to be sporadic, erratic, and invisible, making them much harder than formal politics for outsiders to observe in detail, describe accurately, and explain coherently. Nonetheless, there is an overwhelming amount of evidence of the ubiquitous presence and pervasive influence of informal politics in both the scholarly literature and journalistic accounts of politics in wide-ranging societies and organizations.

The chapters that follow will present such evidence from several East Asian societies in considerable detail. Here, let me cite just a few illustrative

---

5 Douglass C. North, *Institutions, Institutional Change and Economic Performance* (Cambridge: Cambridge University Press, 1990), p. 4.

examples from writings on Japanese politics. In a now classic text on the Japanese Diet, Hans Baerwald took pains to emphasize the wide gaps that separated formal institutions and actual practice in Japan's parliamentary politics.[6] In a best-selling book published two decades later, one of the most prominent and shrewdest insiders of that politics, Ichiro Ozawa, echoes Baerwald's observation by declaring that institutions based on the Japanese constitution and other laws are only formal (*tatemaejo no*) sets of rules that have little to do with actual practice.[7] For example, Diet resolutions that have no constitutional basis are often used to block controversial government actions, because, while a statute may be revised by a majority vote, under the customary rule a Diet resolution may be revised or repealed only by a unanimous vote.[8] Likewise, while the Budget Committee of either house is in session, no other standing committee of that house may meet; questions asked from the floor during a meeting of a Diet committee are answered not by ministers but by senior officials of various ministries, and so on.[9]

Informal politics is as pervasive, if not more so, in the Japanese world of law itself, according to Frank Upham. Detailed case studies of the politics of environmental protection, civil rights movements, and industrial policy lead him to conclude that legal informality overwhelms formal processes of litigation in Japan:

> Meetings may be scheduled and public testimony received, research commissions formed, reports published, elaborate plans of action drafted and approved by competent government officials, and concrete action urged by powerful ministries; but nothing in the process will rise to the level of a legally cognizable act that could become the object of litigation challenging the process as a whole or any step therein.[10]

FORMAL POLITICS AS STATE-CENTRIC POLITICS

Despite the prevalence of informal politics and the widespread recognition of the phenomenon in the literature, formal politics has been treated by most social scientists as the normal and orthodox form of politics, while informal politics, such as factionalism and cronyism, is often treated as if it were an abnormal and deviant form. This is probably because most social scientists

6 Hans H. Baerwald, *Japan's Parliament: An Introduction* (New York: Cambridge University Press, 1974), pp. 121–126.
7 Ichiro Ozawa, *Nihon kaizo keikaku* [A plan for reforming Japan] (Tokyo: Kodansha, 1993), p. 56.
8 Ibid., pp. 42–43.
9 Ibid., pp. 63, 79.
10 Frank K. Upham, *Law and Social Change in Postwar Japan* (Cambridge, MA: Harvard University Press, 1987), p. 22.

associate politics exclusively or nearly exclusively with the state. They understand by politics, as Max Weber put it, "only the leadership, or the influencing of the *state*," or, as the authors of a popular introductory political
science textbook put it, activities that are "centrally, even though not exclusively, concerned with the state . . ."[11] This singular concentration on the state
as the arena or matrix of politics is not surprising, considering the facts that
the state is a political organization par excellence, that politics is far more
extensively and effectively formalized in the state than in any other type of
organization, and, above all, that the modern state is accorded sovereign
power and status.

The sovereignty of the state has been "a defining element" of the Euro-
centric international order since the seventeenth century.[12] The conception
of the sovereign state was in fact inherent in the process through which the
modern state was created in early modern Europe, in the age of the Thirty
Years' War (1618–48) and the Treaty of Westphalia (1648). The absolutist
state in early modern Europe established its authority by conquering and, to
a large extent, absorbing all other types of organization, such as the guild,
estate, and, above all, church, that had not only enjoyed extensive autonomy
but maintained effective control of large territories and populations in
medieval Europe. The Catholic church in particular had exercised strong secular as well as religious power and competed with the medieval empire until
the rise of the modern state.[13] The latter's claim to sovereign status gave birth
to "a vision of the state, or rather of the crown, as a 'public' authority standing for some general principle or interest over and above the myriad 'private'
interests which made up society."[14] This process coincided with the emergence of the concept of the "political," a concept that had not existed before
the thirteenth century. The absence of the concept accounts, to an important
extent, for the autonomy and power of the pope vis-à-vis kings and emperors in medieval Europe. The simultaneous births of the concepts of the sovereign state and that of the political in the history of Western thought thus
lies behind the close bond between the two concepts in contemporary political science writings.

The absolutist state of seventeenth-century Europe has since evolved into
the modern democratic state. The American and French revolutions of the

---

11 For the quotation from Weber, see H. H. Gerth and C. Wright Mills, eds., *From Max Weber: Essays
in Sociology* (New York: Oxford University Press, 1958), p. 77; and for the second quotation, see Roland
J. Pennock and David C. Smith, *Political Science: An Introduction* (New York: Macmillan, 1964), pp.
8–9.
12 Gidon Gottlieb, *Nation Against State: A New Approach to Ethnic Conflicts and the Decline of Sovereignty*
(New York: Council on Foreign Relations, 1993), p. 19.
13 John Breilly, *Nationalism and the State* (Chicago: University of Chicago Press, 1985), p. 46.
14 Ibid., pp. 50–52.

eighteenth century played a catalytic role in this evolutionary process. Throughout Western Europe and North America, and increasingly in other regions of the world, the process has involved the supersession of monarchical sovereignty by popular sovereignty. It has not, however, involved any significant decline in the formal power and prerogatives of the state as such, whether internally or externally. The contemporary state has in fact become "the standard form" of political organization at the expense of all other forms and standards, and it attempts "to regulate a far greater sphere of human transactions in far greater detail than its predecessors ever attempted."[15]

The expansion of the power of the state has been underpinned by the increasingly universal belief that the state, and the state alone, can provide public security and advance public interests for a people in the modern world. Many peoples outside of Europe, including all in Asia, have adopted both the concept and the standard institutions of the modern state modeled on the European sovereign state, thanks either to imposition by colonial rulers or to imitation by Asia's own elites.[16] Wherever it is found, the contemporary state claims and exercises the sovereign right not only to allocate public goods and services but, more importantly, to set authoritative rules, criteria, and standards for the allocation of values. It is the central vehicle for the delivery of *bonheur public* in the contemporary world.[17]

Despite its vaunted status and reputation, however, the state is a notoriously slippery concept that is subject to diverse and often mutually contradictory interpretations. In his famous definition, Weber identified it as "a system of order (that) claims binding authority" over all of its members and their actions.[18] A more contemporary definition identifies it as a set of institutions endowed with coercive power and control of a territory within the boundary of which it monopolizes rule-making and rule-enforcement authority.[19] Either definition, however, permits the creation of a virtually infinite variety of states: They may be large or small, strong or weak, independent or dependent, monarchical or republican, democratic or autocratic, liberal or authoritarian, religious or secular, national or ethnic, unitary or federal, ad infinitum.

15 Robert H. Jackson and Alan James, "The character of independent states," in Robert H. Jackson and Alan James, eds., *States in a Changing World: A Contemporary Analysis* (Oxford: Clarendon Press, 1993), pp. 4, 5.
16 Lucian W. Pye, *Asian Power and Politics: The Cultural Dimensions of Authority* (Cambridge, MA: Harvard University Press, 1985), p. 285.
17 Laura Balbo, "Family, women, and the state: Notes toward a typology of family roles and public intervention," in Charles S. Maier, ed., *Changing Boundaries of the Political: Essays on the Evolving Balance Between the State and Society, Public and Private in Europe* (Cambridge: Cambridge University Press, 1987), pp. 202–203.
18 Max Weber, *Economy and Society: An Outline of Interpretive Sociology*, ed. Guenther Roth and Claus Wittich; trans. Ephraim Fischoff et al. (New York: Bedminster Press, 1968), Vol. 1, p. 56.
19 John A. Hall, "State," in Joel Krieger, ed., *The Oxford Companion to Politics of the World* (Oxford: Oxford University Press, 1993), p. 878.

As Easton once put it, the state thus serves as "a symbol for unity . . . a myth," rather than as a tool of a scientific investigation.[20] It should therefore be treated as "a conceptual variable," as J. P. Nettl suggests,[21] and examined, as Timothy Mitchell argues, "not as an actual structure, but as the powerful, metaphysical effect of practices that make up such structures appear to exist."[22] In other words, the modern state is more an ideological product than an empirical phenomenon. It may be created, transformed, or destroyed almost at will by its members, its leaders, its friends, or its enemies. A single unified ethnic state of Germany or Korea may be divided into two rival ideological states; a single unified multinational Soviet or Yugoslavic state may be divided into multiple separate ethnic states; two rival ideological Korean or Chinese states may be united someday into single national states; a part of a binational Canadian state might be turned into a separate national state. "Stateness" is thus a matter not only of degree but of will, faith, and strategy.

Similar elements of elusiveness and arbitrariness characterize the boundary and relationship between the state and society. The idea that the two ought to be distinct and separate from each other has prevailed since the eighteenth century in both liberal and Catholic streams of Western political thought, especially in Catholic liberalism.[23] The idea springs partly from the belief that, as Alexis de Tocqueville put it, so as to maintain Christianity "at any cost in the bosom of modern democracies," the priesthood must be "shut up within the sanctuary" rather than allowed to step beyond it.[24] The belief in the separation and dichotomy between public political and private social spheres is a twin to the belief in the separation and dichotomy between a liberal state and Christian society.

In practice, however, the conceptual distinction between the state and society in Western political thought has been steadily eroded by the progressive intrusion of state power into society until the two spheres have been virtually fused. The process reached its peak in the emergence of the welfare state in the middle of the twentieth century. In Great Britain, for example, state power penetrated into wide-ranging areas of what had been considered private domain in the 1950s and 1960s.[25] This development led

---

20 Easton, *The Political System*, pp. 111–112.

21 Cited in Hagen Koo, "Strong state and contentious society," in Hagen Koo, ed., *State and Society in Contemporary Korea* (Ithaca: Cornell University Press, 1993), p. 235.

22 Timothy Mitchell, "The limits of the state: Beyond statist approaches and their critics," *American Political Science Review* 85:1 (March 1991), p. 94.

23 Alain Touraine, "An introduction to the study of social movements," *Social Research* 52:4 (Winter 1985), pp. 775–776.

24 Alexis de Tocqueville, *Democracy in America* (New York: Random House, 1945), Vol. 2, Book 2, Chap. 15, p. 156, quoted in Susanne Berger, "Religious transformation and the future of politics," in Maier, *Changing Boundaries*, pp. 122–123.

25 Balbo, "Family, women, and the state," p. 208.

to a blurring of the conceptual and ideological boundary between state and society.

The development also led, belatedly, to the realization that the boundary between state and society is, like the state itself, not an empirical fact but a purely conceptual creation. It is, as Mitchell puts it, "not the perimeter of an intrinsic entity, which can be thought of as a free-standing object or actor," but just "a line drawn internally, *within* the network of institutional mechanisms through which a certain social and political order is maintained," that is, it *"never marks a real exterior."*[26] Many contemporary social issues are then, as theorists of new social movements argue, neither a priori private and non-political nor a priori public and political.[27] There can also be a "space of 'political action within civil society'" that such movements may claim.[28] Civil society thus becomes "a domain of struggles, public spaces, and political processes . . . the social realm in which the creation of norms, identities, and social relations of domination and resistance are located."[29]

The fusion of state and society, however, has always been the part and parcel of Asian, particularly Confucian, theory of politics. As Hagen Koo points out, the two "constitute a moral and ethical unity, inseparable from each other."[30] Moreover, society, and the household in particular, is the model for the state, rather than the other way around, in this theory. A sixth-century Chinese scholar-official, Yan Zhitui, thus observed: "when the father is not kind, the son is not filial, ... The gentleness tempered with severity used in governing the household is indeed like that which is required in governing the state."[31] The tradition has survived to varying degrees in most East Asian societies, including North Korea under Kim Il Sung's rule. Bruce Cummings comments: "In Kim's praxis, like Confucianism, the family unit becomes a model for structuring the state, the ultimate metaphor for organizing everything under heaven, including international relations."[32]

Interestingly, the conceptual fusion and interpenetration between the state and society in Asian societies has not led, as has the conceptual separation between the two in Western societies, to the domination of society by the state. In South Korea, for example, civil society has remained resistant, and

---

26 Mitchell, "The limits of the state," p. 90.
27 Claus Offe, "Challenging the boundaries of institutional politics: Social movements since the 1960s," in Maier, *Changing Boundaries*, p. 69.
28 Ibid., p. 72.
29 Jean L. Cohen, "Strategy on identity: New theoretical paradigms and contemporary social movements," *Social Research* 52:4 (Winter 1985), p. 700.
30 Koo, "Strong state and contentious society," p. 238.
31 Cited from Arthur F. Wright, ed., *The Confucian Persuasion* (Stanford: Stanford University Press, 1966), pp. 6–7, in Pye, *Asian Power and Politics*, pp. 41–42.
32 Bruce Cumings, "The corporate state in North Korea," in Koo, *State and Society*, pp. 212–213.

even subversive and combative, toward the state throughout its history. In fact, this was true even during the Japanese colonial rule. According to Koo, the colonial state failed to eliminate "subterranean networks of resistance movements, peasant and labor organizations, and intellectual circles. . . ."[33] Nor did the Chinese communist state manage to subjugate a defiant society in implementing its key policies. The one child per family policy, for example, was resisted and sabotaged not only by many villagers but also by local cadres of the Chinese Communist Party itself. As Tyrene White points out, many cadres were "villagers first and cadres second," and both violated the law themselves and chose to "interpret the guidelines loosely in line with local people's wishes."[34]

Even if we accepted the state-centric definition of politics, we would thus be compelled to conclude that politics has crossed the boundary between the state and society in modern Western societies, in premodern and modern Confucian societies in East Asia, and inferentially in many others. As we suggested at the outset, however, politics is found not only in the state but in any and every type of organized social group. Competition and conflicts between the state and various social groups within it are also important forms of politics that are played out in "a sphere that overlaps civil society and the state, a sphere where the relationship between the two is fought out."[35]

Nor are we alone in finding "infrastate politics" in a variety of organizations within a state. For example, in a perceptive comment on the nature of politics in many African societies, Naomi Chazan writes: "Politics . . . takes place well beyond the narrower public domain in African nations. Power . . . may legitimately be vested in local social structures as well."[36] According to Lucian Pye, *bapakism*, which refers to a fictive relationship between a father figure (*bapak*) and a circle of "children" (*anak buah*), pervades the Indonesian bureaucracy and "may be a factor in linking together different principal figures along lines which may or may not follow the formal hierarchy of the bureaucracy."[37] Pye also notes that each of the 2,000 or so subdivisions (*jati*) in the Hindu caste system "could handle its own problems of discipline through its respective panchayat, or council of elders."[38] In a provocative study of Japan's industrialization, David Friedman argues that the politics that had significant bearings on its process had little to do with

33 Koo, "Strong state and contentious society," pp. 232, 237.
34 Tyrene White, "Postrevolutionary mobilization in China: The one-child policy reconsidered," *World Politics* 43:1 (October 1990), pp. 67, 70–71.
35 Paul Starr and Ellen Immergut, "Health care and the boundaries of politics," in Maier, *Changing Boundaries*, p. 222.
36 Naomi Chazan, "Patterns of state-society incorporation and disengagement in Africa," in Donald Rothchild and Naomi Chazan, eds., *The Precarious Balance: State and Society in Africa* (Boulder: Westview Press, 1988), p. 123.
37 Pye, *Asian Power and Politics*, p. 306.   38 Ibid., p. 47.

the state but much to do with worker careers, subcontractor coordination, regionalism, and the like."[39] He then concludes: "Ultimately, Japan sustains the idea that we must address politics throughout society if we are to address a country's economic change."[40]

If the concept of infrastate politics is a little hard for some people to grasp, that of suprastate politics should not be. International politics has been as real and as widely recognized a form of politics as state-level politics since long before the Peace of Westphalia. Moreover, both the reality and importance of suprastate politics have vastly increased in the last few decades, as states have increasingly intervened in each other's domestic affairs while more and more suprastate organizations have been formed and come to play roles that are nearly equal, if not superior, to those of individual states as mechanisms for determining "who gets what, when, how, at whose expense" within as well as among states. The United Nations as well as the European Union today enjoy a legal and diplomatic standing among, but increasingly independent of, the individual states of which they consist. In many ways, in fact, suprastate organizations stand above and dictate to many states, if not to the most powerful among them, as may be witnessed from the United Nations' peace-keeping operations, the International Atomic Energy Agency's on-site inspections of local nuclear facilities, the International Monetary Fund's imposition of stringent conditionalities on its loans to member states, and so on.[41] International politics at the end of the twentieth century is thus decreasingly interstate politics and increasingly suprastate politics. Moreover, the distinctions between state-level politics on the one hand and both infrastate-level and suprastate-level politics on the other are increasingly irrelevant in a world where, as Ken Booth puts it, "the global is local and the local is global."[42]

Some authors even argue that the state today is withering away. Alberto Melucci, for example, writes:

> nation-states are extinguishing themselves not because of socialism . . . but because they lose authority; from above, a planetary, multinational political and economic interdependence shifts the center of actual decision-making elsewhere; from below, multiplication of autonomous centers of decision gives "civil society" power it never had during the development of modern states.[43]

---

39 David Friedman, *The Misunderstood Miracle: Industrial Development and Political Change in Japan* (Ithaca: Cornell University Press, 1988), pp. 17–20, 209–210.
40 Ibid., p. 211.
41 Gottlieb, *Nation Against State*, pp. 18, 39.
42 Booth, "75 years on," p. 330.
43 Alberto Melucci, "The symbolic challenge of contemporary movements," *Social Research* 52:4 (Winter 1985), p. 808.

In the same vein, Gidon Gottlieb speaks of a "deconstruction of (state) sovereignty and the reallocation of its attributes" as "a key feature of the architecture of the new European Community."[44]

These observations are provocative and may well be quite correct. It is not our intention, however, to endorse these views but simply to argue that, first, the traditional state-centric view of politics is unwarranted both empirically and theoretically; second, politics at either the infrastate or suprastate level does not differ qualitatively from politics at the state level; and, third, informal politics is as important as formal politics at all three levels. We believe that our preoccupation with state-level politics predisposes us to concentrate on formal politics at the expense of informal politics and of a deeper and sounder understanding of politics as such. To our minds, the basic rules of politics, "who gets what, when, how, at whose expense," at those three levels are identical and can be examined by identical methods and approaches.

The shift of our attention from state to both infrastate and suprastate arenas of politics and from formal to informal forms of politics is probably pertinent in the study of politics in any part of the world. If we believe Pye's observations, however, such a shift seems particularly apposite to the study of politics in East Asian societies. He speaks of "a wide divide" in the Chinese polity "between formal government emanating from the imperial and national capital, and the private governance that rules the daily lives of people through family institutions, clan associations, secret societies, trade and professional organizations, and a variety of *hui-guan*, or co-provincial clubs."[45] If we are "to uncover the actual flow of power," then we must "look through the formal arrangements of authority to the dynamics of the informal relationships, which generate the substance of power that is ultimately decisive in determining political developments."[46] Likewise, in Indonesian politics the formal structures of government may seem tidy and the people may seem to understand hierarchy and defer to superiors; however, "the rules that govern the operation of the formal structures of government are not abstract laws and regulations, but they usually reflect the influence of the informal power relationships."[47]

FUNCTIONS AND ORGANIZATIONAL FORMS OF INFORMAL POLITICS

Why are informal politics so pervasive, particularly in East Asian societies? One plausible explanation is suggested by Pye when he writes about Chinese politics:

44 Gottlieb, *Nation Against State*, pp. 38–39.   45 Pye, *Asian Power and Politics*, p. 292.
46 Ibid., p. 285.   47 Ibid., pp. 310–311.

> In most situations, whether in the party, the bureaucracy, or in nongovernmental institutions such as schools and factories, too many people are waiting in line for advancement and too few openings exist for the formal procedures to do the job of selection. Therefore everyone must prudently seek *guanxi* ties . . . within the (Chinese) bureaucracy the formal regulations tend to be overly constrictive, producing cumbersome procedures and little effective action. Communication, to say nothing of coordination, among offices and bureaus tends to be slow. Hence the informal structures of power built through the *guanxi* networks often serve as the most effective way of getting the state's business done.[48]

A more fundamental reason may be the patent impossibility for the central authority of an organization at any level – state, infrastate, or suprastate – to make and enforce formal rules for all actual and potential conflicts over "who gets what, when, how, at whose expense" that may occur between individuals and groups within the organization. Only in an ideal totalitarian organization is it conceivable for the central authority to be so omnipresent and omnipotent. In real-world organizations, including the state, there must remain a large number of political disputes, whether overt or covert, that are not and cannot be resolved by formal rules and procedures, that is, by means of formal politics, and therefore are necessarily left to informal rules for resolution. In other words, an important function of informal politics is to fill in lacunae in the reach of formal politics. This function must be particularly critical in organizations with a weak tradition of the rule of law, such as most states in East Asia. An important function of informal politics is thus to complement formal politics.

The relationship between formal and informal politics is, however, far more diverse and complex, as the authors of the chapters that follow point out in a variety of contexts. Benjamin Ostrov's study, for example, shows that formal relationships formed between individuals within a particular Chinese government office may evolve into lasting informal ties, which may in turn lubricate transactions between the different offices where those individuals end up. The close and interdependent relationship may be "mutually enhancing at best and mutually corrupting at worst," as Samuel Kim remarks. An example of a mutually enhancing relationship may be found in the way in which the renovation movement (*doi moi*) in Vietnam has been based and spurred on by actions at the grass roots, as pointed out by Douglas Pike. A good example of a mutually corrupting relationship, on the other hand, may be found in the use of the powers of the state by South Korea's ruling party and governments, not only to win elections but even to punish their opponents, as is documented by Soohyun Chon.

48 Ibid., p. 296.

The relationship between the two types of politics, however, may be competing or even antagonistic, in a sort of "fixed-sum, balance-of-power" relationship, as Lowell Dittmer puts it in his concluding chapter. Joseph Fewsmith, too, notes subversive, rather than reinforcing, effects of informal politics on the operations of formal, particularly bureaucratic, structures. In a similar vein, Tyrene White characterizes the Chinese government's attempt to mobilize the public for the population control program as an elite-directed "disruption of social, personal, institutional, and psychological" routines.[49] The politics that governs the routines that get disrupted is informal politics and a target of assault by formal politics represented by the government's mobilization program. Formal politics in Maoist China often culminated in government-directed mass mobilization campaigns, while informal politics has often triumphed over formal politics and forced Beijing to abandon such campaigns in post-Maoist, postrevolutionary China.

Functioning under and in conformity with informal institutions and rules, sometimes in alliance but often in competition with formal politics, informal politics tends to operate through organizational forms that are different and distinctive from those associated with formal politics. If government offices and party organs are representative of the latter, then kinship groups, such as the patrilineal lineage called *ho* in Vietnam, as mentioned by Pike, or groups based on regional and friendship ties in Korea, as discussed by Chon, are typical of the former; and so are the patron–client relationships formed between government or party officials, as Ostrov's study shows.

A variant of the organizational form based on patron–client relationships that is familiar to many East Asian societies is the faction, as noted by both Dittmer and Peter Lee in their discussions of Chinese cases, by Tun-jen Cheng and Tein-cheng Chou in theirs of legislative politics in Taiwan, by Pike in his of transitional politics in Vietnam, and by Haruhiro Fukui and Shigeko Fukai in theirs of electoral politics in Japan. The clique in Chung-fang Yang's description of the politics in the Chinese imperial court refers to a very similar form. The faction is in fact so generic a form that factionalism is often equated with informal politics. It should be noted, however, that, as suggested above, the faction is by no means the only organizational form in which informal politics manifests itself; as Dittmer points out in the concluding chapter, all factions are far from identical but vary widely, for example, in the degree of institutionalization and the size and character of membership.

Like any other social phenomenon, informal politics undoubtedly changes over time. A faction may in time be replaced or absorbed by a bureaucratic organization or policy group. What is so remarkable and interesting about

49 White, "Postrevolutionary mobilization in China," p. 55.

informal politics is that it has not appreciably declined in any East Asian society that we know of, nor is it likely to do so in the foreseeable future. As Fewsmith points out, it remains robust and important in Chinese politics even as formal political institutions grow increasingly effective. When suppressed by the formal authority, informal politics may simply go underground; and when subjected to the pressure of marketization, it may only breed "money politics" and nepotism, as Dittmer and Lu Xiaobo suggest. As South Korean politics becomes democratized, informal groups (*sajojic*) become more, rather than less, visible, active, and influential, as Chon observes. According to Cheng and Chou, factions have become increasingly active and entrenched in Taiwan's legislative politics as it has become increasingly democratized.

It is thus hard to escape the conclusion that not only is informal politics functionally inseparable from formal politics, but most, if not all, of its organizational forms discussed in this book are likely to remain for the foreseeable future as visible and potent as they are in the East Asian societies and inferentially in many other parts of the world. It is thus a subject deserving the serious political scientist's focused attention.

THE ORGANIZATION OF THE BOOK

The eleven substantive chapters that follow this Introduction are divided into four parts. Part I consists of three chapters that discuss informal politics in democratic polities in the region, namely, Japan, Taiwan, and the Republic of Korea (South Korea). Part II comprises four chapters that deal with informal politics in general in the People's Republic of China (China), while Part III presents two case studies in Chinese corporatism. Part IV includes two chapters on informal politics in the Democratic People's Republic of Korea (North Korea) and Vietnam, the two authoritarian regimes on China's periphery. The conclusion by Dittmer summarizes and ponders the theoretical implications of the general themes and major arguments that run through many, if not all, of the substantive chapters.

Part I begins with a discussion of Japanese electoral politics, mainly at the infrastate level, by Haruhiro Fukui and Shigeko N. Fukai. In a set of three case studies, they show that the one candidate in Japan's lower house elections and two in the upper house elections whose cases they studied in great detail all won largely by playing by the informal, rather than the formal, rules of the nation's electoral and party politics. The key to their success was reliance on, for example, informal campaign and fund-raising groups, spousal and factional ties, and/or sponsorship by special interest groups. They conclude that money, reputation, the campaign machine known as *koenkai*, and personal and factional connections are the "stuff" of the informal politics of elections in contemporary Japan.

Tun-jen Cheng and Tein-cheng Chou identify factionalism as the common form of informal politics in general. They then proceed to discuss the structures and functions of the legislative factions in the Nationalist Party, or Kuomintang (KMT), in newly democratizing Taiwan. After tracing the ups and downs of the earliest postwar KMT factions, they look more closely at those formed in the late 1980s and 1990s. They then argue that Taiwan's legislative factions, as "soft" as they are with no fixed leadership and only loosely affiliated members, are not KMT leaders' agents but, rather, the principals who use the leaders for their own benefits. They also point out a number of institutional constraints on the form of informal politics played by Taiwan's legislative factions, as compared to those observed in Japan and South Korea. Nonetheless, as the quintessential organizatinal form of informal politics in contemporary East Asia, the faction has now become nearly as permanent a feature of Taiwan's increasingly democratic legislative and electoral politics as that of Japan's and South Korea's.

In the last chapter of the section, Soohyun Chon begins her discussion of state-level politics in South Korea with the observation that most political transactions in the country are based on informal relationships and networks in the absence of viable formal institutions, such as an effective political party system. She then provides a detailed account of the highly personalized and centralized power that leaders of the South Korean government and political parties, on both sides of the aisle, exercise in raising and dispensing political funds. Moreover, and as has already been mentioned, she suggests that informal primary groups based on kinship, regional, and friendship ties tend to play increasingly, rather than decreasingly, important social and political roles as South Korea modernizes, as is illustrated by the salient role and influence of the *sajojic* groups observed in recent presidential elections.

Part II opens with a wide-ranging discussion by Chung-fang Yang of the cultural and psychological foundations of state-level politics in China with important implications for politics in all polities in the Confucian cultural region. She seeks to explain how "persons in culture" in Confucian societies solve or try to solve problems faced in times of far-reaching environmental change. She first traces the evolution and explores the ramifications of the foundational precepts of Confucian politics, such as public, private, loyalty, sincerity, and trust. By highlighting historical continuities in Chinese political culture, she draws attention to the duality between the formal Confucian deference for gentlemanly, selfless, and public-minded behavior on the one hand and the selfish, interest-driven, and exchange-mediated behavior in actual life on the other. Formalities interpenetrate and intermingle with practical and informal relationships; and political influence is exerted in subtle, culturally sanctioned ways through, for example, exchanges of favors and repayment of obligations. Yang then shows how the old Confucian precepts may help us to understand and explain watershed political events in recent Chinese history, such as the fall from grace of Liu Shaoqi, Hu Yaobang, and Zhao Ziyang.

Lowell Dittmer's chapter that follows focuses on state- and infrastate-level politics in a party state, namely, politics played at the pinnacle of the Chinese Communist Party (CCP) hierarchy. The study begins with a critical review of the literature on modern Chinese politics. Dittmer thus goes over Andrew Nathan's model of the CCP faction; Tang Tsou's and Lucian Pye's criticisms, as well as his own, of that model and their own rival models; and Frederick Teiwes's work on the norms of discussion and decision making within the CCP. Dittmer then proposes a pair of models of key relationships – personal and official – in an attempt to reconceptualize the basis of power in the elite politics of CCP leaders. An official relationship serves as a formal but often vulnerable base of one's power, while a personal relationship serves as an informal but often more potent and durable base of one's power. The interplay between the two types of relationships is both complex and deli-cate, and Dittmer documents the complexity and delicacy with a number of specific examples involving the CCP's past supreme leaders, Mao Zedong and Deng Xiaoping. He then argues that cleavages among top CCP leaders typi-cally develop along two axes – distribution of agreement and distribution of power – and cites a series of intraelite disputes among the top CCP leaders to illustrate the interplay between these two variables.

Dittmer concludes his chapter with the observations that, in the post-Mao reform era, bureaucratic interests and policy commitments increasingly dom-inate intraelite relationships among the top CCP leaders, while CCP factions have been replaced by increasingly overt and competitive policy groups. As the liberalization and marketization of the Chinese economy proceeds, then, Chinese politics comes to resemble what is known as bureaucratic politics in capitalist polities. Meanwhile, informal politics persists, paradoxically, as a "progressive" force to help bring about rapid policy changes with relative ease and, at the same time, as a "reactionary" force to perpetuate the role of tra-ditional personal and hierarchical relationships in policy disputes and per-sonnel decisions at the highest levels of the CCP leadership.

Joseph Fewsmith forcefully and persuasively argues that, to understand and explain contemporary Chinese state-level politics, one must focus not so much on either formal political structures or informal politics in isolation as on their interplay. He cites Deng Xiaoping's relationships with his major rival, Chen Yun, and his subordinates, Zhao Ziyang and Hu Yaobang, as well as the sources of each leader's political power and role as examples of the com-

plex ways in which bureaucratic institutions and informal politics intermingle and interact. In fact, formal institutions and informal politics interact not only with each other but also, and as importantly, with ongoing
political issues and ideology. Fewsmith illustrates this complex four-way pattern of interaction with the example of Deng's rise to power at the expense
of Hua Guofeng on Mao Zedong's death and the arrest of the Gang of Four,
an example that also draws our attention to the central importance of legitimacy in contemporary Chinese politics, and presumably in politics in all
times and places.

Peter Nan-shong Lee zeroes in on the politics of leadership succession in
the CCP. He first proposes four types of leadership found in the CCP that
combine the leadership characteristics identified in two dichotomies: formal
versus informal and functional versus dysfunctional. For example, a formal
and functional combination is found in democratic centralism and an informal and dysfunctional combination in personality cult and factionalism. He
then takes a brief and critical look at the literature on informal politics in
China before launching a detailed investigation into the evolution of the
rules, norms, and problems of leadership succession in the CCP under Mao
Zedong and Deng Xiaoping. He pays special attention to the circumstances
under which Hu Yaobang and Zhao Ziyang were first chosen as heirs apparent to Deng and then were dropped under the concerted pressure brought on
by other senior CCP leaders amidst controversy over repeated attempts, insti-
gated by Deng himself, to institutionalize rules governing the retirement of
older leaders and the promotion of younger ones. This investigation demonstrates the power and tenacity of the traditional informal rules dating back
to the early revolutionary period.

In the first of the two chapters in Part III, Lowell Dittmer and Lu Xiaobo
subject to close and careful scrutiny the changing structures and functions of
the *danwei* (unit), the basic work unit and the common arena of infrastate-
level politics in China under communism. Their analysis, which is based
largely on information derived from personal interviews conducted in 1993
and 1994 with individuals experienced in a variety of danwei in Shanghai
and Shijiazhuang, shows that, once a powerful and effective means of the
party-state to control and monitor citizens' lives and provide a variety of social
services, the danwei is now shedding its control functions while still retaining many of its social service functions. They also observe the tendencies for
multiple subunits based on informal ties to emerge within a danwei, for vertical personal connections (guanxi) to become less important and horizontal
ones more important, for both types to be replaced by money ("marketization") and for nepotism to spread ("familiarization"). These observations lead
Lu and Dittmer to suggest that reform tends to loosen and reduce state con-

trol but breeds informal politics and corruption. They conclude their study with a sketch of a binary model of organization and organizational transformation: "evolutionary" (formal) and "involutionary" (informal). The latter type prevailed in pre-reform China and apparently continues to thrive in reform China.

In the second of the two chapters in this part, Benjamin C. Ostrov's chapter is concerned with informal politics in the Chinese government as seen, specifically, in patron–client relationships among officials in its national defense research and development (R&D) sector. The study shows how such relationships between a prominent official in that sector and his subordinates had their origins in their formal relationships formed in several government organs as early as the 1930s and then were deliberately revived during the Cultural Revolution for mutual protection from attacks by common enemies, both new and old. The study leads Ostrov to suggest that it is difficult to verify even the existence, not to mention the intensity, of a patron–client relationship between particular individuals and drawing a clear line between a formal organization and an informal group. The case study also shows, however, how clientilistic ties may help organizations procure the resources that are necessary for their success even when they lack formal legal authority or competence to do so.

In the last part of the book, and in an extraordinarily detailed yet sharply focused study of state-level politics in North Korea, Samuel Kim demontrates that informal politics accounts for the bulk of politics in the country both under and after Kim Il Sung's rule. Relying, in the absence of documentary evidence, on inferences from announced policy and ideological decisions and changes, he diagnoses the nature of politics in Pyongyang as so extremely personalistic and charismatic that anybody's political power and role can be accurately measured by his or her personal proximity to the Great Leader. Kim then traces the emergence of the "Kim Il Sung family state" through three historical stages: the consolidation of Kim's power and leadership in the 1945–1972 period; the occupation and control of all leadership positions by members of Kim's extended family in the 1973–1994 period of preparation for father-to-son succession; and the period of a systemic crisis and rampant expansion of unauthorized – that is, informal, ideological, political, economic, and cultural – spheres since the early 1990s. The regime has thus been faced lately with formidable challenges in the areas of leadership and succession, national identity, and national security.

In the last chapter of the book, Douglas Pike depicts Vietnamese political culture as one characterized by a deep distrust of politics and cynicism about political leadership, traditionalism, clandestinism, weak formal political institutions, and sharp geographical and religious divisions. The country's political system has been traditionally divided or, rather, torn into three separate spheres: the imperial court, the village, and the household. In this system, the court represents the weak state-level formal political structure, while the village with its council of elders and especially the household with its emphasis on filial piety constitute the durable bedrock of pervasive infrastate-level informal politics. Pike attributes the important changes that have taken place in Vietnam's national politics and political economy in recent years, particularly the rise and progress of the reform and renovation (*doi moi*) movement, not to directives issued by the state's central authority but to initiatives taken and pressures applied by local informal political groups.

The eleven chapters briefly sketched above thus address informal politics found at different levels and in diverse contexts of politics and society in historical and contemporary East Asia. Both individually and collectively, they represent a first-cut attempt to introduce a conceptual perspective and framework for a new approach to the study of comparative and international politics. Dittmer's conlusion that follows them recapitulates and synthesizes the major themes and arguments of that approach.

PART I

INFORMAL POLITICS IN INDUSTRIALIZED ASIAN DEMOCRACIES

CHAPTER 1

— Read This
~~&~~ Notes in Notebook

THE INFORMAL POLITICS OF
JAPANESE DIET ELECTIONS:
CASES AND INTERPRETATIONS

HARUHIRO FUKUI AND SHIGEKO N. FUKAI

As suggested in the Introduction to this volume, informal politics both complements and competes with formal politics in complex and dynamic patterns of interaction. Recent Japanese Diet (parliamentary) elections illustrate this subtle but often powerful role that informal politics plays vis-à-vis formal politics. We examine in this chapter the power and pattern of informal politics primarily in Diet elections held in the late 1980s and early 1990s under the multiple-seat election district system, known as a single non-transferable vote (SNTV) system, as seen in three candidates' experiences.[1] As we will argue, however, our arguments and conclusions also apply to the more recent Diet elections without any significant modifications.

Before we present the case studies and discuss their implications, it will be helpful to reiterate a cliché about Japanese politics in general and Japanese elections under the SNTV system in particular: They were both very expensive. As we pointed out in our previous discussion of a related topic,[2] a candidate could legally spend only so much – a little less than ¥16 million on average in the 1990 lower house general election – during a legally prescribed campaign period of about two weeks. The amount was not insignificant, but neither was it totally beyond the average adult citizen's reach in a nation with a mean per-capita gross national product (GNP) of nearly

---

1 The 1995 electoral reform replaced the SNTV system with a combination of a single-member district (SMD) and proportional representation systems. See Haruhiro Fukui and Shigeko Fukai, "Japan in 1996: Between hope and uncertainty," *Asian Survey* 37:1 (January 1997), pp. 23–24. See also Eugene L. Wolfe, "Japanese electoral and political reform: Role of the young Turks," and Steven R. Reed, "The nomination process for Japan's next general election: Waiting for the *Heiretsu-sei*," both in *Asian Survey* 35:12 (December 1995), pp. 1059–1074 and 1075–1086.
2 Haruhiro Fukui and Shigeko Fukai, "Nihon ni okeru infomaru politikkusu to itto yui taisei: kesu sutade to shoho riron" [Informal politics in Japan and the predominant-party regime: A case study and rudimentary theory], *Leviathan* 9 (Fall 1991), p. 58. Article 194 of the Public Office Election Law limited the amount of money that any candidate could legally spend in an election to a multiple of the number of registered voters per seat in the given election district plus an amount determined on the basis of the total voter population of the district. See Ibid., p. 65; *Asahi shinbun*, February 6, 1990.

¥3.5 million in 1990.[3] In reality, however, a Liberal Democratic Party (LDP) candidate in a Diet election in the late 1980s and early 1990s typically spent between ¥100 and ¥200 million.[4] The actual costs thus exceeded the legal limits by at least six times and as much as by thirteen times. Moreover, the average LDP lower house member spent about ¥100 million per year to keep his or her campaign machine, generically known as a *koenkai* (support association), alive and active for future elections.[5] Winning and retaining a Diet seat, especially in the lower house, was thus an extremely expensive proposition.[6]

Candidates spent huge amounts of money both because they had to win and because they could do so without getting themselves into trouble with the law. They had to pay not only for office space, staff salaries, transportation and communication expenses, and other costs commonly associated with an election campaign in a democratic society, but also for gifts, in one form or another, to constituents and, often, their families and friends. That campaigns cost such large amounts of money was not only a widely known but also a widely accepted fact, especially in rural districts. Whatever the rules of formal politics may have said, candidates did what they felt they had to do to survive within the limits of legitimacy that were defined by rules not of formal politics but of informal politics. The following three case studies, all based primarily on information derived from personal interviews conducted in the summer of 1991, illustrate the logic of informal politics that pervaded Japanese Diet elections under the SNTV system.

We do not claim that any of these three cases were necessarily typical of candidates in recent Diet elections. In fact, we find it very difficult even to define, much less find, the "typical" candidate, since every candidate is unique in one important way or another, such as his or her conception of and attitude toward politics, the kind and amount of politically significant resources at his or her disposal, relationships with constituents, and so on. Nonetheless, we do believe that the three cases capture some of the electoral approaches and strategies common to most candidates in Diet elections under

---

3 Asahi shinbunsha, *Asahi nenkan 1993* [Asahi yearbook 1993] (Tokyo: Asahi shinbunsha, 1993), p. 488.
4 Ronald J. Hrebenar, *The Japanese Party System*, 2nd ed. (Boulder: Westview Press, 1992), p. 61.
5 Tomoaki Iwai, *Seiji shikin no kenkyu* [*A Study of Political Funds*] (Tokyo: Nihon keizai shinbunsha, 1990), p. 127; Jiro Honzawa, *Daigishi hisho zankoku monogatari* [*A Tale of the Cruelty Inflicted upon Diet Members' Staffs*] (Tokyo: Eru shuppansha, 1991), p. 16; Michisada Hirose, *Seiji to kane* [Politics and Money] (Tokyo: Iwanami shoten, 1989), pp. 31–36; Utopia seiji kenkyukai, *Nagatacho kakyu bushi tachi no kekki* [*The Uprising of the Lower Samurai in Nagatacho*] (Tokyo: Kodansha, 1989), pp. 186–188; interview with Masayoshi Takemura, July 19, 1991.
6 In fact, Japanese Diet elections were almost the most expensive in the world, matched only by U.S. Senate and House elections. See Fukui and Fukai, "Nihon ni okeru infomaru politikkusu," pp. 62–63; Haruhiro Fukui, "Japan," in Pippa Norris, ed., *Passages to Power: Legislative Recruitment in Advanced Democracies* (Cambridge: Cambridge University Press, 1997), pp. 103–104.

the SNTV system, with the exception of those affiliated with either the Japan Communist Party (JCP) or the Clean Government Party (CGP).

CASE I: SDP LOWER HOUSE MEMBER, TOMIKO OKAZAKI

Tomiko Okazaki was a Social Democratic Party (SDP) of Japan candidate who ran for and won a lower house seat in the Miyagi-1 district for the first time in the 1990 general election and was reelected in 1993. A native of the neighboring prefecture, Fukushima, she had worked by 1990 for some twenty-seven years since her graduation from high school as a radio and television journalist – as a newscaster for Radio Fukushima for the first several years and then as an anchorwoman for special programs for Tohoku Broadcasting Corporation for the last twenty years or so.[7] During her long career as a radio and television journalist, she not only had reported on but also had been personally involved in investigations into a series of controversial political and social issues, such as the construction of a nuclear power plant and the arrest and detention of a resident Korean on disputed, and unproved, charges of manslaughter. These activities had made her a highly visible and popular local celebrity, with known sympathy for social underdogs and minorities, and a winnable opposition candidate in 1990.

When invited by the local SDP branch, reportedly at the instigation of the leader of the conservative faction in the branch, Kiyotaka Sakashita, to run for a lower house seat on the party's ticket in the middle of 1989, Okazaki delayed her final decision for nearly a year.[8] She may not have been very worried about campaign funds. The LDP was mired in one of the worst scandals in the nation's history and the SDP was expected to win two seats in the district, rather than simply retaining the one that it had won in previous lower house elections. She was sure she could win one of them without a very large campaign war chest. She was worried, however, that she might lose in the following general election, when the LDP might have regained its popularity and strength. She might thus lose both her good job now and her parliamentary seat in a few years. Only informal assurances given by the Tohoku Broadcasting Corporation that, should she lose in her reelection bid in the near future, she could get back her old job at the company may have made her decide to run after the long period of agonizing indecision.

---

7 Shugiin sangiin [House of Representatives and House of Councillors], eds., *Gikai seido hyakunenshi: Shugiin giin meikan* [*A One-Hundred-Year History of the Diet System: Roster of House of Representatives Members*] (Tokyo: Okurasho insatsukyoku, 1990), p. 145. Unless otherwise noted, the following account is based on notes taken during our interview with Okazaki in her office in the House of Representatives Members Office Building on June 20, 1991, and at her local office in Sendai City on June 28, 1991.
8 We owe much of the information used in this section to Professor Hideo Otake.

Notwithstanding the LDP's apparent vulnerability in an election called in the shadow of a well-publicized scandal, Okazaki faced tough competition; since the last (1986) general election, the five-member district had been represented by three LDP, one CGP, and one SDP men. Of these five, the three LDP and the SDP incumbents were known to be planning to run again, while the CGP was expected to field a new candidate in place of its incumbent and the JCP, whose male candidate had been the runner-up in 1986, planned to field a woman candidate this time. Moreover, they were all very strong candidates: The three LDP men were backed by three rival LDP factions (Takeshita, Abe, and Komoto), each of which was expected to spend huge amounts of money for its candidate as usual, and the CGP candidate had the support of the local Democratic Socialist Party (DSP) branch, which did not have its own candidate, as well as the sectarian Buddhist group of coreligionists affiliated with the Sokagakkai organization. Nor would the SDP incumbent help a rival candidate from his own party win at his expense.

Despite the daunting prospects, some 175 local supporters met in the summer of 1989 to urge Okazaki to make up her mind to run. This was the beginning of her unofficial campaign. In the next six months, the campaign expanded rapidly until, a few weeks before election day, both the national and local press had begun to rank Okazaki among the top three contenders, behind one of the LDP candidates, neck and neck with another, and ahead of the third LDP candidate and, possibly, the other SDP candidate as well.[9] The actual result was even better: Okazaki ended up a very close second to the other SDP candidate (149,740 to 150,339 votes) and ahead of all three LDP candidates, who also won, not to mention the CGP, JCP, and independent candidates who lost.[10]

The impressive result of the new woman candidate's campaign, however, hid serious conflicts within her campaign organization. In fact, there were two separate and competing groups involved: an old-style local SDP/labor alliance on the one hand, and a newly formed and still inchoate citizen group on the other. The core of the first group was unionists from the local chapters of the two labor federations that had played key roles in the SDP's triumph in the 1989 upper house election, namely, the Federation of Local Government Employees Unions and the Federation of Telecommunication Workers Unions. The second group consisted of sundry citizen activists involved in a variety of oppositionist campaigns and movements, ranging from opposition to nuclear power plants and the public display of the national flag to opposition to political corruption and war.

9 *Yomiuri shinbun*, February 5, 1990.   10 *Asahi shinbun*, February 20, 1990.

Fund raising was an important and difficult task for both groups, even though Okazaki's campaign was "embarrassingly" cheap compared to a typical LDP candidate's, thanks importantly to the candidate's own public visibility and popularity. The LDP's Abe faction candidate, for example, received ¥10 million from the faction and raised, either in outright donations or in loans, several times as much from his own and allied local firms. In addition, and consistent with a standard practice among LDP candidates, he staffed his campaign offices with people loaned by those firms free of charge. By comparison, Okazaki's SDP/labor group received a modest fund allocation from the SDP's central treasury and raised some additional funds from unionists' contributions. The bulk of her campaign funds was raised by the citizen group, some by soliciting contributions in ¥100 units from ordinary citizens but most by selling inexpensive merchandise contributed by supporters. The group sold, for example, some 14,000 "organic" soap bars, in sets of two, at ¥200 a set. The group grossed about ¥8 million, far more than the party group raised. Since the citizen group's campaign office was rent-free, was manned almost entirely by volunteers, and, as a result, cost no more than about ¥350,000 a month to maintain, the ¥8 million went a long way.

The funds raised by the citizen group were not shared with the party group that managed Okazaki's official campaign headquarters housed in one of the SDP's branch offices. In fact, there was considerable tension and jockeying for control of the campaign between the two groups that often put Okazaki in an awkward position. The citizen group activists shared a deep distrust of all established political parties, including the SDP, and the belief that only a completely autonomous nonpartisan grassroots movement could help solve any of the pressing political and social problems in contemporary Japan and the world. Seasoned and sophisticated experts on specific issues, such as the environment and human rights, supported and campaigned for Okazaki, not for the SDP. Okazaki's own sympathy was clearly with this group; she was dismayed by the SDP's ineffectual local organization and the allied unions' conservatism. Moreover, she believed that the union leadership was quickly losing, if it had not already lost, control of the rank-and-file unionists and could no longer be relied on to commit and deliver a significant number of votes as it used to. She hoped eventually to build a permanent network of block-level citizen groups to which one out of every five or ten adult residents on each block would belong to tackle a variety of pressing local issues.

Okazaki defied and violated the basic rule of informal politics in the largest opposition party of the period, the SDP, which expected all party-endorsed candidates to rely for the conduct of their election campaigns on local party branches and allied local labor unions and let them plan and direct all of the important details of their campaigns. She relied instead mainly on the nonpartisan, or antipartisan, citizen group for fund raising and campaigning. Moreover, she had her own policy agenda infused with ideas and visions on a number of issues close to the constituents' hearts but not necessarily approved by either the SDP leadership or the major allied unions. The agenda did include an SDP-approved position on the rice import issue; becoming a citizens' representative from one of the areas that produced the highest grade, and the most expensive, rice brands, *sasanishiki*, she stoutly defended Japan's rigid protectionist policy on rice trade. She would argue not only that Japan's ratio of its domestic supply of foodstuffs to its total needs was already dangerously low, at about 30 percent overall, but that rice agriculture helped the land hold water and thus conserve the healthy natural environment.

Okazaki was, however, also concerned with a host of other issues that hardly received any attention, much less an explicit commitment, from the SDP leadership. Opposition to golf courses was one example, which she characterized as a transformative issue, and while discussing it she wistfully referred to the better organized and more effective campaign carried on by the local JCP branch and to the recent election of two JCP candidates to an important town assembly within Okazaki's constituency. She was deeply concerned about the steady deterioration of the environment and blamed it on the conservative government's, especially the Ministry of International Trade and Industry's, continuing obsession with economic growth at all costs and refusal to publish key data on the environmental costs of the policy.

Okazaki was as deeply concerned about problems facing children, the elderly, and the handicapped. She was upset by the cruelty inflicted on school children by the "examination hell" and the prevalence of "bullying" in and out of school, both of which teachers were powerless to control. She also objected to the enforcement by school authorities of out-of-date rules about students' uniforms and hairstyles and wanted to have a children's and students' human rights declaration drawn up. The care for the elderly was totally inadequate; many had no pension income and survived on their meager personal savings. The government's plan to train 100,000 volunteers to attend to the needs of the elderly would not meet their growing needs, and a large number of new nursing homes and care facilities were urgently needed. For the handicapped, it was not enough to provide wheelchairs; streets and buildings had to be redesigned to provide to those in wheelchairs easier access and use. For example, the street overpasses with steep steps at both ends, which were common in most Japanese cities, paid no attention to the needs of the handicapped.

On these and many other issues – married women's right to retain their maiden names, abortion, sexual harassment, the rights of foreign workers, and so on – Okazaki was a quintessential citizens' movement representative with a vision of government and politics that was quite different from the one associated with Japan's organized labor and only tangential to the main preoccupation of the union-dominated SDP leadership. Why, then, did she not stop working with the SDP and its traditional allies and become an independent advocate for citizens' interests? The norms and rules of formal politics found in the Public Office Election Law and other relevant laws clearly gave her the right to run as an independent. Moreover, the impressively broad support she evidently enjoyed among her constituents seemed to promise her success without either the SDP's endorsement or labor's support. The political realist in Okazaki, however, led her to continue to work with the party and unions essentially because a few votes made a difference in an election, and the SDP and the unions still could deliver more than a few votes.

As was suggested above, the citizen group that all but overshadowed the party/union organization as the driving force behind Okazaki's successful campaigns in both the 1990 and 1993 lower house elections was a distinctively informal organization. It had no identifiable leadership group or structure, only a loosely defined and bounded group of "members" who neither paid any fixed membership dues nor performed any common and regular roles apart from casting their own ballots for their common candidate and soliciting nonmembers' votes for her as well. It was the kind of organization that closely fitted Claus Offe's description of the new social movements that emerged in Western Europe in the 1980s:

> the new social movements consist of participants, campaigns, spokespeople, networks, voluntary helpers, and donations. Typically, in their internal mode of action, new social movements do not rely . . . on the organizational principle of differentiation, whether in the horizontal (insider vs. outsider) or in the vertical dimension (leaders vs. rank and file members). To the contrary, there seems to be a strong reliance upon de-differentiation, that is, the fusion of public and private roles, instrumental and expressive behavior, community and organization, and in particular a poor and at best transient demarcation between "members" and formal "leaders".[11]

Despite, or because of, such informality verging on amorphousness, however, the group managed to win an impressively large and loyal following that proved to be not only a reliable block of votes for Okazaki at the polls but even the provider of a substantial war chest. Its members were bound to their candidate and to each other, not by formal rules or norms imposed by an organization but purely by a shared set of beliefs and sense of mission. To them, it

---

11 Claus Offe, "New social movements: Challenging the boundaries of institutional politics," *Social Research* 52:4 (1985), pp. 829–830.

was not just legitimate but imperative to elect or reelect their candidate to reform and cleanse the politics of a nation polluted and corrupted under a perennial conservative rule. An organization that depends for its survival and success on this kind of belief-based loyalty and sense of mission may be as subject to dissatisfaction among its members as an organization based on its members' shared material interests. An ideological or cultural group is, however, likely to be far less vulnerable to losses of members due to their exit from the organization. Informality helps reduce the vulnerability on this score: The boundary between a member and a nonmember is so unclear and flexible that "exit" does not mean much in any case. Dissatisfaction would thus more likely lead to "voice" than to "exit" among members of Okazaki's informal citizen group, while dissatisfaction among members of a more formal organization, such as the SDP branch and local union involved in her campaigns, would more often lead to "exit." This difference assumes a special significance in a campaign organization if we assume that many, if not all, of those who exit from one organization may move to rival candidates' camps.[12] The informality of Okazaki's citizen group was thus a source of its strength, rather than of its weakness, and a key factor in the success of Okazaki's campaigns in 1990.

Okazaki's campaign organization and strategy stood her in good stead again in the 1993 general election, in which both the SDPJ and the LDP suffered a disastrous defeat. Three years later, she left the SDPJ to join the newly formed Democratic Party of Japan (DPJ) and ran as one of its candidates in the 1996 general election held under a new set of rules that combined contests in 300 single-seat districts and those in 11 proportional representation (PR) regions. She lost in this election, but a year later she ran again and won by a landslide in an upper house by-election. Her victory, which again was owed mainly to the support of nonpartisan citizen groups, came on the heels of the victory of an independent incumbent in the Miyagi gubernatorial election, a candidate who declined offers of help by all major parties and ran a campaign very much like Okazaki's.[13] A *Mainichi shinbun* poll conducted in the prefecture during the campaign period had found 71 percent of the respondents supporting none of the existing parties. The rising nonpartisanship apparently changed the informal rules of electoral politics in the prefecture in a direction favorable to Okazaki's campaigning style and strategy.

12 The *locus classicus* for this discussion is Albert O. Hirschman, *Exit, Voice and Loyalty: Responses to Decline in Firms, Organizations and States* (Cambridge, MA: Harvard University Press, 1970). On the meaning and implications of the "move to rival camps," see his "Exit, voice, and the state," *World Politics* 16:1 (October 1978), pp. 90–107.

13 *Japan Times*, October 19, 1997; *Mainichi shinbun*, November 18, 1997.

CASE 2: LDP UPPER HOUSE MEMBER,
MAYUMI MORIYAMA

Like Okazaki, Mayumi Moriyama was one of the few women Diet members and one of the even fewer women LDP Diet members.[14] A graduate of the University of Tokyo law faculty, one-time director-general of the Ministry of Labor's Bureau of Women's and Minors' Affairs, and the wife of a veteran LDP member of the House of Representatives, she ran for the first time for an upper house seat in the 1980 "double" election because she was invited to do so by the LDP leadership.[15] With a bare majority of the upper house seats under its control, the LDP was anxious to try to win as many additional seats as possible in that house. She declined the invitation at first, mainly because she thought that she had neither the campaign funds nor the public visibility needed for a successful bid for a Diet seat. She had, however, served as a bureau director in the Labor Ministry for five years and had played a prominent role in mobilizing Japanese government and public support for the United Nations Decade of Women, 1975–1985. (In 1985, she led the Japanese delegation to the World Women's Congress in Nairobi to mark the end of the Decade of Women.) That experience had given her name some visibility. Moreover, she had reached as high a position in the bureaucracy as a woman in Japan's central government bureaucracy could realistically hope to reach. These circumstances and considerations changed her mind.

Once she decided to run in the 1980 upper house election, it was easy to decide to run in her home territory, Tochigi Prefecture, which embraced her husband's bailiwick in the Tochigi-1 lower house election district. This was a prefecture with four upper house seats, two of which were filled every three years by new or reelected members serving a six-year term. Prior to 1980, the prefecture had been represented in the upper house by two LDP and two SDP members. One of the LDP and one of the SDP members were at the end of their six-year terms and would fight for reelection in 1980. Moriyama had to defeat one of them to win a seat of her own. Combined with her limited but useful public visibility as a rare female senior bureaucrat and leader of the government-backed women's movement, there were signs of conservative upsurge in the nation at large and in Tochigi Prefecture in particular. Moreover, Moriyama could presumably ride on her husband's coattails in a

---

14 On the rarity of women among Japanese members of parliament and the formal and informal rules of Japanese electoral and party politics that account for it, see Fukui, "Japan," in Norris, ed., *Passages to Power.*

15 Unless otherwise noted, our discussion in this section is based on notes taken at our interview with Moriyama in the Personnel Bureau Director's office of the LDP headquarters on June 19, 1991.

"double election," in which a lower house and an upper house election were held at the same time. Neither any Japanese law nor any formal rule of the LDP had anything to say about collaboration between spouses or, for that matter, between any relatives or friends in election campaigning. Such collaboration may have smacked of nepotism or cronyism, but it was not only perfectly legal but very common and uncontroversial. In other words, it was, if available, a perfectly acceptable and sensible arrangement for any new candidate to seek.

When Moriyama launched her unofficial campaign in early March 1980 for the June 1980 upper house election, she did rely heavily on her husband's *koenkai* and his allies in the Tochigi-1 lower house election district, as an upper house election district embraced an entire prefecture. In the other half of the prefecture, which constituted the Tochigi-2 district, however, she had to build her own *koenkai* virtually from scratch within a few months. From the beginning, Moriyama's main rival was not so much the SDP incumbent as the LDP incumbent, Tomoji Oshima, who was a member of the LDP faction led by Yasuhiro Nakasone and closely allied with her husband's traditional rival in the Tochigi-1 district and a Nakasone faction affiliate, Michio Watanabe. Her husband belonged to the LDP faction led by Toshio Komoto, and Moriyama therefore also ran as that faction's prospective member. On the other hand, the third LDP incumbent from the Tochigi-1 district, a young first-termer, Hajime Funada, who was a member of Kakuei Tanaka's faction and whose father and Tochigi's governor at the time had long been her husband's ally, lent Moriyama a helping hand. One of the two LDP lower house incumbents from the Tochigi-2 district, Toshiyuki Inamura, interestingly a Nakasone faction member like Watanabe, was also an old ally of her husband's and helped Moriyama run her campaign in that part of the prefecture.

Widely condemned as an important cause not only of disunity in the ruling party, but also of money politics and corruption, an LDP faction was, as far as LDP candidates were concerned, such an influential actor in any Diet election that it could be ignored only at one's peril. This basic rule of the informal politics of Diet elections under the SNTV system was not lost on Moriyama in 1980 or, for that matter, on any other serious LDP candidate in any Diet election since the founding of the party in 1955. Even more important than the factions, however, was the candidate's own personal campaign organization, that is, *koenkai*, the formation of which might be significantly facilitated by an allied faction.

While Oshima's *koenkai* dominated the rural hinterland of the prefecture, Moriyama's enjoyed greater support and popularity in the prefectural capital, Utsunomiya City, especially among women voters. Known as *Mayumikai*

(Mayumi Association), her fledgling *koenkai* had a predominantly female membership, with its largest chapter in that city, but also with a chapter of more modest size in each of the prefecture's forty-nine municipalities. In the three-and-a-half months between early March and late June, when the election was held, Moriyama visited and spoke at rallies, each attended by about thirty people, in nearly seventy different neighborhoods throughout the prefecture. Most of these rallies were organized with the help of her husband's *koenkai*. The result of all of this effort was Moriyama's impressive victory; she beat both Oshima and the SDP incumbent by large margins (288,104 to 250,769 and 209,448, respectively).[16]

Moriyama was reelected in 1986 and 1992 with similar margins.[17] By the last of these elections, she had become politically far more visible than back in 1980, having now served not only as a twelve-year veteran member of the upper house, but also as parliamentary vice minister for foreign affairs, chief cabinet secretary, and minister of education. She had also started an eight-page quarterly newsletter, *Ayumi* (walk), to report her parliamentary and other political activities to members of her *koenkai*. While her *koenkai* continued to be led largely by those older supporters, mostly women, who had helped found it in 1980, she now enjoyed substantial support among younger voters as well, and among as many men as women. A group of current and former Ministry of Labor employees had become part of the *koenkai* organization, as had a variety of women's groups devoted to "cultural" activities such as flower arrangement, cooking, and so on. Like most other Diet members, Moriyama routinely spent Friday through Monday back in the constituency and tried to attend all weddings and funerals to which she was invited. The maintenance and activities of her *koenkai* were financed mainly by contributions from three fund-raising organizations – one in the constituency and two in Tokyo – each with corporate members who paid ¥10,000–20,000 monthly dues apiece.

That employees of a government agency, or even a private company for that matter, should support their current or former boss in an election was, needless to say, nowhere mentioned, much less required, in a law or any other statement of an official intent of the state. On the contrary, such a relationship between a boss and his or her subordinates was generally frowned upon under the rules of formal politics as verging on political corruption. So was a Diet member's involvement in a constituent's private affairs, such as a wedding or a funeral service. The collection of political contributions in the name of membership dues from local corporations was not illegal but ethically

16 Yaozo Kikuoka, ed., *Kokkai benran* [*Diet Handbook*] 64 (Tokyo: Nihon seikei shinbunsha, 1982), p. 311.
17 Kikuoka, ed., *Kokkai benran* 78 (1988), p. 310; 89 (1993), p. 323.

questionable. All of these practices, however, were quite commonplace and nearly universally accepted among Japanese politicians and voters alike in the 1980s and early 1990s.

In its organizational structure and pattern of collective action, Moriyama's *koenkai* had some remarkable resemblances to Okazaki's citizen group: Their structure and rules were extremely informal, loose, and flexible. An important difference was that, as an organization based more on members' shared material or materialistic interests, rather than on a set of beliefs or ideals, Moriyama's *koenkai* required a commitment of far more time, energy, and, above all, money from the candidate or her representatives than did Okazaki's citizen group.

Moriyama's husband died in the wake of the 1986 double election and left his seat vacant to be filled by a successor. The inheritance of a Diet seat by an incumbent's relative or friend was a very common practice, especially among LDP politicians. As we pointed out elsewhere, the so-called *nisei* (second-generation) members accounted for 31 percent of the entire lower house membership and 46 percent of the LDP contingent in that house in 1990.[18] In other words, the inheritance of a Diet seat was not subject to any rule of formal politics in this period and was a perfectly acceptable practice under the rules of informal politics. Moriyama therefore could have asked to inherit her late husband's seat in the 1990 general election, but she did not, partly because the LDP had suffered devastating losses in the 1989 upper house election and was loath to lose another seat in that house, and partly because Moriyama herself did not feel ready to run for a lower house seat. She instead had a younger local politician, Susumu Yanase, run in her place, and he won, along with her late husband's inveterate rival, Watanabe, and ally, Funada. In 1993, Yanase and Funada both ran and won again, but not as LDP candidates; Yanase ran as a candidate of the New Party Sakigake (NPS), which had split from the LDP on the eve of the election, while Funada ran as a candidate of the Japan Renewal Party (JRP), which had also split from the LDP at about the same time. Moriyama wisely did not try to switch her seat from the upper house to the lower house in an election in which the LDP suffered an unprecedented defeat due largely to widely publicized revelations of a series of scandals. The daily headlines on those scandals made almost any candidate of a "new" party preferable to any LDP candidate, as far as most voters were concerned. Had Moriyama run in that election, her loosely organized campaign organization would have lost many of its members and might have run a serious risk of disintegration. She avoided such a risk by knowing and

18 Haruhiro Fukui and Shigeko N. Fukai, "Elite recruitment and political leadership," *PS: Political Science & Politics* (March 1992), p. 30; Fukui, "Japan," in Norris, ed., *Passages to Power*, p. 105.

respecting the rules of the informal politics of elections in Japan in the early 1990s.

In the 1996 general election, held under the new electoral rules, Moriyama finally switched her upper house seat for a lower house seat, not as a winner in a new Tochigi district but as a winner in one of the eleven regional PR contests among the parties, each with a ranked list of its candidates. A senior member of the party and the upper house, Moriyama was ranked third on the LDP list for the northeastern region and comfortably among the seven LDP winners in the region. Which candidates should run in a PR region, rather than in one of the 300 single-seat districts, and how they should be ranked on their party's list were decisions made by each party according to strictly informal rules and largely on an ad hoc basis. The results of such decisions, however, determined who were to write, amend, or repeal the basic rules of the nation's formal politics.

CASE 3: SDP UPPER HOUSE MEMBER, MASAO KUNIHIRO

Masao Kunihiro was one of the forty-six SDP candidates elected in the 1989 upper house election and one of the twenty elected from the single national constituency under the PR system installed in 1983 for upper house elections. He had earned his bachelor of arts degree from the University of Hawaii and his master of arts degree in cultural anthropology from Columbia University in New York. Back in Japan, he had become a well-known and popular television personality, first as an English teacher on the air in a Japan Broadcasting Corporation (NHK) educational program, and then as a newscaster for a private television network. He had also served on a foreign minister's policy staff and as a consultant for the Ministry of Foreign Affairs. In 1989, he was an international relations professor at a private university.[19]

In the memorable 1989 electoral upset, the SDP beat the LDP in a Diet election for the first time since 1955, when both the LDP and the SDP's antecedent, the JSP, were founded; and, even more impressively, the socialists beat the conservatives for the first time since a parliamentary system was introduced in Japan in 1889. To many observers, this appeared to mark the beginning of a new era in Japanese parliamentary and party politics. In the previous (1986) upper house election, the SDP had lost nine seats, down to

---

19 See Shugiin sangiin [House of Representatives and House of Councillors], eds., *Gikai seido hyakunen-shi: Kizokuin sangiin giin meikan* [*A One-Hundred-Year History of the Diet System: Roster of House of Peers and House of Councillors Members*] (Tokyo: Okurasho insatsukyoku, 1990), p. 299. Unless otherwise noted, the following account is based on the notes of our interview with Kunihiro in his office in the House of Councillors Members Office Building on June 20, 1991.

22, to the LDP in the PR-based nationwide contests; this time, however, the SDP beat the LDP twenty to fifteen. Ranked third on the SDP's party list of candidates, Kunihiro was an easy winner; in fact, in the position in which he was placed on the party list, he would have been an easy winner even without an upset. The only interesting question here then is how and why he was ranked third on that list.

Kunihiro's enormous public visibility and popularity was unquestionably an important consideration on the part of the SDP's top leaders, who compiled the official candidate list. His visibility and popularity alone, however, would not have earned him the third place on that list; sponsorship by one of the nation's largest labor organizations and the SDP's key ally, the All Japan Federation of Telecommunication Workers Unions (Zendentsu), did. Like other influential union organizations allied with the SDP, Zendentsu was an enormously important source of both votes and funds for the party; it contributed about 10 percent of the SDP's total membership. Without the intervention by this sponsor, Kunihiro might still have made it to a relatively high place on the list and thus been elected. It is very unlikely, however, that he would have been placed as high as third.

Kunihiro was not the only new SDP candidate who was "adopted" by a major labor organization in the 1989 upper house election. Kiyoko Kusakabe, who was a graduate of London University, a professor of social work at a well-known private university and ranked fourth on the SDP's list of PR candidates, was "adopted" by another large labor group, the Federation of Local Government Employees Unions.[20] Of the remainder of the party's twenty-five PR candidates, sixteen were new candidates. All but four of these sixteen, however, were either representatives of special interest groups with substantial nationwide memberships or SDP functionaries who would have either not needed the support of particular patron labor organizations or already had long-standing prior relationships with such organizations.[21] The four exceptions were, respectively, a reporter of a private television network, a lawyer, a pharmacist, and a social worker. It is almost certain, although we are unable to document it at this point, that all or most of these four were, like Kunihiro and Kusakabe, "adopted" by major labor organizations.

"Adoption" of an SDP candidate by a particular labor federation or federations was not mentioned in any official rule of the party. Nor, for that matter,

20 For her background, see Shugiin sangiin, *Gikai seido hyakunenshi: Kizokuin sangiin*, p. 297. Our attribution of her rank on the SDPJ candidate list to the labor federation's sponsorship is based on Kunihiro's testimony.
21 Six of them, all ranked at the bottom of the list, were party functionaries; the rest were officials of, respectively, the All Japan Federation of Farmers Unions, Japan Women's Congress, Japan Medical Association, National Association of Retired Persons, National Federation of Small and Medium-Sized Enterprises, and Otani Group of the Shinshu (Buddhist) Sect. See *Yomiuri shinbun*, July 6, 1989.

were the SDP's nearly total dependence on public sector labor groups and the latter's dominance of the party's policy and policy-making part of the formal relationship between them. Nonetheless, the intimate relationship with organized labor was a widely known and accepted fact of life for the SDP, and the "adoption" of an SDP candidate by a labor federation was a routine practice. In short, both were informal but well-established rules of opposition politics in Japan.

Each patron labor group must have had some reason to "adopt" a particular candidate. It appears that the candidate's visibility and popularity were far more important considerations than his or her policy or ideological position. Kunihiro was an avowed "citizens' representative," as were Tomiko Okazaki and most other women candidates endorsed by the SDP in the 1989 election. With the then SDP leader, Takako Doi, they shared interest in such broad global issues as the environment, human rights, Third World poverty, nuclear hazards, arms control, and so on. At the top of their domestic policy agenda was, as a rule, the defense of the postwar Japanese constitution, particularly its controversial "peace clause," against the conservatives' repeated assaults. On the other hand, the leaders, and presumably also the rank and file, of most of the major Japanese labor federations, including Kunihiro's patron group, Zendentsu, had long since recanted their erstwhile radicalism and had embraced "pragmatism," which translated into a willingness to cooperate with management, not only in the private sector but, increasingly, in the public sector as well. They were, by and large, indifferent, if not hostile, to citizen groups and their causes.

Ironically, the SDP's spectacular success in the 1989 election, including the victories of an unprecedented number (ten) of its women candidates, was owed importantly to the continuing support of the party's traditional ally, organized labor. Despite the media hype about its miracle rebirth under a latter-day Joan of Arc's (Takako Doi's) heroic leadership, the party remained de facto in the grip of the few influential labor federations. Not surprisingly, as labor leaders in general and those in the private sector in particular had over the years become increasingly "pragmatic" and "corporatist," the SDP leadership and rank and file, too, had moved in the same direction. By 1989, Doi's hardline antirearmament, anti–Self Defense Forces, and anti–U.S.-Japanese military alliance position had become a minority view in the party. They found themselves increasingly at odds with and alienated from both their patron union bosses and the "pragmatist" majority in their own party, led by, among others, Makoto Tanabe, who succeeded Doi as the SDP leader in July 1991. The victory of the citizens' representatives in the 1989 upper house election thus introduced a new ideological fault line in a party that so far had been kept afloat almost entirely by the support and under the dominance of Japan's increasingly conservative organized labor. The ideological

falling out was bound to have deleterious impacts on SDP candidates'
performance in future Diet elections. In the 1989 upper house election,
however, Kunihiro and others who placed at the top of the SDP's PR list did
not have to worry about either votes or money, thanks to their sponsors' commitment of both to their success. Few of them would have been able to raise
enough funds and win enough votes on their own.

The privilege to free-ride on a sponsor's financial and organizational power
did not extend to SDP candidates running in multimember prefectural districts in upper or lower house elections; each candidate had to raise most, if
not all, of the money and woo most of the votes that he or she needed to
win.[22] In such a situation, tension and conflict between the demands of and
pressures from, on the one hand, the SDP's old ally, organized labor, and, on
the other, some individual SDP candidates' new allies, citizen groups and new
social movements, would inevitably raise sticky problems, as in Okazaki's
case. While Okazaki survived the test in 1993, Kunihiro did not in 1995.
In early 1994, he had opposed and voted against the electoral reform bills,
in defiance of the SDP's official policy, and had consequently been expelled
from the party. He then joined a newly formed mini-party, called the Party
for Peace and Citizens (Heiwa, Shimin), ran at the top of its PR list in the
1995 upper house election, without union support, and lost. Informal politics thus made or broke a candidate, depending on how he or she accommo-
dated and availed him- or herself of its potent power. Kunihiro's case shows
that such accommodation was not always easy, especially when the candidate
was committed to an ideological belief or principle.

SUMMARY AND CONCLUSION

The three case studies presented in this chapter illustrate the complex pattern of conflict and accommodation between formal and informal politics at

22 Only 100 of the 252 upper house members were elected from the nationwide constituency under the
party list–based PR system, while the remainder were elected from 47 multimember prefecturewide
constituencies by a plurality method. A voter in an upper house election thus cast two ballots, one
for a party list in the nationwide competition and the other for an individual candidate running in
the voter's own prefecture. In a lower house general election before the 1994 revision of the electoral
law, all but one of its 512 members were elected from multimember constituencies, some coinciding
with prefectures but many with subdivisions of a prefecture. For a discussion of the pre-1994 lower
house election systems and their effects on party politics in prewar and postwar Japan, see Haruhiro
Fukui, "Electoral laws and the Japanese party system," in Gail Lee Bernstein and Haruhiro Fukui,
eds., *Japan and the World* (London: Macmillan Press, 1988), Chap. 7; Sadafumi Kawato, "Senkyo seido
to seitosei: Nihon ni okeru 5-tsu no senkyo seido no hikaku bunseki" [A comparative analysis of five
electoral systems used in Japan], *Leviathan* 20 (Spring 1997), pp. 58–83. For discussions of the 1994
electoral reform and its effects as seen in the results of the 1996 general election, see Albert
L. Seligmann, "Japan's new electoral system: Has anything changed?" and Masaru Kohno, "Voter
turnout and strategic ticket-splitting under Japan's new electoral rules," both in *Asian Survey* 37:5
(May 1997), pp. 409–428, 429–440.

the state and infrastate levels in Japan in the late 1980s and early 1990s. The following are some of the most interesting aspects of this interplay as seen from the perspective of an effort to construct an empirical theory of informal politics.

First we note that, as the conventional wisdom about Japanese politics has long emphasized, money was an extremely important element of politics, especially electoral politics.[23] The SDP candidate, Okazaki, and the LDP candidate, Moriyama, both carefully weighed the possibility and difficulty of finding enough of it to make their candidacy realistic before they decided to run for a lower and an upper house seat, respectively, in response to an invitation from party leaders. Other Japanese citizens who met all of the formal requirements of candidacy as easily as either of them, but could not hope to find several times the legally prescribed amounts of campaign funds, could not have run and won. It was thus a fundamental and fundamentally important rule of informal politics in Japan in the last decades of the twentieth century that money reduced the number of Japanese citizens who were actually, rather than theoretically, qualified to run in a Diet election to a tiny fraction of the nation's adult population.[24]

Second, however, money alone did not determine whether one could run in a Diet election as a viable candidate. One's visibility and reputation – both the quintessential stuff of informal politics that is not subject to regulation or control by law or any other formal rule of the state, infrastate, or suprastate organization – played a key role in the success of all three candidates. Both Okazaki and Kunihiro were well-known television personalities, while Moriyama was a rare woman who had graduated from Japan's most famous university and attained a top position in the nation's male-dominated central government bureaucracy. One's reputation that had little to do with formal politics went a long way in Diet elections, whether as a substitute or as an inducement for campaign funds.

Third, an active and efficient campaign organization, *koenkai*, was even more critical to a candidate's success. It did not matter whether the organization was built by the candidate him- or herself, as in Okazaki's case and, partially, Moriyama's, or supplied by others, as in Kunihiro's. Nor did it matter whether it was an organization with a well-defined membership and a rigid boundary, as the labor groups that supported Kunihiro's campaign and, partially, Okazaki's, or one with a much looser structure, as the citizen group in Okazaki's campaign and some elements of Moriyama's campaign network. What mattered was that the organization was extensive and active enough to

23 In addition to the sources already cited, see also Michisada Hirose, *Seiji to kane* [*Politics and money*] (Tokyo: Iwanami shoten, 1989).
24 For amplification of this point, see Fukui, "Japan," in Norris, ed., *Passages to Power*.

reach and mobilize a large number of occupationally diverse and increasingly finicky voters. Kunihiro's defeat in the 1995 upper house election testifies to the enormous handicap that a campaign without a viable organizational base suffers. It is interesting and significant to note in this regard, however, that an extremely loosely organized group of the new social movement type beat a much better organized and established coalition of party activists and union members in both voter mobilization and fund raising in Okazaki's campaign and, to a lesser extent, in Moriyama's. Informality, to the extent that it encourages voluntary activism, can be a strength rather than a weakness in real-world politics.

Fourth, a number of much older and more familiar forms of informal politics also played an important part in Diet elections of the period. Electoral alliances between spouses and collaboration between one of them and the other's political allies, as seen in Moriyama's case, were good examples. Faction-based rivalries and collaboration among LDP candidates, again as seen in Moriyama's case, were just as common. So was orchestrated support by the employees of a government agency or private firm for their current or former boss. Many of the oldest and best-known bases of informal politics, such as kinship, factionalism, and workplace relationships, were thus still very much alive and visible in Japanese electoral politics in the last decades of the twentieth century. Sponsorship of SDP candidates by labor groups, as in Kunihiro's case, was an oppositionist variant of the same type of old-fashioned informal politics that was dying hard, if it was.

Fifth, the foregoing case studies provide ample evidence of the strength and tenacity of informal politics. Its durability is all the more remarkable when we compare its manifestations in the Diet elections of the late 1980s and early 1990s with those observed by Curtis in the 1967 lower house election.[25] The *koenkai* used by LDP candidates, the crucial role of money in their campaigns, the union support for a JSP (today's SDP) candidate, and so on, described by Curtis have all too familiar rings to us. These and other attributes of old-style informal politics have proven more tenacious and durable than Curtis believed a quarter-century ago; in the conclusion of his 1971 book, he foresaw a shift in the conservative candidates' campaign strategy away from reliance on *koenkai* and toward greater reliance on voluntary associations and, eventually, on direct appeal to the electorate.[26] Such a shift may have been under way, but apparently only at a glacial pace, especially in rural areas. Our own case studies suggest that the *koenkai*-based machine politics is going to be the rule rather than the exception for many LDP and other

25 Gerald L. Curtis, *Election Campaigning Japanese Style* (New York: Columbia University Press, 1971).
26 Ibid., pp. 251–253.

conservative Diet members for a long time to come. So is SDP politicians' reliance on unions. It is worth noting that the extensive changes in the formal electoral rules embodied in the 1994 revision of the lower house election law have so far failed to change the informal but decisive roles played by *koenkai* and labor unions, as several studies of the 1996 general election demonstrate.[27]

Finally, however, it is also true that, as Okazaki's and Moriyama's cases suggest, in many urban areas looser knit networks of voters are formed around particular policy issues and demands, which are often cemented by personal trust in the candidate and/or shared ideological beliefs and commitments. The impressive effectiveness of the new social movement type of groups in Okazaki's campaigns may well reflect the rising undercurrent of yearning for more open and participatory politics among Japanese voters. Normally hidden under the surface current of traditional machine-centered campaigning and camouflaged as an epidemic of voter apathy, the undercurrent may prove to be powerful enough to sustain new forms of campaign organization to compete with, if not replace, the traditional forms typified by *koenkai* and labor unions. Okazaki's victory in the 1997 upper house by-election suggests that, under certain conditions, loosely knit networks of volunteers speaking for a disaffected public may prove to be more than equal to the entrenched machines. This study thus suggests an increasingly dynamic and complex landscape of informal politics of elections in Japan as the nation prepares to enter the twenty-first century.

---

27 For supporting evidence and arguments, see various chapters in Hideo Otake, ed., *Seikai saihen no naka no sosenkyo* [*A general election amidst an ongoing realignment of political forces*] (Tokyo: Yuhikaku, 1997); Fukui and Fukai, "Japan in 1996," p. 25; and *Yomiuri shinbun*, October 21, 1997.

CHAPTER 2

INFORMAL POLITICS IN TAIWAN

T. J. CHENG AND T. C. CHOU

Academic attention on democratic consolidation is riveted to the making of formal rules, notably the choice of electoral system and the rewriting of the constitution.[1] Formal rules are important for an understanding of the political process. They lay down the basic institutional framework within which political elites compete. They embody an incentive system that shapes the behavior of political elites.

However, politics should be understood in terms of unwritten rules as well. First, formal rules may become completely ritualized, as in pre-1989 European communist regimes. Often, formal rules simply exist on paper, either unenforced or overlooked. For example, political contributions and electoral spending grossly exceed the legal limits in Japan, Korea, and Taiwan. Second, while formal and informal power may eventually converge,[2] this process may be very long. Third, the discrepancy between formal rules and the actual code of conduct can be very significant. Fukui and Fukai show that informal politics in Japan is normal politics, while the making and remaking of formal rules are extraordinary politics that explains what went wrong with informal politics but do not explain what usually occurs in Japan.[3] Hence, once the infrequent drama of remaking formal rules is over, unwritten rules reemerge to guide politics.

In informal politics, factionalism stands out as a particularly salient phenomenon. This is particularly true in some parts of the world, such as

1 Bernard Grofman and Arend Lijphart, eds., *Electoral Laws and Their Political Consequences* (New York: Agathon, 1986); Juan Linz, "Democracy: Presidential or parliamentary. Does it make a difference?" *Journal of Democracy*, 1990; Giuseppe Di Palma, *To Craft Democracies* (Berkeley: University of California Press, 1990).

2 Lowell Dittmer, "Bases of power in Chinese politics: A theory and an analysis of the fall of 'Gang of Four,'" *World Politics* 31:1 (October 1978), pp. 26–60; Andrew J. Nathan, "A factionalism model for CCP politics," in Steffen W. Schmidt, Laura Guasti, Carl H. Lande, and James C. Scott, eds., *Friends, Followers, and Factions: A Reader in Political Clientelism* (Berkeley: University of California Press).

3 Haruhiro Fukui and Shigeko N. Fukai, "Informal politics and one-party dominance in Japan: A case study and a rudimentary theory," *Leviathan* 9 (Fall 1991), pp. 55–79.

caucus- membership is preassigned, not selected

East Asia, the Mediterranean countries, developing countries in general, and, arguably, the pre–civil rights American South and big immigrant cities.[4] Permutations of political power in southern Italy are an epiphenomenon of factional dynamics, and factional ties within America's Democratic Party are the best predictor of gubernatorial races in the American Old South. Factional politics determines leadership selection, the allocation of cabinet positions, and campaign strategy in Japan. Intraparty conflict is even more severe than interparty competition in contemporary Taiwan. In the Sixth Republic of Korea, intraparty politics has prevented the switch from a presidential system to a parliamentary government. Academic debates on the virtues and vices of forms of government are totally irrelevant to Korea's recent constitutional choice.[5] Even the Leninist party in communist China has not been immune from factions, which remain a useful analytical category for political dynamics.

Like political parties and caucuses, factions are political groupings meant to solve collective-action problems, so as to economically create "public" goods that benefit all of their members. With "isomorphic" hierarchical structures, these three kinds of political groupings are different from political coalitions, which are temporary alliances on some pre-agreed-upon and well-specified issues. The units of a coalition do not surrender their autonomy to a central decision-making unit, but simply coordinate their strategies in a largely one-shot political game. Moreover, the members of a coalition are heterogeneous and shifting, and their sizes change according to the issues at stake. In the United States, for example, Jessie Jackson's Rainbow Coalition consists of various minority groups and single-issue groups while the shape of protectionist coalitions in the U.S. Congress varies from one session to another.

Caucuses, factions, and parties are, however, asymmetric in terms of their internal organizing principles. Caucuses are groups based on common attributes, such as the black caucus and the women's caucus, and whose members are preassigned rather than self-selected. (Old-day American caucuses, in the pre–Andrew Jackson or pre-convention era, denoted a closed meeting of a group of people, in a political party, for the purpose of nomination or even policy deliberation.) Factions are, in most cases, leader-oriented, guided by unwritten rules, and based on patron–client networks. In contrast, parties have formal rules and ideology-tinted platforms. Factions are informal,

---

4 See Frank P. Belloni and Dennis C. Beller, eds., *Faction Politics: Political Parties and Factionalism in Comparative Perspective* (Santa Barbara, CA: ABC-Clio, 1978); Schmidt et al., eds., *Friends, Followers, and Factions*; Guy Hermet, Richard Rose, and Alain Rouquie, eds., *Elections without Choice* (New York: John Wiley, 1978), especially the chapter by Alain Rouquie on "Clientelist Control and Authoritarian Contexts."

5 Tun-jen Cheng, "The constitutional choices in newly democratic Korea," International Relations and Pacific Studies, University of California, San Diego, Policymaking process case material, 1992.

personal, opaque, and akin to political machines, while parties are formal, transparent (with the exception of Leninist parties), platform-oriented, with rules codified and amended in due process and hence less susceptible to political bosses. Factions are ideology-free, interest-centered, and power-motivated. Organizationally, a typical faction is cemented by dyadic relations between a patron and several clients, who in turn may be lesser patrons with their own clients.[6] Clients are loyal to their patrons in exchange for rewards or protection. Because dyadic ties are diffuse and transcend specific policy issues, they are also semipermanent, lasting beyond the official association in an institution.

Thus, the patron–client model underlies most analyses of factions. The clientelist model, premised on the exchange of loyalty for rewards, is at its best in analyzing the internal relations of factions. However, this model does not explain how factions exercise power to extract resources from external political actors or sponsors for the purpose of maintaining internal cohesiveness. For the growth and evolution of factions, the principal–agent model may be more useful.[8] When a group of actors (be they national legislators, party delegates, or a local political machine) endorses a contender in a power game (such as the race for president or party head), it appears that the former are followers looking for a boss; in fact, the opposite is true. The former is the principal and the latter the agent. The former delegates power to the latter, as an agent, for the critical task of protecting and expanding factional interests. Delegation of authority does not have to be explicit; the critical test of the principal–agent relation is that the former can remove the latter if agency costs and agency losses become too exorbitant. If the agent fails to deliver political goods, the principals simply designate another agent for the task.

Historically, factions that were not favored by the ruler were regarded as cliques, which is a pejorative concept, and clique activities could mean treason. Modern factions all carry noble names (such as associations, study groups, clubs, and so on) and formally pledge allegiance to the party. Except in the Leninist party, which prohibits factions, nearly "every democratic political party" tolerated, if not permitted, factions.[9] Thus the question is not whether factions exist, but how they emerge. What forms do they take? What

6 Haruhiro Fukui, "Japan: Factionalism in a dominant-party system," in Belloni and Beller, eds., *Faction Politics.*

7 Robert R. Kaufman, "The patron-client concept and macro-politics: Prospect and problems," *Comparative Studies in Society and History,* 16 (June 1974), pp. 284–308.

8 D. Roderick Kiewiet and Matthew D. McCubbins, *The Logic of Delegation* (Chicago: University of Chicago Press, 1991), Chap. 1.

9 Austin Ranney, "Candidate selection," in David Butler, Howard R. Penniman, and Austin Ranney, eds., *Democracy at the Polls* (Washington, DC: AEI, 1981), p. 101.

is the structure (basis) of factions, and to what extent do they become the mainstay of politics?

Factions in some countries are certainly more stable and institutionalized and perform more functions than in others. Factionalism in Japan is often used as a paradigm to measure and discuss factionalism in other countries. Still, not all factionalism is as full-blown, consistent, and long-lasting as Japan's. As Ralph Nicholas argues, factions may persist for a long time, but they are less permanent than corporate political parties or enduring corporate groups such as clans or lineages.[10] The longevity, persistence, and stability of Japanese-like factionalism may well be the exception, rather than the rule. Indeed, even the deeply entrenched factionalism in the Japanese Liberal Democratic Party suffered a near breakdown in 1993 when some factions defected the party, ushering in a period of factional realignment.

This chapter analyzes emerging factions within the ruling party, the Kuomintang (Nationalist Party or KMT), in newly democratizing Taiwan. Factionalism in the principal opposition party, the Democratic Progressive Party (DPP), has long existed and is a problem, but there is nothing special about it. Factionalism tends to arise in any political opposition movement and plagues the major opposition party in the process of its political ascension. Yet factions within the opposition, no matter how intense and fierce, usually are constrained by the necessity to collaborate for survival and to increase their chances of seizing political power. In contrast, factions in the dominant KMT party raise a theoretically interesting question for discussion on democratic transitions: Will factionalization of the ruling party be controlled and become a mechanism for continuous political domination, or will it become a midwife to a two-party or multiparty system? The cohesion or fragmentation of the ruling elite is, as Robert Fishman argues, a critical variable in determining the political structure that will emerge after a democratic transition.[11] This variable is particularly important to one-party hegemonic regimes undergoing democratic change, such as those in Taiwan and Mexico. If the ruling party can maintain some degree of cohesion, it can steer the course of political change from one-party hegemonic authoritarianism to faction-lubricated, one-party–dominant democracies, à la pre-1993 Japan, or a strong-leader–oriented, one-party–dominant system, à la pre-1973 Israel.[12]

10 Ralph W. Nicholas, "Factions: A comparative analysis," in Schmidt et al., eds., *Friends, Followers, and Factions*, p. 58.
11 Robert M. Fishman, "Rethinking state and regime: Southern Europe's transition to democracy," *World Politics* 42:3 (April 1990), pp. 422–440.
12 T. J. Pempel, ed., *Uncommon Democracies* (Ithaca: Cornell University Press, 1990); Tun-jen Cheng, "Exits from One-Party Hegemony," paper presented at International Studies Association Convention, Vancouver, 1991.

Conversely, a grand split of the ruling party could usher in multiple-party competition, à la post-1993 Japan. The case of the KMT will shed light on the process and outcome of democratic transition in one-party hegemonic systems.

We will also focus mainly on new factions in the Legislative Yuan (or branch). This is partly due to data limitation and partly because of the importance of the Legislative Yuan vis-à-vis the other two national representative bodies, the Control Yuan (an oversight organ) and the National Assembly (essentially a presidential electoral college). The emerging factions within the KMT are most dynamic and manifest in the Legislative Yuan, while factional grouping outside this arena is extremely fluid and not readily identifiable in the absence of a power struggle. Moreover, conflict in the nebulous KMT leadership stands out more clearly in the Legislative Yuan. The leadership of each legislative faction interfaces with other factions in the party and government. Members in the Legislative Yuan need to explicitly state their positions to communicate with constituents on the one hand, while on the other hand signaling political leaders engaged in conflict of their loyalty. They do so in an effort to reap concrete benefits from political battles. Hence, studying legislative factions will shed light on the political infighting of the Byzantine KMT leadership.

Factions in the Legislative Yuan are known as "secondary political groups" within the KMT, while conflicts in the KMT's leadership are regarded as factional splits between mainstream and nonmainstream factions. Political conflict in the Legislative Yuan is seen as a proxy war among the KMT's leadership. This chapter, however, will show that legislative factionalism is more entrenched, institutionalized, and permanent than that in the party leadership stratum. We also argue that, far from being agents of the KMT leadership, legislative factions are actually the principals. As principals, these legislative factions pick KMT leaders as agents to expand their political market shares and maintain factional cohesion.

In the following sections we first summarize our views on the now-defunct factionalism in the postwar KMT regime. We then describe the formation of new factions within the legislature. Finally, we analyze the nature of the emerging legislative factionalism and explore possible causes for incipient factional politics. We essentially characterize legislative factions as "soft factions," in that they lack powerful leaders, permit overlapping and multiple membership, practice and tolerate predatory recruitment of members, and cannot impose discipline and sanctions against uncooperative faction members. In accounting for the rise of legislative factions, we underscore the institutional factors, mainly the electoral system and to some extent the preexisting hegemonic party system, in motivating legislators to coalesce into informal groups.

KMT Nationalist- fled from China in 1950 when the communists took over. [handwritten marginalia]

OLD FACTIONS SUBMERGED (1950–1986)

Factional strife – which bred instability and corruption – was a fatal blow to the KMT regime on the mainland.[13] The postwar KMT regime has never been faction-free, but factionalism was subdued until recently. Some factions evaporated or disintegrated during the regime's relocation to Taiwan; those who regrouped in Taiwan were either loyal to or disciplined by a reformed KMT. Factions were most active and observable in the Legislative Yuan; legislators interpellated officials, deliberated bills, and made explicit policy stands revealing factional lines. Factions were not as active in the Control Yuan, where each commissioner exercised power individually. Factions existed, but remained largely dormant in the National Assembly, where most delegates primarily moonlighted. Note that the members of all three national representative organs were made lifetime members after the national elections were suspended indefinitely. Essentially two major factions emerged in the Legislative Yuan in postwar Taiwan: the United Caucus Clique (UCC) and its competitor, the CC Clique (CCC).[14] In the pre-1949 years, constituency groups of the UCC emerged as reform-minded forces targeted at the KMT's dominant and primarily preservative faction: the CCC. In postwar Taiwan, the UCC came to dominate the party state while the CCC functioned as a "liberal" opposition faction that supervised the in-power UCC. Out of power, and sworn not to assume office, the CCC members were very critical of government policies. Although several other factions existed (including one splinter group from the CCC and an interparty club), factionalism was primarily a duopoly consisting of the UCC and the CCC.

Local factions existed in Taiwan and were used by the regime to exercise political control at the local level.[15] With few exceptions, factions in nearly

13 Ch'i, Hsi-sheng, *Nationalist China at War* (Ann Arbor: University of Michigan Press, 1982), pp. 208–213; Lloyd E. Eastman, *Seeds of Destruction* (Stanford: Stanford University Press, 1984).

14 The UCC integrated the Whampoa group (based on the military academy), the *san-min-chu-i ch'ing-nien-t'uan* (Three People's Principles Youth Corps), *fu-hsing-she* (The Renaissance Society, intelligence network), and the followers of *Chu Chia-hua* (who succeeded Chen Cheng as head of Youth Corps and later became head of the Organizational Department of the KMT. The CC clique collected the remnants of the powerful CC faction in the pre-1950 period, previously under the leadership of Chen Kuo-fu and Chen Li-fu. Chen Kuo-fu later died, while Chen Li-fu went to the United States to raise chickens. The UCC has about 146 members, the CCC about 60 members. See Hung-mao Tien, *The Great Transition: Political and Social Change in the Republic of China* (Stanford: Hoover Institute Press, 1989), pp. 149–150. For prewar factional lineages, see Lloyd E. Eastman, "Nationalist China during the Nanking decade, 1927–1937," in Eastman et al., *The Nationalist Era in China 1927–1949* (Cambridge: Cambridge University Press, 1991), pp. 26–32.

15 Lawrence W. Crissman, "The structure of local and regional systems," in Emily Martin Ahern and Hill Gates, eds., *The Anthropology of Taiwanese Society* (Stanford: Stanford University Press, 1981), pp. 105–106; Bruce J. Jacobs, *Local Politics in a Rural Chinese Setting* (Canberra: Research School of Pacific Studies, Australian National University); Arthur J. Lerman, *Taiwan's Politics* (Washington, DC: University Press of America, 1978). For a more updated analysis, see Nai-teh Wu, "Politics of a regime patronage system: Mobilization and control within an authoritarian regime," unpublished paper, University of Chicago, Political Science Department, 1987; and Joseph Bosco, "Taiwan factions: *Guanxi*, patronage, and the state in local politics," *Ethnology* 31:2 (April 1992).

all localities were created and nurtured by local elections that the KMT regime promulgated in 1951. The KMT regime used local factions to manipulate local politics. Factions permitted the KMT to allocate votes to maximize seat gains and to balance the power of county governments versus county councils. Thus, the KMT became an indispensable mediator among rival factions and a coordinator for factional leaders' sequential access to highly circumscribed political power at the local level.

As a strong party, under its supreme leader, Chiang Kai-shek, the KMT was able to contain factionalism at both the national and local levels. At least three unwritten rules prevented faction politics from subverting the authority of the KMT regime in postwar Taiwan. First, local factions were insulated from central politics. Anyone breaching this informal rule invited political purge. The crackdown of Lei Chen in 1961 – a well-connected KMT libertarian, who attempted to coalesce with local leaders to form a new political party – is a good example. It provided a "threshold" case and set a de facto standard of political behavior for all political actors. Moreover, the suspension of national elections was a disincentive for local elites to align with factions at the national level. Highly intensive and often internecine factional conflict at the local level never spilled over to the central level. Second, factions from the three national representative bodies could not coalesce. Sharing the constitutional power of the legislature meant that these three institutions faced turf wars. But it also meant that the three ought to make alliances to collectively check the executive power, a condition that could have made the life of the president and his premier very difficult. Factional alignment across the three houses could have ameliorated turf wars, but the party leadership was averse to permitting this integrative function of factions. Third, factional squabbles were confined to deliberation and interpellation in the Legislative Yuan. Party discipline was enforced in voting; noncompliant members risked excommunication and expulsion from the party. Since the electoral space was sealed, those expelled from the party could not vindicate their case by resorting to popular support.

As in other single-party systems or one-party–dominant systems, factional politics in the postwar KMT regime had the semblance of multiple-party checks and balances. However, the analogy between faction competition and party competition is a specious one. First, the KMT was a quasi-Leninist party; all members were required to declare their loyalty to the party leadership and commit themselves to the party's platform and ideology. As long as the party leadership had disciplinary power and the authority to interpret the ideology of the party, there was a limit to which factionalism could play itself out.

Second, interfactional competition might be likened to interparty competition, if the factional balance of power were validated by electoral verdict, as in Japan. There, the shift in factional balance often leads to personnel changes, although not the drastic policy shifts that characterize interparty competition. However, in the case of the KMT, factional balance could not be electorally adjusted, albeit factional disputes bore some overtones of policy debates.

Third, because they faced no reelection battle and were immune from constituency pressure, legislative factions under the KMT regime had no incentive to defy the party leadership. Factional members did not have to perform their representative functions or deliver "goodies" to their constituencies. Indeed, most CCC legislators settled for "cheap talk." Specifically, they aired dissenting opinions but voted with the ruling UCC faction. After the rise of the CCK, the CCC, as the out-of-power faction, was better treated and its members were co-opted into leadership positions within the Legislative Yuan. Factional balance was maintained through the assignment of committee chairmanships and subcommittee convenorships.

In other political systems, leadership succession is intertwined with the ebb and flow of factions. Until the mid-1980s, however, the KMT regime suffered only one conflict regarding political succession, namely, that between Chen Cheng and Chiang Ching-Kuo (CCK), which was for all practical purposes settled in the latter half of the 1960s.[16] The CCK's followers emerged outside of the Legislative Yuan. This succession process was less a factional struggle than a generational elite substitution. In any case, the battle of succession was fought outside of the legislative arena. The death of Chen Cheng in 1965 led to the decline of the UCC, which made the "opposition" role of the CCC less important than it used to be. Intensive factional strife in the Legislative Yuan petered out after 1965, not to resurface again until the mid-1980s. Meanwhile, old-timers in the three houses of congress emerged as targets of political reform, which the CCK launched.

NEW FACTIONS EMERGE (1986–1991)

Following the crucial decision by the KMT leadership to pursue democratic reform and the formation of the first new opposition party in 1986, Taiwan's democratic transition was set in motion. In the wake of political decontrol, factionalism resurfaced in the Legislative Yuan. As this arena has begun to open up for political competition, it has become an important policy-making arena, as laws, and not decrees, are now needed to govern the country. With the influx of newly elected legislators, new factions took shape in the late 1980s. These new

16 For an analysis of the succession conflict, see Edwin A. Winckler, "Elite political struggle 1945–1985," in Winckler and Susan Greenhalgh, eds., *Contending Approaches to the Political Economy of Taiwan* (Armonk, NY: Sharp, 1988), pp. 154–161.

factions are not an outgrowth of old factions. There is neither institutional lineage nor hereditary membership between the old and new factions. Factional links between these two "generations" are insignificant and transient.

Precursors of these new factions predate the democratic transition in 1986. To replenish the aging 1947 cohorts of members of the three national representative bodies, the KMT regime began to institutionalize "supplementary" national-level elections in 1972. These newly elected national representatives were predominantly Taiwanese, while a smaller number of new members were selected from overseas Chinese communities, mostly non-Taiwanese. New recruits, unlike the 1947 cohorts, needed to renew their terms: every three years for legislators and every six years for assembly persons and members of the Control Yuan. These new members began to coalesce among themselves, but the formation of factions was aborted. There was neither room nor incentive for the newly elected legislators to form groups independent of the old factions. On the one hand, the KMT disallowed any new (that is, Taiwanese) legislator clubs for fear of highlighting the subethnic cleavage and the embarrassingly political underrepresentation of the native Taiwanese.[17] In 1981, Chiang Yen-shi, then secretary general of the KMT, disbanded a mutual assistance club that was organized by new members.[18] On the other hand, it was more rewarding for new recruits to associate with the old-timers than against them. While the number of new recruits gradually increased from 11 to 101 between 1969 and 1989, they were still outnumbered by old-timers (see Table 2.1). New recruits, although still a minority, competed among themselves to ally with old guards, especially members of the UCC, so as to get good committee assignments and other resources that the old guards could spare or would vacate.[19] Not all new recruits were so tempted, however.[20] As the number of old guards shrank (including the drop in their attendance rate due to poor health), more new recruits were added and it became less attractive for the latter to be co-opted by the former. When the numerical balance between the old guards and the new recruits was attained in the late 1980s, the time seemed ripe for the latter to declare their independence from the former.

The Wisdom Coalition (*Jisi hui*) blazed the trail in April 1988.[21] Leaders of this club include Huang Chu-wen, Wu Tzu, Lin Yu-hsiang, and,

---

17 Tien, *The Great Transition*, p. 150.   18 *Chung-kuo shih-pao* [*China Times*], January 1, 1990.
19 *Shih-pao chou-kan* [*China Times Weekly*], March 1, 1989, p. 19.
20 In 1985, the Tsai's Thirteen Brotherhood Club, a small but highly active group of some thirteen new legislators revolving around legislator Tsai Chen-chou, became defunct after the collapse of its leader's Cathay business group. Some old-timers were reportedly enlisted by this group. See Wu Ke-ch'ing, "Chuanyan zhong de 'shisan xiongdi' menglin jieji," [The alleged Thirteen Brotherhood nears break-up]. *Shih-pao tsa-chih* [*Time Magazine*], 39 (September 25, 1985).
21 *Jisi-hui* literally means thought-aggregating club and they call themselves the Wisdom Coalition; coalition is not an appropriate term since members joined this club as individuals and this club is not an aggregation of several preexisting groups.

Table 2.1. *Ratio Between the Supplementary Members and Their Senior Colleagues in the Legislative Yuan*

Years	Senior Members		Supplementary Members	
	Number	Percent	Number	Percent
1969	468	97.7	11	2.3
1972	419	92.1	36	7.9
1975	377	87.9	37	8.6
			15a	3.5
1980	309	76.1	70	17.2
			27a	6.6
1983	270	73.4	71	19.3
			27a	7.3
1986	224	69.1	73	22.5
			27a	8.3
1989	150	53.6	101	36.1
			29a	10.4

Sources: Lei (1992: 167), originally from Ministry of the Interior, *Statistic Data Book of Interior*, various years.

Notes: "a" denotes a subset of supplementary members selected from overseas Chinese communities. Supplementary elections began in 1969; those elected in 1969 faced no reelection and possessed the status of senior members who were either elected in 1947 or selected from those candidates standing for the 1947 election on the mainland. Supplementary members elected after 1971 must renew their mandates through election every three years. All senior members are required to retire by the end of 1991.

before his appointment as party whip, Jaw Ying-chi. The hard-core members of the Wisdom Coalition legislators came from regional electoral districts (as versus "occupational" ones), and at the time of its formation they were first-term legislators. This faction was also mainly a grouping of indigenous legislators (see Table 2.2). It initially had three mainlanders, but all three left in late 1991. With about fifty members, the Wisdom Coalition was the largest political group until late 1991. Its leaders blatantly pronounced their intention of seizing power from the old-timers. This inevitably made the faction a "strategic ally" of DPP legislators in a joint venture to force the old-timers to retire.

The DPP emerged as a formidable opposition after the 1986 legislative election. This was the first time that the KMT regime permitted this newly but illegally formed (viz., against the Martial Law Decree) opposition party

Table 2.2. *Subethnic Background of Members of Seven*
Major Factions (as of December 1991)

Faction	Taiwanese	Mainlanders	Overseas Chinese
DPP	19	–	–
WIC	37	–	8
NKA	7	7	–
CPRC	11	6	15
Concord	7	5	24
RC	20	6	2
CRC	26	11	14

Notes: DPP is included here for comparison. No mainlanders belong to the DPP or WIC now. The WIC had two mainlanders, but they were both NKA members and had switched their membership from WIC to CRC. All except four mainlanders joined the CRC. It seems that there is a premium on having a few mainlanders and overseas Chinese in one's faction so as to signal that this faction is not parochial. DPP = Democratic Progressive Party; WIC = Wisdom Coalition (previously the Wisdom Breakfast Club); NKA = New KMT Alliance; CPRC = Constructive Policy Research Club; Concord = Concord Political Research Association; RC = Renovation Club; CRC = Congressional Reform Group.

to compete with the KMT, without an implied threat of persecution. With fewer than twenty members in the Legislative Yuan, the DPP could not introduce any bills, but it made good use of the legislative forum to set the agenda for removing roadblocks to a democratic transition. Self-defined as the only effective countervailing force against the KMT, the DPP successfully humiliated the old-timers (dubbed as old thieves), trimmed the budget, and in particular highlighted the issue of the acutely obsolete mandate of the old-timers in the three "houses" of the congress.

The challenge of the DPP in the legislature posed both a risk and an opportunity for the newly elected KMT legislators. The DPP's clear-cut policy stand on democratic reform, which was quite popular, could have discredited the newly elected KMT members in the eyes of the electorate. Unless the new KMT legislators asserted themselves, they faced the danger of being identified as junior partners of the extremely unpopular old-timers, an image that would cause them to lose reelections. The Wisdom Coalition used political reform to impress their voters, a bold strategy that differentiated them from the other co-opted new legislators, who used the delivery of political pork, with the assistance of old-timers, to consolidate their constituencies' electoral support.

Once the Wisdom Coalition came into being, other groups mushroomed. Of these, the Constructive Policy Research Club (CPRC) (*Jianshe yanjiu hui*) was the most sizable and began to compete with the Wisdom Coalition.[22] Planned in November 1988 but formally launched in May 1989, the CPRC was a club for new legislators who were closely affiliated with the KMT party caucus in the legislature.[23] Previously associated with old-party elites and old-timers in the UCC faction, the CPRC was antithetical to the Wisdom Coalition.[24] The CPRC included many financially rich members, most of them overseas representatives (who were appointed rather than elected), and a number of representatives from "professional" associations (which had a very small membership); hence its claim of popular support was not as strong as the Wisdom Coalition's, which could claim to command 3 million voters (see Table 2.2). Two-thirds of the CPRC members were incumbents who were reelected in 1986, rather than first-time legislators, and its membership was quite stable. Chaired by Shen Shih-shiung and his deputy, Wu Shien-er, the CPRC was quite active in debating policy issues. Divided into five sections (budget, domestic affairs, economic and transportation, defense and foreign affairs, and the rest), the CPRC held Tuesday lunch meetings to discuss legislative bills.

The formation of the Wisdom Coalition severed the ties between the old guards and the Young Turks, terminated the dependence of the latter on the former, and accelerated the process of pensioning off the old guards from the political scene. Due to the "elective affinity" between the UCC and CPRC, it appears that the WBC could have a tacit alliance with the CC. Had the WBC members chosen to become the minor partners of the CCC (a path of least resistence), then the Legislative Yuan would have been polarized into a UCC–CPRC camp versus the CCC–Wisdom Coalition camp. Under this co-optation model, factional lineage would have been established, new recruits would have remained hostages to old guards, and the pace of political reform in Taiwan would have been slowed down.

The CPRC appeared to have the blessing of the KMT's party whip, which preferred to see a Wisdom Coalition–CPRC cleavage rather than an old-timer–young-Turk cleavage.[25] There was certainly an incentive for the CPRC to join the emerging broad coalition among the new recruits to force out the

22 The *Jianshe yanjiu hui* call themselves the National Policy Research Association; but association is not an appropriate term since this is not a formal organization or legal entity.
23 *Shih-pao chou-kan*, March 1, 1989, #211, pp. 19–20.
24 The leading established old faction, the UCC, has been recruiting new legislators and as such violating its agreement with other old factions, thus inviting criticism from the CCC.
25 The CPRC has a publication bearing the scripture of the last old-time speaker, Liang Su-jong.

old guards, which would have drastically expanded electoral space and made the reelection battle of the incumbents much easier. Nonetheless, the CPRC was very supportive of the conservative party leadership in the Legislative Yuan, which often caved in to old-timers' pressure for gradual rather than accelerated retirement.[26] The CPRC was discredited when old-timers from various factions formed a democratic constitutional research club in September 1989 for a rear-guard battle or glorious retreat and to strike a good deal for their retirement.

In contrast, the Wisdom Coalition often stood against the then-conservative KMT party whip and speaker (themselves old-timers). For example, it defied the KMT's Central Standing Committee's demand for large-scale organizational expansion of the Executive Yuan to increase administrative capacity. The Wisdom Coalition also suggested excluding overseas Chinese legislators from decision making (e.g., legislative voting), although not from policy deliberation. More significantly, the Wisdom Coalition often strategically sided with the DPP to urge for accelerated democratic reforms. Yet, the Wisdom Coalition also mediated between senior KMT legislators and the DPP on three important bills, thereby keeping the DPP off the streets and in the Legislative Yuan. The three bills in question were the election and recall law, the civic association law, and the retirement ordinance.[27]

The 1989 December legislative election marked the end of the Wisdom Coalition–CPRC bipolarity. The expansion of new seats allowed the KMT to nominate a number of second-generation mainlander candidates, who then formed the core of a small but highly potent club, called the New KMT Alliance (NKA) (*Xin Guomindang lianxian*).[28] The NKA was predominantly, but not exclusively, a mainlanders' club, as it also hosted a few Taiwanese legislators who were primarily party cadres, distinct from Taiwanese professional-managerial and business elites, who were frequently found in the Wisdom Coalition. Originally formed as a coalition during election campaigning in December 1989, the NKA was a small but homogenous group of unification activists and clearly identified with the nonmainstream faction (explained below) of the KMT leadership. Many NKA members were affiliated with the Democracy Foundation, a policy institute that was founded by former KMT Secretary General John Kuan and funded by Hua Long (a leading mainlander) group, which functioned as the brain trust of the nonmainstream KMT elite. Leaders of the NKA were You Mu-ming, Ke Yu-chin,

26 *Chung-shih wan-pao* [*China Times Evening News*], September 27, 1989.
27 *Lien-ho Pao* [*United Daily News*], December 16, 1989.
28 *Xin Guomindang lianxian* calls itself the new KMT coalition, but it is more than a coalition. It is a rather closely knit alliance that has binding commitments from its members; given the high degree of collective action, cohesiveness, and mobilization for mutual support among the members of this group, it may more aptly be seen as an alliance.

Li Sheng-feng, Chen Kuei-miao, and Chao Shao-kang. The NKA has twin advantages, small size and homogeneity of its membership, facilitating its collective action. Its members' expectations or actions easily converged even without formal communication and coordination. The NKA thus quickly displaced the CPRC as the main protagonist of the Wisdom Coalition. While the CPRC continued to function as the most staunch supporter of the party, it took a neutral stand on conflicts within the KMT leadership kindled by the March 1990 presidential election, a political battle to be detailed below.

Apart from the Wisdom Coalition, the CPRC, and the NKA, there were three kinds of less active factions. The first type were those that were sizable, but uncommitted to a particular position, and yet could be decisive in floor voting. The Concord Political Club (*Xiehe wenzheng yanjiu hui*, which called itself the Concord Political Research Association) and the Renovation Club (*Chuanxing hui*) were examples. The former emerged on March 8, 1990, mainly representing the military, overseas Chinese, and some big enterprise groups, while the latter was organized by Huang He-ching and formed on May 1, 1990, consisting mainly of local bosses throughout the Taiwan province, but also some big enterprises. These two factions were derived from the short-lived One Mind Club (*Yixing hui*) organized by Liao Fu-bun and Huang He-ching, two major fund providers of the club. The second type contained those that were small and single-issue—oriented, addressing one type of policy that their members were especially concerned with, for example, the medical doctor's caucus, the overseas Chinese legislators' caucus, and the women's caucus. The third kind were small, but transcended either the party or factional lines, and their members attempted to act as intermediaries between parties, for example, the seven-member interpellation group.

The Wisdom Coalition and the NKA were engaged in three rounds of conflicts. The first round pertained to the campaigning for the presidential election in March 1990, during which the candidate team of the mainstream faction (the incumbent President Lee Teng-hui and Vice Presidential nominee Li Yuan-tsu), endorsed by the central committee of the Kuomintang, was challenged by another self-nominated KMT candidate team (Lin Yang-kang and Chiang Weigo) that was supported by the nonmainstream faction. The bifurcation of the KMT leadership into two factions originated in the disagreement between those central committee members unconditionally promoting then Vice President Lee Teng-hui's succession to just-deceased Chiang Ching-kuo as the president of the party in 1988 and those who showed hesitancy or reluctance on this issue. The conflict between these two factions escalated in early 1990, when President Lee avoided choosing from leaders of nonmainstream factions for his running mate in the upcoming election. Second, there were two "scandals" that involved the alleged business influence on politics in the first half of 1991. One scandal implicated a mainlander business maverick who was a main supporter of the nonmainstream faction. The other scandal involved a Taiwanese shipping magnate who was allegedly connected to the mainstream faction. Finally, the division of power between the president (a position held by a Taiwanese since Chiang Ching-kuo died) and the premier (a position held by mainlander and nonmainstream KMT leaders until 1993) became a controversial issue that began to loom large in the second half of 1991, in association with the constitutional reform and the making of Taiwan's policy toward Mainland China. These three rounds of conflict were cumulative in that their effects reinforced rather than negated factional differences. Thus, the lineup of protagonists was clearly drawn. The Wisdom Coalition and the NKA had taken sides in the first and third rounds of conflict while triggering the second round. While it would appear that the Wisdom Coalition and the NKA picked President Lee and Premier Hau Pei-tsun as their "bosses," in fact they were selecting their agents for the overriding task of increasing political resources for their members. We shall come back to this issue later.

The fight between the NKA and the Wisdom Coalition was fierce and relentless. Their mutual attacks were virulent and their verbal abuse vitriolic. For example, the NKA used the most sinister language to denounce Lee on practically every decision he made during the difficult task of democratic reform and did its utmost to hobble Lee on the eve of the presidential election.[29] The Wisdom Coalition, for its share, implied that the new "leader" of the nonmainstream faction, premier Hau, might betray Taiwan's interest and come to terms with the mainland authority. While abrasive, the NKA was after all a small group and outvoted by the Wisdom Coalition. However, it is important to note that the NKA joined hands with the Wisdom Coalition as well as the DPP to amplify the massive social protest against the old-timers' resistance to retirement.

The "bipolarity" of the Wisdom Coalition and the NKA was soon compounded by the advent of another active legislative grouping, the Congressional Reform Coalition (CRC) (*Guohui gongneng gaige hui*), which was initiated by a few first-term legislators in November 1991. The CRC defined itself as a club for novices who claimed to be suffering from lack of leadership and interpellation opportunities as well as from the tarnished image of the paralyzed legislative branch as a result of the misdemeanor of many flamboyant legislators. The CRC thus claimed to aim at reinvigorating the "function of the Congress" (*guohui gong neng*) and deliberating and passing legislation that could

29 *Taiwan shih-pao* [*Taiwan Times*], March 18, 1990.

enhance its members' abilities in seeking nomination and reelection in December 1992.[30] Forming a new club also enabled the organizers of the CRC to bid for legislative leadership positions (such as the speaker of the Legislative Yuan and the chairperson of the Central Policy Commission, a liason body between the executive and legislative branches) vacated by the old-timers who were finally compelled to retire in December 1991.[31]

The CRC was a sort of "countervailing organization" for those legislators resisting the dominance of the Wisdom Coalition while aspiring to the glamor of the NKA. Meant to be a united front to counter the Wisdom Coalition, the CRC was an open shop, extending invitations to nearly every legislator while following democratic principle in its organizational management.[32] Thirteen freshmen legislators (out of a total of fifty-seven) did not join the CRC, while more than ten Wisdom Coalition members did (without forsaking their original membership). With one single exception, the NKA members joined the CRC and became a crucial source of its leadership team. Members of other legislative factions also contributed to the growth of the CRC. Despite its heterogeneous membership, though, the CRC managed to check and balance the Wisdom Coalition. As the latter aligned with the mainstream KMT elite and the president, the CRC echoed with the non-mainstream KMT elite and the premier.[33]

WHY FACTIONS?

The incipient legislative factionalism documented above stems from the very process of democratic transition under a hegemonic party. The passing away of a strong man (Chiang Ching-kuo) triggered succession battles from which the new leadership (Lee Teng-hui) emerged. Not only was the new leader politically weak, and hence in need of sharing power with other contenders for some time, he also faced a tough reelection challenge, thanks to the democratic change. Meanwhile, political decontrol and electoral competition with the opposition loosened the KMT's grip over its rank and file, especially those with local networks and vote-mobilizing capabilities. The uncertainty of leadership succession and the loosening up of party discipline portended a sort of Hobbesian condition within the KMT. As countries form alliances for the defense and promotion of national interests in the anarchical international order, members of the Legislative Yuan – the most competitive political market – coalesced into factions to enhance individual interests.

---

30 *Chung-kuo shih-pao* [*China Times*], October 5, 1991.
31 The manifesto of the CRC was primarily a wish list of new jurisdiction of the Legislative Yuan.
32 *Lien-ho wan-pao* [*United Evening News*], October 28, 1991.
33 *Tsu-li wan-pao* [*Independent Evening News*], November 15, 1991; *Tsu-li tsao-pao* [*Independent Morning News*], November 18, 1991.

Factionalization did not lead to the disintegration of the KMT. No KMT factions or their members had bolted the KMT before the summer of 1993, when the NKA broke away from the KMT to establish the New Party. The exit of the NKA did not trigger any further exodus from the KMT. The huge resources commanded by the KMT (including government positions, lucrative party-owned enterprises, and name recognition) kept nearly all of its factions and factional members from exercising the option of exit. Despite intensive competition and conflicts, the KMT factions colluded whenever necessary so as to ensure the party's monopoly of power. Obviously, if the rewards for staying in the fold are not forthcoming, or if "voices" are not heeded, defection becomes less costly. However, as long as these resources continue to be available for distribution, we can hypothesize that the KMT factions in Taiwan's legislature can only procreate rather than diminish.

The rise of legislative factionalism in Taiwan is also attributable to its peculiar electoral system: the single, nontransferable vote (SNTV), multiple-member district system. Elections under the SNTV system tend to be more volatile, expensive, and conducive to "family feuds" than other systems, such as proportional representation or the single-member district system. The source of volatility lies in the fact that the number of candidates nominated by both the ruling and opposition parties is quite unpredictable, as are the patterns of vote distribution (a landslide winner may absorb so many votes that the vote-getting order of all of the other candidates can be easily unseated by a small number of swing votes). The experience of pre-1995 Japan, the other country adopting the SNTV system, shows that it is not infrequent for five- or six-term heavyweights or other senior Diet members to lose their seats to newcomers. Since each voter casts only one vote under this electoral system, all candidates need to compete with one another (including others from the same party) in the same district. Because the party label cannot distinguish one candidate from the competing candidates of the same party, a candidate needs to create his/her own specific, easily recognizable image; forge a distinct reputation; and build up a personal network, often called a *Hou yuan hui* in Taiwan or *Koenkai* in Japan (Chinese characters of these two terms are the same), so as to prevent one's support base from being eroded by others. It takes effort and money, usually from endless gift-giving for a variety of occasions, to cultivate one's own electoral base. When multiple-member competition becomes extremely keen, candidates may even be tempted to purchase swing votes that may drastically increase the probability of winning.[34]

34 For the impact of the SNTV system on Japanese electoral politics, see Gerald L. Curtis, *Election Campaigning Japanese Style* (New York: Columbia University Press, 1971) and Mark Ramsayer and Frances Rosenbluth, *Political Market in Japan* (Cambridge: Harvard University Press, 1993).

Factional affiliation conceivably can help a candidate solve the problems under the SNTV system: It can enhance one's chance for renomination, raise political funds, enhance one's image (for the purpose of "product differentiation"), and reduce attrition in electoral mobilization. Under the SNTV system, a political party needs to nominate an "optimal" number of candidates, as too long or too short a list means wasted votes that do not translate into seats for a party. As the primary system is not fully established, the nomination for KMT candidates results from negotiation among party leaders based on all sorts of considerations, such as public opinion polls, voting in primaries, reputation, and local support bases of the candidates-to-be. Given that every aspirant has some sort of comparative advantage, faction membership conceivably will improve one's odds in the battle of nomination. Factional ties may also assist a candidate in campaign financing. It is widely known that factions in Japan secure ties to business and provide their members with money pipelines. In Taiwan, factions do not perform this function (see discussion below), but factional membership does affect the distribution of KMT-controlled resources, including funds raised from KMT enterprises and the allotment of votes from reliable bases, such as residential compounds for families of the military. These resources are essential to those candidates without deep pockets and local support bases.

Factional membership in Taiwan's legislature means sharing political information, lending support in the interpellations, and improving the chances of becoming convenors or coconvenors of legislative committees, all without any obligation attached, such as bloc voting, as discussed below. As the largest faction, the Wisdom Coalition got more committee chairs or cochairs than other factions (see Table 2.3). Factional association can also help a candidate communicate to potential supporters and economize the cost of building his/her image and reputation (for which group membership is a proxy). Given the volatility of elections under the SNTV system, one needs to be assured of effectively communicating to constituencies one's political stand and policy contributions, relative to potential competitors in the same electoral district. It is thus little wonder that KMT legislators from the same electoral district rarely participate in the same faction.[35] A candidate can expect unreserved support from fellow factional members if they are located in different districts. An agreement between factions can also reduce cutthroat competition among fellow party candidates in the same district.

35 *Ji-yu shi-pao* [*Freedom Times*], November 8, 1991. The NKA offers the best example. This faction was originally a coalition formed during the election with members from different electoral districts. For other factions, there are legislators from the same district belonging to the same faction – a phenomenon found in less than one-fourth of the electoral districts, but in this case these legislators all have their respective solid and clearly identifiable support bases.

Table 2.3. *Factions and Their Control of Committee Chairmanship*

	Exclusive	Share with other factions
DPP	1	—
WIC	4	7
NKA	—	4
CPRC	1	6
Concord	1	8
RC	—	8
CRC	2	12
Other	1	—

Notes: There are 12 committees and 25 chairpersons and cochairpersons.

The mass media in Taiwan often conceive of the KMT legislative factions as temporary agencies created by the more permanent "political bosses" within the high command of the KMT to fight wars by proxy. For example, the Wisdom Coalition was often depicted as a group of clients forged by their patron, President Lee Teng-hui, while former Premier Hau Pei-tsun commanded the NKA. The connection between the legislative factions and KMT leaders is correct, but the direction of causality is misspecified. As was shown in a previous section, legislative factions long predated conflicts within the KMT leadership. Moreover, one can argue that legislative factions act on behalf of, rather than at the behest of, KMT leaders in expecting the latter's promotion of the political interests of a given faction. Legislators owe their positions to voters, not party leaders, while party leaders are often in need of support from legislative factions to keep their government positions and to get their policies made. In appearance, political leaders are always on political markets and, as a legacy of the KMT nomenclature system, still hold some positions and are hence seen as permanent actors in the game; legislators, on the other hand, who are required to renew their tenure every three years, seem to be actors in the game for a short, fixed, although renewable, period of time. However, in actuality, in the absence of term limits, legislators can be semi-permanent incumbents, as in the United States. In contrast, political leaders can be very transient and easily marginalized; those who are not on the rise will be swept aside in the game of political competition. Given the fact that the Legislative Yuan has become an indispensable axis of newly democratized

Table 2.4. *Overlapping Membership of Legislative*
Factions as of December 1991

Factional membership	No. of legislators
Nil	10
Single	58
Double	24
Triple	24
Quadruple	9
Fivefold	4
Total	130

Notes

1. Of 58 legislators who belong to one faction only, 19 are DPP members and belong to the DPP party caucus, 19 belong to the Wisdom Coalition, 7 belong to the CPRC, 7 belong to the Concord, 3 belong to the CRC, and 1 belongs to the RC.

2. Of 10 no-factional legislators, 4 do not belong to any political party and 6 are from the KMT.

3. Of 130 legislators required to renew their terms every three years, 29 are selected from overseas Chinese while 101 are elected from Taiwan; and of the 101, 18 are elected from the occupational associations, such as business, farmers, fishermen, teachers, and labor.

polity, KMT leaders will need more support from their legislative factions than the other way around. KMT leaders are more like agents than the principals of legislative factions.

SOFT FACTIONS

The factions in Taiwan's legislature lack internal discipline, as reflected in multiple or overlapping memberships, the predatory recruitment of faction members, and, until now, the absence of bosses. A cross-listing of factional membership is pervasive (see Table 2.4). Among 100 non-DPP legislators who joined a faction, nearly a quarter of them have double memberships; another quarter of them have triple listings, and nine of them have four memberships, while four of them each belong to five factions. Some core members of factions even have multiple memberships. There is no informal rule of one-person–one-faction membership, unlike the cases of Korea and Japan.

All of the factions are trying to recruit new members from the first-term legislators. However, the fact that faction members may have multiple memberships, the formation of the CRC, and the response of the Wisdom Coalition show that major factions are still engaged in predatory recruitment. Finally, the bosses of factions are still lacking. Major factions are led by three or four core members, who do not have the stature of national leaders yet, again unlike the cases of Japan and Korea. Taiwan's new factions are bossless (*yu pai wu fa*); the "leadership team" can convene regular meetings in the factions' conference locations, but they cannot enforce faction obedience.[36] Members are equal and do not pay allegiance to their coordinators. Taiwan's legislative factions are more like leagues based on collegiality than on dyadic links to the boss. In fact, rank-and-file members frequently criticize their leaders in public. All told, these factions are soft, with neither a fixed membership to count on coherent group action nor a compliance mechanism to enforce discipline.

Multiple membership is a hindrance to a faction's collective action because it leads to information leakage and undermines group cohesion. Leaders of some factions (including those of the Wisdom Coalition) have attempted to enforce the informal rule of exclusive factional membership by registering itself as a civic association. Such a process of formalization would turn a faction into a legal entity, which then could legitimate fund raising,[37] require a pledge of allegiance from members, and extract binding commitments to joint action. But exclusive membership has to be enforced by all major factions; otherwise, those that enforce it will suffer and shrink. Smaller factions are naturally unwilling to go along with the bigger factions for a cartel-like agreement. And from the viewpoint of faction members, an association that compels joint action and enforces discipline is probably less preferable to one that permits ample room for individual actions while providing mechanisms for coordination and consultation among members.

Legislative rules in Taiwan also help to keep factions soft. Voting in committees and on the floor is secret; hence factional loyalty is not observable. The core members of a faction thus cannot verify their fellow members' loyalty to the faction. But even when its members' actions were verifiable, legislative factions did not have effective mechanisms to ensure their members' allegience. As was mentioned above, faction membership may improve the odds of renomination by the KMT, but no faction can guarantee the outcome, given that so many other factors (opinion polls, evaluation of legislators by KMT leaders, primaries, etc.) all impinge on the choice of party candidates.

---

36 Gunter Schubert, "Constitutional politics in the Republic of China: The rise of the Legislative Yuan," *Issues and Studies* (March 1992), p. 35.
37 Interview with Tsai Ming-feng, December 20, 1991.

Factions (or, for that matter, parties) in Taiwan are not conduits for the flow of political funds from the private sector, which is not as concentrated or organized as in Japan and Korea. Political contributions in Taiwan usually flow from individual donors to individual politicians.

The form of government also prevents the empowering of factions in Taiwan. A parliamentary system, à la Japan, would enable legislative factions to command obedience from their members as the makeup of the cabinet reflects the factional balance of power. Unless a Diet member is proven to be a trusted member of a faction, he or she cannot expect to receive a cabinet appointment. This is not so in Taiwan, where, due to its French-style, semi-presidential system, cabinet portfolios are usually beyond the reach of legislators. The only kind of position a legislative faction in Taiwan can possibly offer to its members is committee convenorship. Unless legislative factions can "harden" themselves by broadening resources or opportunities for their members (for example, positions in the party caucus in the Legislative Yuan or membership in the Central Standing Committee), legislators will continue to hold multiple memberships while withholding loyalty.

POSTSCRIPT

This chapter hypothesizes that KMT legislative factions are formed to assist their members in their electoral battles and career advancement. We also hypothesize that factional members within the legislature are principals searching for an outside agent (a party leader) so as to acquire political resources and improve the odds for renomination and reelection under the volatile SNTV system. The legislative election in December 1992, the first full-house election in postwar Taiwan, provided an excellent opportunity to test these hypotheses. While all of the seats were up for grabs, there were massive entries into the race, creating an explosion of participation. Party nomination, endorsement, and support mattered more to the candidates than ever. While 25 percent of the total seats were designated as at-large seats to be distributed proportionally according to the voting share of parties that obtained at least 5 percent of the total votes, 75 percent of the seats were still being competed for under the SNTV system.

Being the most active and powerful faction in the legislature, the Wisdom Coalition was given insufficient "quota" in the nomination for KMT candidacy, proportionally less than the quota allotted to the NKA. Initially, the KMT planned to use performance and "loyalty" to the party as major criteria for nomination, while the results of the party primaries would be only minor factors. Such a policy would have favored incumbents in general and the Wisdom Coalition in particular, a reward for the faction's support to

President Lee. Yet as NKA members and many nonmainstream KMT elite successfully mobilized support in the KMT primaries, the nomination policy was overturned. In finalizing the roster for the KMT, President Lee yielded to then Premier Hau Pei-tsun, who endorsed winners in the KMT primaries at the expense of many Wisdom Coalition members. While many Wisdom Coalition and a few NKA members were not renominated, they were "permitted" to run without the KMT's endorsement or punishment.

Most NKA members were returned, while many Wisdom Coalition members were defeated. After the election, the NKA as a faction not only remained intact, but it acquired an ally – newly elected, nonmainstream KMT legislators. The Wisdom Coalition disintegrated; those who managed to get reelected joined new factions. Other former factions either declined or became inactive as their core members suffered electoral defeats and their alliances with old-timers came to a natural end. Two new factions emerged, though, the Yushan Club (named after the summit in Taiwan, signifying its indigenous orientation), organized by a business tycoon turned legislator from central Taiwan and predominantly a Taiwanese club, and the People's Will Association (*Minyi Hui*), headed by a former speaker of the Taiwan provincial assembly and primarily joined by former representatives at sub-national levels, including some mainlanders.

Despite the permutation of factions, factionalism still persists in the Legislative Yuan. The factional lineup is helpful to the allocation of legislative committee convenorships. The game of image-making continues, and the issues that are used to create one's image are expanding; they are no longer limited to questions of national identity and policy toward Mainland China. Issues such as the environment, welfare, and local development loom large, suggesting the coming of pork-barrel politics. However, factions remain "soft," without exclusive membership, bosses, or discipline.

There is a learning process, however. The plight of the Wisdom Coalition seems to have taught the KMT's legislative factions a lesson on their support of and ties to KMT leaders. The failure of the Wisdom Coalition to reproduce of itself as a legislative faction was to a great extent attributable to its ineffective electoral campaign, which focused primarily on the issue of subethnic cleavages rather than on policy issues. But its debacle was also due to its over-estimating the support and resources that its "agent" could deliver. Thus, in the absence of some credible promise or reward, the People's Will Association has been hesitant to endorse any particular political power contenders on the occasion of intraparty leadership conflicts. Even the Yushan Club, headed by an avowed friend of President Lee, avoids lending unconditional support to policies advanced by the mainstream KMT. The NKA was equally calculating in its ties with nonmainstream KMT leaders. As Hau

Pei-tsun faltered in an intensive political struggle within the KMT and was removed from premiership in early 1993, the NKA rebelled against the KMT, now that this faction could no longer find an "agent" within the KMT leadership to protect, not to say enhance, its political interest and claim its due share in the allocation of KMT-controlled political resources. In the summer of 1993, the NKA members resigned from the KMT to form the New Party, although they adopted a similar party emblem and claimed political lineage of Dr. Sun Yatsen, the founder of the KMT. Meanwhile, newly elected, nonmainstream KMT legislators began searching for promising KMT leaders, such as Lin Yang-kang, former head of the Judiciary Yuan and a presidential hopeful, to be its "agent" in preparation for subsequent political battles. For the 1995 legislative election, most incumbent factional members were renominated and reelected. One can anticipate that legislative factions will be instrumental to the forthcoming leadership battle for the succession to President Lee. Constrained by term limits, KMT leaders in key political positions come and go, but legislators can be elected indefinitely. To renew their mandates under the SNTV system, legislators coalesce into factions and select KMT leaders as their agents to improve the odds of reelection, and they do change their agents. The KMT's legislative factions are soft but indelible.

ACKNOWLEDGMENTS

The authors thank Haruhiro Fukui, Peter N. S. Lee, and Brian Woodall for their comments, and Chung-ling Chen and Duncan Wooldridge for their competent research assistance.

CHAPTER 3

THE ELECTION PROCESS
AND INFORMAL POLITICS
IN SOUTH KOREA

SOOHYUN CHON

Political institutions determine economic rules in general, although the causality runs both ways. That is, property rights are determined and enforced by political institutions, but the structure of economic interests will also influence political structure. One of the most important political economic structures that has determined Korea's property rights in the past is the tightly knit relationship between the administrative branch of the government and the *chaebol*, the large family-owned industrial conglomerates. The organization of the Korean government endows the executive branch with special privileges that other democratic nations' governmental administrations usually do not enjoy; that is, ministries can change the rules and regulations governing commerce and other matters without the approval of the legislative branch. Using the dominant executive power, Korea's past presidents have developed personalized political exchanges to benefit specific groups. Since ministers are political appointees of the president, he has direct lines of command and authority over the ministries. Businesses and individuals with direct access to the president, therefore, have been able to get the rules and regulations changed in their favor or persuade the government to grant special privileges on their behalf. In return for extending the desired favors, the ruling party leader receives large political contributions from big businesses that he uses primarily to fund elections.

Past political economic exchanges in Korea are largely responsible for the present economic crisis that has collapsed the stock market/exchange rates and dictated the $US57 billion IMF bailout package. The economic crisis of December 1997 was triggered by huge losses incurred by financial institutions in their highly speculative investments in Latin America, Southeast Asia, and Russia, financed mostly by short-term foreign loans. This short-term liquidity crunch combined with a series of bankruptcies of large conglomerates in the last two years drew the attention of foreign investors and financial institutions to fundamental weaknesses in Korea's industrial structure. Korea's present industrial structure, dominated by *chaebol*, is mainly the

66

product of the government's financial policy that provided subsidized financing for selected industries with close connections to presidential power. Subsidized financing, mostly made available in the form of low-cost debt, enabled the *chaebol* to take on higher risk projects and higher leverage than they would have (had they borrowed the debt in a free financial market) and to reap the rewards in the form of higher returns on their equity. In the meantime, the burden of carrying the high risk and low return were born by debt holders, that is, the general public. As the *chaebol* concentrated on accessing the government-subsidized loans and entitlement privileges, the distortion in the market mechanism motivated Korean industries to largely ignore the basic principles that drive most of the world's industries, namely, a high rate of return on investments and advantage over competition. Taking the risk of high leverage paid off handsomely when Korea's economy was growing at a steady pace; however, both the *chaebol* and the government underestimated the downside risk of levering up in economic downturns. The Korean economy, dependent on the *chaebol* structure, started to collapse under the burden of huge debts in high-risk ventures, poor cash flows that could not even meet their interest payments, and excess capacity.

Korea's political economic structure was effective in launching the economic development of the country and played a significant role in the rise of the Korean economy to the eleventh largest in the world – even though the ranking dropped down to twentieth as the Korean won depreciated over 50 percent against the U.S. dollar in mid-December 1997. The country's remarkable economic success in the past was part of the reason that the general public was willing to tolerate the corruption and contradictions in the political economic exchanges between the government and the *chaebol*. However, the sustainability of economic exchanges based on personal and informal relationships rather than on institutionalized market transactions turned out to be limited. The general public increasingly became critical about the level of corruption in Korea's political economic exchanges, and the resulting political mood change in the country led to the arrest of Kim Hyun Chul, President Kim Young Sam's youngest son. Kim was jailed on charges of influence peddling to channel policy loans to the now-bankrupt Hanbo Group. Former Presidents Chun Doo Whan and Roh Tae Woo are also serving sentences under charges of corruption, treason, and accepting bribes while they were in power.

Korea is now at a crossroads where it must rationalize its economic structure and build new political economic institutions, making a transition from informal political economic exchanges based on primary group interest to one based on formalized institutions and market transactions. This chapter will shed light on the potential changes that could facilitate political and eco-

major differances is the PPTz ektion practices vs 1997—

nomic institution building by examining the historical changes in election systems. Since there were important changes in Korean election campaign practices between the 1992 and 1997 presidential elections, the first part of the chapter will describe the system that prevailed until 1992, and the latter part will discuss the characteristics that differentiated the 1997 presidential election from the previous ones.

LEGITIMACY OF THE GOVERNMENT: KOREAN CONCEPT

The Korean public has a simplistic Confucian concept of how power should be conferred to its ruler. According to this concept, a government's legitimacy is judged by whether the ruler has the "mandate of Heaven" to govern (*chonshim*), as derived from the support of the people (*minshim*). Withdrawal of the mandate is manifested in the downfall of rulers. It comes in the form of economic hardships, such as an extended period of famine or excessive exploitation by bureaucrats leading to chaos or revolt (*nan*). In light of this ideal, an alternative political system that permits a strong opposition to replace the existing one is an alien concept to most Koreans. Instead, political support has generally been divided between pro- and antigovernment positions.

Majority support legitimizes a government by giving it a "heavenly mandate," and the election process measures the degrees of political support for candidates. In the elections held by the military governments since 1972, however, the leading parties won elections with less than 40 percent support. With less than a majority, Korean governments in the past tried to maintain their rule by manipulating the election system with the authority of the government – in effect, obtaining an advantage in competition with the opposition through an election system advantageous to the leading party. There are many ways for the leading party to build an advantage into an election system. One way has been to create a system that works outright in its favor by providing access to huge political funds made available exclusively to the leading party. Another way was to use the organizational power of the government's bureaucracy to facilitate the reelection of government-sponsored candidates. Past military governments and to a lesser extent outgoing President Kim Young Sam's government effectively used both of these advantages to claim political legitimacy.

POLITICAL ADVANTAGES GIVEN TO LEADING PARTY CANDIDATES

Financing Elections and the Leading Party

Korean elections, whether legislative or presidential, used to be enormously expensive ventures. Kim estimated the total expenditures of the four elections held in 1992 – a National Assembly election, a presidential election, and local elections in large and small districts – to be about $US3 billion at the current exchange rate of won1,500 to $US1, or equal to about 16 percent of Korea's total annual government budget at the time. About $US1 billion was spent in the 1993 general assembly election alone. However, the rules of the Regulatory Agency for Elections (Sungo Gwali Wiwonhoi) do not really allow expenditures of this magnitude.[2] In effect, Korean election regulations are among the strictest in the world, with candidates allowed only twenty days of campaigning and strictly limited legal campaign expenditures. According to these regulations, the average expenditure permitted for an electoral district is approximately $US50,000. The legitimate sources of the funds are limited to: (1) membership dues paid by party members; (2) huwonhoi (koenkai or candidate support group) contributions; (3) Sungo Gwali Wiwonhoi subsidies; (4) government support; and (5) funds raised by political parties. Accepting political donations from any other source is deemed illegal. The huge campaign expenditures and overly rigid electoral rules gave the ruling party ample room for political intervention and maneuvering in elections. Such intervention in turn led to the creation of a political exchange to connect primary groups with the ruling party.

Korea's "uncommon democracy"[3] places a tremendous concentration of power in the hands of the president. This is due partly to the organizational structure of the government under a presidential system as such and partly to historical developments that are unique to Korea, as is so well described by both Henderson and Choi.[4] President Park Chung Hee, who initiated systematic postwar economic development programs in South Korea, may have found it necessary to concentrate power in the state so that development plans could be effectively and aggressively implemented. Such a concentration of power in the state, and more accurately in Park's own hands, was made possible by the manner in which political funds were raised to finance the prohibitively expensive election campaigns necessary to maintain the government party's advantage and to ensure the reelection of ruling party candidates. It was an easy way for a president to stay in power, and President Park opted for this expediency instead of establishing a democratic election system. Thus, the ruling party, especially during the earlier period of military rule, aggressively raised political funds to maintain its advantage, manipulated the election system, and increased the chances of reelection for its

1 Kwang Hyun Kim, "Sungoe Paguk Matneun Kyongje [Next year's economy in recession due to upcoming elections], *Chosun Ilbo*, November 24, 1991.

2 Jungsuk Yoon, *Hanguk Jonwhangieu Jungchi Kwanjung [Korean Political Process in Transition]* (Seoul: Ingan Sarang, 1991).

3 T. J. Pempel, ed., *Uncommon Democracies* (Ithaca: Cornell University Press, 1991).

4 Choi Tae Kwon, *Pop Sahoi Hak [Social Laws]* (Seoul: Seoul National University Press, 1983); Gregory Henderson, *Korea: The Politics of the Vortex* (Cambridge, MA: Harvard University Press, 1968).

candidates. Most of these funds were administered by the presidents themselves, and a large portion was spent to support ruling party candidates in
various elections and to nurture the presidential power base. Two major ways
of raising political funds were donations from corporations and from individuals seeking nomination in central and local government elections.

President Park received contributions from big corporations in the form
of membership fees in proportion to their revenues. The general pattern of
corporate donations of political funds did not change much from the period
of President Park's rule to that of President Roh Tae Woo's. Political contributions were also made to ministers so that they in turn could donate a portion of the money to the president. This indirect method was used when
businesses wanted to target specific rules and regulations governed by
ministries and sought the specific administrative attention of the ministers.
Another source of political funds was religious institutions, that is, Christian churches and Buddhist temples.

As an alternative source of political fund raising, the president, as ruling
party leader, also accepted money for nominations in National Assembly elections. A nomination for candidacy in the national constituency cost a candidate more than one for a local election district, because nominees for local
districts were expected to spend their own money on their campaigns. Candidates running in the national constituency were elected in proportion to
the number of seats their party won in local district elections. Thus, the higher the ranking a nominee obtained in the national constituency, the higher
were his/her chances of winning a seat in the National Assembly. Nominees
for the national constituency were usually ranked in accordance with the
amount of money that they contributed to the party as well as their political influence within the party itself. Even though candidates' contributions
were smaller than those from businesses, the arrangement clearly demonstrated that the power to finance elections is concentrated in the hands of the
ruling party leaders.

Political fund raising, especially for election campaigns, became the major
vehicle for tying the ruling party's political power to primary group interests and for faction building based on regionalism.[5] The rise of regional economic power in the Kyongsang provinces under the military regime
illustrates this point well. President Park Chung Hee was a farmer's son from
Sunsan, a small village near Andong in North Kyongsang Province. Gaining
power by military coup did not give him much political legitimacy. In a society where primary group connections is of ultimate importance in power

---

5 Soohyun Chon, "Political economy of regional development in Korea," in Richard Appelbaum and
Gregory Henderson, eds., *States and Development in Asia Pacific Rim* (Newbury Park, CA: Sage Publications, 1992), pp. 150–174.

building, Park found himself without adequate political support. His modest background made it difficult to use his clan as his primary support group. Primary group connections based on his military career helped, but military officers were a relatively small group at the time and they did not usually come from elite family backgrounds in Korea. His more reliable support, albeit more distant, came from his geographic ties with North Kyongsang Province. Andong, near his Sunsan birth place, is the home of powerful clans dating back to the Lee Dynasty. With tight-knit connections and a high acceptance factor in Korean society, the elite of North and South Kyongsang – Korea's most populous provinces – became the primary supporters of President Park's power base. The fact that out of ten of the top *chaebol* in Korea, seven of them have their clan origins in Kyongsang Provinces points to the mutual support fostered by the Kyongsang elite and President Park; thus ensued the regionalism in Korea that pitched the Kyongsang Provinces (Youngnam) against the Cholla Provinces (Honam). The fact that President Park's successors, Presidents Chun and Roh, also were generals from North Kyongsang Province perpetuated Kyongsang's regional power and became a powerful political card in elections.

Financing Elections in Opposition Parties

While corporations and religious organizations were expected to contribute money to the ruling party, political contributions to opposition parties were actively discouraged by the bureaucracy. For example, any business that was closely affiliated with an opposition party or that donated money to one was likely to be audited by the tax authorities. South Korea has one of the highest effective corporate tax rates in the world, and it is difficult even for the most profitable businesses to accumulate retained earnings without tax evasion. In a business environment where tax evasion is a means of survival, the government has a powerful instrument to control the political attitudes of businesses through the Internal Revenue Service. Auditing is an indirect statement that the government disapproves of the targeted firm's standing in the country's politics, and it is still used as a means of controlling political opposition.

Since effective government monitoring under the past military regimes barred businesses from contributing to opposition parties, it was difficult for their candidates to raise money. The bulk of their funding either came from personal sources or had to be raised after their election to an assembly seat. Because opposition parties were cut off from most sources of corporate donations, only two sources of funds were available to them. One source became available when an opposition assembly member served on special National

Assembly committees that made important policy decisions affecting the business sector interests. Members of such committees expected donations from corporations in return for promises not to reveal the government's close relationships with certain businesses. The Suso scandal illustrates how kickbacks may breed corruption when the interests of the administration, ruling party National Assembly members, and opposition party assembly members converge.

The other source of funding for opposition parties came from their candidate nomination practice, which concentrated power in the hands of party leaders. When the ruling party cut off corporate donations to opposition parties by applying indirect pressure on potential donors, this had a significant impact on each opposition party's power structure. Traditionally, a nomination for a National Assembly seat could be bought from a party leader in return for a donation. When outside sources of funding dried up, nominated candidates became the most stable source of political funds for the opposition. Opposition party leaders who held the power to nominate candidates also became the only people within their own party with financial resources large enough to support candidates. Consequently, opposition party leader became the center of power outside the ruling party.

The procedures governing contributions to either Kim Dae Jung or Kim Jong Pil during the 1992 presidential election are not very well documented. Since they concern highly secretive transactions, they are known only to a few other than the two Kims and potential candidates. Neither the two Kims nor the potential candidates have an incentive to reveal the nature of such transactions. However, a scandal involving Kim Dae Jung, known as the Chongbalyon incident, revealed his fund-raising practice to the public. Two candidates, Lee Dong Bae and Cho Chan Hyung, competed for a nomination for a National Assembly seat in Namwon (North Cholla Province) during the 1988 election. Lee was a loyal follower of Kim Dae Jung's throughout his political career, and Cho was a prosecuting attorney with substantial influence in the Namwon area. Cho donated large sums of cash and real estate to Kim Dae Jung. When Cho realized that even after contributing such large amounts he might not be nominated because Kim Dae Jung was leaning toward the other candidate, he attempted to blackmail Kim by threatening to reveal his political donation practices to the public. Kim was forced to nominate Cho as a candidate of his party, at the time called *Shinmindang* (New People's Party), in the local Namwon electoral district; he

---

6 *Donga Ilbo*, "Kipo Ganeun Galdeung" [Deepening conflict], July 25, 1991; "Naebun Saebulssi: Namwon Gongchun Jabeum" [New sparkle in internal disputes: Namwon nomination conflict], July 29, 1991; "Shinmin, Cho Youn Hyung Bueujang, Jemyong Kyoljung" [The decision to oust Vice Chairman Cho Youn Hyung from Shinmin Party), July 30, 1991.

nominated Lee as the ninth candidate in the national constituency. Details of this transaction were leaked to the public by Cho Youn Hyung, a leading member of Shinmindang.

ROLE OF GOVERNMENT BUREAUCRACY IN ELECTION CAMPAIGNS

One interesting aspect of the South Korean election process is the way in which the established channels of government bureaucracy were used to apply political pressure on voters to elect ruling party candidates. Up until the 1992 election, the bureaucracy served as an effective campaign machine that assisted the ruling party in elections in five major ways: (1) mobilization of informal groups; (2) electoral organization support; (3) intelligence gathering; (4) personnel support; and (5) support of ruling party assembly members after election.

Mobilization of Informal Groups

During the past elections, it was a prevalent practice to use the government bureaucracy as a tool to mobilize voters affiliated with primary groups. The ruling party, especially during the military rule, recruited local leaders for their election campaigns by applying political pressure and exploiting connections with influential individuals and groups in their communities. Heads of powerful clans and wealthy businessmen were actively recruited. Several months before the election campaigns started, high-ranking government officials would frequently visit local areas to solicit the cooperation of local businessmen, clan members, and political leaders for progovernment candidates' campaigns. It was expected that the informal groups represented by these leaders would support the ruling party. Primary groups in turn sought to maximize their group interests by aligning themselves with the dominant political power.

In addition, numerous civic organizations funded by the government were mobilized during elections to reach primary interest groups. The Korean Youth Organization, the Elderly Citizens Organization, the New Community Movement Society, and the New Community Movement Woman's Society, to name just a few, were such organizations. The Council for the Promotion of Social Purification, an organization run by retired army generals and officers, also played an important role in elections and in defending government interests. Under President Chun Doo Hwan, about twenty such organizations were entirely subsidized or funded by the central government budget.

Specific organizations used for campaigns have changed from government to government, but the general practice remained the same through the 1992 presidential election. For example, the most powerful campaign organization under Presidents Park Chung Hee and Chun Doo Hwan, the New Community Movement Society (Saemaeul Woondonghoi), had an extensive *myon*-level organization nationwide. The arrest of Chun Kyung Hwan – former President Chun Doo Hwan's younger brother and former head of the New Community Movement Society – on the charge of embezzlement was an attempt on the part of succeeding Roh Tae Woo's government to remove any remnant of Chun's political influence in this powerful electoral organization. The use of such organizations to mobilize informal friendship networks works better in areas where a sense of co-unity still exists; thus, support for the ruling party predominates in rural areas where people know each other and have close ties to the community.

In recent years, an effort to pull together clan-level political support has resulted in increasing importance of *jongchinhoi* (clan organizations). Koreans' primary loyalty is to blood ties over ideological interests; therefore, securing the support of clans is important in mobilizing votes. The *jongchinhoi* of influential clans, such as the Kimhae Kims, supposedly attract about 250,000 members in their annual formal gatherings.[7] These big clan organizations represent powerful interest groups, and their incorporation into politicians' support bases is significant, since kinship groups serve as intermediaries for social mobility. This motivates clan members to become a part of the political power structure to partake in the benefits that come from such affiliation.

Electoral Organizational Support

Up until 1992, the ruling party had an extensive and well-funded electoral organization that could easily induct about 10,000–15,000 new party members in each electoral district. By being able to recruit large numbers of party members during the campaign period, the ruling party was able to avoid violating election laws that limit the number of campaign workers who can be legally employed by individual candidates. There was and still is no legal limit to the number of people that political parties can mobilize as party members, and each party member is expected to bring at least three other people to participate in the campaign. The electoral committee can then pay recruits' wages and expenses under the pretext of educating new members for the committee's work. Each recruit serves as a nucleus of a new party cell within his/her primary group.

---

7 Terry McCarthy, "Korea's tangled family trees," *San Francisco Examiner*, April 2, 1992. Park Hee-Sup, "Jipdan Ikijueueu Moonjewa Daechaek" [The problems and solutions of group selfishness], *Hankookeu Shimin Yoonri* [*Civil Ethics of Modern Korea*] (Seoul: Asan Sahoi Bokji Saup Chaedan, 1991), pp. 207–221.

Intelligence Gathering

Government bureaucracy has also been used beyond the limits set by election laws for intelligence gathering during election campaigns. At the top levels, the electoral committee organization and the government administrative organization overlap to some extent. At the grassroots level, electoral committee organizations usually coincide exactly with *myon* and *dong*. In the past, members of election committee informed the *myonjang* and *dongjang* about each voter's choice of his or her favored candidate in their district. Since Koreans are rather straightforward in expressing their feelings, this ingenious organization is believed to have the capability of gathering information that can quite accurately predict election results. Election forecasts were then summarized and analyzed in detail by the Korean Central Intelligence Agency before each election. This intelligence helped leading party candidates in terms of whom to contact and to bribe for swing votes at the last minute.

PERSONNEL SUPPORT

Before an election, close friends or acquaintances of government party candidates were placed in a number of local governments' administrative positions within candidates' electoral districts to support campaign efforts. Their next assignments and promotions were determin by how effectively they supported the ruling party's candidates in the current election. Therefore, large-scale personnel moves before and after major elections put pressure on local officials to cooperate in the government election campaigns.

In the 1992 presidential election, the conflict between Kim Young Sam and Kim Dae Jung over the timing of an election for large-district representatives boiled down to the issue of who would win the right to appoint the heads of the *ku* that would provide support to a candidate in the upcoming presidential election. Under the new governmental organization, district representatives were given authority to appoint the heads of local governments, and the timing of large-district representatives' elections would have a significant impact on the organizational support for either party in the next presidential election.

SUPPORT OF RULING PARTY ASSEMBLY MEMBERS AFTER ELECTION

After an election, bureaucrats and ruling party National Assembly members work closely together so that the assemblymen may project a good public image to his/her constituents. For example, all budgets, including those for construction projects, are prepared by *kun* and governments. If a construction project takes place in a *kun* without being supported by a National Assembly member, the ruling party assembly members from the *do* will receive credit for bringing the project into the district. Ruling party members are also informed about the awards of all construction bids and local government budgets within their district, so that they can obtain a share of the profits from these projects to be used as political funds for the party.

SAJOJIC: DEVELOPMENT OF NEW PRIVATE ORGANIZATIONS

In the 1992 presidential election that brought Kim Young Sam into power, the degree of intervention by the government bureaucracy was reduced significantly, if not completely. For various political reasons, Presdient Roh sought to have the government bureaucracy take a neutral position. Thus, while subtle forms of involvement continued, blatant intervention by the bureaucracy ceased. In Kim Young Sam's successful presidential campaign, as the support of the government bureaucracy started to wane, private and informal organizations played an increasingly important role. Even during President Roh Tae Woo's election campaigns, the role of private organizations had become quite prevalent. These informal organizations, called *sajojic*, consisted of groups of people who shared political interests with the president through various personal connections and were used in addition to the civil and government organizations to reach primary interest groups. In both Roh's and Kim's cases, *sajojic* consumed a large share of the political funds that they raised. At its peak, president Roh's *sajojic*, Wolgeysoohoi (Laurel Association), had more than 1 million members as a private supporting organization.[8] Park Chul Won, Roh's nephew on his wife's side, led Wolgeysoohoi and played a crucial role in Roh's successful 1988 election campaign. Wolgeysoohoi's function after the election was to maintain Roh's power base during his presidency.

While vying for the 1992 presidential nomination, Kim Young Sam attacked Park Chul Won by accusing him of using private groups to support President Roh's personal power. Even though President Kim Young Sam criticized the use of private organizations mobilized by President Roh, during his own presidential election campaign he was known to have relied heavily on informal networks to mobilize mass support. Kim Young Sam had the support of many private elite and mass organizations, including the

8 Doo Won Suh, "Park Chul Won: Wolgeysoohoi and Minjadand Pabol" [Park Chul Won: Wolgeysoohoi and Democratic Liberal Party Faction], *Shindonga*, March 1990, pp. 170–186.

Democratic Mountain Climbers' Organization (Minju Sanakhoi), the Patriotic Activists' Campaign Headquarters (Nara Sarang Silchon Undongbu), and the Youth Organization (Joongchung). The Democratic Mountain Climbers' Organization consisted of Kim Young Sam's old friends from his opposition party days. The Patriotic Activists' Campaign Headquarters included important Christian leaders, and the Youth Organization was made up of the followers of Kim Hyun Chul. The sizes of these private organizations were estimated to be equal to those of the electoral organizations, and they consumed approximately the same amounts of political funds as the official organizations in Kim's election campaign.[9]

One common thread running through all of these informal organizations mobilized for political campaign is the lack of organizational continuity. Once the president is elected and completes his tenure, their power structure disintegrates rather quickly, primarily due to the discontinuation of political funding and the leader's real or anticipated loss of power. The emergence and decline of private organizations with the rise and demise of presidential power illustrate an institutional weakness in the Korean political system. Presidential power does not have deep roots because the power is limited to the tenure of particular presidents. Thus, South Korea's presidential system has become a hindrance to political institution building and formalized political exchange.

IMPORTANT CHANGES IN THE 1997 PRESIDENTIAL ELECTION CAMPAIGNS

There were remarkable changes in the political climate that surrounded the 1997 presidential election from previous elections that made it possible for an opposition party leader, Kim Dae Jung, to be elected president for the first time in Korea's democratic history. Due to various institutional and political climate changes, the two most important election campaign advantages that the leading party had – in raising political funds and in having support from the government bureaucracy – were eliminated for the most part. First, after the Hanbo incident that ended in the arrest of Kim Young Sam's son, political fund donations to political parties were directed through Sungo Gwali Wiwonhoi. With the weakening of presidential power and the leading party's political position through a series of corruption scandals, regulations governing the elections were more strictly enforced than in the past, reducing the direct *chaebol* political contribution to the leading party. Even

9 Byung Gul Kwak, "Daekwon Jooja Kim Young Sameu Sajoji Jungchijaeum" [Leading candidate, Kim Young Sam's private organization and political fund], *Shindonga*, October 1991, pp. 214–224.

though there were still advantages given to the leading party, such as the
threat of IRS audits for those who supported the opposition, the blatant dis-
advantages that the opposition parties used to suffer in raising political funds
were eliminated.

Second, not only was there a more equitable distribution of political funds
between the leading and opposition parties, but the amount needed to win
the election was also much smaller compared to that of the previous elections. Television debates among leading candidates became the single most
important factor in determining each participant's popularity, significantly
reducing the enormous amount of campaign funds needed to buy labor to
attend political campaign rallies.

Third, the establishment of local government elections virtually eliminated the vehicle through which the leading party could use government bureaucracy to its definitive advantage. Since opposition parties also had local
government officials on their side, they were able to compete against the leading party on a much more level playing ground than in the past.

Fourth, President Kim Young Sam, besieged by corruption scandals, had
his presidential power significantly weakened and could neither appoint his
own successor nor support his candidate's election campaign. Lee Hoi Chang,
the former prime minister and a supreme court judge with an impeccable
reputation, was nominated as a presidential candidate because he was popular and the furthest removed from Kim Young Sam within the leading party
power structure. His popularity, however, plunged when it was revealed that
his two sons had evaded compulsory military service. Even though Youngnam regional insecurity about having a Honam president pushed Lee's popularity back up to surpass that of Kim Dae Jung's for a while, the leading
party was blamed for Korea's December 1997 economic collapse and Kim
won the election by a narrow margin of 430,000 votes.

Finally, no single candidate represented the Youngnam region. Realizing
the importance of Youngnam votes in winning the election, Kim Dae Jung
downplayed antagonistic regional politics. He struck a bargain with his
old-time supporters from Honam to take a back seat during the campaign
and surrounded himself with non-Honam advisors. By striking an alliance
with Kim Jong Pil, he secured the support of the Chungchung Provinces.
Park Tae Jun, the former chairman of POSCO (Pohang Steel Company),
brought with him the partial support of Youngnam. In return for their
support, Kim Dae Jung promised 50 and 25 percent of the cabinet seats to
Kim and Park, respectively. In lieu of using the government's administrative branch as the core of presidential power, Kim Dae Jung is presently
forming a faction in his party to share the presidential power base with his
allies. It will be interesting to see whether the incoming president actually

lives up to his promise of doling out cabinet seats to Kim Jong Pil and Park Tae Jun.

CONCLUSION

One salient feature of South Korean politics is the lack of strong political institutions, including an established political party system. Political parties exist, but they consist of factions led by strong individuals. Most political exchanges in South Korea take place in the form of handing out personal favors through informal networks rather than forging consensus in return for rewards within a political party system. Many social scientists have been puzzled over why South Korea has never managed to institutionalize political exchanges and why all of the social interactions are based on personal and informal networks.

Until the 1992 presidential election political exchanges based on primary group interests prevailed. Those processes revolved around intricate systems that allocated privilege and favor to particular informal social groups in return for their political support. These procedures were not institutionalized but remained informal and personalized transactions. Informal groups based on personalized relationships provided calculated consensus in government policies in return for favors done by the government, mostly particularistic benefits made available by the authority of the president.

The centralization of power that enables the president to finance and control elections in effect weakens South Korea's party structure. Whenever presidents change, the ruling party structure that is dependent on presidential power loses its core and disintegrates. This is in spite of the fact that the formal organization of the ruling party is well funded and well established. Opposition parties, on the other hand, have been led by strong leaders and have managed to maintain a higher degree of continuity in their power structures. This is partly because there has been no change in the opposition party leadership in the last three decades, even though there may have been changes in party names and in the composition of their membership. Thus, it is easier for opposition party politicians to realign themselves as needs arise and form new informal groups within the party even though that party's power structure may be no less personalized than the ruling party's.

For both ruling and opposition parties such a political structure makes it difficult for durable intraparty factions to form as power bases independent from the party leader. The fact that only a small percentage of National Assembly members (17 percent in the case of the 13th National Assembly) are elected to their seats more than once means that there is only a weak basis for faction-building in South Korea's party system. This is partly because the centralized power of the president and opposition party leaders prevents any growth of competing power structures, such as durable factions within the party system.

The difficulty of forming vertical patron–client relationships also contributes to the failure of political faction-building in South Korean politics. Since a personalized informal network – that is, a relationship based on kinship, regional, school, and other forms of primary group ties – is much more effective than a patron–client relationship as an instrument with which to build a political power base, it is difficult to form an institutionalized power structure. As South Korea gradually makes the transition to a pluralistic society, informal group structures such as regionalism, kinship networks, and school ties are beginning to predominate over a formalized and institutionalized power structure. Political transactions thus take place within or via informal groups. Patron–client relations can hold tightly within the primary organization; however, due to the dominance of presidential power and the lack of strong political institutions, there are no institutions that can translate such patron–client relations into a formal political structure. This in turn reinforces the power concentration in the hands of the president, enabling him to negotiate political exchanges directly with informal groups.

The 1997 presidential election witnessed several significant changes in the election system that may shed light on how the centralized power of the president can be harnessed through institution-building. The changes in political fund raising – channeling donations through Sungo Gwali Wiwonhoi – took care of some of the corrupt political donation practices. The establishment of a local government election system largely eliminated the government bureaucracy's intervention in elections. These developments indicate that institutional changes could partly, if not completely, eliminate the corrupt process of negotiated political exchange for personal interest. Usually, the existing power structure of a nation does not like to see changes in institutions governing property rights that serve them favorably. The crisis in Korea's economy, however, provides an excellent opportunity to establish new political economic institutions based on market transactions rather than personalized exchanges. The IMF bailout package demanding the restructuring of Korea's economy, in spite of all of its limitations, is a force that can override the country's entrenched political economic interests. Just as the breakup of *zaibatsu* after World War II laid the foundation for Japan's rise as one of the world's major economic powers today, the IMF bailout package with its demand of economic liberalization – if implemented correctly – can potentially serve such a function for Korea's future economic development.

ACKNOWLEDGMENTS

The author would like to thank Professor Haruhiro Fukui, who allowed her to join the Pacific Rim Project and funded her research. Sincere gratitude is also expressed to Mr. J., who provided very useful information on Korean election processes. Professor Yoon Jungsuk gave important assistance in the formation of theoretical framework for the study. Professor Robert Scalapino's letters of introduction opened doors for the author during his field trips to Korea. The author also thanks Dr. Jin Yong Oh, Professor Wooik Ryu, and Richard Schank for their insightful comments and support during his research. Professor Tun-jen Cheng's comments are also appreciated.

PART II

DICTATORSHIP WITH CHINESE CHARACTERISTICS: MACROPERSPECTIVES

PSYCHOCULTURAL FOUNDATIONS OF INFORMAL GROUPS: THE ISSUES OF LOYALTY, SINCERITY, AND TRUST

CHUNG-FANG YANG

While I was ensconced in writing the first draft of this paper, the Hong Kong business community was shaken by the news that Zhou Guanwu, aged 77, head of Shougang, China's largest and most powerful state-owned steel manufacturer, had been forced into retirement and that, the following day, his son, Zhou Beifang, head of a Hong Kong–based holding company of this enterprise, was under arrest and investigation in Beijing for his possible connection to serious economic crimes.[1] Zhou Guanwu was reported to be close to Deng Xiaoping, a relationship that became manifest when Deng visited the company in 1992, a gesture of approval for the company's adherence to Deng's policies. Since then, Shougang obtained exclusive rights to launch businesses bearing no direct connection to the production or marketing of steel. This special treatment was widely seen to be linked to the cordial relationship between Deng and the Zhous. Furthermore, one of the subsidiaries of Zhou's holding company in Hong Kong had among its partners no other than Hong Kong tycoon Li Ka Shing and another Shanghai-based company in which Deng's second son, Deng Zhifang, was a vice managing director. The news broke amid rumors of Deng's deteriorating health. Many speculated that this event represented a showdown between two megapowers. Backed by the intertwined relation network (*guanxi wang*) between the two families, Shougang had reportedly been resisting the new tax reforms initiated by government policy makers, which would drastically reduce the profitability of the giant enterprise. Shougang's resistance set an example for many smaller companies around the country, thus rendering the reform program virtually ineffective for the previous two years. These resistant companies were mainly beneficiaries of earlier liberal economic policies that had however resulted in a high rate of inflation and chaotic problems of man-

---

1 An updated report released on November 8, 1996, stated that Zhou Beifang had been sentenced to death for illegally using state funds and bribery. No official announcement on this case has been issued as of December 31, 1997.

agement and control for the government, along with rapid economic growth. These companies foresaw the same fate that Shougang envisioned for itself if they complied with the new tax reform policies. Government officials responsible for executing the new policies were reportedly immobilized by "interest" groups formed informally among company personnel and some high-ranking powerholders. With Deng's imminent death, current government leaders decided to strike back simply for the purpose of establishing their own credibility.

While reporting the Shougang incident and its implications, Hong Kong media also revealed other problematic business activities implicating Deng's children. Although the latter might not be directly responsible for the incidents at issue, their involvement in high-power deals was indicated by such incidents.[2] With Deng Rong's recent high-profile world tour promoting her biography of her father and her elder sister Deng Lin's earlier trip selling her own paintings, people could not avoid the impression that the Deng children were busy cashing in on their father's political capital before his death. Among sinologists, the incident begs the questions, Who is actually running China? How are these powerful informal groups formed? How do they operate? Meanwhile, many old questions have resurfaced, such as how the Chinese people could have switched from accepting the ideology of radical Maoism during the Cultural Revolution to embracing the headstrong pursuit of self-interest so fast and with such ease.

In this chapter I plan to offer a psychocultural foundation for the analysis of Chinese political behavior in general and for understanding the way informal groups function in particular. After first proposing a new framework within which to examine the Chinese political activities in general, I will divide the remaining chapter into three sections, outlining three cultural meaning systems based on which, why, and how informal groups are essential to Chinese political functioning can be appreciated. In the first section, a two-tier social interaction system will be introduced providing the specific cultural backdrop against which the words "trust" and "sincerity" derive their special meanings. Within this cultural context, in the second section I will elucidate a leader/subordinate/group system in which the problem of loyalty becomes particularly acute and thus bring in the significance of informal groups in helping to solve this problem. Finally, I will explain a social influence system that demonstrates how informal groups are normally formed and how they operate. While laying these foundations, I hope in the meantime to answer some of the questions raised above and to provide

2 *Hong Kong Economic Journal* (newspaper), Feb. 21, 1995, p. 8. A similar but more updated report and analysis was published in *Newsweek*, Nov. 4. 1996.

interpretations for some other political events that have happened in Chinese societies.

FRAMEWORK USED FOR ANALYSIS

In the pursuit of an understanding of the relationship between culture and political behavior, one needs to adopt a specific point of view pertaining to how culture and the individual are related. In this chapter I adopt a "person in culture" perspective, a perspective that puts people in their own social/cultural/historical context and explores how they live under the conditions and constraints of that particular context, especially with respect to the types of problems that they may face in running their everyday lives and in times of environmental change, how they come to solve those problems, and exhibit certain characteristic behavior patterns as a result. Culture, in this framework, is defined as a set of meaning systems whereby people interact with one another. The way to understand political behavior in a particular culture is to examine how meanings are given to some key words by local people, what functions these words serve, how they are used, and how meaning changes reflect the experiences of people trying to make a better living in an ever-changing environment.[3] Cultural members are viewed as active beings; besides abiding by prescribed values and rules, they often choose to get around them, or to borrow outside help (from another culture), or to invent new alternatives to solve emerging problems. Their activities, political or otherwise, thus should not be simplistically construed as demonstrating some static and everlasting characteristics of cultural modal personality; nor should they be sweepingly viewed as variations of the same cultural theme. Instead, they are conceived as ways by which cultural members, using their particular coding systems, communicate and deal with the particular complex of problems arising in their lives. Our job is to find the meaning systems and decipher these activities with them so that a coherent understanding can be derived beneath often seemingly contradictory surface phenomena.

From this perspective, I propose here that political events in Chinese societies today should be conceptualized as a continuation of those of Imperial China and the Republic of China (often called Confucian China), rather than as part of a new Leninist China, for instance, in the case of the People's Republic of China. The Leninist political structure should be viewed as something

---

3 Many works in anthropology have influenced my taking this position to examine the relationship between culture and person. For example, Clifford Geertz, "From the native's point of view: On the nature of anthropological understanding," in R. A. Shweder and R. A. LeVine, eds., *Culture Theory: Essays on Mind, Self, and Emotion* (Cambridge: Cambridge University Press, 1984), pp. 123–136, and Roy G. D'Andrade, "Cultural meaning systems," Ibid., pp. 88–122.

borrowed (from another culture) to help solve the problems facing China at the time. Many of the key concepts in operation today in the political arenas of Chinese societies originated in the pre-Qin feudal era and went through a drastic meaning change beginning with the Qin Dynasty, when the country became a united autocratic state. Although taking this frame of analysis necessitates a thorough historical review of the transformations of the meanings of some key concepts, space limitation does not permit me to do so here.[4] In the following sections, I will simply lay out three sets of key concepts and meaning systems that I deem useful in helping us to understand why and how informal groups operate in Chinese political activities. Although these systems are derived from adopting the historical approach, historical accounts will be given only when deemed necessary, and, in those cases, examples illuminating how the concepts operate in the current politics of contemporary Chinese societies will follow.

THE TWO-TIER SOCIAL INTERACTION SYSTEM

In this section I will sketch a social interaction system that is considered fundamental to the understanding of all Chinese social behavior. I have expounded elsewhere that this system represents a conciliation between what is expected of the individual on the one hand and psycho/social/political reality on the other.[5] The expectation has been derived from a particular shared worldview concerning how individuals and groups (state, society, etc.) relate to one another. Contrary to the beliefs of Western scholars, the traditional Chinese conception of individual/group relationships has been characterized by local scholars as acknowledging the importance of the individual.[6] However, the individual is not valued in the same way as in modern Western cultures. That is to say, the individual is not valued for his or her own merit, but for his or her ability to develop or to realize an inborn social nature, that is, to love other people and to live with them harmoniously. Confucian prescriptions concerning how this could be achieved are to have the individual relegate the private and individuated self (*xiaowo*, the small self) and to

4 A more comprehensive discussion can be found in an early version of this paper: Chung Fang Yang, "Psychocultural foundations of informal groups: The issue of loyalty, sincerity and trust," paper presented at the 47th Annual Meeting of the Association of Asian Studies, April 6–9, 1995, Washington, DC.

5 Chung Fang Yang, "How to study the personality of the Chinese?: An indigenous perspective," in K. S. Yang and A. B. Yue, eds., *The Psychology and Behavior of the Chinese* (Taipei: Gueiguan, 1993), pp. 319–440. (In Chinese.)

6 A comprehensive review of different views on this issue can be found in Chung Fang Yang, "Are the Chinese really collectivistic?: Toward a reconceptualization of the Chinese value systems," in K. S. Yang, ed., *The Values of the Chinese: A Social Science Perspective* (Taipei: Gueiguan, 1994), pp. 321–434. (In Chinese.)

embrace the larger collectivity to which he or she belongs, the operating self (*dawo*, the large self), in a given situation. The individual was encouraged to begin by including family members into the large self (loving and serving one's family), then friends and associates, the country, and finally the world.[7] By cultivating oneself through this route, one gradually opened the boundary of the individuated self to include all others. The ideal end state of the developing self is "sagehood," in which one is united with heaven and earth; that is, one evolves through the *dawos* to become a "sage." Note that the self was conceived as the center of one's relationships with others, rather than a separate entity. The significance of this point will become apparent in our discussion on the "leader/subordinate/group" system in the next section.

On his way to sagehood, Confucius set up a role model for his disciples to emulate: *junzi* (gentleman). *Junzi* was said to differ from another type of person, *xiaoren* (mean person) in that the former practiced the principle of *yi* (reasonableness) and the latter the principle of *li* (self-interest).[8] In his discussion of the model of Confucian personality, Zhu Yilu accounted that in later historical development, *junzi* had come to carry the extra meaning of "selflessness."[9] Ironically and problematically, since the Han dynasty, upward mobility had largely been achieved through becoming imperial officials and climbing the bureaucratic ladder. The criteria for official selection had been invariably associated with either practicing the model behavior of *junzi* or excelling in knowledge of the Confucian classics, in which how to become a *junzi* was the major theme. Therefore, on the one hand, the selfless *junzi* had been the shared ideal self of the Chinese elite and ruling class; on the other hand, being *junzi* could be the only means to make a "selfish" but good living.

The Issue of Sincerity

In a culture in which a difficult role model is established and a heavy-handed reward and punishment scheme is practiced to enforce it, it is easy for people to be lured into feigned compliance, becoming *junzi* by name only.[10]

---

7 In *Da Xue* (*Big Learning*), one of the Four Books dispatching Confucian thoughts, a path of self-development was designed for the individual: *xiu shen* (self-cultivation), *qi jia* (raise a family), *zhe kuo* (run the country), and *ping tienxia* (conquer the world).

8 *Confucian Analects, Book VI*, Chap. 16: "The mind of the superior man is conversant with righteousness; the mind of the mean man is conversant with gain."

9 Zhu Yilu, *Confucian Modal Personality and Chinese Culture* (Shanyang, PRC: Liaoning Educational Books, 1991). (In Chinese.)

10 The traditional Chinese method of education and socialization emphasized modeling the "correct" behavior first and appreciating it later. Through relentless practice, one gradually experiences the modeling of the "correct" behavior first and appreciating it's goodness later. For descriptions of the Chinese socialization method, see David Y. F. Ho, "Chinese patterns of socialization: A critical review," in M. H. Bond, ed., *The Psychology of the Chinese People* (Hong Kong: Oxford University Press, 1986), pp. 1–37.

Furthermore, with *junzi* as the ultimate goal of a long process of self-cultivation (until one's death), it is reasonable to assume that most of the people, however sincere they are in their pursuit, are still in the process of pursuing this ideal, with various degrees of success. In other words, they still have personal desires and individuated interests that have not been eradicated. They thus have to find other ways to meet their *xiaoren*'s needs and desires that are harbored underneath while they have their external behavior modeled after that of a selfless *junzi*.

Based on the above-described cultural background, I have proposed a resulting two-tier social interaction system adopted by the Chinese to handle this conflict of motivation.[11] On the top layer, people say and do things following *li* (rituals or formalities) as prescribed by *junzi*, that is, being loyal to and considerate of one another and interacting purely based on the principle of propriety. At the next layer, however, people's personal needs and desires are pursued and fulfilled through some carefully calculated exchanges, while they are cultivating themselves to have less such demands. During such instrumental exchanges, attention is not focused on looking after one's self-interests, since pursuing such goals is considered selfish and thus undesirable. Individual goals are achieved through the culturally acceptable route: "I do it for you and you do it for me." Of course, no formal social contracts are signed at any time, but they are embedded in a strong belief in *bao*, an indigenous version of the norm of reciprocity and a complex social influence system that will be taken up in the last section of this chapter. This kind of indirect instrumental exchange requires good communication and a shared understanding of the unspoken rules between the two parties to ensure that each clearly recognizes the needs and desires of the other. Ironically, this requirement cannot easily be met within a social interaction structure in which meanings operate at a deeper layer and in which one's own needs and desires can only be expressed vaguely and equivocally (lest they should be deemed selfish). One's ability to have his needs and desires fulfilled therefore depends on the other party's ability and willingness to grasp them beneath a facade of formalities, usually labeled as *keqi* (taking the attitude of a guest), and to meet them skillfully without embarrassing oneself (by making them explicit).

Consequently, the most important factor influencing the success of such social exchanges is one's ability to pick the "right" persons on whom one can rely to perform the duties of the other end in the hidden contracts. This brings up the issue of trust: its meaning and its function in this social inter-

---

11 Chung Fang Yang, "A theory of the Chinese self," in C. F. Yang and H. S. R. Kao, eds., *The Chinese Mind and the Chinese Heart: A Collection of Papers on Indigenous Chinese Psychology* (Taipei: Yuanliou, 1994), pp. 93–146. (In Chinese.)

action system. In the last section of this paper, I will demonstrate that a *guanxi* (personal relationship) network, based on which one can form his or her informal groups, becomes a vehicle to secure such a trust. In the meantime, a constant assessment of sincerity is to be carried out by both parties throughout their interactions until mutual trust is fully established. A recent instance of a "sincerity" debate illustrates the point. After Hong Kong's last colonial governor, Chris Patton, announced a political reform plan unilaterally without consulting the PRC negotiation team, he was accused of breaching the "sincerity" code. Since then, the sincerity issue had became the constant refrain between Patton and Chinese officials during the Sino-British negotiations concerning the future of Hong Kong.

One more point that needs to be addressed in regard to social interaction is that the social exchanges just outlined appear to be too much like cold-blooded manipulations, involving no emotions or affections at all. Then, how do feelings and affections fit into this picture? Or do they fit at all? Besides concluding that the Chinese are deprived of emotional intimacy experiences, as some sinologists have already claimed, I have explained elsewhere that the instrumentality and expressiveness dichotomy of human relationships is false and that the two types of exchanges operate simultaneously in social interactions, but not necessarily in opposing or compensatory fashion.[12] In other words, while two persons are engaged in such instrumental exchanges as described in the system, affections can flow as well. Rarely do we see pure instrumental or pure affective exchanges in real-life social interactions. This is especially true for the Chinese because *qing* (emotion or affect) has always being an important component accompanying *li* (propriety) in constituting the "proper" behavior in social interactions and interpersonal relationships. Exactly how *qing* becomes part of this social interaction system will be illustrated in the last section as well.

To summarize, there are four major characteristics reflecting the two-tier structure of Chinese social interaction: (1) indirectness – the real meaning is underneath the surface formalities; (2) interdependence – "I for you and you for me" is the way to fulfill one's goals and desires; (3) obligation-based personalism – one's behavior toward another is guided by obligations perceived in a specific dyadic relation; and (4) situation-dependence – one's *dawo* and social behavior are determined by "with whom" and "under what occasion" one is interacting.

This conceptualization of Chinese social interaction as a two-tier structure opens up a new perspective for examining Chinese political activities and

---

12 Chung Fang Yang, "Toward a reconceptualization of *Guanxi* and *Renqing*," to appear in *Indigenous Psychologied Studies in Chinese Societies*, 11. (In Chinese.)

events. As has been pointed out correctly by many political scientists, there is a need to make a distinction between official norms and their realization in studying the PRC's political behavior;[13] a similar, but further, argument made here is that there is not only a need to distinguish between what is said and what is done, but also between these and what is meant. For instance, Lucian Pye observed that, "In China, people can become instant 'old friends,' a status that is supposed to represent the ultimate of shared intimacies."[14] From this he inferred that such behavior demonstrates the Chinese hunger for intimacy. Taking the two-tier-structure framework, "old friend" over-zealously addressed to a total stranger or light acquaintance would not be interpreted as "intimacy-seeking" but more likely as *keqi* (Pye's formal respectability), meant to create a friendly surface atmosphere for the occasion. Sometimes it is intended to *tao jinhu*, to create an "instant" *guanxi* for possible future instrumental exchanges.[15]

THE LEADER/SUBORDINATE/GROUP SYSTEM

In the previous section, the Chinese conception of an individual/group relationship was laid out and the concepts of *dawo* and *xiaowo* were introduced. In this section, the relationship between an individual and a group will be further expanded, with special attention paid to the dynamic relationship between the leader and the subordinate of a group (*dawo*), whether it be a state, an organization, or an enterprise, of which both are members and/or with which both identify themselves. From there the problem of loyalty will be brought out and the significance of informal groups will become even more apparent.

Figure 4.1 shows the relative positions of an individual (the small self) and the groups (the large selves) with which he or she is associated. The figure clearly illustrates a culturally specific conception of what constitutes *si*, the "private," and *gong*, the "public." Japanese scholar Mizoguchi Yuzo recently compared the differences between the Japanese and the Chinese conceptions of *gong* and *si* and concluded that the Chinese conception obliterates the boundaries between them and allows one (*gong*) to contain the other (*si*).[16]

13 For example, D. G. Goodman, *Groups and Politics in the People's Republic of China* (Cardiff, England: University College Cardiff Press, 1984), p. 3.
14 Lucian Pye, *The Mandarin and the Cadre: China's Political Cultures* (Ann Arbor: Center for Chinese Studies, The University of Michigan, 1988), p. 47.
15 Researchers from North American or European countries have to be aware of the fact that the people they are studying may behave and interact quite differently with them than when they do with local people. I suspect that the researchers are often approached as "good friends" for their instrumental values.
16 Mizoguchi Yuzo, "A comparison of the Chinese and Japanese conceptions of *Gong* and *Si*," *Twenty-first Century*, (February 1994), pp. 85–97. (A Chinese translation.)

Thus, when one acts one always acts for both *gong* and *si* simultaneously because one is always encompassed by a larger collective (*dawo*, the group or the public), as is shown in Figure 4.1. In addition, this conception of the relationship between *gong* and *si* posits that, if one works for the benefits of *gong*, one's *si* is also supposed to be taken care of. However, the reverse is not considered true. This "fallacy" necessitates the addition of a moral undertone to the two words. When one is said to be *weigong* (for the public or a entity larger than oneself) one is expected to work for the benefits of everyone in the entity without thinking about one's personal gains and losses. If one does so as expected, one is said to be morally good and correct. However, if one thinks about one's own interests while working for the collective entity, one is considered to be *weisi* (for oneself) and morally bad and incorrect. The way *gong* and *si* are used in *weigong* and *weisi* clearly demonstrates how the meanings of *gong* and *si* are motivational rather than territorial.

The main distinction between working for *gong* and for *si* lies in whom one has in mind while working for a collective entity. This distinction of course is often very difficult to make from outside the expressed behavior. It becomes even more difficult when a moral tone has been added. People have to rely on what one has actually gained for him- or herself to decide whether this person is working or has been working for the collective or for him- or herself. This criterion of judgment forces any public official who wants to maintain high moral standards to avoid any policy decision that will benefit him- or herself, even if the decision is most beneficial to the collective entity that he or she works for.

Meanwhile, before one has been morally cultivated to the point of total selflessness, one has personal needs and wishes to be addressed. Consequently, one must resort either to servicing those needs indirectly (through the help of others) or to carefully disguise one's *weisi* by pretending that one is *weigong*. Especially for those holding public positions, who constantly carry an identifiable operating *dawo* (i.e., the state), the need for such solutions is even stronger than ordinary citizens because, for them, *weigong* must be shown at all times. In the end, it becomes extremely difficult to tell who is truly *weigong* and who is actually *weisi*. A set of attributional procedures (tests of sincerity) must be developed to help solve this problem.

Even in modern Chinese societies, there remains a plethora of phrases reflecting how people are constantly reminded of the predicament caused by this *gong/si* conflict: "*da gong wu si*" (be fair to all without self-serving biases), "*gong er wang si*" (go all the way for the public and forget the self totally), "*jia gong ji si*" (seek self-interest in the name of public interests), "*gong bao si chou*" (revenge for private grudges with public excuses), and so on. This conception of the relationship between the public and the private and their operation in self/group relationships helps to explain how people could change from "working for the country" so swiftly and easily to "working for oneself," as demonstrated in the instances outlined in the beginning of this chapter. After the Cultural Revolution, documents, anecdotes, and reports gradually disclosed a different picture from what the people were told previously. They had become disillusioned after realizing that what they had been led to believe since the establishment of the new People's Republic and what they had been taught in their textbooks about patriotism, altruism, and self-sacrifice were nothing but schemes employed by powerholders to mobilize support, which was then used as a resource for personal power struggles. The people realized that they were just pawns in the power struggles and wasted not only their enthusiasm but even their lives. This disillusionment set many free from the *dawo*, for which they had been sacrificing their *xiaowo* for all those years, and resulted in a shift in the opposite direction, totally forgetting about the party, the country, and the public and concentrating on working for the betterment of their own lives. This makes it easier for a people who at all times are wearing both the hats of *dawo* and *xiaowo*.

The Issue of Loyalty

The problem of not being able to tell whether the performed act is *weigong* or *weisi* creates yet another problem for people (henceforth called "the subordinates") working for a large collective under another person's leadership (henceforth called "the leader"); this is especially true for public officials working for the autocratic state. It is about the issue of loyalty. Ji Yiou Liu gave a comprehensive historical account of the problematic development of the meaning of *zhong*, the Chinese version of loyalty.[17] He stated that since the change of political structure (to an autocratic state) during the Qin Period, a loyalty dilemma had constantly bothered many imperial officials and their contemporary counterparts: Toward whom should one be loyal? The head of state who appointed him? Or the state for which he was supposed to work? The problem would not have been particularly acute if the head of state considered himself a person working for the same people as the officials. However, since the Qin Dynasty, up to and including the present government of the PRC, the head of state has invariably been determined by a contest of military forces. In other words, the state has always been "earned" by the founding leader and his followers in every change of dynasty. It is only natural in this case for the head of state to think of the state as his own private property, rather than that of the people, and to treat his appointees as

---

17 Ji Yiou Liu, "Gong and si: The ethical implications of loyalty," in C. J. Huang, ed., *New Perspective of the Chinese Culture: Traditional Thoughts*, vol. 2 (Taipei: Lienjing, 1982), pp. 171–208. (In Chinese.)

his own private employees. Conflicts therefore often arise for state officials when they are asked to obey orders from the leader that are considered, by themselves, to be detrimental to the welfare of the people. Liu labeled this loyalty problem a conflict of *gongzhong* (loyalty to the public) and *sizhong* (loyalty to the leader privately). This conflict may not pose a big problem if the officials in question are simply mundane and selfish *xiaoren* who obey orders from any rice provider. In that case, they would be conflict-free to be the leader's private, loyal followers. However, those who have internalized at least part of the Confucian ideology of serving both the state and the people as one's path toward sagehood often find the conflict tormenting, for one of the meanings of loyalty confers on them responsibility for giving advice, however unpalatable, to their superiors when they see the latter not acting in the best interest of the state and the people.[18] In their attempts to assume this responsibility, some officials have received death penalties for themselves or their families, or the termination of a lifelong career (when the admonition angered the superiors). Some lucky others, however, were rewarded with fame and promotions as brave fighters for the state and the people (in cases when the act was seen by the emperors as an act of ultimate loyalty).[19]

The problem of loyalty arises not only for the subordinates of a group or a state, but also for their superiors. The leaders undeniably need their subordinates to serve as extensions of themselves, but they also need assistance in reflecting the feelings of the people toward their policies and giving counteradvice about how to run the state better. However, because of the absolute power that the heads of the state have over their officials, it becomes virtually impossible for the officials to speak the truth, lest they be demoted or killed. Therefore, among those people who show deference and obedience, the superiors usually cannot easily tell whether they speak with the best interests of their employers in mind, that is, with private loyalty to the leaders; with the state and the people in mind, that is, with public loyalty to the state; or simply *weisi*, with their own interests in mind, period. This problem again brings up the issue of sincerity and how to decide which officials are telling the truth while they are performing some seemingly loyal acts. Unfortunately, the ultimate and surest test of sincerity is through the official's remonstrance, because the superiors can almost always be certain that officials who are willing to risk their lives must be sincere about what they have said. Ironically, and unfortunately for the leaders, those officials who do take it on themselves to remonstrate were exactly those who were more loyal

18 The most recent surge of debate on this loyalty dilemma was aroused by Liu Binyan, whose book in the late 1980s called remonstrance a loyalty of the second kind, the first being "deference."

19 In later dynasties, many scholars (such as Li Zhe, in the Ming Dynasty) were also very critical of those remonstrators and considered remonstrance an instrumental act.

to the state and the people than to the superiors themselves. In the event of a conflict between the interests of their employer and the people, they would be the most likely ones to desert the former for the latter![20] In sum, the leaders in this leader/subordinate/group system often develop ambivalent feelings toward their elite subordinates in the formal hierarchical structure. On the one hand, they want these officials to be loyal to them by speaking more truthfully through remonstrance; on the other hand, those who do speak up are distrusted and feared because, in case of conflict, they tend to desert the leaders for the state and the people. In modern Chinese societies, the same kind of distrust of outspoken intellectuals among leaders remains for practically the same reason. The best illustration of this ambivalent feeling is a report that quoted Mao Zedong as saying that he liked the "rightists" because they spoke the truth; he abhorred "leftists" because they always lied. Another good example is the ubiquitous labels given to political dissents, "*li tong guo wai*" (treason) or *dian fu* (subversion), which reflects the same kind of distrust and fear that these dissenters are more loyal to another group (country) or another cause than one's own.[21] From this perspective, we can also see that the *dawo*, like the political party, the country, and the people, can be manipulated to serve as excuses with which either the leader demands the obedience of his subordinates or the subordinates defy the superior's orders. In addition, the defiance of the subordinates can be deemed as either treasonous or patriotic, depending on who looks at it and who has ultimately won the power struggle.[22] During the Cultural Revolution, Mao Zedong repeatedly employed this same script to get rid of political enemies such as Liu Shaoqi and Peng Dehuai.[23]

In Need of Qinxin: Informal Inner Cliques

This distrust of their official employees often led to the leaders' reliance on a clique of private and close confidants, called *qinxin*,[24] who serve the role of

---

20 Here I try to provide some explanations to a thought-provoking question raised by Lucian Pye in *The Mandarin and the Cadre*: "What is it in Chinese culture that makes it seem self-evident that people who are skilled are unlikely to have strong attachments, but also that it is inappropriate to raise questions about the technical competence of intensely dedicated and loyal people?" (p. 50).

21 This example also reflected the logic on the part of the ruling government of equating itself with the state and the people. The trials of Wei Jingsheng, Wang Dan, etc., are some of the most recent examples.

22 A recent report about Dr. Li Zhisui, the private physician of Mao for twenty-two years, illustrates vividly the role that "the state and the people" play in the moral reasoning of the Chinese. When asked whether he felt that he betrayed the trust inherited in a doctor/patient relation when he published a memoir detailing the private life of Mao, Dr. Li replied that, keeping Mao's life secret demonstrated his loyalty to one man, but making it public demonstrated his loyalty to the state and people of 1.2 billion (*Hong Kong Economic Journal*, January 25, 1995, p. 8).

23 Yang, "Psychocultural foundations of informal groups" (the early version), pp. 26–27.

24 *Qin* means close; *xin* means confidante in Chinese.

"private employees" to the leaders. The major qualifications for these *qinxin* are (1) their physical closeness to the leaders so that they could be called on at all times; (2) their ability to follow through on the orders given by the leaders without questioning; and (3) their absolute loyalty to their employers and to them only. This last requirement demands them to be void of ambition to become leaders themselves. The responsibilities of these *qinxin* included: (1) to do what the leaders cannot do as the head of the state (because they are not expected to do anything other than *weigong*, for the state and the people); (2) to take care of or to fight for their personal and private interests (sometimes by means that are not allowable in the official capacity of the emperors); and (3) to serve as the scapegoat in times of trouble. These *qinxin* are held accountable only to the leaders personally, bypassing the bureaucratic apparatus that has often been considered as being controlled by untrustworthy elite officials who have the potential to replace them to become the leaders in the name of public goodness. In his paper describing the power struggle in Imperial China between emperors and their bureaucratic apparatuses led by the prime minister, Y. S. Yu stated that, due to the qualifications specified for these *qinxin*, the inner cliques of the emperors often included their blood and affinal relatives, eunuchs, private secretaries, and an independent secret police force.[25] These people usually were less educated and easily became corrupt once they became powerful. However, Yu quoted a Japanese scholar as saying that there was also a tendency for these people to want to become part of the apparatus, thereby making their power legitimate, but by their doing so they also make themselves untrustworthy to the emperors. At that time, the emperors would try to get rid of them and seek a new wave of *qinxin*.

What has just been described concerning the dynamic relationships among the head of state, his elite officials, and the state holds true not only for their modern counterparts, but also for all other leader/subordinate/group contexts in many modern Chinese societies. However, nowhere is this dynamics more clearly and vividly evident than in the PRC, where *wei renmin fuwu* (serve the people) is on the front door of practically every government building, let alone with every breath public officials exhale. Party members are repeatedly told to be loyal "to the party, to the country, and to the people," In the head/worker/factory context, the profits gained by the factory are supposed to be divided equally among "country, *danwei*, and the individual." The individual in this quotation does not mean an individual person but workers in

---

25 Ying-shih Yu, "The imperial power and the prime minister's power under '*juen zuen chan bei*,'" in Y. S. Yu, *History and Thoughts* (Taipei: Lienjing, 1976), pp. 47–76. R. Y. Huang's *1587, A Year of No Significance* (New Haven: Yale University Press, 1981) illuminates the struggle between a Ming emperor and his Confucian officials very well.

the factory as a group. When asked recently by Hong Kong reporters what constituted a Hong Kong resident after 1997, a PRC government official's answer to this question included a "patriotism" condition. Patriotism meant considering China as one's *dawo* and subjecting one's *xiaowo* to this *dawo*. This instance indicates that, regardless how "resident" is defined according to international laws, the cultural meaning system still plays an important part in its practical use. While this same "*dawo* precedes *xiaowo*" logic continues to be prevalent in modern Chinese self/group relationships, it is no wonder that the leader of any group always needs to establish small groups of *qinxin* whose loyalty he or she can count on. These inner cliques are especially useful in the event of factional conflicts within a group because, at that time, the normative resolution is to consider such conflict as *neibu zhengdun* (internal conflict), and thus it should be handled with an open mind and with a goal of maintaining group harmony. Power struggles between factions thus must be settled beneath the surface with the help of these inner cliques.

THE SOCIAL INFLUENCE SYSTEM

As the significance of informal groups has been elucidated in the previous section, the remaining question concerns how these informal groups are formed and how they function. In this section I will briefly present a social influence system that I think provides the answer. Social influence refers to the processes whereby one affects and is affected by others. More specifically, it refers to the processes through which one makes others do as one wants them to do. In a paper explicating this social influence system, I postulated that social influence is achieved through the dynamic interplay of *guanxi*, *renqing*, *bao*, and *mianzi*.[26] *Guanxi* (relation or relationship) operates in a weblike interpersonal network in which each Chinese is embedded, with the self at the center.[27] It reflects how much influence one can exert on related others and how one can get one's wishes and needs actualized through such influence. Of course, it also reflects how much one can be influenced by others. *Renqing* (human emotion) is an even more complex term than *guanxi*, carrying many meanings reflecting its importance and omnipresent in Chinese social life. Specifically relevant to the discussion here are its two meanings, one as an object (such as a gift), a resource, or a favor with which one proceeds or facilitates social exchanges and ensures one's influences on those people included in one's *guanxi* network. The other meaning is an obli-

---

26 Yang, "Toward a framework for the study of Chinese social interaction."
27 For a good description of this network, see Fei Xiaotong, *Rural China* (Shanghai: Guancha She, 1948), pp. 22–30.

gated feeling or emotion that one shows to others in social interactions; the expression of it follows the principles of *bao*, a variation of the norm of reciprocity that entails giving, receiving, and repaying.[28] This obligated dimension of *renqing* allows the use of *renqing*-granting (like gift-giving or favor-offering) as a tool to oblige the receiver to repay in ways that he or she demands.[29] *Mianzi* (face or social prestige) serves as a regulator; it enhances or amplifies influence, but also contains and controls abuses of influence (lest one lose face if the demand is too much and rejected.[30]

The Chinese system of social influence is thought to include three major routes:

1. Eliciting from the other party affective and behavioral obligations that are prescribed in many ascribed relations in the societies;
2. Eliciting from the other party repayment of *renqing* obligations inherited in principles of *bao*, which prescribe general rules applicable to all social interactions (regardless of the type of relationship that existed between the two parties);
3. Eliciting genuine feelings of affection and intimacy, which characterize the *zijiren* (inner circle) relationship, which in turn binds the other party to give help voluntarily and unconditionally when needed.[31]

Explanation of these three routes requires an elucidation of the Chinese conception of relationship, *guanxi*.

Assumed Qing and Real Qing in *Guanxi*

Scholars have long been interested in the operations of *guanxi* in Chinese social interactions:[32] Many deemed it the most unique characteristic of Chinese society. This has attracted many scholars to try to conceptualize *guanxi* and to find the behavioral rules governing the different types of *guanxi*

---

28 A good explanation of this concept can be found in Lien-sheng Yang, "The concept of *Pao* as a basis for social relations in China," in J. K. Fairbank, ed., *Chinese Thought and Institutions* (Chicago: University of Chicago Press, 1957), pp. 291–309.
29 A good explication of this concept is provided by Ambrose Y. C. King, "An analysis of *Renqing* in interpersonal relationships: A preliminary inquiry," in *Proceedings of the International Conference on Sinology* (Taipei: Academia Sinica, 1980), pp. 413–428. (In Chinese.)
30 This concept was thoroughly investigated by Hsien-Chin Hu, "The Chinese concept of face," *American Anthropology* 46, pp. 45–64.
31 Kuo-Shu Yang, "Social orientation of the Chinese: A social interactive perspective," in K. S. Yang and A. B. Yu, eds., *The Psychology and Behavior of the Chinese People, 1992* (Taipei: Gueiguan, 1993), pp. 87–142.
32 For examples, see Chien Chiao, "*Guanxi*: A preliminary conceptualization," in K. S. Yang and C. I. Wen, eds., *The Sinicization of Social and Behavioral Science Research in China* (Taipei: Academia Sinica, 1982), pp. 345–360 (in Chinese); Mayfair M. H. Yang, *The Art of Social Relationships and Exchanges in China*, Ph.D. dissertation, University of California, Berkeley, 1986; Ambrose Y. C. King, "*Kuan-hsi* and network building: A sociological interpretation," *Daedalus* 120 (1991), pp. 63–83.

discernible by local people.[33] Integrating their efforts and formulations, I conceptualized *guanxi* as a summary of the status of one's ties with another person.[34] It is construed to have come from two aspects of mutual interaction: ascribed (*jiyou guanxi*) and interactive (*jiaowang guanxi*). The former is similar to Bruce Jacobs' "*guanxi* base"; it refers to a collection of institutionally ascribed relations shared by the interacting dyad (such as locality, kinship, colleague, etc.) either by way of blood association or by interaction.[35]

These relations are recognized by all Chinese societies as meaningful, and each of them is prescribed with a specific affection (*qing*) and a set of mutual obligations to express such an affection. This type of *guanxi*-specific affection has been labeled as "assumed *qing*" by Hsien Chin Hu.[36] It is deemed to be different from real *qing*, the affection derived spontaneously from actual interactive experiences between two parties. For different ascribed relations in the *guanxi* base, the degree of pressure toward expressing the assumed *qing* is different. In a normal situation, the pressure toward conformity is the strongest in parent/child relations. Another such highly obligated relation is the patron–client dyad, which will be taken up shortly due to its special relevance to our discussion here.

The interactive aspect of a *guanxi* refers to what is accumulated through actual interaction experiences between the two parties. It can be further decomposed into two components: instrumental and affective. The former refers to what comes out of the exchanges following the "I for you, and you for me" scheme, and the status of it is judged by the extent to which each fulfills the other's personal needs and wants. The latter refers to the standing regarding the exchanges of real affection between the two. Each of these two components is also seen to have a set of affective and behavioral rules governing its operation. Instrumental exchanges are regulated by *renqing* obligations, whereas affective exchanges are regulated by real *qing* and the need principle.

I have maintained in this *guanxi* conceptualization that the major function that *guanxi* serves in social interactions is that its prescribed affective and behavioral rules guarantee the trust needed at different stages of a relationship's development. Ascribed *guanxi* gives assurance during initial interactions; the trust is provided by the obligations inherited in those ascribed

33 For example, Kuang-Kuo Hwang, "Face and favor: The Chinese power game," *American Journal of Sociology* 92 (1987), pp. 944–974.
34 Yang, "Toward a framework for the study of Chinese social interaction."
35 J. B. Jacobs, *Local Politics in a Rural Chinese Cultural Setting: A Field Study of Masu Township in Taiwan* (Canberra, Australia: Contemporary China Center, Research School of Pacific Studies, Australian National University, 1980).
36 Hsien-Chin Hu, "Emotion, real & assumed, in Chinese society," unpublished manuscript on file with Columbia University Research in Contemporary Culture, Doc. No. CH 668, 1949.

relations shared between the two. As interactions continue, actual experiences take over to supply the needed guarantee. The guarantee comes from knowing that the other person will indeed comply with the *renqing* obligations and thus ensure repayment in instrumental exchanges, or that he or she will demonstrate genuine affections by providing needed help spontaneously.

The three aspects comprising the Chinese conception of *guanxi* – that is, the ascribed *guanxi* base, the instrumental, and the exchange of genuine affection – correspond to the three social influence routes outlined earlier in this section. One of the routes takes advantage of the strong pressure toward complying with *guanxi*-specific obligations, another with *renqing* obligations inherited in all, but especially in instrumental exchanges. The third route mobilizes the other party with the trust and the affection implied in a closeknit and family-like relationship. In the remainder of the chapter I will use two *guanxi* categories to demonstrate the forming and functioning of informal groups.

Patron–Client Relationships: The Influence of *Enqing*

As stated earlier, for some of the ascribed relations in the Chinese *guanxi*, a wide range of obligations with very strong compliance pressures are implied, such that a forceful and enduring bond is established between the two that overrides other experiences derived from their interactions. Patron–client *guanxi* serves as a good example. The assumed *qing* prescribed for this *guanxi* is *enqing*, and this *qing* often gets further enhanced in the course of interaction, during which the patron plays a protective and sponsorship role, called *bao* (guarantor) and the client a protected and docile one, not unlike that in a parent–child relation.[37]

Enqing is originated between two persons, one of whom has granted a significant favor by making a pivotal positive impact on the recipient's life. In such a case, the grantor is considered to have bestowed on the recipient an *en* and the latter is said to owe an *enqing* to the grantor. For instance, if a person has recommended another person for an important career position, sometimes to replace him- or herself, the latter is said to owe a *zhi yu zhi en* (indebtedness due to patronage) to the former and is obliged to comply with whatever is demanded by the former.

A modern illuminating example of this concept in operation happened in Hong Kong, when two of the contenders for the Chief Executive Officer for the Special Administration Region (SAR) government were questioned by the Hong Kong press in terms of their abilities to keep Hong Kong's

---

37 *En* is also used to describe the *qing* between a parent and child. One is said to owe one's parents an *en* for giving birth and nurturing him or her.

independence from the PRC after 1997. Both of these two candidates for the highest ranking position of post-1997 Hong Kong come from prominent families running successful businesses in Hong Kong, but the family businesses of both had allegedly, at one time, been "rescued" by the PRC government from bankruptcy. Such an *en* granted by the PRC government to their families has been widely deemed as having the effect of making it impossible for them to resist any demand that may be asked by the grantor in the future.

In the succession case the *enqing* often becomes even stronger if the *en* grantor also chooses to serve as the guardian for the appointee at the beginning of the appointee's tenure in office, when his own credibility has not yet been established. This is an act of *bao* (protection) on the part of the grantor. In this kind of patron–client relationship, whenever the appointee is faced with challenges and resistance by his rivals and his subordinates, the *en* grantor needs to bale him out by lending his own prestige and credibility. This continuous *enqing* that is owed usually is repaid by the appointee's deference and obedience to the orders or advice of the *en* grantor. The *en* grantor can then use this *enqing* owed by the appointee as a vehicle and a guarantee for expanding his own personal influence.

Unfortunately, this act of *bao* on the part of the *en* grantor is a double-edged sword for the appointee. On the one hand, it makes the appointee's job easier by reducing opposition and resistance; on the other hand, it undermines his effort to build his own credibility. Any significant independence shown away from the *en* grantor's instructions can help him build his own credentials, but it can also be interpreted by the *en* grantor as an ungrateful and betraying act. Several such moves will lead to the *en* grantor's "deserting" (*qi*) the appointee and replacing him with a new client. With this fear of being deserted the appointee is constantly in double jeopardy. For this same grievous reason, most of the appointees who outlived (literally or politically) their *en* grantors often are the conforming type whose credibility becomes a problem immediately after the grantor's death or downfall. A power-defense war usually follows.

This dynamic interaction of *en* and *bao* is reflected in most of the transitions of power in China past and present. This also helps to explain why, in the 1980s, an informal group led by Deng Xiaoping, who held no influential official positions, can become the most powerful clique. Deng's desertion of Hu Yaobang and Zhao Ziyang serves as a good example of how a patron–client relationship went sour because the *en* receivers became too independent. It also explains why the more docile Jiang Zemin and Li Peng kept their positions up to Deng's death and are now facing credibility problems.

The patron–client *guanxi* discussed above reflects the fact that each of the ascribed ties in a *guanxi* can, during the course of interaction, become, or be manipulated to become, a strong interdependent bond between two persons. This bond usually is a mix of ever-growing obligations and genuine emotions, and thus it ensures an interpersonal transmission of influence.

Sincerity Assessment: The Making of *Zijiren*

In finding a way to guide behavior in dyadic interactions, the Chinese often distinguish between *zijiren*, those who are parts of oneself, and *wairen*, those who are outside of oneself. *Zijiren* are people who belong to one's intimate circle and are treated just like he or she treats him- or herself. Francis L. K. Hsu has argued that, for the Chinese, this inner circle of a person normally includes only his or her family members.[38] Within this circle, members treat each other casually, with all of the formalities relaxed. They help each other on the basis of need rather than *renqing* owed. Members feel close, safe, and secure with each other, even though affections are rarely expressed explicitly with words or body language. Expressions of love are shown by what they do for each other in times of need and how much they sacrifice for the welfare of other members in the family. Lin Tuan, however, disagreed with Hsu and stated that people who are not family members can become members of this *zijiren* circle through the evolvement of a genuine affection (*ganqing*) during interaction.[39] He called this evolvement the process of "family-zation" (to become a family member). One way to cultivate more social influences in the Chinese social interaction system is thus to expand one's own *zijiren* circle and/or to make sure that one is included in many influential persons' *zijiren* circles. Becoming a godparent to someone's son or daughter, or a godson or daughter to someone older than oneself, or through marriages are some of the quick ways to become "family members"; but whether the two become real *zijiren* to each other has to be determined after some sincerity assessments as mutual interactions continue.

The evolution of *guanxi* in the course of social interactions hedges on three kinds of sincerity assessment, during which actions expressed by another party are evaluated in terms of three meanings of sincerity: authenticity, intention, and commitment. Two persons can interact with each other without seriously getting into a "meaningful" *guanxi* if they simply follow the normative codes of conduct regulating interactions with *wairen* (outsiders) in

38 Francis L. K. Hsu, "Eros, affect, and *Pao*," in F. L. K. Hsu, ed., *Kinship and Culture* (Chicago: Aldine, 1971), pp. 439–475.
39 Tuan Lin, "Confucian ethics and action theory: A dialogue with Professor Kwang Kuo Hwang," *Contemporary* (April 1992), pp. 82–103.

social occasions (such as a host inviting the appropriate guests and the guest giving a gift that is appropriate for the occasion). During this phase of a *guanxi*, each person's sincerity is being assessed by the other in terms of whether one means what one says, and one passes the authenticity test if he delivers what he or she has promised. Once this test is passed, the two then enter into a new phase of their *guanxi*, during which a "meaningful" *guanxi* involving instrumental exchanges with or without affection take place. In this new phase, another kind of sincerity assessment is under way. For example, a person's "friendly" gesture offered beyond complying with the *renqing* obligations governing instrumental exchanges (such as giving an exorbitant gift on a wedding occasion to a person with only a distant *guanxi*) can be attributed either as a signal or pressure for a future instrumental exchange (if the assessor finds that he or she possesses some resources that the *renqing* grantor may deem valuable as repayments) or as an expression of affection (if the above possibility is eliminated). This assessment of intention guides the assessor either to maintain a cordial businesslike relationship with the assessed or develop a cozier friendship. While both parties enter a more affectively involved phase of a *guanxi*, a third kind of sincerity assessment is also under way whereby the level of commitment of the two is determined. During this assessment period, the assessor regards the assessed as genuinely committed when an action taken by the latter is considered as involving self-sacrifice. Passing this test of commitment leads both parties into the final phase of a *guanxi*, in which they become *zijiren* to each other.

With the above meanings and assessment processes attached to the word "sincerity," the ultimate criterion for sincerity judgment behind one person's action toward another person is the degree of self-sacrifice, that is, the extent to which an action is coming from deep within one's heart. It implies that the actor really treats the other as oneself. Since the highest level of self-sacrifice is to give up one's life, an act involving life-sacrificing is often considered to be the utmost sincere act. The hunger strike during the June 4th movement serves as a good illustration of this reasoning; the people of Beijing poured out their emotions after the students at Tienanmen Square wrote their wills to their parents and determined to starve themselves to death to demonstrate that they meant what they said.[40] Another excellent example of this show of sincerity took place in Taiwan when a legislator stabbed his own arm in front of his fellow members in the legislature to demonstrate the sincerity of his words. In October 1994, he was implicated in a stock market scandal in which he was accused of having "protected" a tycoon colleague

40 Chung Fang Yang, "Conformity and defiance on Tiananmen Square: A social psychological perspective," in P. Li, S. Mark, and M. H. Li, eds., *Culture and Politics in China: An Anatomy of Tiananmen Square* (New York: Transaction, 1991), pp. 17–224.

allegedly involved in that case. He denied the allegation with a fling of a knife onto himself.[41]

CONCLUSION

In this chapter, I have introduced three cultural coding systems with which the significance and the operation of informal groups can be examined and understood. These three interrelated systems provide reasons for explaining why the issues of trust, loyalty, and sincerity become grueling problems in Chinese social interactions and, specifically, why the elite members occupying positions in the formal bureaucratic structure are not entrusted with jobs fulfilled by the informal groups. They also inform about ways to investigate the informal groups that currently exist in the political arenas in Chinese societies. I hope that readers of this book will be able to use the systems described here to assist them in gaining a deeper understanding of the political activities reported in other chapters included in this volume.

41 *Ming Bao* (newspaper) (October 12, 1996), Section B, p. 1.

CHAPTER 5

INFORMAL POLITICS AMONG THE CHINESE COMMUNIST PARTY ELITE

LOWELL DITTMER

The informal dimension has always played an extremely important part in Chinese leadership politics.[1] This is due in part to the unsettled nature of the Chinese political scene throughout the twentieth century, which makes it difficult for any political arrangement to become securely institutionalized, and in part to the traditional aversion to law and preference for more moralistic, personalized authority relations. Although usually not part of the explicit analytical framework, the informal dimension has been implicitly taken into account in the biographical analyses of the lives of prominent leaders or thinkers and in the study of leadership coalitions and cleavages ("factionalism"). Informal politics per se did not, however, become the basis of social science theory until relatively recently – specifically, with the publication of Andrew Nathan's pioneering article on factionalism and in Tang Tsou's rebuttal, which coined the term.[2]

While such contributions have taken us a long way toward a consensually acceptable analytical framework, a critical review will be necessary before beginning our own analysis. The following chapter consists of three parts: Following a brief review of the literature, we introduce our own attempt at conceptual synthesis. We then attempt to apply that schema to the leadership politics of post-Liberation China, focusing on the reform era.

NOTIONS OF PERSONAL POLITICS

The central variable in Nathan's pioneering model was the faction, which he uses to explain patterns of conflict and coalition among CCP elites. Taking

---

1 A relatively comprehensive bibliography can be found in Lucian Pye, *The Dynamics of Chinese Politics* (Cambridge: Oelgeschlager, Gunn & Hain, 1981), pp. 267–276.
2 Andrew Nathan, "A factionalism model for CCP politics," *China Quarterly* 53 (1973), pp. 33–66; Tang Tsou, "Prolegomenon to the study of informal groups in CCP politics," *China Quarterly* 65 (1976), pp. 98–114; "Andrew Nathan replies," *China Quarterly* 65 (1976), pp. 114–117.

off from Franz Schurmann's distinction between elite "opinion groups" on the one hand – temporary issue-based coalitions that contain their disagreements within the officially demarcated decision-making arena (without mobilizing outside constituencies) and resolve their differences through reasoned "discussions" (*taolun*) – and "factions" on the other, which conspire for power and plot to mobilize outside organizational forces to overthrow the consensus,[3] Nathan launches a wide-ranging tour through the comparative social science literature to arrive at a universal model. He then applies this construct to China – and finds, *mirabile dictu*, that it fits! Recent CCP elite political history is then ransacked to find evidence supporting the model. A "faction" is defined as a vertically organized, patron–client network linked by personal (face-to-face) "connections" (*guanxi*). It is external to but dependent on the formal structure along which it extends, like a "trellis." Altogether, a faction has no fewer than fifteen "structural characteristics," including a "code of civility" governing normal intraelite relations (as factions discover that they can never really eliminate one another, they learn mutual toleration), an overarching ideological consensus that subsumes hairsplitting wrangles over policy or "line" differences, and so forth. Contrary to popular usage, the Cultural Revolution represents an exception to Nathan's conceptualization, given Mao's determination to overcome and destroy the factional balance-of-power system. Mao's attempt, however, ultimately fails, according to Nathan, permitting Chinese elite politics to revert to the factional *status quo ante*.

Tang Tsou first subjects Nathan's model to a thorough critique and then erects his own rival conceptualization upon its debris. He begins by substituting "informal group" for "faction," explicitly because the former term is more easily universalizable, implicitly because it avoids a pejorative taint (which is even more pronounced in the Chinese usage, *paibie, paixing*; Tsou is averse to Chinese cultural exceptionalism). The new term has the additional advantage of highlighting the relationship between formal and informal organization, thereby facilitating interdisciplinary cross-fertilization with the rich post-Weberian literature on informal organizations (agreeing with Nathan's "trellis" analogy, Tsou emphasizes that a formal structure is assumed to be the "precondition rather than the product" for the development of informal groups). Although theoretically his concept also includes "opinion groups," in his own discussion of empirical cases this structurally legitimate grouping silently fades away and Tsou in effect uses "faction" and "informal group" interchangeably.

---

3 See Franz Schurmann, *Organization and Ideology in Communist China* (Berkeley: University of California Press, 1968), pp. 54–57, 196ff.

Tsou makes three criticisms of Nathan. First, whereas Nathan argues for "rampant" factionalism (i.e., factions operating independently of formal structures), Tsou argues that structures place various constraints on factions. For example, the latter share the ideology of the "host" organization, including many of its goals, norms, and interests (not to mention personnel). Although the factions within an organization may differ sharply, their differences are couched in the same (or minutely differentiated) public language. Second, in contrast to Nathan's assumption of an overarching ideological consensus, Tsou contends that ideology is up for grabs, with the victor claiming a monopoly on legitimacy and roundly denouncing the loser in both ideological and moral terms. (This claim stands in some tension with the first point, which assumes that all factions derive their legitimacy from the host organization.) Third, and most fundamentally, Tsou denies the hypothesized "live-and-let-live," "no-win" pattern of factional contests. Factional fights normally end in the clear-cut victory of one faction over the other, whereupon the former seizes control of the formal organization, breaks the decision-making logjam, and rams its own policy and personnel preferences through. Without altogether denying the existence of a "code of civility" governing intraelite relationships during certain periods, Tsou reconstrues its meaning: This is not a compromise among rivals, but merely the looser form of domination exercised by a triumphant faction chief over subordinates who are also informal clients. To be sure, Tsou concedes that a "balance-of-power" type of arrangement was obtained when the leadership split into first and second "fronts" in the early 1960s, but he considers this a mere tactical armistice pending later opportunities to renew the struggle and finally prevail.

In addition to Tsou's points, we might highlight a number of other unresolved problems in Nathan's construct. First, Nathan's "fifteen characteristics" are really too numerous to function as practical criteria and should be reduced to a few essential points. Some of his characteristics are not specific to factions (such as the "climate of civility"), but normative features of CCP intraelite relations in general, for example. Second, although the point that factions are based on "connections" (*guanxi*) generated through face-to-face interactions is a valid insight (which also helps to explain the persistent closed, elitist bias in PRC politics), we would make two qualifications. Albeit initially generated via face-to-face contacts and prone to attenuate relatively quickly with social distance, connections are nonetheless transferrable to third parties, making it possible for entire factional networks to be transmitted intact from one patron to another. Thus the remnants of Liu Shaoqi's political base seem to have shifted allegiance successively to Zhou Enlai and to Deng Xiaoping during the 1970s, just as Hu Yaobang's faction migrated (in each case with a few defections) first to Zhao Ziyang upon Hu's demotion in early 1987 and thence to Zhu Rongji on Zhao's fall at Tiananmen. The second qualification is that despite the *guanxi*-based, elitist bias of Chinese politics there have been occasions when elite factions have been augmented by mass constituencies – and it is obviously impossible to account for such an extension based purely on face-to-face contacts. To a limited extent such mobilizations may be *mediated* by factional links between central and local leaders, as when Zhou Enlai or the Cultural Revolution Small Group (*wenhua geming xiaozu*, hereinafter CRSG) members summoned Red Guard faction leaders to Beijing (or met with them in tours of the countryside), or when Mao went on tour in the summer of 1971 seeking support for his move against Lin Biao, or when Deng Xiaoping convened intensive meetings with PLA leaders in May 1989 to concert the mobilization of troops for the June 4 crackdown at Tiananmen. In other cases the link may be initiated from below based on elective affinities, as when democracy wall activists mobilized in support of Deng Xiaoping in the fall of 1978, or when democracy protesters in May 1989 similarly gravitated to the support of Zhao Ziyang after Hu Yaobang's death. In either case, factional theory may need to be supplemented by a principal–agent model to account for such coordinated, large-scale political action, even when the latter seems to adhere to the factional logic of the small group.[4]

Third, are factions always organized on a vertical, patron–client basis? This does seem to have been true in the case of the initial targets of the Cultural Revolution – Peng Zhen, Luo Ruiqing, Lu Dingyi, and Yang Shangkun (who, whatever their previous connections, certainly colluded to restrain public criticism of Wu Han) – or of the Gang of Four, in which Jiang Qing was the patron (by dint of seniority as well as her own empowering "apron-string relationship" [*chundai guanxi*] to Mao) of Zhang Chunqiao, Yao Wenyuan, and Wang Hongwen; or in the case of Hua Guofeng's "small gang of four" – Wang Dongxing, Ji Dengkui, Wu De, and Chen Xilian. All three of these quartets are invariably listed in the same name order, reflecting their relative informal ranking. The rank order is likewise implicit in the conventional listing of the Gao Gang–Rao Shushi coalition of the early 1950s and the Liu Shaoqi–Deng Xiaoping alliance of the early 1960s.[5] This generalization, while plausible, requires further empirical analysis, particularly regarding

4 D. Roderick Kiewiet and Matthew D. McCubbin, *The Logic of Delegation* (Chicago: University of Chicago Press, 1991), Ch. 1; as cited in Tun-jen Cheng and Tein-cheng Chou, "Legislative factions on Taiwan: A preliminary analysis," unpublished paper presented at the annual AAS Convention, Washington, DC, April 4, 1992, p. 8.

5 The Liu-Deng alliance, based on a compatible ideological outlook and work style rather than any anti-Maoist conspiracy, was reinforced by such acts as Liu's suggestion that Deng be appointed secretary-general when Mao complained of excessive workload in December 1953, and Deng's nomination of Liu as chief of state in 1959. Teiwes, *Mao's Court*, p. 26ff.; Hei Yannan, *Shi nian dong luan* [*Ten years of chaos*] (Hong Kong: Xingzhen, 1988), p. 50.

those interesting test cases in which there was a clear discrepancy between formal and informal ranking – such as the Gang of Four[6] or the group whose cooperation (indeed, successful conspiracy) led to the coup against the Gang in September 1976 (viz., Hua Guofeng, Ye Jianying, and Wang Dongxing).[7]

Lucian Pye's contribution to the analysis of factionalism (he reverts to Nathan's original term) is essentially critical. Pye rejects the premise that factions are defined either by "primordial" ties such as shared generational class or geographical origins, or by ties based on common achievement such as early bonding experiences, old school ties, organizational links, and even ideological affinity, pointing to exceptions to each generalization.[8] Factionalism, he argues, is a central, even modal pattern of Chinese political behavior that is deeply rooted in psychocultural security drives (unfortunately not providing much insight into the latter). The faction-riven reality of Chinese politics is obscured by a "veil of consensus," which stems from an equally powerful cultural need to identify political authority with unchallenged moral and doctrinal correctness. In China's conflict-averse political culture, norms of consensus predominate, but at the same time the search for personal security generates a ceaseless countermobilization of informal loyalty networks. It is the intimate and indissoluble linkage between these contradictory imperatives that is the key to the political process; the failure of Western analysts to grasp it, Pye suggests, is what accounts for the alternating adoption and rejection of conflict and consensus models of Chinese leadership politics. Because factions are power-maximizing entities constrained only by the moral imperative to affirm a nominal leadership solidarity, factional struggle does not serve as a vehicle for rational policy debate, organizational interest articulation, or aggregation of political demands and supports. China emerges as a "bureaucratic polity without bureaucratic politics" – a system in which policy conflict is perpetual, but policy issues become mere symbols of hidden personal rivalries. The "Alice in Wonderland" quality of Chinese politics is typified for Pye in the 1970s paradoxes of a technology-intensive air force exalting "men over machines" and an industrially advanced Shanghai lobbying on behalf of China's rural poor. Such symbolic transpositions frustrate policy debate and obscure accountability on behalf of a purely nominal, normative consensus.[9]

6 During their active careers, the Gang of Four were listed in hierarchical order of their formal positions: Wang Hongwen, Zhang Chunqiao, Jiang Qing, and Yao Wenyuan. When legal proceedings were initiated against them in 1980, they were listed in order of informal power base: Jiang, Zhang, Yao, and Wang.
7 On the Hua–Deng–Ye connection, see Lin Qingshan, *Fengyun shinian yu Deng Xiaoping* [*A decade of turmoil and Deng Xiaoping*] (Beijing: Liberation Army Daily Press, 1989), p. 440.
8 Pye, *Dynamics*, pp. 7, 77–126.
9 Pye, *Dynamics*, passim.

INFORMAL POLITICS AMONG THE CCP ELITE

Whereas Pye deftly illustrates the paradoxical and arbitrary relationship between formal and informal power in Chinese politics, these contradictions also provide useful starting points for the positive analysis that he tends to forgo. There are several assumptions implicit in Pye's critique that might fruitfully be sifted out and linked to specific hypotheses for further empirical research. Hence we might distinguish:

(a) Those informal ties that are relatively self-sufficient, that is, can stand on their own in an institutional vacuum, such as the coalitions between radical Red Guard faction leaders and the CRSG, or between moderate faction leaders and regional PLA commanders, during the Cultural Revolution. Such factions may be expected to function independently from the formal structure, as demonstrated by the tenacious power of Deng Xiaoping and certain other leaders, even when completely bereft of formal power bases. Other factions, such as Lin Biao's "571" clique, proved to be far weaker when forced to operate outside of their formal base.

(b) Informal ties as the independent variable and formal organization as the dependent variable – for example, the informal networks that led to the formation of the Central Advisory Committee in August 1982 or to the reconstitution of the CCP Politburo in October 1987. In such cases the formal structure can be artificially inflated (provisionally) by the recruitment of strategic personnel. The appointment of an informally powerful leader can particularly energize a formal organ, as in Liu Shaoqi's appointment as chief of state in 1959, Peng Zhen's appointment as chairman of the NPC in June 1983, or Qiao Shi's appointment as his successor in 1992.

(c) Formal organization as the independent variable and informal ties as the dependent variable – for example, the cultivation of *guanxi* or the acquisition of additional personalized power on the basis of the personal appropriation of official ties and perquisites. This is illustrated in the studies of rural and urban patronage networks in Oi's and Walder's studies, respectively.[10]

The central focus of Frederick Teiwes's historical analyses[11] has not been factions or informal groups per se, but the normative framework or "rules of the game" he perceives as regulating the process of intraelite conflict and "rectification." This normative framework, which permits open discussion and

10 See Jean Oi, *State amd Peasant in Contemporary China: The Political Economy of Village Government* (Berkeley: University of California Press, 1989), Chaps. 7 and 9; and Andrew Walder, *Communist Neo-Traditionalism: Work and Authority in Chinese Industry* (Berkeley: University of California Press, 1986), Chaps. 4 and 5.
11 See his *Politics and Purges in China: Rectification and the Decline of Party Norms, 1950–1965* (White Plains, NY: M. E. Sharpe, 1979); *Politics at Mao's Court: Gao Gang and Party Factionalism in the Early 1950s* (Armonk, NY: M. E. Sharpe, 1990); and, with Warren Sun, eds., *The Politics of Agricultural Cooperativization in China: Mao, Deng Zihui, and the "High Tide" of 1955* (Armonk, NY: M. E. Sharpe, 1993).

vigorous debate of conflicting proposals before a decision is made, followed
by maintenance of iron discipline during subsequent implementation, was
allegedly introduced during the Zhengfeng movement in the 1940s to replace
the "ruthless struggles and merciless blows" type of rectification associated
with the Returned Students' leadership and lasted (with momentary lapses,
such as the Gao-Rao purge) from the late 1940s through the mid-1950s.[12]
"Mistaken" viewpoints were tolerated and even allowed to persist so long as
organizational discipline was maintained, that is, there was no conspiratorial activity and no mobilization of outside organizational resources. As
long as conflict was conducted according to the norms, elite solidarity behind
a decisive leadership could be maintained while permitting a full airing of
views. Teiwes credited this new pattern of rectification primarily to Mao
Zedong, with whose rise to power it coincided – at the same time blaming
Mao for its lapse at the Lushan plenum in 1959 and, more explosively, during the Cultural Revolution. Whereas in his earlier studies Teiwes attributed
considerable independent efficacy to the "rules of the game," his more recent
work has tended to subordinate this code to the historical prestige attained
by individual players by dint of their achievements in the revolutionary period. Status ranking, according to this more recent perspective, tends to
eclipse policy orientation or bureaucratic base as a source of power, to become
more significant than formal "rules of the game" in sustaining (or disturb-
ing) a climate of civility.

It goes without saying that any attempt to review and assess these varied
formulations is still tentative. Nathan's model was clearly seminal and
remains a primary reference point, although it seems flawed in excluding from
its ambit the very period to which it might have been considered most relevant. Tsou's central criticism of Nathan – that his "code of civility" is based
on an intrafactional balance of power that is empirically exceptional and that
a hierarchical intraelite relationship is more typical than pluralism – seems
largely correct. It is borne out in Teiwes's more recent findings, which liken
high-level politics during the early Maoist period to "court politics," that is,
"a process dominated by an unchallenged Chairman surrounded by other
leaders attempting to divine his often obscure intentions, adjusting their
preferences to his desires and trying to exploit his ambiguities to advance

12 This generalization is qualified in *Mao's Court*, which finds that the confrontation with Gao Gang–Rao
   Shushi took place in considerably more rough-and-tumble fashion than previously assumed. Based on
   new documentary evidence plus interviews with Chinese scholars and bureaucrats, Teiwes finds that,
   "Such phenomena as attacks by proxy, vague and politically loaded accusations, exaggerating past
   'errors' without regard for historical circumstances, and collecting material on political enemies, which
   would become such a feature of the Cultural Revolution, were already present in the Gao–Rao affair"
   (p. 151).

their bureaucratic and political interests, and squabbling among themselves when Mao's actions exacerbated old tensions or created new ones among them."[13] But are we justified in assuming, with Tsou, that intraelite conflict inevitably culminates in a showdown resulting in the clear-cut victory of one group and its establishment in a position of hegemony?[14] Such a generalization calls for two qualifications.

First, there do seem to be periods, sometimes fairly extended, when a certain level of elite pluralism or balance-of-power politics does obtain. One of these was the post-Leap recovery period preceding the Cultural Revolution, and a second includes the first several years of the post-Mao period, during which time Deng was obliged to share power with a series of strong rivals, including Hua Guofeng, Ye Jianying, Li Xiannian, and Chen Yun; even after consolidating his supremacy at the Third Plenum of the 11th Central Committee, Deng's relationship to Chen Yun was less than unequivocally vertical (as Fewsmith demonstrates in his chapter). Collective leadership is a norm among CCP elites that members of a minority may use in self-defense, as Teiwes has emphasized: Autocratic leadership is in contrast subject to censure as a "cult of personality," "hegemonism," and the like (Mao himself, stung by Deng Xiaoping's alleged failure to consult him, once stormed: "What emperor decided this?"). This norm has strong cultural and ideological sanctions and is repeatedly invoked. To assume that norms are always adhered to would of course be naive, yet norms are a not-unimportant component of a given organizational subculture. One may dismiss periods of apparent calm and apparent elite consensus as mere window-dressing concealing subterranean factional maneuvering that anticipates later opportunities for renewed struggle, as some analysts of elite factionalism do, but that seems to be arbitrarily attributing a higher level of "reality" to conflict than to consensus. If periods of compromise are preparatory to renewed conflict, are bouts of struggle not also motivated by a need for subsequent periods of stability to consolidate gains? Clearly both phases are part of the Chinese political reality, and there is no a priori reason to privilege one over the other.

Second, even in those cases in which factional struggle culminates in the victory of one faction and the destruction of its rival, this is typically followed by the recurrence (often quite promptly) of a new factional power balance in which new actors step into the position of the eliminated faction — tempting one to infer that opposition is almost a "functional requisite" of the

---

13 Personal communication from Teiwes.
14 Cf. Joseph Fewsmith's contribution to this volume and, more specifically to the current point, his "The impact of reform on elite politics," in Roderick MacFarquhar and Merle Goldman, eds., *Paradoxes of Reform* (Boston: Harvard University Press, 1998).

system.[15] Thus, within a few months of the demolition of the Liu-Deng "bourgeois reactionary line" during the Cultural Revolution, first Zhou Enlai and then an ostensibly rehabilitated Deng Xiaoping reemerged to assume ideological and organizational leadership of a moderate policy alternative that many of the leading radicals deemed analogous to the Liu-Deng line.[16] Nor has the purge of Zhao Ziyang at the 4th Plenum of the 13th Party Congress in June 1989 resulted in the destruction of his line, which seems to have survived with the help of Li Ruihuan, Zhu Rongji, and Qiao Shi. Deng Xiaoping himself found it useful to resuscitate this group in the spring of 1992, after having brought it to the brink of ruin. So if Nathan was wrong to assume that a factional balance of power is a normal state of affairs, it is also mistaken to assume that just because one faction decisively destroys a rival, this will result in an enduring, monolithic elite consensus. The available evidence may warrant the somewhat weaker inference that a major outbreak of factional conflict is likely to be followed by a period of consolidation that we might term "contained factionalism."

Finally, Pye has made an important contribution in pointing to the psychocultural insecurity at the root of factional affiliation and maneuver. Yet to conclude this by dismissing all objective bases for such affiliation is to throw the baby out with the bathwater. Just because no one node (e.g., generation, region, old-school tie) can function as an invariably reliable indicator of factional linkage does not mean that all of them may be dispensed with. These may function as interchangeable options, at least one being necessary but not sufficient, with the specific selection likely to be based on situational needs. Further research is needed to discriminate among these nodes: Unlike a former teacher–student relationship, old-school ties or common regional origins [*tongxue, tongxiang*] offer no basis for hierarchical ranking, for instance.

TOWARD A CONCEPTUAL SYNTHESIS

Any new conceptualization should avoid the problems of vagueness and overweening ambition that have plagued earlier definitional efforts. In the former case, we are given a purely negative definition of the central term, defining *informal politics* not in terms of what it is but in terms of what it is not – that is, formal politics (which usually remains undefined). Clearly it is important to note the interdependency between formal and informal politics,

---

15 This thesis is elegantly formulated in Avery Goldstein, *From Bandwagon to Balance-of-Power Politics: Structural Constraints and Politics in China, 1949–1978* (Stanford: Stanford University Press, 1991).

16 This compresses events slightly: In 1969–1971, Zhou aligned with Lin to shut out the radicals (thus earning Jiang Qing's ire and triggering the "anti-Lin Biao and Confucius" movement). In this capacity he shepherded the economy through a phase of heavy investment in small-scale rural industry that was somewhat redolent of the Great Leap Forward.

but informal politics should not be derogated to the status of a shadow category, dependent on the definition of its positive counterpart. The opposite problem is the tendency to strive for prematurely ambitious conceptualizations – to aim at a model of factionalism that is valid throughout the Third World, for example, or even applicable to Chinese organizational life in general – and then to interpolate from these general models to the political situation within the CCP Politburo. This sort of abstract model-building is understandable, in view of the paucity of hard empirical evidence about the inner workings of the Politburo and other powerful leadership organs. Yet a definition that is valid for a universal or even comparatively broad range of informal political behavior cannot be expected to capture the *differentia specifica* of the CCP leadership. A more prudent strategy would seem to be to set a middle-range boundary for inquiry – say, the arena enclosing the several score of top members of the Chinese Party-State elite – and then see to what extent the findings derived from this limited sample can be more broadly generalized. Given limited time and resources, this is a good place to start even if our findings should not turn out to be generalizable, given the commanding and norm-setting role of the "center" in Chinese politics.

The central term in our conceptualization of Chinese personal politics is *relationships*; as Liang Shuming noted long ago, Chinese culture is neither individualistic (*geren benwei*) nor group-oriented (*shehui benwei*), but rather relationship-based (*guanxi benwei*).[17] Ambrose King has postulated that, in contradistinction to Japanese relationships, which are based on fixed frames or *ba* (the family, workplace, or village) that set a clear boundary and give a common identity to all individuals within that frame, Chinese relationships are formed on the basis of attributes (e.g., kinship, classmates, school ties) that are infinitely extendable.[18] Attributes provide a pluralistic basis for identification depending on the specific attribute shared; thus the more attributes a person has, the more relationships one is able to establish.[19] To qualify this valuable insight, while it is certainly true that Chinese attributes sometimes reticulate into vast networks, other Chinese attributes are also enclosed by fixed frames, such as those within the same parochial village or "basic work unit" (*jiceng danwei*). Perhaps the ultimate criterion determining how far

17 Liang Shu-ming, *Chung-kuo wen-hua yao-yi [An outline of Chinese culture]* (Hong Kong: Chi-cheng t'u-shu kung-ssu, 1974), p. 94.
18 Cf. Chie Nakane's analysis in *Japanese Society* (Berkeley: University of California Press, 1970); and Ambrose Yeo-chi King, "*Kuan-hsi* and Network Building: A Sociological Interpretation," in *Daedelus* 120:2 (Spring, 1991), pp. 63–85.
19 *Caeteris paribus* and *mutatis mutandis*, of course; the cultivation of *guanxi* takes time and effort. See Mayfair Yang, *Gifts, Favors and Banquets: The Art of Social Relationships in China* (Ithaca: Cornell University Press, 1994).

attributes extend within a given culture is the amount of social mobility (i.e., in cases in which mobility is tightly constrained for prolonged periods, attributional networks beyond the "frame" may wither). In any case, the Chinese political scene seems to include both types of connections, not always clearly differentiated.

Analytically, we would draw a key distinction between two "ideal types" of relationships: those in which the relationship with the other is valued as an end in itself, to use the Kantian language, or "value-rational" relationships; and those purpose-rational relationships in which the other is merely a means to other ends. Empirically, these two ideal types are mixed – value-rational relationships often harbor ulterior purposes, and purpose-rational relationships may become valued; the distinguishing criterion in any instance is whether one is willing to forfeit the relationship for the sake of purpose, or vice versa. We may term the former relationships "personalized" and the more functionally specific, purpose-rational relationships "official." Both personalized and official relationships are useful in high-level elite politics, but in different ways. An official relationship is typically formed with those colleagues, subordinates, and superiors with whom one has routine professional contacts. These relationships may be mobilized in support of career objectives so long as they are in the collective interest of the organization of which all are a part; thus we may refer to this ensemble of relationships as one's *formal base*. By mobilizing one's formal base, one is able to exert "official power," which the Chinese refer to as *quanli*. Some high-level leaders seem to have relied exclusively on official power, either out of principle, as seems to have been the case for Liu Shaoqi or Deng Xiaoping,[20] or because they lacked sufficient opportunity to build a strong informal base, as seems to have been true in the cases of Hua Guofeng or Zhao Ziyang.

Yet there are two important limitations to what one can do with official power. First, it is in most cases a relatively simple matter to be divested of one's formal base: a job rotation, purge, or demotion and it is gone. Chinese cadres do not have "tenure" or (until quite recently) legally stipulated terms of office, and their positions are hence far more tenuous from a strictly formal perspective than those of a civil servant (whether elected or appointed) in the West. Thus when Hu Yaobang failed to crack down energetically enough on young protesters in December 1986, he was promptly relieved of

20 Liu did nothing to protect Peng Zhen when the latter came under fire during the Cultural Revolution, for example, and Deng did little on the same occasion to support Wu Han, his bridge partner, or Li Jingchuan. Nor is there much evidence that the informal groups below the party center rallied to the support of their putative patrons – they were too busy defending themselves. Although Deng rehabilitated Liu posthumously, his failure to support clients Hu Yaobang and Zhao Ziyang when they came under fire is well known. See also my *Liu Shaoqi and the Chinese Cultural Revolution* (Armonk, NY: M. E. Sharpe, 2nd ed., 1998).

his position as general secretary (*zong mishu*); although he remained a full Politburo member, he was in effect in internal exile, for without a hierarchical organization under his jurisdiction that he could convene in meetings and thus mobilize in support of his interests his ability to exert official power was sharply curtailed. When the cadre responsible for one's official demotion is also one's informal patron (as in the Deng-Hu and Deng-Zhao clashes, but *not* the Mao-Deng or Hua-Deng confrontations), dismissal is normally a career-ending event. Kang Sheng is an interesting variant: In the course of overzealously "rectifying" suspected ideological deviants during the Zhengfeng campaign of the early 1940s in his capacity as head of the six-person campaign committee, Kang became so unpopular within the party that in the late 1940s he was (like his contemporary, Beria) divested of control of the security apparatus and rendered politically impotent. Relegated to the governorship of Shandong Province, Kang took "sick leave" throughout the early 1950s, yet still his power continued to ebb, finally (at the first session of the 8th Party Congress in 1956) falling to candidate membership within the Politburo. Yet though he may have lost Mao's favor, he retained an alternate "connection" to the chairman through Mao's wife, Jiang Qing. He used this conduit to regain favor in "court" when the Mao–Liu rift began to emerge in the early 1960s by involving himself in the Sino-Soviet polemical dispute – and by editing, with Chen Boda, the "little red book" of Mao quotations. Thereby he succeeded in being named again to various ad hoc committees, including the CRSG (first under Peng Zhen and then Chen Boda), culminating in his comeback as a high-level advisor during the Cultural Revolution.[21] Formal positions are thus normally a prerequisite to informal power, but there are important exceptions to this generalization, which will merit consideration when the issue of the relationship between formal and informal politics is more closely examined below.

The second limitation of a formal base is that one cannot rely on it to defend one's personal political interests. For example, if I should come under attack for some serious ideological transgression, it would not be in the interests of my official associates to jeopardize their own careers and the interests of our organization to come to my defense, for to do so would be to become implicated in my alleged crime. Under such circumstances the prudent course for my official associates would be to repudiate and ostracize me – especially in view of the presumption that public accusation is often tantamount to conviction. If my career is jeopardized by an assault on my character, I have but two recourses: allay the accuser's attacks through a persuasive self-

21 Cf. John Byron and Robert Pack, *The Claws of the Dragon: Kang Sheng* (New York: Simon & Schuster, 1992).

criticism (by definition well-nigh impossible in the case of an "antagonistic contradiction") or mobilize my unofficial backers to resist.

Thus most members of the CCP elite find it useful to cultivate personalized as well as official relationships, which typically have more long-term utility and can be mobilized if their life chances or career is at stake. Such relationships comprise a political base (*zhengzhi jichu*), on the basis of which one can exercise informal power (*shili*). A political base may be gauged in terms of its *depth* and *breadth*: A "broad" base consists of a network of cronies diffused throughout the party, military, diplomatic, and governmental apparatus, whereas a "deep" base consists of supporters going all the way back to the early generations of revolutionary leadership, hence having high seniority and lofty positions.[22] Whereas some formidable politicians such as Zhou Enlai or Ye Jianying had political bases both broad and deep, others have had bases that are deep but narrow (e.g., Chen Boda) or broad but shallow (e.g., Tian Jiyun) – which has tended to limit their options.

How is an informal base assembled? It is put together through the incremental accretion of discrete "connections." People have a large but finite number of potential affinities (or *gongtongdian*), including kinship; common geographic origin; former classmates, teachers, or students; or common former Field Army affiliation – at least one of which is usually necessary to form a "connection" (*guanxi*). A cadre assigned a new task or post will immediately canvass the area for such potential links and proceed to activate them, rather than just waiting for them to emerge haphazardly. An objective basis for an affinity does not necessarily create one, however, as demonstrated for example by Mao's wholesale purge of fellow Hunanese of his generation during the Cultural Revolution or Chen Yun's loathing for Kang Sheng, whom he knew all too well; it is no more than a starting point. An informal base must be "cultivated." To do so, an initial bonding episode is useful, such as the bond formed among certain "white" area cadres when Liu Shaoqi authorized confessions to spring them from KMT prisons, or the bond formed between fellow Shandong natives Kang Sheng and Jiang Qing when he vouched for her admission to the CCP and her marriage to Mao (not to mention his rumored seduction of the ambitious young woman in Shandong much earlier).[23] If such bonding involves an experience common to a whole

22 See Dittmer, "Bases of power in Chinese politics: A theory and an analysis of the fall of the 'Gang of Four,'" *World Politics* 31 (October 1978), pp. 26–61.

23 There is circumstantial but by no means conclusive evidence that Jiang Qing became Kang Sheng's lover when her mother was employed in the Zhang household in Shandong. See John Byron and Robert Pack, *The Claws of the Dragon: Kang Sheng* (New York: Simon and Schuster, 1992), pp. 18, 48–49; also Ross Terrill, *The White-Boned Demon: A Biography of Madame Mao Zedong* (New York: William Morrow, 1984), pp. 18, 136. Yet the fact that such rumors are so widely credited by Chinese sources (e.g., Terrill quotes Hu Yaobang on the "depravity" of the liaison) is significant per se.

group of cadres, we might refer to this as privileged category forging, an occasion that may be publicly commemorated later when the participants become established – thus December 9 is typically used to celebrate the so-called White Area clique that emerged to lead this urban anti-Japanese student movement, just as August 1, originally an occasion for celebrating Nanchang Uprising alumni, became the anniversary of the founding of the PLA. But connections may also be recruited on an idiosyncratic basis, as Mao recruited Chen Boda at Yanan in the early 1940s, or Hua Guofeng in Hunan in the mid-1950s. And of course it is quite possible to have connections with patrons who later have a falling out, thrusting a client into a cruel dilemma (as Chen Boda was forced to choose in early 1966 between Liu Shaoqi, his first patron, and Mao Zedong).[24]

Cadres with an informal base can resort to this resource in the case of a serious threat to their careers, that is, an "antagonistic contradiction" that would normally lead to purge or permanent sidelining. An informal base may be mobilized in the most extreme case via clandestine meetings or informant networks, as in the case of Chen Duxiu's "Leninist Left-Wing Opposition," Zhang Guotao's alleged organization in the 1930s of a rival Central Committee, Peng Dehuai's "Military Recreation Club" that Mao claimed conspired to draft his critique of the Leap prior to the Lushan plenum, Zhang Chunqiao's "'244 Secret Service Group," whose purpose was ironically to frame other leading cadres on charges of belonging to secret conspiracies, or Lin Biao's commission of his son Liguo to set up a "Joint Fleet Command" to plot an attentat against Mao.[25] But because factional manipulations are ipso facto illegitimate, more subtle tactics are often used, such as Aesopian language (e.g., commissioning rival writing groups to reconstrue Chinese history, a stratagem used by both the moderates and the radicals in the mid-1970s),[26] or the more passive manifestation of support by sitting on one's

---

24 When Liu was in charge of the Northern Bureau during the anti-Japanese war period, he recruited Peng Zhen as director of the organization department and Chen Boda as director of the propaganda department, thus giving Chen his first important post since joining the party. Chen's subsequent collaboration with Liu included helping to edit several of his manuscripts for publication. Chen became Mao's "pen" at Yanan, allegedly saving his life during a Nationalist air raid at Fuping in 1948, compiling (with Kang Sheng) the "little red book" for publication. Jiang Qing alerted Chen to his dilemma while he was editing the draft of the *May 16* (1966) *Circular* [*wuyiliu tongzhi*] in Hangzhou. When Chen and Kang Sheng found that Mao had added the phrase "Khrushchev-like persons sleeping beside us," Chen asked Jiang Qing for guidance. Jiang rolled her eyes and said, "You really don't know who China's Khrushchev is? You helped him edit and publish his *How to Be a Good Communist*. . . . You should be cautious." Ye, *Chen*, pp. 103–104, 157–159, 234–278.

25 This was a twenty-member network based at 244 Yongfu Road in Shanghai during the 1970s, which allegedly succeeded in destroying more than 1,000 of Zhang's enemies. As cited in John Wilson Lewis, "Political networks and policy implementation in China," unpublished paper, Stanford University, 1983, pp. 43–44.

26 Cf. Dittmer, *China's Continuous Revolution* (Berkeley: University of California Press, 1987), pp. 197–205.

hands during a criticism campaign (e.g., Ye Jianying, Xu Xiangqian, et al. conspicuously failed to join in criticizing Deng in the spring of 1976). This last tactic has been employed with increasing frequency and boldness during such mobilizational efforts as the antispiritual pollution campaign of 1983–1984 or the antibourgeois liberalization movements of 1987 and 1989–1990. Because informal bases are not mobilized for the sake of routine bureaucratic policy making but for informal, sometimes purely personal power-political reasons, the bases normally have little specific policy relevance – although given the prevailing assumption that politics is a moral crusade, the factional gist of a dispute may be dressed up in ideological rhetoric. (Thus Deng Xiaoping, looking back at the history of "line struggles" in the CCP, dismissed the existence of diverging policy "lines" in most cases.)[27]

The relationship between formal and informal politics is fluid and ambiguous – informal groups are often absorbed into formal structures, and formal structures in turn operate with a great deal of informality[28] – but the distinction remains relevant in at least three respects. First, the distinction appears in the recruitment and utilization of "base" members. There are two types of base members: those who are relatively pure cases of informal "connections," and those who also have impressive formal credentials (*zige*). An example of the former is apparent nepotism (e.g., spouses Jiang Qing, Wang Guangmei, Ye Qun, and Deng Yingchao; the children of Deng Xiaoping, Ye Jianying, or Chen Yun). Still more "informal" are extramarital romantic liaisons.[29] Personal secretaries are included in this category as well (e.g., Chen

27 "The struggle against Comrade Peng Dehuai cannot be viewed as a struggle between two lines. Nor can the struggle against Comrade Liu Shaoqi," he chided the authors of the Resolution on Party History. While absolving Chen Duxiu, Qu Qiubai, Li Lisan, and others of conspiracy, he did accuse Lin Biao, Gao Gang, Jiang Qing, et al. of conspiracy – yet not of championing a divergent "line." For example, "But so far as Gao Gang's real line is concerned, actually, I can't see that he had one, so it's hard to say whether we should call it a struggle between two lines." Deng Xiaoping, "Adhere to the party line and improve methods of work" (February 29, 1980), in *Selected Works of Deng Xiaoping* (Beijing: Foreign Languages Press, 1984), pp. 278–279.

28 Due to the members' long-term association with one another, their relative lack of lateral contact with members of parallel organizations, the comprehensive regulation of participants' roles, and a perceived sense of common threat from the "outgroup," informal bonds often develop among members of the same formal unit.

29 These reportedly included an actress introduced to Mao in 1948 by Wang Dongxing named Yu Shan, with whom Mao was so smitten that he installed her in the palace of Zhongnanhai and had Jiang Qing sent to the USSR for rest and recuperation (like her predecessor, He Zichen); and a beautiful young woman (also introduced by Wang) named Zhang Yufeng, with whom he became infatuated in the 1970s. Both affairs had an incidental impact on policy, the first by temporarily severing Kang Sheng's connection to Mao, and the second by exacerbating the estrangement between Mao and Jiang Qing in the mid-1970s. See Roger Faligot and Remi Kauffer, *The Chinese Secret Service*, trans. Christine Donougher (London: Headline Books, 1989), pp. 216, 262, 389. Terrill claims that Jiang Qing also indulged in extracurricular affairs, as with Zhuang Zedong, "the dashing young table tennis champion (who found himself rewarded with a meteoric rise to the post of Minister of Sports)." *White-Boned Demon*, pp. 316–317. My other informants however discredit this: Jiang's tenuous relationship with Mao and fear of total banishment from court would have precluded any such behavior.

Boda and Hu Qiaomu had been Mao's secretaries, Deng Liqun was Liu Shaoqi's secretary, Zhang Chunqiao was Ko Qingshi's secretary;[30] after 1956, Jiang Qing became Mao's "fifth secretary in charge of international affairs");[31] as well as miscellaneous long-term staff personnel, such as Mao's former body-guard, Wang Dongxing.[32] An example of the latter type (i.e., informal recruits with their own bureaucratic bases) was the membership of Bo Yibo, Peng Zhen, Yao Yilin, An Ziwen, and others in Liu Shaoqi's White Area faction; or Hu Qili, Rui Xingwen, and others in Hu Yaobang's Youth League faction (*Gongqingpai*). The main difference is that whereas the former are exclusively dependent on their patron, the latter have other options for career security or mobility. Thus the former are apt to be more personally loyal, as their patron is their lifeline and they are apt to find it difficult to extend their base beyond it (cf. Lin Biao's recruitment of Chen Boda, arousing Mao's enmity). As "court favorites," they may hence be entrusted with maverick personal missions. Indeed, favorites may deliberately cultivate those items on their patron's agenda that are apt to exacerbate friction with the bureaucrat-ic apparat and thereby enhance their own indispensability (e.g., Zhang Chun-qiao, Yao Wenyuan, and other members of the CRSG boosted their own career prospects by promoting Mao's antibureaucratic impulses).[33] Career bureau-crats (e.g., Peng Zhen) are more apt to try to balance their patron's more dis-ruptive requests against their own bureaucratic interests.

There are also mixed types, such as Kang Sheng, who had a distinguished revolutionary record (*zige*), but it was exclusively in an area of secret police and cadre screening that alienated him from most of his colleagues. Hence he behaved as a favorite, retaining access to the chairman through Jiang Qing.

30 Zhang Chunqiao utilized his connection to Ke Qingshi to gain access to Mao, Ke's patron. By reading Ke's report to Mao, he was able to divine Mao's intellectual interests, and on this basis proceeded to draft an essay ("Destroy the bourgeois right") for publication in Shanghai's *Jiefang* [*Liberation*] daily. Mao read the essay, liked it, and instructed that it be published in *People's Daily* (October 13, 1958), with his own commentary attached. Ye Yonglie, *Chen Boda* (Hong Kong: Wen-hua jiaoyu chubanshe, 1990), pp. 105, 208–209.

31 On Jiang Qing's appointment, see Ye Yonglie, *Chen*, p. 163; on the more general importance of secretaries in Chinese politics, see Lucian Pye and Wei Li, "The ubiquitous role of the *Mishu* in Chinese politics," *China Quarterly* 132 (December 1992), pp. 913–937.

32 Mao first recruited Wang as a personal bodyguard in the Jinggang mountains when Wang was only 17, and Mao became almost a father to him. Wang cared for Mao when he was sick; Mao taught Wang to read and write. As Mao's career advanced, he took Wang with him: first to leadership of the grow-ing security contingent (eventually the "8341" team), and then (on Yang Shangkun's purge in the Cultural Revolution) to director of the General Office of the CPC Central Committee. Wang became an alternate Politburo member at the 9th CPC Congress and a full member at the 10th. Du Feng, "Wang Dongxing, wei shemma hui xia tai?" *Zheng ming* (Hong Kong) 30 (April 1980), pp. 34–40.

33 For example, Chen Boda reportedly promoted the concept of the "people's commune" in print even before Mao uttered his famous oral endorsement at Zhengzhou (in the article "Entirely new society, entirely new people," published in *Hongqi* 3 [July 1, 1958]). Thus, when criticized by Peng Dehuai at Lushan, Mao declared: "I have no claim to the invention of the people's commune, though I made some suggestions." Ye, *Chen*, pp. 203, 208–209.

An interesting mixed type to have emerged since the 1980s is the beneficia-
ry of the third line of cadre recruitment – and, following them, the so-called
princelings' party (*taizi dang*). On the one hand, these young cadres fit the
category of formal, categorical recruitment, as their upward mobility was
launched by the policy of bureaucratic rejuvenation introduced by Deng
Xiaoping and Hu Yaobang in the mid-1980s; on the other hand, a rather
conspicuous minority of them are related to veteran cadres, beginning with
Li Peng and Zou Jiahua, giving rise to suspicions of an underlying informal
bias.[34] These "hybrids" may be expected to behave like favorites so long as
their patronizing relatives are still politically potent, and then to sink or swim
based on the personal power bases and *zige* that they have been able to amass
in the meantime.

Unlike most Western countries, where formal politics is clearly dominant
over informal politics and the relationship is one of "imposition and resistance,"[35] the Chinese informal sector has been historically dominant, with
formal politics sometimes providing little more than a facade. Informal politics plays an important part in every organization at every level, but the
higher the organization the more important it becomes. At the highest level
– because the tasks to be performed are relatively unstructured, the area of
discretion large, personal judgment crucial, the demand for quick decisions
great, and secrecy imperative – informal politics prevails. This informal
sphere is distinguished from relations within the host organization as a whole
by its more frequent contacts, greater degree of goal consensus, loyalty to the
informal group, and ability to work together. An astute leadership, while
using informal politics to cobble together a majority within the formal apparatus, will then turn to formal politics for public policy implementation. The
resort to formal politics as legitimation seems to have increased since the
death of Mao, following the repudiation of the personality cult and diminu-
tion in the relative importance of ideology. Whereas previously an official
could be dismissed on grounds of ideological deviation (as defined *ex cathe-*

34 Among the Third Generation, Li Peng is of course Zhou Enlai and Deng Yingchao's adoptive son;
Zou Jiahua, vice-premier and (since the 14th Party Congress) a full member of the Politburo, is Ye
Jianying's son-in-law; Ye Xuanping, Ye's son and former governor of Guangdong province, now chairs
the Chinese People's Political Consultative Conference; and so forth. Jiang Zemin's relationship to Li
Xiannian was so close that Chinese rumors (inaccurately) imputed kinship. *China Information*, 4:1
(Summer 1989), pp. 64–68; *South China Morning Post*, April 11, 1992; for a comprehensive analysis,
see M. S. Tanner and M. J. Feder, "Family politics, elite recruitment, and succession in post-Mao
China," *Australian Journal of Chinese Affairs* 30 (July 1993), pp. 89–119; and He Ping and Gao Xin,
Zhong gong "taizi dang" [*Chinese Communist "Princes' Party"*] (Hong Kong: Ming Qing, 1992). Two qualifications: First, along with favoritism there is also evidence of widespread resentment of it; and, second, the "princelings" are often highly competent.
35 Haruhiro Fukui and Shigeko Fukai, "Election campaigning in contemporary Japan," unpublished
paper presented at the 44th Annual Meeting of the Association for Asian Studies, April 2–5, 1992,
Washington, DC, p. 1.

dra by a Caesero-papist leader), now the way must be paved for downward mobility by formal procedure (cf. the cases of Hua Guofeng or Zhao Ziyang) and sometimes even legality (as in the public trial of the "Gang of Ten" in 1980 or the 1995–1997 prosecution of Chen Xitong's Beijing gang). The overall thrust of development since the advent of political reform in 1978 (despite such interruptions as Tiananmen) has been toward increasing formalization, as measured by the frequency, length, and regularity of meeting sessions and the number of people and procedural steps involved in drafting legislation. Thus the 13th Congress in 1987 even announced a system of regular meetings of the Politburo, its Standing Committee, the Central Secretariat, and a system whereby the Standing Committee would report regularly to the Politburo and the Politburo would report to the Central Committee.

Formal norms also serve a gate-keeping function, defining who can play. As noted above, without a formal position an informal base has little leverage; thus normally a factional network can be destroyed simply by removing its leader(s) from the formal positions in the organizational structure that enables it to extend its informal relations and loyalties. There are two apparent exceptions to this generalization that deserve scrutiny: the two political resurrections of Deng Xiaoping, and the power plays against Hu Yaobang and Zhao Ziyang by the gerontocrats who had "retired" in the mid-1980s. But Deng's first and second comebacks, in 1973 and 1977, while greatly facilitated by informal connections, were both achieved in conformance to the normative rules of the game (i.e., by throwing himself on the mercy of the Supreme Leader). True, neither self-criticism (the text, needless to say, has not been included in his *Selected Works*) was really "sincere." After helping to bring the PLA to heel by rotating Military Region commanders, Deng gravitated into the orbit of Zhou Enlai, promoting the latter's Four Modernizations so as to undermine or even eclipse the radical program of "continuing the revolution under the dictatorship of the proletariat." Surely he violated the spirit of the terms of his second rehabilitation under Hua Guofeng by subtly differentiating his own position from Hua's on various issues (e.g., treatment of the intellectuals, the Mao cult), thereby presenting himself as an alternative to the existing line and eventually wresting de facto leadership from Hua's grasp. Deng's informal base certainly played an important role, specifically in two respects: Some of his connections (e.g., Zhou Enlai and Ye Jianying) undoubtedly lobbied on behalf of his return, and Deng's value to Mao (or to Hua) was not exclusively personal but a package deal that included his military and civilian political contacts. But that is not the point: Neither comeback was a *pure* case of informal politics overcoming a formal verdict; formal "rules of the game" were also skillfully manipulated to legitimate a reversal of verdicts.

The second case, the comeback of the "sitting committee" from positions of nominal retirement in the Central Advisory Committee (or even from positions of complete retirement from formal positions), can be explained by three circumstances. First, Deng's own retirement was only pro forma, thereby setting an example that legitimized others' reactivation. Second, their retirement was predicated on their right to name their own successors, a tacit deal in which the appointees continued to welcome their predecessors' "advice." Last, but by no means least, their comeback was not a pure case of informal influence overcoming formal power, but rather a convergence of informal and formal power. Their informal patron could be assumed to be Deng Xiaoping, which explains their willingness to be pushed into retirement in the first place. But the coin had two sides: Just as Deng obliged them to retire, he could now invite them back. This was formally legitimated by the device of the "expanded" meeting, which any qualified official could attend as an observer at the invitation of the convener. In view of the fact that votes are not usually taken in such sessions and the agenda is set by the chair, the distinction between full members and observers is minimal.[36] Most important and controversial issues are decided by such enlarged meetings at which participation is arranged to ensure the outcome.[37] Thus at the January 1987 meeting urging Hu Yaobang to resign, no fewer than seventeen cadres attended from the Central Advisory Commission and two from the Central Disciplinary Inspection Commission to augment eighteen Politburo members, two alternate members, and four Secretariat members; Bo Yibo, although no longer a member of the Politburo, was allowed to present the case for the prosecution. Deng, who convened the meeting, determined the roster and set the agenda.[38] Ostensibly retired cadres played an even more crucial role in the events leading to the crackdown at Tiananmen and the purge of Zhao Ziyang at the Fourth Plenum of the 13th Central Committee.

Although the historical trend is toward political formalization (e.g., compare the death of Lin Biao with the trial of the Gang of Four or the unconstitutional demotion of Hu Yaobang with the Central Committee's plenary dismissal of Zhao Ziyang), informal politics remains much more powerful than in other countries and may be expected to prevail at the highest level well after formal legal rationality has been superimposed at subordinate levels. The formal rules of the game have the best chance of prevailing

36 Chen Yizi et al., eds., *Zhengzhi tizhi gaige jianghua* [*Talks on political restructuring*] (Beijing: Renmin chubanshe, 1987), p. 46; also *Deng Xiaoping Wenxuan* [*Selected works*] (Peking: People's Pub., 1984), p. 290.
37 See Suisheng Zhao, "The feeble political capacity of a strong one-party regime: An institutional approach toward the formulation and implementation of economic policy in post-Mao Mainland China," *Issues and Studies* 26:1 (January 1990), pp. 47–81.
38 My assumption is that the impetus to demote Hu came from Deng, with the enthusiastic support of other veterans whom Hu had pressed into retirement.

when they coincide with an informal balance of power; when they do not, a clash may occur, in which the depth and breadth of one's informal base is likely to be the most decisive factor. Yet even in the event of a clash so resolved, the winning faction will probably (1) use formal legal norms and organizational levers (e.g., Deng's self-criticisms) to augment informal resources prior to the clash, and (2) legitimate victory post hoc via constitutional engineering and the proclamation of new formal norms.

What do we know about how informal politics is actually conducted at this empyrean political altitude? Politics is supposed to proceed according to what Teiwes calls "rules of the game," some of them written in such canonical texts as Mao's 1941 speech calling on cadres to rectify their methods of study or Liu Shaoqi's *On Inner-Party Struggle*, which was published the same year. Among these are the norms of collective leadership and democratic centralism. It is true that all Politburo members are formally equal in the sense that each (including the chair) has but one vote, each has access to the same confidential information streams, and so forth. Each member may be assumed to have not only a relatively broad and deep informal base but to preside over a formal hierarchy as well (e.g., Zhou Enlai for many years controlled both the State Council and the foreign ministry, Mao the PLA, Liu and Deng the Party apparatus, and Kang Sheng the security apparatus; after the September 1997 15th CCP Congress, Jiang Zemin was assumed to control the party apparatus, Li Peng the NPC, Chi Haotian and Zhang Wannian the PLA, Qian Qichen the foreign ministry, and Zhu Rongji the government bureaucracy). Although the combination of formal and informal power bases makes each member of this elite extremely powerful, there seems to be an intraelite balancing process in perpetual motion, in which the functional division of labor and a rough equality consonant with the formal norms of collective leadership are in constant tension with the hierarchical imperative.

This need for hierarchy is an informal norm that seems to have been cemented by patron–client relationships within the leadership and activated by a fear of "chaos" (*luan*): Hierarchy implies order. Paradoxically, although collective leadership is indeed a party "norm," it is deemed unstable and a source of potential vulnerability by Chinese participant-observers. Thus the "normal" relationship among CCP elites is hierarchical, as indicated by the punctilious observance of protocol (who appears in public ceremonies, who mounts the dais in what order, who speaks in what sequence, who stands next to whom, the sequence in name lists, and so forth). Hierarchy implies monocratic personal leadership, referred to by Deng as the party "core,"[39] but which

---

39 In an "internal" [*neibu*] speech on June 16, 1989, Deng classified Mao as the leadership core of the first generation and himself as the leadership core of the second generation and designated his client Jiang Zemin as the leadership core of the third generation. *Zhongguo wenti ziliao zuokan* 14:392 (November 20, 1989), p. 36.

we term (more precisely) the "Paramount Leader" (PL).[40] The CCP hierarchy is somewhat looser than the imperial court, partly because it is informally based and in constant tension with the formal norm of collective leadership, partly because of the ongoing "musical chairs" competition for reallocation of formal offices, and partly because the question of succession is never permanently settled. Yet the need for hierarchy has deep cultural roots, and any challenge to it is apt to provoke panic and extreme responses. *The perceived stability of this leadership hierarchy*, we submit, is the *decisive determinant* of whether leadership differences will be settled through *negotiated compromise* or through *zero-sum struggle*, possibly involving mass publics and resulting in major organizational or "line" changes. We term the former "periods of elite hegemony" and the latter "periods of hierarchy disturbance."

Second, it would seem that the distribution of power bases within the CCP leadership is highly skewed, relative either to elected (or appointed) executives in pluralist systems or even to Communist Party leaderships in other socialist countries, such as the erstwhile Eastern European "people's democracies" or the former Soviet Union. There is ample data demonstrating that the PL has privileged access (i.e., more than anyone else) to the intramural levers of bureaucratic power, to the media, and to the ideological symbolism capable of moving the masses in the public arena. In this sense we would agree that the CCP indeed is governed by an informal *Fuehrerprinzip*, albeit in tension with the formal norms of collective leadership.[41]

Innerparty Debate. – Mao has expressed himself frequently on the need for full and open debate within the party, and at the Lushan conference in 1959 he began his counterattack on Peng Dehuai by enjoining his supporters to "listen to bad words." He tried to maintain the impression that there had been full and free debate even at Lushan: "You have said what you have wanted to say, the minutes attest to that. If you do not agree with my views, you can refute them. I don't think it is right to say that one cannot refute the views of the chairman." Yet close scrutiny of the available records reveals that there were many limits on freedom of discussion. First, Mao had an irascible and

---

40 Ironically, much of the responsibility for this is Mao Zedong's, who immersed himself deeply in such dynastic histories as the *Shi ji* (*Records of this historian*, which covers the period from the Yellow Emperor through the Han dynasty) and *Zizhi Tongjian* (*General mirror for the aid of government*, compiled in the eleventh century, which covers 1,300 years of imperial history, from 403 B.C. to A.D.. 959), quoted generously from the classics, and generally modeled himself after China's great emperors. Harrison Salisbury, *The New Emperors: China in the Era of Mao and Deng* (Boston: Little, Brown, 1992), pp. 8–9. In his final year Mao was going through the *General mirror* (which in its standard modern edition runs to 9,612 pages) for the eighteenth time, according to Guo Jinrong, *Mao Zedongde huanghun suiyue* [Mao Zedong's twilight years] (Hong Kong, 1990), as cited in W. J. F. Jenner, *The Tyranny of History: The Roots of China's Crisis* (London: Allen Lane, Penguin Press, 1992), p. 38.

41 See Leonard Shapiro and John Wilson Lewis, "The roles of the monolithic party under the totalitarian leader," in J. W. Lewis, ed., *Party Leadership and Revolutionary Power in China* (London and New York: Cambridge University Press, 1970).

domineering personality; he could explode in anger and be abusive, as he was in the summer of 1953 in response to some remarks by the venerable Liang Shuming, shouting that Liang had "stinking bones", or as he was in his testy response to Peng Dehuai's relatively mild and cautious criticisms at Lushan.[42] Although Chen Yi claimed in his Cultural Revolution self-criticism that he had "opposed Chairman Mao several times," he contradicted himself later: "Who dares to resist Chairman Mao? No one can do that, because Chairman Mao's prestige is too great." Indeed, if the conversations published in the *Mao Zedong sixiang wansui* volumes are analyzed to determine the role of Mao's interlocutors, the chairman rarely heard any discouraging words, even from those "XXX's," presumably so designated because they were later discovered to be his enemies. Zhang Wentian complained to Peng Dehuai that Politburo meetings "were only large-scale briefing meetings without any collective discussion," and Peng agreed that, "in reporting to the Chairman on the current situation, one talks only about the possible and advantageous elements."

Deng disliked Mao's patriarchal leadership style so much that he never sat near him during meetings, even though he was deaf in one ear, a fact that Mao took note of. Yet Deng himself, once rid of Hua, claimed Mao as his guardian angel and showed that he had learned from the "Helmsman."[43]

42 The system of hierarchy and the tradition of respect for one's superior put critics in a disadvantageous position. Those in a subordinate position assume a respectful attitude and understate their case, while those in a superior position can take advantage of their position to use forceful language to display their power or even temper. Thus in his letter Peng began by saying, "whether this letter is of value for reference or not is for you to decide. If what I say is wrong please correct me." He then confirmed the achievements made in the Great Leap, before pointing out the shortcomings and errors committed by the party. Even regarding the backyard furnaces, which everyone (including Mao) agreed were a disaster, he merely said, "there has been some loss and some gains," making his point subtly by reversing the usual order. And he went out of his way to declare these shortcomings and errors unavoidable and that there were always shortcomings amid great achievements. He attributed these mistakes not to Mao, but to the misinterpretation by officials and cadres of Mao's instructions. He asked for a systematic summing up of achievements and lessons gained in the several months since mid-1958, but said, "on the whole, there should be no investigation of personal responsibility." He said finally that now the situation was under control, and "we are embarking step by step on the right path." At the end of his letter he quoted Mao's assessment: "The achievements are tremendous, the problems are numerous, experience is rich, the future is bright." In contrast, Mao's criticism of Peng was direct and blunt. His letter "constituted an anti-Party outline of Rightist opportunism. It is by no means an accidental and individual error. It is planned, organized, prepared and purposeful. He attempted to seize control of the Party and they wanted to form their own opportunist Party. Peng Dehuai's letter is a program that opposes our general line although it superficially supports the people's commune . . . His letter was designed to recruit followers to stage a rebellion. He was vicious and a hypocrite."
43 "The second fall, it is known, took place at the beginning of the Cultural Revolution. . . . Well, this time, too, Chairman Mao tried to protect me. Without success, though, because Lin Biao and the Gang of Four hated me too much. Not as much as they hated Liu Shaoqi, but enough to send me to Shanxi province to do manual labor. . . . Even when I was sent to Shanxi . . . Chairman Mao had someone watching over my security. Foreign friends often ask me how it was possible for me to survive all those trials and tribulations, and I usually answer: 'Because I am the sort of person who does not get discouraged easily, because I am an optimist and know what politics is.' But this answer is not the real answer, the complete answer. I could survive because deep in my heart I always had faith in Chairman Mao." Cf. Deng's 1980 interview with Oriana Fallaci, reprinted in *SW*, pp. 326–335.

Indeed, Deng was probably a more proficient bureaucratic infighter than Mao, who repeatedly had to resort to outside forums (e.g., provincial cadres, the "broad masses") to trump his colleagues. Deng's gradual seizure of power from a seemingly solidly entrenched Hua Guofeng in 1978–1982, for example, was a masterpiece of bureaucratic intrigue. His very bureaucratic virtuosity has made him a rather unreliable supporter of political reform, however, not hesitating to flout many of the reform institutions that he had helped to establish when he found it expedient to do so. Thus, paradoxically, he seems likely to leave the supreme leadership role whose prerogatives he originally decried (and whose formal office he never occupied) nearly as strong as he found it. Deng's chosen successor, Jiang Zemin, despite leaving little imprint on policy in his first eight years, made his intention to consolidate stable hegemony clear with the early ouster of four potential rivals from the Politburo: Yang Shangkun, Chen Xitong, Qiao Shi, and Liu Huaqing.

Public contests. – The PL can use his formal authority to undercut the authority of an opposing faction, the clearest illustration of which is provided by the way Mao handled the case of Lin Biao. At the 2nd Plenum of the 9th Central Committee at Lushan in August–September 1970, a dispute unexpectedly surfaced over whether the post of chief of state should be reestablished, after Mao thought he had disposed of the issue by disavowing interest in the post during preliminary negotiations. After that, Mao systematically used his control over the communication of important documents to lower level organizations and his power of appointment to undermine the influence of Lin and his supporters. "Throwing stones" referred to various documents that had important bearing on the conflict. Mao took various documents written by Chen Boda, added his own comments, and distributed both to the lower levels. He also approved the distribution of other documents (such as the self-criticisms of Huang Yongsheng, Wu Faxian, Li Zuopeng, and Qiu Huizuo, with his marginal criticisms) that expressed his views on the issues involved. In contrast, the informal channels of communication that were available to the opposition reached only a very limited number of persons, as the need for secrecy constrained their communications. "Blending sand with soil" referred to Mao's use of his power of appointment to put his own men in the "management group" of the CMC, which had been staffed exclusively by Lin's followers. "Digging up the cornerstone" referred to his reorganization of the Beijing Military Region. He also made an inspection trip during which he criticized Lin Biao and Chen Boda and presented his views to local cadres and commanders. He could do so openly and officially, whereas his opponents had to communicate exclusively through clandestine channels.[44] Since the informal groups depend on the formal organizational structure as a "trellis," in Nathan's words, they can be undermined by invoking formal organizational sanctions to clip short the trellis.

Although this was not Deng's preferred modus operandi, and he had less need to do so in view of his consummate mastery of innerparty political tactics, Deng has also been quite capable of manipulating the *vox populi*. Thus he gladly accepted public support during the first Tiananmen incident of 1976 and in the 1978 phase of the Democracy Wall movement, giving his young fans clandestine backing. (Thus the article launching the "criterion of truth" debate was written in close collaboration with Hu Yaobang, just as Yao Wenyuan's article launching the Cultural Revolution had been reviewed by Mao.) Deng's gradual retirement from formal positions after 1986 put him in a somewhat more awkward position to command public support, as the mass media are normally monopolized by formal incumbents. Yet just as Mao created an alternative channel to the media from his informal base in Shanghai, in 1991 Deng arranged through his daughter Maomao (Deng Rong) for a Shanghai newspaper to publish pseudonymous articles attacking conservative policy arguments. And just as Mao took advantage of the (somewhat misleading) impression that he had prematurely been shoved aside by ungrateful colleagues to launch the Cultural Revolution, in his spring 1992 voyage to the south (*nan xun*) Deng used his lack of formal positions to play the outsider and incite guerrilla warfare against an entrenched center. Although his conservative opposition did not surrender without resistance, Deng had chosen his symbolic weapons shrewdly, positioning himself in favor of "reform" and accelerated economic growth; like the emperor, no one could challenge him with impunity but had to proceed by indirection (e.g., attack a surrogate or heir apparent).

In sum, the (informal) role of the PL is equipped with the following formidable assets: (1) a public image (symbolized since the imperial era by the sun) of not just good will but political flawlessness (Red Guards deemed any reference to "sunspots" as evidence of *lèse majesté*); (2) the final word in construal of official ideology; (3) free ambit to act in concert with any assortment of colleagues or subordinates at any level in the hierarchical network without fear of accusations of "factionalism" (which might be made of anyone else); and (4) sovereign control of both internal bureaucratic document distribution systems and public media networks. This has been true throughout the reigns of both Mao Zedong and Deng Xiaoping, and there is no indi-

---

44 See Michael Y. M. Kao, *The Lin Piao Affair: Power Politics and Military Coup* (White Plains, NY: International Arts and Sciences Press, 1975), introduction *et passim*.

cation that Jiang Zemin means to forfeit any of these advantages. The impli-
cation is that if and when a cleavage occurs, the PL is more likely to prevail
than any conceivable challenger.

This is not to say that other members of the leadership are completely lacking autonomous power; were that the case, no elite cleavage would ever mate-
rialize. The PL's colleagues' resources are sufficient to stymie his initiatives
protractedly during periods of stable hegemony or (at risk of purge) to mount
a frontal challenge during a hierarchy disturbance. The relative power of other
Politburo members is determined by a combination of (1) their informal connections (*guanxi*) to the PL, retaining his "favor"; (2) their formal command
positions beyond Politburo membership (e.g., Premier, NPC Standing Committee chair, CMC chair); (3) their career credentials (*zige*); (4) the depth and
breadth of their informal bases; and (5) adventitious situational opportunities (e.g., the PL's absence from the capital, serious illness). The PL might be
thought to monopolize the first two of these levers by dint of his power of
appointment and dismissal. But appointments once made are not easy to
undo, as a purge may be politically costly – particularly if a Politburo member has high prestige and a broad informal base (e.g., the purges of Peng
Dehuai, Liu Shaoqi, and Lin Biao alienated many cadres in their respective
"tails"). Thus a veteran cadre may mount sufficient formal and informal power
for a sitting PL to postpone a showdown (as Deng Xiaoping and Chen Yun
avoided confrontation) or to wage a fairly fierce struggle if open cleavage
should eventuate. Yet the power distribution is such that the ultimate outcome is not normally in doubt.

The basic leadership configuration within the Politburo may thus vary
along two axes: the distribution of agreement and the distribution of power.
Although both are continua with many intermediate positions, the polar
alternatives may be depicted as shown in Table 5.1.

Intraelite cleavage tends to surface when the PL becomes engaged in the
dispute; otherwise, rivalries may fester for years (like the Kang Sheng–Chen
Yun or Jiang Qing–Wang Guangmei grudges). The single issue with the
greatest potential to generate cleavage is that of succession, a triangular affair
involving the PL, his heir apparent, and other would-be successors. The PL
is not necessarily the original focus of the dispute. If we review the ten "great
line struggles" frequently listed during the Maoist era in CCP history texts,
few of those five that took place since liberation (i.e., since the consolidation
of the PL position) involved an obvious attempt to usurp power from an
incumbent PL; the more typical pattern was for controversy over the line of
succession to focus on the designated heir apparent, leading the PL to purge
either the latter or his challengers. (As in traditional imperial court politics,
which lacked Western primogeniture rules, succession is pivotal during a PL's

Table 5.1. *Distribution of Agreement*

		Cleavage	Solidarity
Distribution of Power	Hierarchy Collegiality	Hierarchical Factionalism	Primus inter Collective Leadership

later years, but the issue can emerge at any time.) The purge of Gao Gang and Rao Shushi followed the latter's attempt to displace Liu and Zhou at a time when Mao was introducing arrangements to retire to a "second front" after bouts of illness; the Lushan plenum occurred immediately after the formal appointment of Peng Dehuai's old nemesis, Liu Shaoqi, as chief of state (consolidating his heir apparency);[45] and the Cultural Revolution involved (inter alia) Lin Biao's displacement of Liu Shaoqi from that position. Contrary to the public story, recent evidence indicates that the "September 13 Incident" was precipitated by conflict between the Gang of Four and the left wing of the PLA (exacerbated by friction within Lin's family), which escalated to a threshold at which Mao was obliged to choose.[46]

In the reform era, there have been at least two elite cleavages involving succession. Whereas the purge of Hu Yaobang occurred in the context of a generalized resentment among veteran cadres who resented Hu's party reform program (resulting in their retirement) and anticorruption drive (resulting in the prosecution of some of their children) and was reportedly anticipated by friction between Hu and Zhao (who criticized Hu's work style in a late 1984 letter to Deng that was read at the meeting to decide Hu's demotion),[47] the decisive factor in his fall was Deng's willingness to abandon him to his enemies, probably due to his exasperation with Hu's attempts to ease Deng himself into retirement.[48] Zhao Ziyang's fall came in the context of clear signals

45 Peng's antipathy for Liu apparently dated back to 1940, when Liu presided over a long and grueling criticism session of Peng after the Hundred Regiments campaign. (Teiwes, *Mao's Court*, p. 68.) Of course, Lushan involved many issues, some of them far more salient; the point is merely that succession was among them.

46 See the memoirs of Lin's former secretary: Jiao Hua, *Ye Qun zhi mi: Ye Qun yu Lin Biao* (Hong Kong: Cosmos Books, 1993); also personal communication from Jin Qiu. Ye appears to have been a proud and ambitious woman, which may have helped precipitate the 1966 fall of Lu Dingyi (due to friction between Ye and Su Huiding) and later brought her into conflict with both Jiang Qing and her own daughter, "Doudou."

47 See Ruan Ming, *Deng Xiaoping diguo* (Taiwan: Shibao wenhua chuban qiye youxian gongsi, 1992), pp. 188–191. Hu Qili reportedly also provided information critical of his erstwhile patron for the January meeting.

48 Hu, having been appointed CCP secretary-general, was apparently under the delusion that he was really in command. So he reportedly went to Deng and asked him to cede his power: "Be an exam-

of his sympathy for democracy activists who were publicly calling for Li Peng's purge and Deng's retirement, and was anticipated by a sharp Zhao–Li rivalry dating from Li's takeover of Zhao's economic portfolio after an inflationary binge the previous summer (though Li had been Zhao's choice to succeed him). One distinguishing feature of Chinese succession crises is that so far all have been premortem struggles, in which the incumbent has figured prominently.

A second type of hierarchy disturbance may occur when the PL seeks to delegate or reassign authority as a way of exploring policy options, circumventing bureaucratic impediments, testing loyalties, or even justifying an intended dismissal – a sort of "unguided missile" launch. A PL may thus assign different elites to do contradictory things, delegate several people to perform the same task, violate the chain of command and hold briefings with subordinates without informing their chief, and cultivate a rival "favorite" – Mao did all of these and more. For example, Mao reportedly complained to Gao Gang about Liu Shaoqi, Zhou Enlai, and other White Area cadres at the time he was setting up the "two fronts" within the Politburo, giving Gao grounds to hope that he might displace them.[49] He consulted with Bo Yibo in formulating the Ten Great Articles without first consulting Bo's superior, Zhou Enlai.[50] At the outset of the Cultural Revolution, Mao delegated a central work conference in October 1965 to look into the case of Wu Han while simultaneously instigating an informal group in Shanghai to launch its own inquiry and write a polemical article assailing Wu (keeping his involvement with the Shanghai group secret from Beijing). He set up the Cultural Revolution Group under Peng Zhen's chairmanship, which circulated its February (1966) Outline only after Peng traveled to Wuhan (on February 5) to seek Mao's approval (he responded ambiguously); but in the meantime Mao personally supervised the rival February Summary (*Eryue qiyao*) based on the more radical meeting on literary and art work in the armed forces conducted February 2–20 by Lin Biao and Jiang Qing, personally revising the document three times before having it circulated through innerparty channels. A few months later he repudiated the February Outline and disbanded the Cultural Revolution Group. At a time when he was covertly encouraging a

ple. I cannot work efficiently while you are still in power." Moreover, he allowed his ambitions to become public. When Lu Keng asked him in 1986, "Why do you have to wait to become chair of the Central Military Commission until Deng dies?" Hu was silent. Not too long afterward, when a *Washington Post* reporter asked: "Who is going to replace Deng as chair of the CMC?" Hu replied: "We will solve this problem once and for all at the Party's 13th Congress. No one can be in a post forever." Pang Pang, *The Death of Hu Yaobang*, trans. Si Ren (Honolulu: University of Hawaii, Center for Chinese Studies, 1989), pp. 42–43.

49 Du Feng, "Can the Gao Gang Dilemma Be Resolved?" *Zheng ming* 37 (November 1, 1980), pp. 18–19.
50 I am indebted to Peter N. S. Lee for this point.

Red Guard insurrection against the work teams launched by the "bourgeois reactionary headquarters" of Liu Shaoqi and Deng Xiaoping (whose dispatch he had also endorsed), he was also apparently suspicious of his next chosen successor, Lin Biao, as he confided in a confidential letter to Jiang Qing.[51] While naming Lin Biao his successor in the constitution of the 9th CPC Congress, he also made a bid to the radicals, telling Lin that as he was getting old and that he, too, should have a successor – Zhang Chunqiao would be a good candidate.[52] He apparently permitted the Gang of Four to formulate a slate of government appointments for the Fourth National People's Congress in early 1975, while to his senior colleagues he expressed nothing but scorn for these efforts. During Mao's final year in power his actions were typically ambivalent: He backed Deng's measures to carry out the Four Modernizations program and defended him from the Gang, but he simultaneously allowed his own inflammatory ideological comments to be propagated while sanctioning the efforts of such would-be theorists as Zhang Chunqiao and Yao Wenyuan, who wrote major exegeses on class struggle and proletarian dictatorship that could not have been so widely publicized without his endorsement. Both Liu Shaoqi, during his various struggle sessions in the Cultural Revolution, and Jiang Qing, during her trial a decade later, insisted resolutely that they were doing only what Mao had told them to do. Although Mao repudiated each, both may have been right.

Deng Xiaoping seems to have been less apt to delegate various subordinates with conflicting (or identical) assignments, but he was no less willing to give them relatively "hot potatoes" for which he would then claim credit if they succeeded or scapegoat them if they failed. Certainly Hu Yaobang had grounds to assume that he had Deng's support in his campaign to rejuvenate the CCP and retire party elders; Zhao Ziyang also claimed Deng's authorization to pursue a soft line toward the protesters during the first two weeks of May 1989. Yet both found themselves abandoned by the PL when circumstances gave their opponents the opportunity to counterattack. Both the 1986 campaign for political reform and the summer 1988 experiment with price reform could be said to have originated with Deng, who then, however, joined the critics of those policies in cashiering first Hu and then Zhao.

A third type of elite cleavage consists of the continuation of policy debate by other means, to parody Clausewitz. Policy disputes tend to escalate when the leadership is in a "quandary," that is, an open-ended situation offering

---

51 Mao wrote the letter revealing his uneasy state of mind on July 8, 1966, although it was not publicly revealed until after Lin Biao was killed on September 13, 1971. He was apparently perturbed by Lin Biao's speech warning against *coups d'état* at an extended meeting of the Politburo on May 18. Ye, *Chen*, p. 280.

52 Wang Nianyi, *1949–1989-nian de zhongguo: datong luande niandai* (Henan: Henan renmin chubanshe, 1988), pp. 387–388.

several feasible options on which the PL is still noncommital, in which various factions have chances for relative gains. Indeed, the more serious the problems confronting the CCP, the greater the legitimacy of raising differing views and alternatives about which groups might contend. Thus in the National Conference of 1955, which formally resolved the Gao–Rao affair, speeches were made only in support of the purge and there was no debate. At Lushan no one challenged the principles on which the commune system rested; the question was one of timing, the haste with which it was implemented and the failure to test it in selected spots before implementation on a nationwide basis. In the first half of 1962, in contrast, even the alternative of redistribution of land to the individual household was suggested, as was the foreign policy alternative of reconciliation with imperialists, revisionists, and reactionaries and cutting off aid to national liberation movements. As we now know, this was at a time of perhaps the gravest crisis in CCP history, when people were starving to death as a consequence of the Great Leap (some 13.5 million according to PRC statistics, twice that according to Western demographers). The issues raised by the democracy marchers in April–May 1989 were also far-reaching, involving the legitimation of autonomous associations and the birth of a civil society. It would seem that the secular trend is for disagreements to escalate to include sharp cleavages on an increasingly wide-ranging panoply of policy alternatives, reflecting the deideoligization of politics.

Informal politics is thus not unrelated to policy, but policy alone is not a reliable guide to the positions of the contending parties. Thus Zhou Enlai's position on the Cultural Revolution (as on most policy issues) coincided more closely with Liu's and Deng's than with Mao's, but he switched in time for the 11th Plenum of the 8th CC and threw his lot in with the radicals. In policy disputes, at some point fairly early in the struggle, a weighing of the political capital wielded by the various contenders occurs and parties to the conflict then choose sides strategically. The more evenly matched the factional contenders, the more protracted and bitter the struggle is likely to be (cf. the 1930s conflict between Mao and the Returned Students). The greater the imbalance, the shorter and more easily resolved the dispute (cf. the Deng-Hu and Deng-Zhao splits). In such confrontations, the faction chief with the broadest and deepest base and most distinguished *zige* is likely to prevail. As was noted above, this tends to skew the outcome in favor of the PL. Yet even at the height of polarization there is a large group of individuals who do not belong to any of the principal factions. Most leading cadres are neither "leftists" nor "rightists," but somewhere in between. The existence of this "freefloating" (*zhuzhong tiaohe pai*) uncommitted bloc exercises a certain constraint on the minority of passionate activists who typically demand more radical departures from the status quo. Finally, policy disagreements are "normally" resolved within the elite without including outside forces – that has been the norm since the publication of Liu's *On Inner-Party Struggle*, and since the Cultural Revolution the CCP has sought to underline that norm. Yet the most explosive confrontations are those that are publicly vented, giving at least one faction the option of manipulating the masses against the other. In such cases (cf. the 1966, 1976, 1978, 1986, and 1989 clashes) rhetorical and "public relations" skills may play a significant role in the outcome. Such showdowns, being in violation of the norms, are likely to be chaotic, "win all or lose all," although not exclusively so – zero-sum conflicts may also be settled internally (e.g., Gao Gang and Qiao Shi).

THE IMPACT OF REFORM

The question of the impact of reform on informal politics is of course a complex one deserving far more empirical research than has yet been conducted,[53] but a few preliminary hypotheses may be suggested. First, the overall decline in the status of ideology (with the perhaps inadvertent assistance of the regime) and the increasing importance of purpose-rational relationships seems to have had both an emancipatory and a corrosive impact on *guanxi* – emancipatory because, with the relaxation of constraints on lateral communication brought by the end of class struggle and the spread of the market, personal contacts of all types are multiplying. At the same time the reform's impact is corrosive in the sense that such connections have become suffused with utilitarian considerations. As a consequence, the dichotomy introduced earlier between personalized and official ideal types has tended to break down. A new type of connection has emerged that is more instrumental and less sentimental. It is shown in tabular form in Table 5.2. In this table, the "pure" types of relationships are either official (highly purposive, low in value: "commodified") or personalized (low in purpose, high in value: "sentimental"). "Bureaucratism" (a pejorative term for relationships neither personalized nor purpose-rational) has been (for obvious reasons) negatively valued in both the Maoist and reform eras. The new hybrid *guanxi* is however *both* personalized and purpose-rational, to the consternation of those who deplore the freighting of personal relationships with considerations of short-term material utility. Here one uses connections sentimentalized for their intrinsic value as an instrument to achieve other ends, or even cultivates "connections" with ulterior gain in view. This is particularly noticeable at the lower levels, where cadres with direct responsibility for managing the econ-

---

53 See Peter Lee's chapter in this volume.

Table 5.2. *Mixed Relationships*

		Purpose	
		High	Low
Value	High	*Guanxi* (new) "hybrid"	*Guanxi* (old) "sentimental"
	Low	Market "commodified"	Bureaucratic (neutral)

omy are constantly offered new opportunities for rent-seeking behavior. The other tendency is for networks of connections to metastasize throughout society at large with the corrosion of the previously impermeable boundaries of the "basic unit." The upshot of these two trends is that *guanxi* become increasingly indistinguishable from collegial or other superficially affective professional or business associations.

At the highest elite levels, which are still protected from the market by a combination of relatively high salaries and a comprehensive free-supply system, material interests have not yet adulterated personalized relationships in any obvious way. Yet increasing purpose-rationality has also made its appearance here. Previously, factions were primarily motivated by personal security considerations, as Pye has noted. But in the course of reform, security is no longer in such short supply; on the contrary, there has been an attempt to legalize tenure arrangements and restore popular respect for officialdom. The bloody crackdown on the "masses" at Tiananmen should not blind us to the fact that *elite* disciplinary sanctions have become, with certain well-publicized exceptions, milder than before. The Liuist barriers shielding the party from populist monitoring (e.g., from mass protests and big-character posters) have been restored; and whereas rectification campaigns and purges have not been altogether discontinued, they have been far less protracted and intensive than before, sparing most "human targets" from public humiliation and other severe sanctions.[54] Hua Guofeng retains a seat on the Central Committee, Hu Yaobang died a full member of the Politburo, and even Zhao Ziyang retained party membership and has been seen on the golf course. Moreover, the secu-

---

54 For a review of party rectification under the 1980s reforms, see Ch'i Hsi-sheng, *Politics of Disillusionment: The Chinese Communist Party under Deng Xiaoping, 1978–1989* (Armonk, NY: M. E. Sharpe, 1991), pp. 170–257. In this connection it is noteworthy that when Liu Shaoqi's works on party rectification were republished after his posthumous rehabilitation, the "unity" [*tuanjie*] and conciliatory themes (already ascendant) were emphasized, while discussion of contradiction and innerparty struggle were toned down.

Table 5.3. *The Evolution of Informal Groups*

	Action	
Structure	General	Particular
Formal	Bureaucratic politics	Independent kingdom
Informal	Policy group	Faction

larization of Mao Zedong Thought that has accompanied Deng's pragmatic focus on growth at any cost, and the attendant banning of the specters of an elite "struggle between two lines," or "people in the Party taking the capitalist road," have reduced the ideological inhibitions on the operation of factions. Although still denied and forbidden,[55] factional behavior has become somewhat less clandestine. The upshot is that contemporary elite informal groups have begun to engage in the active pursuit of policies perceived to enhance the interests of their constituencies, not merely in clandestine self-defense and power seizure plots (as shown in Table 5.3).

In the course of reform, the dominant trend has been clockwise from factions toward bureaucratic politics. Independent kingdoms have always been taboo, and their empirical incidence seems to have declined since liberation, given the center's enhanced power to rotate cadres. At present the prevailing operational type seems to be the "policy group." This is informally constituted but takes coherent positions on policy issues of interest to its constituency. The group responsible for China's acquisition of nuclear weaponry in the early 1960s, as related by Ostrov, is a good example. Another example is the so-called petroleum faction (Yu Qiuli, Gu Mu, Li Shiguang, and Kang Shi'en): Although classically constituted via loyalties formed while exploiting the Daqing oil fields in the early 1960s, this grouping cohered in defense of energy, heavy industry, and central planning; although fomally censured in the mid-1980s, it then merged into a new functional grouping that was first headed by Chen Yun and then Li Peng. There was also the 1980s coalition of Deng Liqun's propaganda apparatus with Chen Yun's planning and heavy industry group in defense of complementary bureaucratic inter-

---

55 E.g., Zhao Ziyang, Li Peng, and Deng Xiaoping all emphasized the nonexistence of factions within the CCP leadership in speeches immediately after the 13th Party Congress. Suisheng Zhao, "The feeble political capacity of a strong one-party regime: An institutional approach toward the formulation and implementation of economic policy in post-Mao Mainland China" (Part One), in *Issues and Studies* 26:1 (January 1990), pp. 47–81.

ests.[56] The policy group is a mixed type: Recruitment is still based on personal patronage, with loyalty to the patron still expected in the event of elite cleavage. Yet issue commitment and departmental esprit de corps play an increasingly vital role in group cohesion. This, then, is a "half-rationalized" (i.e., policy-oriented but still personalized) form of factionalism roughly corresponding to the "half-reformed" status of the Chinese political system.

The seemingly inexorable trends toward increasing decentralization and market autonomy seem to presage a bright future for informal politics of every sort, given the continued interdict against formal organization beyond the scope of the party-state. There may thus be conflict among informal relations: splits among groups based on repressed cleavages – class background, geographic origin, Tiananmen, Democracy Wall, the Cultural Revolution – or conflict between formal and informal bases (Deng Xiaoping mobilizing his old cronies to purge Hu and Zhao). The tendency toward increasing regional autonomy from the center is in part based on economic decentralization, in part on revised formal game rules (such as the rule permitting the center to appoint only "one down" instead of "two down"), but also in part on informal politics (specifically local networking). It seems likely that informal group or coalition formations and intergroup competitions (e.g., east coast vs. interior, rural vs. urban, commercial and service sectors vs. heavy industry) will be increasingly openly bruited rather than repressed, as in the past. First, the waning of ideological dogmatism makes more interests (trade associations, avocational gatherings such as stamp collectors or *qigong* devotees) and more arguments admissible. Second, the extraordinary growth of the market and the even more rapid growth of extrabudgetary funds, foreign investment capital, and local tax assessments suggests that there will be ample resources behind various unofficial or quasiofficial political actors. Third, the impact of Tiananmen has not only dampened the zeal of would-be protesters, but a national leadership increasingly dependent on international commodity and capital markets has an enhanced stake in avoiding sanctions.

CONCLUSION

To sum up, informal politics in the PRC can be defined on the basis of a combination of behavioral, structural, and cyclical criteria. Behaviorally, it con-

---

56 See Charles Burton, *Political and Social Change in China since 1978* (New York: Greenwood, 1990), pp. 63–64: It soon became clear to Deng Liqun that most threatening to the interests of the constituency of propaganda workers was devolution of authority to lower levels, because maintaining an "orthodoxy" demands uniformity through central coordination (i.e., the "party's unified leadership"). This threw Deng Liqun into the arms of Chen Yun. The conditions defined by the reformers as necessary to economic development were seen to be antagonistic to those required for effective political and ideological work.

sists of manipulating both personalized and official relationships to construct a "political base." Informal politics tends to be implicit and covert (*neibu*) rather than explicit and public, and flexible, casual, and irregular rather than institutionalized. Informal politics tends to be vertically, monocratically structured, relying relatively heavily (although not exclusively) on face-to-face contacts, sometimes mimicking the form of the formal organization in which it is nested. In terms of function, it may be assumed to impact leadership more than routine administration and high-level leadership more than low-level (where there is less discretionary latitude). The circumstances that are most conducive to informal politics are those in which the leadership is beset by a crisis that is not soluble through standard operating procedures, permitting the existing hierarchical monopoly to break down into more open and intense elite networking. Informal politics tends to occur at those points in the political-economic cycle when this type of structural breakdown is most likely to occur – particularly leadership successions, of course, but other national crises as well. Is the political cycle of stable hegemony interrupted by hierarchy disturbances correlated to the business cycle that has emerged in the course of reform? This question will require further analysis, as we seem to have elite cleavages during both economic peaks (Gao Gang, the Cultural Revolution, Hu Yaobang) and valleys (Deng Xiaoping's second comeback in December 1978, Zhao Ziyang's fall). More important than top or bottom, perhaps, is whether the cycle has reached the end of the curve, at which point at least one faction within the leadership is prepared to fight hard ("against the current") for a radical policy departure.[57]

As a political form, informal politics in contemporary China is Janus-faced. It tends to be "progressive" in terms of policy, as its flexibility facilitates more rapid reform by offering shortcuts to time-consuming bureaucratic procedures. This has helped to make China, despite its vast size and numerous problems, an extraordinarily well-led country, compared to many others in the Third World (albeit not always wisely governed). Paradoxically, it is at the same time "reactionary" in its power-political implications, tending to reinforce traditional hierarchical relationships (including the "cult" of leadership inherited from the empire) and culturally embedded relationships more generally (e.g., nepotism and other time-honored primordial "connections") at the expense of more rational legal and meritocratic personnel arrangements. Corrections to these tendencies have perforce been in the formal realm.

Forecasting the future is complicated by the fact that informal politics must be assumed to evolve along with everything else. Generally speaking,

57 See L. Dittmer and Yu-shan Wu, "The modernization of factionalism in Chinese politics," *World Politics* 47:4 (July 1995), pp. 467–495.

we would conclude that informal politics seems also to have been undergoing a process of rationalization, with a tendency to backslide during crises. This is partly due to the tradeoff between formal and informal politics, as reform has brought a growing institutionalization of various bureaucratic "systems," which are increasingly dependent on explicit rules, procedural regularization, and legislation.[58] Second, as noted above, informal groups have themselves become increasingly oriented not merely to power plays and the minimization of personal risk, but to the promotion of policies designed to enhance bureaucratic interests. Thus, at the mass level, informal groups seem to be undergoing a transition to official, avocational, and business groupings, while at the elite level the transition is toward political pressure groups or even policy-oriented coalitions (viz., "reformers" vs."conservatives").

Thus we may end this speculative glimpse into the future on an optimistic note. Yet this will be a "march of 10,000 *li*," beset by detours and pitfalls. That was clearly evident in the ejection of first Hu Yaobang and then Zhao Ziyang from the leadership, resulting in a politically irrational splintering of the policy group most committed to reform.

ACKNOWLEDGMENTS

An earlier draft of this chapter was presented at a conference on "Informal Politics in East Asia" at the Chinese University of Hong Kong, August 17–18, 1992. The author is deeply indebted to the publications and unpublished insights of the late Tang Tsou on this topic.

58 Cf. Shiping Zheng, *Party vs. State in Post-1949 China: The Institutional Dilemma* (New York: Cambridge University Press, 1997).

CHAPTER 6

FORMAL STRUCTURES, INFORMAL POLITICS, AND POLITICAL CHANGE IN CHINA

JOSEPH FEWSMITH

Western studies of China have offered sometimes dramatically different images of the way the political system works and how policy decisions are made. In recent years, studies of China's political system have drawn on Western understandings of bureaucratic processes to develop a picture of a highly institutionalized, albeit fragmented, administrative system.[1] In particular, Lieberthal and Oksenberg's monumental study of the energy bureaucracy depicts a system in which there is an elaborate division of labor and institutionalized operating procedures that direct the paper flow and greatly influence the decision-making process.[2] Their work, as well as that of others, has highlighted the fragmentation of power and consequent bargaining that takes place in the system.[3] The richness of this work suggests the intellectual mileage that can be gained by looking carefully at the formal, institutional structure of the system. Yet as Lieberthal and Oksenberg clearly recognize, China's political system is far less institutionalized at the highest levels of the party, and there are policy arenas in which bargaining models are far less useful. As Jonathan Pollack remarked in a recent article on the People's Liberation Army, "The closer to the acme of the system, the less command derives from specified rules and norms. . . ."[4] Lieberthal has similarly noted that the "fragmented authoritarianism" model was largely constructed around stud-

---

1 Harry Harding, "Competing models of the Chinese communist policy process: Toward a sorting and evaluation," *Issues and Studies* 20:2 (February 1984), pp. 13–36.
2 Kenneth Lieberthal and Michel Oksenberg, *Policy Making in China: Leaders, Structures, and Processes* (Princeton: Princeton University Press, 1992).
3 David M. Lampton, "Chinese politics: The bargaining treadmill," *Issues and Studies* 23:3 (March 1987), pp. 11–41; David M. Lampton, ed., *Policy Implementation in Post-Mao China* (Berkeley and Los Angeles: University of California Press, 1992); and Kenneth Lieberthal and David M. Lampton, eds., *Bureaucracy, Politics and Decision Making in Post-Mao China* (Berkeley and Los Angeles: University of California Press, 1992).
4 Jonathan Pollack, "Structure and process in the Chinese military system," in Kenneth G. Lieberthal and David M. Lampton, eds., *Bureaucracy, Politics and Decision Making in Post-Mao China* (Berkeley: University of California Press, 1992), p. 169.

ies of investment projects and does not necessarily have the same utility in other areas.[5]

In contrast, other studies that draw explicitly or implicitly on notions of Chinese political culture stress the informal nature of the Chinese political process and the importance of "relation networks" (*guanxi wang*).[6] Viewed from this perspective, laws, regulations, and institutions count for little; what matters is who knows whom. The present volume systematically explores this dimension, stressing the importance of informal politics for "who gets what, when, and how." As Dittmer and others emphasize, however, informal politics is given shape in large part by the "trellis" of formal politics. It is, in other words, the interaction between formal and informal politics that should be the focus of our attention. Western studies of organizational behavior have long recognized the importance of this interaction, but studies of the Chinese political system have generally neglected this interaction. Yet even a cursory glance at the Chinese political system suggests the importance of both factors. This chapter thus makes a modest effort to address this interaction by looking at the way formal and informal politics interacted in the 1980s.

It seems evident that certain interests in Chinese society do find institutional expression in China's bureaucracy, and thus efforts to reform China's bureaucracy are often successfully resisted. For instance, in 1988, the State Council abolished the State Economic Commission, but beginning in 1993 it was gradually resuscitated until it had reappeared, in a more powerful form, as the State Economic and Trade Commission. On the other hand, many important policy decisions apparently receive only a cursory review, at best, by China's bureaucracy. For instance, personal relations and political interests were critical in the promotion of the rural reforms in the late 1970s and early 1980s. The interaction between formal and informal structures of power is also apparent in the difficult-to-measure, but nonetheless real, ebbs and flows of power over the course of time. Viewing the policy-making process over time, it seems apparent that power shifts from one individual or institution to another according to the issue involved and the overall political atmosphere. To take but one dramatic example, between 1983 and 1984 neither the composition of the Politburo nor that of the Central Committee of the Chinese Communist Party (CCP) changed significantly, yet the politics of the two periods differed dramatically. In 1983, the party launched a campaign against "spiritual pollution," whereas in 1984 it adopted a landmark decision on economic structural reform. Such rapid shifts along the political spectrum from "left" to "right" are not explicable by reference to bureaucratic

POLITICAL CHANGES IN CHINA

or bargaining models. Bureaucratic models would lead one to expect slow, incremental shifts in policy, but in fact the policy behavior observed is rapid and nonincremental.

One could argue that the reason the campaign against spiritual pollution, like the campaigns against bourgeois liberalization in 1987 and 1989–1990, did not last was because bureaucratic interests reasserted themselves. But such a line of reasoning only underscores the question of why bureaucratic interests were overruled in the first place. It seems apparent that there is a large element of nonbureaucratic politics that needs to be examined and explained. Bargaining models are not of much help in explaining such campaigns as that against spiritual pollution precisely because such campaigns have an ideological component that does not lend itself to the sort of bargaining that goes on in other areas, such as capital construction. A factional model seems potentially more helpful, but there is no known explanation for the shifts in factional alignments in this period.[7] Moreover, the factional model is not compatible with the ideological components of either the campaign against spiritual pollution or the subsequent Decision on the Reform of the Economic Structure. It is important to recognize that reform decisions, like the movements that have interrupted the reform process, have an important ideological dimension. Such ideological components are not compatible with the "culture of civility" said to typify factionalism.

Moreover, whether one is looking at such policy shifts as that from 1983 to 1984 or at other periods of political change, such as the emergence of reform in the late 1970s, it seems that there are factors other than bureaucratic or factional politics involved. In particular, it seems that one cannot explain such shifts without an understanding of how broad issues affect the decision-making process, yet discussions of Chinese politics have rarely discussed how issues get into the political system. In his wonderful study of the American political system, Hedrick Smith used the term "power float" to suggest the way in which power flows among the individuals and institutions in Washington.[8] It seems that power "floats" in Beijing as well as Washington, albeit in quite different ways. This chapter cannot offer a complete explanation for the ways in which power floats in Beijing; it can simply suggest that any explanation of the Chinese political system and policy-making process must take account of informal politics, formal structure, and political issues. Moreover, as Smith's study of American politics suggests, one wants to try to understand how these elements change over time. Looking at how these elements interact may help us to understand

---

7 Andrew J. Nathan, "A factionalism model for CCP politics," *The China Quarterly* 53 (January–March 1973), pp. 34–66.
8 Hedrick Smith, *The Power Game: How Washington Works* (New York: Ballantine Books, 1988).

not only past transformations of the political system but also the post-Deng transition.

INFORMAL POLITICS AND FORMAL STRUCTURE IN THE INAUGURATION OF REFORM

Chinese politics in the period following the death of Mao and the subsequent arrest of the Gang of Four can be seen as a period in which formal structures, battered but not destroyed by the Cultural Revolution, overlapped and interacted with informal politics, party norms (which continued to exist as an ideal), uncertain ideology, and burgeoning social issues. When one looks back at the political transition that took place in China fifteen years ago – the only political transition to have taken place since the establishment of the PRC until the recent death of Deng – one sees that reform emerged from a complex process in which Deng Xiaoping used a set of issues that could mobilize a constituency, distinguish him from Hua Guofeng, and thereby legitimate his own displacement of Hua as the paramount leader of China. It is important to emphasize, as Teiwes does, the revolutionary legitimacy that Deng possessed by virtue of his long participation in and major contributions to the victory of the CCP and the administration of the PRC prior to the Cultural Revolution.[9] Nevertheless, despite such revolutionary legitimacy, Deng did not challenge Hua Guofeng in an intraparty meeting and then articulate an agenda but rather the other way around, underscoring the importance of issues in legitimating leadership.

If one thinks counterfactually for a moment about alternative scenarios, perhaps it can shed some light on the implicit "rules of the game" by which Chinese politics are played, at least in this period. Given Hua Guofeng's rather junior standing in the party, his weak personal network, and his apparently modest work capabilities, it might seem logical to suppose that a group of veteran leaders would get together, either formally or informally, and decide to oust Hua and replace him with someone more acceptable. This could have been done in an extralegal fashion, as with the ouster of the Gang of Four, or legally through the convening of a party plenum. Having disposed of Hua, Deng and the new leadership could then consider the direction of policy. Indeed, given the strength of Deng's leadership credentials – his party experience, his extensive personal connections, and his links to the military – this seems a logical scenario. The fact that the political situation evolved along rather different lines tells us a great deal about Chinese politics.

---

9 See Frederick C. Teiwes, "The paradoxical post-Mao transition: From obeying the leader to 'normal politics'," *The China Journal* 34 (July 1995), pp. 55–94.

The first point that this counterfactual scenario brings out is the degree of legitimacy that Hua Guofeng possessed, both because of Mao's endorsement of his leadership ("with you in charge, I am at ease") and Hua's holding of formal office. The Gang of Four had been seen as so dangerous that they had to be removed by extralegal means; even then, without the legitimization provided by Hua Guofeng's approval as the formal head of the party, the plotters might have desisted. Hua Guofeng was hardly regarded in the same category as the Gang of Four, and removing him needed to be legitimated. Whatever the party constitution said about the members of the Central Committee electing the head of the party, it was clear that Hua had to be delegitimated before he could be removed.[10]

The need to first delegitimate Hua highlights a second point in this counterfactual scenario, namely, the link between personal leadership and the political line. If Chinese politics were either more formalized or more informal, the line would not be so important. The political line is what connects individual leaders to policy direction and to a broader ideological framework. As is well known, Hua attempted to secure his leadership by vowing to continue the policies of Mao Zedong (even if he modified them in practice). The Dazhai model, which emphasized collective labor, was confirmed in agriculture, as was the Daqing model, which similarly emphasized ideological incentives in industry. Most of all, Hua vowed to uphold the results of the Cultural Revolution and the "all-round dictatorship of the proletariat." These policies, summarized as the "two whatevers" ("whatever decision Chairman Mao made, we resolutely support; whatever instructions Chairman Mao made, we will steadfastly abide by"), were intended to legitimize Hua's position as Chairman Mao's revolutionary successor and to limit the return and influence of those veteran cadres purged during the Cultural Revolution, particularly Deng Xiaoping (after all, Mao had "instructed" that Deng be purged).[11] Without challenging this line, it would have been difficult if not impossible to remove Hua Guofeng, much less inaugurate a new line of reform and opening up.

The process of delegitimizing Hua Guofeng and legitimizing Deng Xiaoping illuminates the interconnections between formal position, informal politics, political issues, and ideology. Frequently we think of Chinese politics as dominated by informal politics, but clearly there are limits to informal politics (just as Hua Guofeng could not be removed through informal means). A closer look shows the ways in which the formal structure, informal processes,

10 See Tang Tsou, "Chinese politics at the top: Factionalism or informal politics? Balance-of-power politics or a game to win all?" *The China Journal* 34 (July 1995), p. 115.
11 "Study well the documents and grasp the key link," *Renmin ribao* (February 7, 1977), trans. Foreign Broadcast Information Service, Daily Report-China (hereafter, FBIS-Chi), February 7, 1977, pp. E1–3.

and broader ideological framework interact. At least three issues were vital to Deng in this quest: rural policy, enterprise policy, and ideology.

Rural Reform

The inauguration of rural reform is too complex to discuss in detail here, but some aspects that underscore the interaction between the formal and informal processes in Chinese politics can be mentioned. Although many people played an important role in rural reform, perhaps no one was more critical than Deng's close associate, Wan Li. Wan was appointed as Anhui Party secretary in June 1977, a month before Deng's rehabilitation, although there is every reason to believe that Deng and his colleagues were behind Wan's appointment. Almost as soon as Wan arrived in the province, he began challenging the then-prevailing Dazhai model; Wan was openly contemptuous of the commune system, dismissing communes as "labor camps." Wan completely ignored the provincial "learn from Dazhai" office and sought help from people like Zhou Yueli, who was then holding a sinecure position as head of the provincial policy research office. Zhou had previously been the personal secretary to Zeng Xisheng, the former provincial CCP secretary of Anhui who had first enthusiastically endorsed the policies of the Great Leap Forward, bringing famine and death to millions, but then with equal enthusiasm endorsed the household responsibility system. By the end of 1961, shortly before Zeng Xisheng was criticized and transferred out of Anhui, some 80 percent of the province was practicing the household production responsibility system.[12]

Wan's actions in Anhui were "aided" and spurred on by the severe drought that hit the province in 1978. A Xinhua film crew reportedly went to Anhui and caught graphic pictures of horrific suffering. Shown to a meeting of the Politburo, the film allegedly brought tears to the eyes of the viewers. The film had brought into stark relief the contradiction between the youthful ideals of those former revolutionaries and the present reality of continued privation, thus contributing to the salience of rural poverty as a political issue.[13] Of course, the political leadership was not moved just by pictures of wretched suffering in the countryside; leaders were concerned as well about the possibility of widespread social disorder. Thus, Chen Yun warned the central work conference that immediately preceded the 1978 Third Plenum that if the

12 Joseph Fewsmith, *Dilemmas of Reform in China: Political Conflict and Economic Debate* (Armonk, NY: M. E. Sharpe, 1994), Chap. 1. See also Dali Yang, *Catastrophe and Reform in China* (Stanford: Stanford University Press, 1996).
13 Wang Lixin, "Life after Mao Zedong: A report on implementation of and major consequences of major Chinese agricultural policies in CCP politics," *Kunlun* 5 (December 1988), trans. Joint Publication Research Service, JPRS-CAR-89-079 (July 28, 1989).

livelihood of the peasants were not bettered, rural party secretaries would lead peasants into the cities to demand food.[14] As Luo Xiaopeng has observed, "The astonishing reality of the rural poverty not only proved to be an effective weapon for Deng and Chen in their political fight with Hua Guofeng, it also created a sense of crisis within the new leadership."[15]

Wan Li's protection of early reform efforts in Anhui and the film produced by Xinhua were actions that took place within the structure of formal politics,[16] but informal politics were also critical in gaining central support for rural reform. One story that exemplifies the important role of personal relationships and the salience of poverty as a political issue in the early rural reform is that of Guo Chongyi. Guo, a member of the Anhui Provincial People's Congress, came to Beijing in the summer of 1979 with a report on the success of the early implementation of the household responsibility system in parts of that province. Because that system was still contrary to party policy, several high-level officials refused to meet Guo or to read his report. Finally, he was introduced to Chen Yizi, then a researcher in the Agricultural Institute of the Chinese Academy of Social Sciences (CASS). Chen was excited by the report and took it that evening to both Hu Yaobang and Deng Liqun. Hu immediately wrote a note supporting continued implementation of the household responsibility system on an experimental basis.[17] Guo's report would never have made it through the bureaucratic channels to rise to the top of the system, especially if the bureaucracy had been charged with overseeing the implementation of Cultural Revolution–era agricultural policies, as any institution prior to the inauguration of reform would have been.

Informal politics was also in great evidence in the role that young reformers played in the promotion of rural reform. Whether one looks at the role of the so-called "four gentlemen"[18] or that of the Rural Development Group, it is apparent that informal politics was central to their activities. On the one hand, the members of these groups came together on the basis of personal relationships, either because they had known each other during the Cultural Revolution or because someone introduced them as they and others were returning to Beijing following the end of the Cultural Revolution. Personal

14 See Chen Yun, "Jianchi an bili yuanze tiaozheng guomin jingji" (Readjust the national economy in accordance with the principle of proportionality), in *Chen Yun wenxuan (1956–1985)* (*Selected Works of Chen Yun, 1956–1985*), p. 226.

15 Luo Xiaopeng, "Rural reform and the rise of localism," in Jia Hao and Lin Zhimin, eds., *Changing Central-Local Relations in China: Reform and State Capacity* (Boulder, CO: Westview, 1994), p. 115.

16 Wan's formal position as party secretary was no doubt important, but clearly his loyalties were to Deng Xiaoping rather than to Hua Guofeng or Ji Dengkui, then in charge of rural policy. Thus, Wan's position was formal, but his alliances and policy positions reflected informal structures.

17 Joseph Fewsmith, *Dilemmas of Reform in China*, pp. 32–33.

18 The four gentlemen (*si da junzi*) was the name given to Huang Jiangnan, Wang Qishan, Weng Yongxi, and Zhu Jiaming, four young reformers who contributed both to the early rural and enterprise reforms.

relationships formed quickly, and these became the basis for promoting various reform policies. On the other hand, such groups would have been impotent had they not quickly formed relationships with senior political leaders. The presence of Wang Qishan, the son-in-law of Yao Yilin, and the patronage of Ma Hong guaranteed the "four gentlemen" access to very high levels of the party leadership. Similarly, the relationship between Chen Yizi and party leaders Hu Yaobang and Deng Liqun; the participation of Deng Yingtao, son of Deng Liqun; and the close relationship between various group members and He Weiling, a close friend of Deng Xiaoping's son, Deng Pufang, all gave the nascent Rural Development Group access to high-level leaders within the party. Throughout the early reform period, the Rural Development Group played a critical role as a source of new information and policy innovation, yet it existed on the fringes of China's bureaucratic system. The Rural Development Group was initially formed by a group of young intellectuals and had no formal standing within China's bureaucratic system (which made it unique within China's policy-making structure). It was not until late 1981 that the CCP Secretariat formally affirmed the work of the group and gave it bureaucratic standing by attaching it to the Agricultural Institute of CASS. Even then, the group members maintained separate identity, separate funding, and regarded themselves – as they were regarded by others – as outside the regular bureaucratic structure. This brief description of the origins of rural reform is not meant to suggest that either Deng or Wan had a blueprint for reform that Wan took with him to Anhui. The reality was a complex mixture of high-level support for innovation and a bottom-up push by peasants and lower level cadres to break free of the confines of collectivization. But Wan did focus quickly on rural issues and made no effort to support the then prevailing policy of the center, which suggests his desire to undermine policies associated with Hua Guofeng.

Enterprise Reform

The inauguration of enterprise reform inevitably involved a more bureaucratic process than rural reform. Whereas rural affairs had been overseen primarily by the Rural Work Department of the CCP Central Committee, industrial affairs were supervised by the various commissions and ministries of the State Council that oversaw the administration of the planned economy. Despite the disruption and decentralization that had taken place during the Cultural Revolution, this was still an extensive bureaucratic apparatus. Moreover, the industrial economy – particularly that which involved the large- and medium-sized state-owned enterprises that made up the core of the planned economy – was interrelated and interdependent in ways that the rural economy was not. It was possible to experiment with rural reform in one area (particularly a poor and backward area) without it affecting directly rural production in other areas. The same was not true of the industrial economy. With the economy already faring poorly and central government finances severely strained, the risk of enterprise reform was simply greater – one part of the industrial economy could not be easily isolated from other parts, so disruption in one area might have major repercussions for the overall economy. The combination of a more bureaucratic structure and the potential risk of enterprise reform generally produced a more centralized decision-making process.

Nevertheless, the inauguration of enterprise reform involved formal structure, informal politics, and ideology just as rural reform did. At the same time that Wan Li was undermining the Dazhai model in Anhui, Hu Qiaomu and others were working on a theoretical critique of the theories behind the economic policies of the Gang of Four, but that had implications for Hua Guofeng's economic policies as well. This effort resulted in Hu's July 1978 report to the State Council, "Act in Accordance with Economic Laws, Step Up the Four Modernizations." This report was drafted by Hu and others in the Political Research Office (*Zhengzhi yanjiu shi*) of the State Council. This office, established by Deng in 1975 when he was fighting the Gang of Four, was responsible for the drafting of the policy documents that were later denounced as the "three poisonous weeds."[19] The office was never formally closed after Deng was purged in 1976. As the political climate shifted following the arrest of the Gang of Four, the staffers – including Hu Qiaomu, Deng Liqun, and Yu Guangyuan – could go back to the office. Even before Deng's own rehabilitation, the people in this office apparently provided Deng with up-to-the-minute reports on the political atmosphere at the highest levels of the party. In the end, it was this office that drafted Hu Qiaomu's report. The purpose of Hu Qiaomu's report was to justify in Marxist ideological terms the reform of the Chinese economy. Drawing on the economic thought of Sun Yefang and others, Hu refuted such Cultural Revolution charges as that paying attention to material incentives would lead to "economism." Hu's report also laid out the case for emphasizing the "law of value" and for "proportionate development in a planned way." In short, Hu Qiaomu's report laid out the basic ideological premises of reform and thereby undermined Hua Guofeng's policy line.[20]

19 On the Political Study Office, see Tan Zongji and Zheng Qian, eds., *Shinianhou de pingshuo* [*An evaluation ten years later*] (Beijing: Zhonggong dangshi ziliao chubanshe, 1987), and Su Shaozhi, *Shinian fengyu: Wenge hou de dalu lilunjie* [*Ten years of storms: Mainland theoretical circles after the Cultural Revolution*] (Taipei: Shibao wenhua, 1996).

20 Hu Qiaomu, "Act in accordance with economic laws, step up the four modernizations," *Xinhua* (October 5, 1978), trans. FBIS-Chi, October 11, 1978, pp. E1–22.

The irony is that, despite the ideological issues involved in enterprise reform being joined (successfully from Deng's point of view) earlier and at a higher level than was the case with rural reform, enterprise reform proceeded more slowly than rural reform. It got underway in Sichuan Province in the fall of 1978 and was extended the following spring (following Deng's victory at the Third Plenum), but the reforms undertaken were modest and had little impact initially. The pace of reform, such as it was, slowed even further following the December 1980 Central Work Conference, which called for the implementation of retrenchment policies. Undoubtedly, the reason that enterprise reform proceeded more slowly was the interdependence and greater bureaucratization of the industrial economy mentioned above. This process confirms the ability of formal structures – China's bureaucratic apparatus – to resist changes that they do not like, just as the work of Lieberthal, Oksenberg, Lampton, and others suggests.

Ideological Reform

As many have noted, the cornerstone in the effort to delegitimize Hua Guofeng was the discussion on practice as the sole criterion of truth. Promoted by members of Hu Yaobang's intellectual network in the Central Party School, at the People's Daily, and elsewhere,[21] the discussion on practice as the sole criterion of truth reflected the relationship between power, political line, and policy. The issue of practice was raised in opposition to Hua Guofeng's "two whatevers," which were, in turn, rooted in an effort to prevent Deng Xiaoping from challenging Hua for power.

At the National Propaganda Symposium on November 18, 1976, Wang Dongxing sharply attacked Deng, saying, "This person Deng Xiaoping is wrong, and his errors are very serious. He did not listen to Mao Zedong, and continued to do those things that he had done before."[22] Shortly thereafter, Wu Lengxi told a meeting of the National People's Congress (NPC), "Whatever Chairman Mao instructed or Chairman Mao affirmed, we must strive to do and strive to do well." He also tried to link criticism of Deng Xiaoping to that of the Gang of Four on the grounds that both were opposed to Mao. Shortly thereafter, Wang Dongxing ordered Li Xin and his Central Theoretical Study Group to write the February 7 editorial, publishing it prior to the March Central Work Meeting in an effort to parry demands for Deng to return to work. Apparently it was Li Xin who penned the famous sentence

---

21 Merle Goldman, "Hu Yaobang's intellectual network," *The China Quarterly* 126 (June 1991), pp. 219–242; and Michael Schoenhals, "The discussion on practice as the sole criterion of truth," *The China Quarterly* 126 (June 1991).
22 Su, *Shinian fengyu*, p. 65.

about the two "whatevers" and inserted it into the draft of the editorial.[23] In a joint report to the 1979 Theory Conference, *People's Daily* editor-in-chief Hu Jiwei and his colleagues argued that "The roots of the divisions over line, orientation, and policies the past two years lie in division over the theoretical line."[24] Without challenging Hua Guofeng's theoretical line, it was impossible to justify Deng Xiaoping's return to power or the adoption of reform.

The discussion on practice as the sole criterion of truth, launched in May 1978, was thus the linchpin linking the reform agenda that was implicit in Wan Li's permissive attitude toward rural reform in Anhui and in Hu Qiaomu's report to the State Council to a broader ideological framework that could delegitimize Hua Guofeng and justify Deng Xiaoping's return to power. Had this campaign been defeated, the Dengist reforms would likely have been stillborn, and Hua Guofeng would have remained in power. The connection between policy and political line was very close.

This very brief overview of the inauguration of reform brings out several analytical points. First, although the competition between Hua Guofeng and Deng Xiaoping can be called a power struggle, it was not simply a power struggle. The policies and ideologies articulated by each side were not just used cynically but rather marked distinctly different political lines. The struggle for power was a struggle to implement very different policy visions. Second, despite the fluidity of the political situation following Mao's death, the formal political structure still had meaning. This was evident in the need for Hua to authorize the arrest of the Gang of Four, in the bureaucratic processes involved in early enterprise reform, and in the use that reformers made of their formal political positions to push their agenda. Thus, Wan Li was Anhui Party Secretary, Hu Qiaomu and others were assigned to the Political Study Office of the State Council, and Hu Yaobang was Vice President of the Central Party School.

Just as clearly, however, the formal political structure was not determinative. Wan Li's actions in Anhui violated the policies of his formal superiors and supported Deng Xiaoping's rise to power. Similarly, the activities of Hu Qiaomu and his colleagues in the Political Study Office were undertaken on behalf of Deng Xiaoping rather than the head of the State Council, Hua Guofeng. Likewise, the actions of Hu Yaobang and his intellectual network were based on the informal ties that existed among individuals and were intended to subvert rather than reinforce the formal structure by campaigning for Deng Xiaoping to replace Hua Guofeng. Moreover, political issues, such as rural poverty, could enter the system and be promoted through infor-

23 Ibid., pp. 44, 65.   24 Ibid., p. 64.

mal ties such as those that linked the Rural Development Group to high-level party leaders. Thus, in the political transition from Hua Guofeng to Deng Xiaoping one can see that informal politics was critical, even predominant, but that nevertheless party norms (including the importance of ideology), party traditions (which linked power to policy), and formal structure still played important roles.

CHINA'S POLITICAL SYSTEM IN THE 1980S

As the Dengist coalition replaced Hua Guofeng and his colleagues at the center of China's political system, it moved to reinforce long-held (and long-ignored) party norms and to strengthen the formal structures of the system. There was a greater emphasis on collective leadership (at least rhetorically and to some extent in reality), on not wielding "big sticks" in criticizing opponents (which did not stop such campaigns as that against spiritual pollution or bourgeois liberalization but may have limited them), on intraparty supervision and control (through a reestablished Central Discipline Inspection Commission), routinizing cadre promotion, and establishing a retirement system. The NPC and the Chinese People's Political Consultative Congress (CPPCC) were restored and began to take on a greater role, particularly as the NPC became more active in formulating economic legislation. The policy-making process, while ultimately still tightly controlled, became more open and consultative than it had ever been under Mao or Hua.

Although there seemed to be clear movement toward the strengthening of formal institutions and the routinization of politics, the process was far from complete. In particular, the notions of a political "core" with a corresponding political line remained deeply embedded. These notions, which are inherently incompatible with procedural rationality, skewed the political process by perpetuating the perception that political conflict necessarily involves the struggle for power, that the struggle for power is ultimately a "game to win all,"[25] and hence the belief that compromise should be tactical rather than an integral part of the political process.

As Deng emerged as the core of the political system, a role that combines both formal position and informal networks, his power was constrained by other party elders, most notably Chen Yun. There were many areas of agreement between the two party elders, including the need to turn away from class struggle to emphasize economic construction, to rejuvenate party ranks, and to strengthen party norms. But there were also many areas of disagree-

25 Tsou, "Chinese politics at the top."

ment. As one policy researcher described their relationship, Deng and Chen were "opponents within cooperation" (*hezuo zhong de duishou*).[26]

Although Chen initially sought to give greater emphasis to market forces, by the winter of 1980 he was reemphasizing planning. This gave rise to a debate over the relationship between planning and markets. Conservative economists apparently allied to Chen emphasized the primacy of planning; they called for integrating the planned economy with market regulation. Market-oriented reformers derided this form of integration as *bankuai jiehe* ("board and plank integration"), suggesting the effort of conservatives to maintain a separation between the central, planned core of the economy and the limited role that market forces that would be allowed to operate around the periphery. In contrast, market-oriented reformers such as Liu Guoguang called for an "organic" integration (*youji jiehe*) between the planned economy and the market economy, suggesting both that planning and markets should have equal status and that they should be encouraged to permeate each other so that planning would take the market economy into account, and vice versa. By 1981 market-oriented reformers had raised internally the concept of a "planned commodity economy." The notion of a commodity economy, by suggesting that exchange of equal value should predominate, flew in the face of Marxist orthodoxy and the belief that the planned economy was the sin qua non of socialism. Conservatives won this first round. Liu Guoguang made a self-criticism, and the resolution of the 12th Party Congress enshrined Chen Yun's formulation regarding the integration of the planned economy and market regulation (which was also written into the party and state constitutions).

The reason for going into this otherwise obscure debate is that it makes very clear that in endorsing the commodity economy as the central concept of the 1984 Decision on Economic Structural Reform, Deng was clearly rejecting Chen's consul and adopting a different development strategy. It is true that Chen did not openly oppose this decision (in this and much else that Chen did vis-à-vis both Mao and Deng, Chen would make known his views internally but then maintain silence if the decision went against him), but Chen gave only qualified support. Chen has been quoted as stating: "I agree with Zhao['s letter outlining the reform decision] but I would like to point out our practice in the past is not simply copying the Soviet model. We have our own development and very good experience. Now, the only thing we should do is change it, improve it, and develop it to comply with the new situation."[27] Thus, Chen apparently rejected the reformers' charge

---

26 Author's interview.
27 Fewsmith, *Dilemmas of Reform in China*, Chap. 3, esp. pp. 109–116.

that China's economic system had been copied from the Soviet Union and suggested that incremental improvement on China's own developmental experience would be better than rejecting that experience in favor of new models of development (which is apparently what Chen believed that the 1984 decision was doing). As China's economy encountered problems of one sort or another in the ensuing years, Chen and conservative economists allied with him did not hesitate to criticize the failings of reform. Following the Tiananmen tragedy, when Deng again endorsed the integration of the planned economy and the market economy, conservatives edited his remarks to call for the integration of the planned economy and market regulation.[28] The return to the pre-1984 formulation was hardly accidental.

Chen's disagreement with Deng was most apparent in the economic area, but it extended to the ideological and organizational spheres as well. Chen, it seems, not only feared that the emphasis on markets would destroy the socialist economy, but also that markets and opening up to the outside world would undermine the ideological legitimacy of the system and the organizational integrity of the party. In short, Chen Yun did not simply disagree with this or that policy or with the pace and scope of reform; he and his supporters disagreed with the direction of reform and presented a systematic alternative to Deng's vision. To Chen's credit, he always chose to abide by the norms of the party and seems genuinely never to have wanted to challenge Deng's role as core of the party. Nevertheless, when the opportunity arose following Tiananmen, Chen and other conservatives did take the initiative to implement a policy line that was quite distinct from that of Deng. It took Deng three years of sometimes rather strenuous infighting before he could once again dominate China's policy agenda.[29]

The relationship between Deng and Chen had a major impact on the distribution of power below the apex of the system and on the decision-making process. It is important to note that Deng's subordinates, Hu Yaobang and Zhao Ziyang, who were charged with carrying out the reforms, existed on a distinctly different political level from that of Deng, Chen, and the other elders. According to associates of both men, neither was in a position to go to see Deng and chat about the economic or political situation on a more or less equal basis. Some old cadres such as Wang Zhen could do that, but Hu and Zhao could only make reports and ask for instructions (*huibao*, *qingshi*); there was a very real difference in status, and Deng apparently took pains to maintain that status differential.

At least in part because of the status differential between Deng (and the other elders, particularly Chen Yun) and second-echelon leaders such as Hu

28 Author's interview.   29 Baum, *Burying Mao*, p. 294.

Yaobang and Zhao Ziyang, the most important personnel decisions were not in the hands of those charged with implementing policy, namely, Hu and Zhao. For instance, as head of the party organization, Hu Yaobang had ultimate responsibility for ideological affairs. Yet throughout the period, Hu had to contend with Deng Liqun, who headed the Propaganda Department until 1985 and who obviously thought himself more qualified than Hu Yaobang to be general secretary.[30] The fact that the party head, charged with overseeing ideology, could neither appoint nor remove the head of the Propaganda Department may have violated the principle of democratic centralism, but it certainly reflected the informal structure of power.

Hu was not the only one who suffered from this inability to oversee the apparatus that he was charged with running. From September 1980 until the 13th Party Congress in October 1987, Zhao Ziyang was premier of the State Council, but the evidence suggests that Zhao never dominated this apparatus. In part, Zhao's problem was that his career had been in the provinces and he had never developed the extensive ties throughout the bureaucracy that were needed to manage it. But the bigger part of Zhao's difficulties stemmed from the same source as Hu Yaobang's. Because Zhao was a second-echelon leader and senior appointments were controlled at a level higher than his own, he could never control the most important bureaucratic elements of the State Council, particularly the State Planning Commission. The State Planning Commission, headed at various times by Yao Yilin and Song Ping, remained loyal to Chen Yun; Zhao could pressure, cajole, and compromise with the State Planning Commission, but he could not command it and he could not have its leaders changed.

At the risk of considerably oversimplifying political relations in China, one can heuristically sketch the power structure of Chinese politics in the mid- to late 1980s, as shown in Figure 6.1.

As schematic as this diagram is, it nonetheless suggests two important aspects of politics in the Dengist period. First, it highlights, as discussed above, Chen Yun's role as the proponent of a policy line, perhaps one should say latent policy line, that differed significantly from that espoused by Deng. Second, the diagram suggests the very carefully constructed balances that Deng established to maintain the stability of the party while still biasing the structure toward his own policy agenda. One can also see from the diagram both how Deng balanced reformers off against conservatives and even maintained rivalries between reform leaders, including Zhao Ziyang and Hu

---

30 Joseph Fewsmith, "Reaction, resurgence, and succession: Chinese politics since Tiananmen," in Roderick MacFarquhar, ed., *The Politics of China: The Eras of Mao and Deng*, 2nd ed. (Cambridge: Cambridge University Press 1997), pp. 472–531.

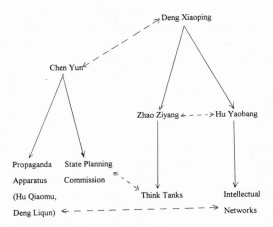

Figure 6.1. Schematic Diagram of Informal Power Relations

Yaobang.[31] To say that Deng maintained a balance among different forces within the party neither suggests that those forces were fixed and unchanging (as a factional model implies) nor that Deng acted simply as one of many forces within the party. On the contrary, the balances constructed or maintained by Deng were intended to reinforce Deng's role as the core of the party and therefore to support his policy line (even as the existence of different forces suggested the difficulty of maintaining and implementing a consistent line). As was suggested above, no one leader or group was able to control all of the instruments of policy that "rightfully" belonged to him. As the diagram illustrates, this system of checks and balances was crafted out of an intermingling of informal politics and bureaucratic institutions; indeed, it frequently juxtaposed informal politics and bureaucratic institutions.

This system was viable in the mid-1980s because it reflected a certain balance of power within the party, but it was not sustainable over the long run for two reasons. First, the very structure of power meant that policy decisions could not be optimal. Indeed, policy decisions are rarely, if ever, optimal. The point is that policy decisions that are suboptimal because they are designed to parry opponents, rather than to reach compromise, are almost certain to lead to counterattacks when their flaws become evident in the implementation process. In thinking about economic reform, Zhao Ziyang had to constantly keep in mind the power and opposition of the State Planning Commission and other conservative organs. This meant that thoughts about price and ownership reform had to be trimmed back to what was politically viable — which meant that their chances of working smoothly were corre-

31 On the rivalry between Hu Yaobang and Deng Liqun, see Richard Baum, *Burying Mao: Chinese Politics in the Age of Deng Xiaoping* (Princeton: Princeton University Press, 1994).

spondingly diminished. Second, and more important, is the basic assumption of Chinese politics that power is monistic and indivisible, and hence that compromise is tactical rather than fundamental. As Tang Tsou put it in his eloquent and insightful article on the Tiananmen tragedy:[32]

> It is true that at times there were compromises, concessions, admissions of defeat, negotiations, and even cooperation with such opposing forces, but those were tactical measures that did not lead to permanent institutions and fundamental processes according to which all political forces would have to conduct their contestations, promote their interests, and accept the results.
>
> In other words, Chinese political culture has not yet accepted the politics of compromise that are so vital to democratic governance.

This suggests that informal politics plays a significantly different role in Chinese politics than it does, say, in American politics. In the American context, informal politics is frequently seen as ameliorating political conflict. Backroom deals, logrolling, and the venerable Washington institution known as "let's do lunch" are all seen as ways of working things out among divergent interests and opinions – sometimes at the expense of the American public. They are, for better or worse, ways in which political conflict can be contained. Chinese politicians certainly cut deals just as their American counterparts do, but sooner or later political conflict in China seems to result in political rupture.

To refer back to the schematic diagram of the Chinese power structure shown above, it is apparent why, given the opposition of the State Planning Commission to market-oriented reform and given the relationship of that organization to Chen Yun (an instance of a bureaucratic organization being tied to a political patron through informal means), Zhao Ziyang was forced to rely increasingly on his think tanks and to adopt policy measures that went around the limits of control of that organization. In other words, Zhao had to rely on a series of informal relationships to maintain the momentum of reform and his own position within the system.

Although the use of think tanks enlivened policy debate and led to policy innovation, it also led to political competition with such bureaucratic organs as the State Planning Commission that was, in the final analysis, a struggle for dominance. If Zhaoist-style reform were successful, the State Planning Commission and Chen Yun would inevitably lose politically, just as problems in reform would diminish Zhao Ziyang and Deng Xiaoping while enhancing the influence of Chen Yun. Thus, conservative planners never missed an opportunity to criticize a variety of sins, including inflationary pressures, loss of revenue to the central government, and so forth. The deba-

---

32 Tang Tsou, "The Tiananmen tragedy," in Brantly Womack, ed., *Contemporary Chinese Politics in Historical Perspective* (Cambridge: Cambridge University Press, 1991), p. 319.

cle of the 1988 price reform effort gave them a ready-made issue, and Zhao
Ziyang paid the price. Thus, it was not so much informal politics per se that
was so debilitating for Chinese politics as the combination of informal politics and ingrained assumptions about the role of "line" and political core, and
the corresponding rejection of the politics of compromise, that led to the esca-
lating tensions within the party that finally exploded during the protest
movement of 1989.

CHINESE POLITICS IN THE 1990S

Tiananmen left China's political system badly shaken. Recriminations rico-
cheted through the party as people tried to lay the blame for what had happened at the feet of their political opponents. The fall of socialism in Eastern
Europe in the fall of 1989 exacerbated intraparty tensions in China, even as
international tensions fed domestic doubts about China's policy of opening
up. Restoring inner party stability was the most difficult domestic political
task that Deng Xiaoping had undertaken since 1978.

There were several factors that facilitated stabilization. The simple fact that
the collapse of socialism in Eastern Europe and subsequently in the Soviet
Union did not cause any major domestic upheaval in China perhaps gave
party leaders a confidence that they could in fact survive. Indeed, it can be
argued that the collapse of the Soviet Union facilitated the restoration of
political stability in China by making it evident to many, most notably to
Deng, that the CCP's only chance of political survival lay in further reform
– a conclusion that Deng pushed by way of his dramatic trip to Shenzhen in
early 1992.

Domestically, the most important factor was the complete inability of the
conservatives, under the leadership of Li Peng, to implement a successful economic program. After years of carping about the various failings of reform,
conservatives at last had a relatively free hand to implement their preferred
policies. The failure of the so-called "double-guarantee" system (which
restored greater central control and planning of over 200 major industries),
the escalation of interenterprise debts, and the dramatic decline in the profits of state-owned enterprises punctured conservatives' illusions about the viability of a restoration (even a partial restoration) of the old planning system.[33]
At the same time, the continued vitality of the township and village enterprise sector (under a less than ideal policy environment) underscored the suc-
cesses of market-oriented reform. Although new debates over the role of the

33 Barry Naughton, *Growing Out of the Plan: Chinese Economic Reform, 1978–1983* (Cambridge: Cambridge
   University Press, 1995), p. 286.

large- and medium-sized state-owned enterprises would soon emerge, the debate over planning and markets as it had been cast in the 1980s was basically over; for all intents and purposes, the planned economy was dead.

These international and domestic factors were accompanied by generational change. Deng Xiaoping gave up his last major position, that of head of the party's Central Military Commission (CMC), in September 1989. Although Deng was still the paramount leader (and indeed his continued presence in the early 1990s was critical to the restoration of political stability and the vigorous reassertion of reform), his retirement as head of the CMC marked the beginning of the shift in power from the generation that had fought and won the revolution to the first postrevolutionary generation. This generational shift was given a push by the deaths of several major conservative leaders: CPPCC Deputy Secretary Wang Renzhong in March 1992, former President and CPPCC Chairman Li Xiannian in June 1992, former Mao secretary Hu Qiaomu in September 1992, and Chen Yun in April 1995. By 1996, Deng Xiaoping appeared incapable of further intervention in the political system, and in February 1997 he finally passed from the scene. Some eight years after Tiananmen, the shift to the so-called third generation of leaders (with Mao Zedong and Deng Xiaoping representing the first and second generations, respectively) was complete.

The question that hangs over the Chinese political system is whether the trends just sketched foreshadow a more stable, institutionalized system in the future or whether China's political traditions (such as viewing power in monistic terms) and the party's history of ideological cum power conflict will lead to renewed instability and, perhaps, the collapse of the system. Put in the terms that we have been using in this chapter, the question is whether the formal aspects of the system are becoming more institutionalized so that conflict within the party can be resolved through procedural means.

This is obviously a very complex question, and opinions within the field vary tremendously.[34] No doubt the trends that seem so ambiguous now will appear self-evident a few years hence. Instead of trying to foretell the future, perhaps one can outline the contingencies on which the future will hang by making a few comparisons with the trends of the reform period that have been sketched in the previous pages.

Perhaps the most consistent, and indeed ominous, feature of Chinese politics in the reform era has been the continuation of the interrelated notions that power is monistic, that one person must emerge as the "core" of the political system, and that policy is linked to power through political "line."

---

34 The range of opinion stretches from William H. Overholt's optimistic scenario in his *The Rise of China* (New York: Norton, 1993) to James Miles' pessimistic portrait in his *The Legacy of Tiananmen: China in Disarray* (Ann Arbor: University of Michigan Press, 1996).

Such a political system inherently rejects a politics of compromise, resists institutionalization, and is antagonistic to procedural rationality. These features were very evident in the political transition from the death of Mao to the emergence of Deng as the new core. Moreover, these features continued to characterize Chinese politics through the first decade and more of reform. They affected the structure of the political system (that is, the real distribution of power), distorted the reform process, and exacerbated tensions within the elite (not just between conservatives and reformers, but also among reformers). They certainly contributed to the tragedy of Tiananmen.

It must also be noted, however, that the existence of these features did not lead to the breakdown of the system as it did during the Cultural Revolution. Conflict was real and had a major impact on the second echelon, but it did not trigger a "struggle to win all" at the highest level. This was no doubt due in part to Chen Yun's personality. Perhaps more than any other high-level political leader, Chen took party norms concerning the expression of political differences seriously. This reticence did not go so far as actually refraining from interference in reform measures that he disagreed with, but it did stop him from openly criticizing Deng or challenging Deng for the core position. For his part, Deng tolerated Chen's criticisms of the problems of reform and the interference of the State Planning Commission in the implementation of reform. There was perhaps a mutual recognition that the party could not survive another "struggle to win all."

If the scope of conflict between Deng and Chen was bounded, consciously or unconsciously, by such a recognition, there was also a more positive element that restrained conflict, namely, an emphasis on party norms. Perhaps the most important of these norms was that party meetings would be held on a regular basis. Thus, since 1977, party congresses have met every five years, as required by the party constitution, and plenary sesssions of the Central Committee have met at least once a year, also as required by statute. Given the history of the CCP, this is a remarkable record. The convention of regular party conclaves does not mean the complete routinization of party affairs. After all, both Hu Yaobang and Zhao Ziyang were dismissed without benefit of a party plenum (in Zhao's case one was called within a month of his effective dismissal), and three weeks prior to the convening of the 4th Plenum of the 13th Central Committee, Deng Xiaoping called in Premier Li Peng and Politburo Standing Committee member Yao Yilin to inform them that Jiang Zemin would be the next general secretary (following Zhao's ouster). Deng said that he had checked with Chen Yun and Li Xiannian — giving a fairly accurate account of the range of consultation needed to make the most critical decisions in the party. Nevertheless, the regular convening of party meetings suggests a broader range of consultation on a wider range of issues (but not including top leadership issues!) than ever before in party history.

Another factor that has affected the conduct of elite politics (even if tracing its impact is difficult) is simply the growing complexity of managing a nation with a large and rapidly growing economy, diverse and frequently conflicting interests, and a wide range of international interests and commitments. Efforts to manage an increasingly complex social and economic system have led to the growing importance of the NPC, to a growing emphasis on law (although there is still a very long way to go), to a far more consultative policy-making process, and perhaps, although it is difficult to tell, to a greater emphasis on institutions to manage society. When most problems are complex and technical in nature, ideological formulas are not very helpful. Moreover, if (and it is a big if) there is greater consensus at the elite level on the general direction of reform (which is to say, if disagreements really are over the pace and scope of reform measures rather than fundamental issues of orientation), then the salience of "line" issues seems likely to decline. If power is no longer so closely linked to policy, political competition is more likely to be "normal" (more about competence than ideology, as Michael Dukakis once put it).

If these trends suggest that the formal political structure and norms limiting political conflict have gained ground over the past two decades, it must still be recognized that they exist on shaky ground. China is not simply an authoritarian system undergoing democratization; it is a Leninist system undergoing both political change (one dare not call it democratization) and economic reform.[35] This is a formidable challenge that no Leninist system has yet successfully negotiated. If China has managed the process of economic reform without political collapse better than the Soviet Union or other socialist states did, it nevertheless remains true that marketization undermines the legitimacy of the CCP. This may not be a problem as long as economic development remains strong and social conflicts remain under control, but it is easy to envision scenarios in which economic or social problems prompt questions of legitimacy and/or generate intense intraelite conflict. In such an event, the lack of institutionalization at the highest level could yet prove to be a fatal flaw. Even in the absence of such system-threatening conflict, there are a variety of issues that could trigger elite conflict. The perilous state of state-owned enterprises, the influx of peasants into the cities, growing income

---

35 Minxin Pei has emphasized the importance of dual transition (economic and political) in Leninist systems, as opposed to authoritarian systems. See his *From Reform to Revolution: The Demise of Communism in China and the Soviet Union* (Cambridge, MA: Harvard University Press, 1994).

inequalities, corruption, and rising nationalism have already generated a growing neoconservative movement.[36]

CONCLUSION

This overview of the interaction of formal structure and informal politics in the reform era suggests some of the ways in which these and other factors have interacted to produce political outcomes. Although informal politics has always been important, even dominant, formal structure has nevertheless played an important role. Thus, as noted above, Hua Guofeng's endorsement of the arrest of the Gang of Four was important more because of Hua's formal status as head of the party than because of any informal influence he wielded. Perhaps conversely, Deng Xiaoping's position as the core of the party has depended first and foremost on his extensive personal connections throughout the party, but Deng has never neglected the formal bases of power. Even though Deng declined the positions of chairman or general secretary, he accepted a position on the Politburo Standing Committee and headed the party's powerful Central Military Commission. When Deng gave up his position on the Politburo Standing Committee, as we know from Zhao Ziyang's revelation to Gorbachev, the 13th Party Congress passed a secret resolution to refer major issues to him as the "helmsman" of the party.[37] This action suggests that party norms were sufficiently institutionalized that Deng needed such a formal resolution to justify his continued access to important documents and his continued involvement in the political system.[38]

Just as Deng combined formal position and informal influence, so did Chen Yun. Indeed, Chen was such a formidable rival to Deng largely because of Chen's own extensive personal relations throughout the bureaucracy, particularly the planning system. But Chen's power was not based solely on personal politics and influence; until his death, he was either on the Politburo Standing Committee, head of the Central Discipline Inspection Commission, or head of the Central Advisory Commission.

Informal politics, of course, is not wholly negative. Indeed, it has provided Chinese politics with a degree of flexibility, even vitality, that the formal political structures alone could not provide. The great virtue of informal politics is that low- or midlevel officials can cut through or go around bureaucratic organizations, taking new information or policy proposals quickly to

---

36 Joseph Fewsmith, "Neoconservatism and the end of the Dengist era," *Asian Survey* 35:7 (July 1995), pp. 635–651.

37 Beijing television, May 16, 1989, trans. FBIS-Chi, May 16, 1989, p. 28; and *Renmin ribao* (May 17, 1989), trans. FBIS-Chi, May 17, 1989, p. 16.

38 Precisely what powers were conferred by such a resolution was obviously ambiguous, as the contention over publicizing Deng's views during his 1992 trip to Shenzhen revealed.

the highest levels and sometimes getting immediate decisions. Informal politics has been vital to reform because reform is necessarily characterized by rapid change and the transformation of institutions. It is a process that almost by definition cannot be carried out through bureaucratic channels; indeed, one of the critical differences between the reforms in the former Soviet Union and in China is the far higher level of institutionalization in the former, something that turned out to be a disadvantage.

Throughout China's reform, informal politics has been critical for identifying and raising issues, for bringing new information to bear on the analysis of problems, and for proposing new policy recommendations. The emergence of reforms in the late 1970s certainly cannot be understood as the outcome of bureaucratic politics, and the current political transformation will necessarily involve more than bureaucratic politics as well. The difference is that if the current political transformation is to be successful, the role of formal politics vis-à-vis informal politics will have to increase.

Indeed, as Dittmer suggests in his Conclusion to this book, the role of informal politics in the PRC appears to be diminishing – although by no means disappearing – over the course of the reforms. Party conclaves are held regularly, the bureaucracy is larger but better led, and economic and other legislation have acquired an unprecedented importance. Moreover, the role of the Central Committee seems to be gaining in political importance, as Susan Shirk has argued.[39] At the same time, however, informal politics remains important. As Dittmer and Lu point out in their contribution to this same volume, formal structure and informal politics can expand at the same time.[40] Teiwes has argued persuasively that the reduction of party demands on society and the open-ended nature of the reform process has resulted in a corresponding reduction of demands on party members, thus allowing them to maintain, and express, differences of opinion.[41] Similarly, Walder has argued that reform has changed the incentive structure for cadres so that those at the lower reaches of the state have more interests in common with the local society than with the central state, thus reducing their willingness to comply with orders from above.[42] Whether such trends will undermine the growing importance of formal politics or complement their functioning is one of the major questions that China must ask as it heads into the twenty-first century.

---

39 Susan Shirk, *The Political Logic of Economic Reform* (Berkeley: University of California Press, 1993).

40 Lowell Dittmer and Lu Xiaobo, "Personal politics in the Chinese *Danwei* Under Reform," *Asian Survey*, vol. 36, no. 3 (1996), pp. 246–267.

41 Frederick Teiwes, "The paradoxical post-Mao transition."

42 Andrew G. Walder, "The auiet revolution from within: Economic reform as a source of political decline," in Andrew G. Walder, ed., *The Waning of the Communist State: Economic Origins of Political Decline in China and Hungary* (Berkeley: University of California Press, 1995).

ACKNOWLEDGMENTS

The ideas in this chapter were first presented at the Shorenstein symposium on "East Asian Development Strategies and International Conflict: Issues for the 21st Century" in Berkeley, California, and at the 47th annual meeting of the Association for Asian Studies in Washington, DC, in 1995, and were published as "Institutions, Informal Politics, and Political Transition in China" in *Asian Survey* 36:3 (March 1996), pp. 230–245. The present version has been extensively revised from these earlier versions. I have greatly benefited from the comments of Lowell Dittmer, Brantly Womack, Dorothy Solinger, and others.

CHAPTER 7

THE INFORMAL POLITICS OF LEADERSHIP SUCCESSION IN POST-MAO CHINA

PETER NAN-SHONG LEE

For more than seven decades from 1921 on, the top leadership structure of the Chinese Communist Party (CCP) has taken shape in an informal and organic process. There were several attempts at leadership succession during Mao's era, but they were not successful at installing a new political leader of the party-state. Examples include such cases as Liu Shaoqi, Lin Biao, Wang Hongwen, and Deng Xiaoping. Hua Guofeng was chosen and groomed for leadership succession in the last days of Mao Zedong in 1976, precluding other candidates, such as Deng Xiaoping and the "Gang of Four." Yet although Hua managed to acquire almost all of the top formal leadership posts, he failed to hold onto them after the death of Mao Zedong.

Although an unsuccessful candidate for (premortem) succession, Deng Xiaoping was among the first to explicitly recognize the succession issue under Mao as problematic. As soon as he reassumed power in 1978, he took initiatives to carry out the retirement of the massive cohort of veteran revolutionaries and to engineer the process of leadership succession. In the CCP, political leadership is dealt with as an informal structure that is neither explicitly stated in the party's charter nor in any other official document. In Deng's view, political power is more than the holding of top formal posts in the CCP; the central leadership team led by the leadership core exercises it.[1] That is, the leadership core is an informal status as well as an informal set of commanding and leading relationships. In the CCP's conception, the "core" is expected to provide effective leadership, to maintain political integration for the entire party-state hierarchy, and to take policy initiatives for the transformation of society.

1 Deng Xiaoping, *Deng Xiaoping Wenxuan (Disanjuan) (Selected essays of Deng Xiaoping*, vol. 3), (Beijing: Renmin chubanshe, 1993), pp. 296–301, 309–314. Tsou Tang provides an analysis of Deng's view on the "leadership core" by taking advantage of Deng's first explicit statements on the subject matter during and after the June 4th incident. See Tsou Tang, "Chinese politics at the top: Factionalism or informal politics? Balance-of-power politics or a game to win all?" *The China Journal*, No. 34 (July 1995), pp. 100–102, 107.

During the reform era, leadership succession also involves some explicit and even formal requirements, for example, the criteria of age limits; educational qualifications and professional competence; and the demonstrated loyalty, proven ability, and effectiveness of the chosen successor. But more important than these formal elements, not only does the top Chinese political leadership exhibit many salient informal characteristics, but also leadership succession itself is an informal and often organic process. Thus leadership succession in post-Mao China is more than a mere change of the topmost formal posts. It is equally important to build up an informal power base to provide sufficient political support for the new leadership core. In short, the selection and installation of the top political leadership in post-Mao China take place in a fluid situation where the rules of the power game have not been explicitly laid down.

This chapter is devoted to the study of the informal politics of the Chinese Communist ruling elite, with special reference to the function of leadership succession, focusing on the post-Mao period. The chapter starts with a discussion of the informal dimension of political leadership, coupled with the CCP's self-conception of leadership. We then examine how Deng tried to install and cultivate his successors in three cases. This will be followed by an analysis of the tensions, cleavages, and conflicts within the current leadership circle.

THE INFORMAL DIMENSION OF LEADERSHIP

Professor Haru Fukui suggests in his Introduction that political power does not assume a mere formal form, adding that the informal dimension often carries greater weight than its formal counterpart. Fukui's generalization is valid and relevant to the study of leadership succession in modern China, where political institutions are often challenged, dismantled, and rebuilt; they are fluid, variable, and ever changing; and they are often the end results of drastic and violent transformations. When one tries to answer the question of how power changes hands in China, one has to tackle some preliminary questions, for example: What form does power tend to assume in the Chinese context, formal or informal? How is it acquired, accumulated, and transferred? We shall try to answer these questions below. It is assumed that the structure at the top echelons of the party-state hierarchy tends to be informal. Our discussion will focus on two perspectives: structural-functional and evolutionary.

From a structural-functional perspective, political leadership tends to be informal in the top echelons of the power hierarchy of such a large-scale organization as the CCP. One may also assume theoretically that the fusion of formal and informal structures is a constant occurrence in such a large and complex organization. In his general theory of organization, Philip Selznick states that leadership is a natural process within a formal hierarchy, deeming leadership an integral part of "informal structure" within which fuller and more spontaneous human behavior takes place. In contrast, within a formal structure, tasks, powers, and procedures are set out according to some officially approved pattern.[2]

By the same token, Henry Mintzberg asserts that, in a modern organization, the "strategic apex" that occupies the topmost echelon tends to be informal, whereas the "operating core" (or "machine bureaucracy") in the lower echelons is often formal, dealing with work directly related to the production of products and the provision of services.[3] From the perspective of organizational design and logic, the strategic apex is charged with the strategy of the organization, the relationship with the environment, overall responsibility and coordination, and control over organization and resources. Furthermore, in Mintzberg's view, the relationship between power and communication tends to be "organic" at the strategic apex, as such relationships are simply too fluid to formalize; the structure has to evolve naturally and shift continually to ensure that the structure is "functional" in terms of the fulfillment of the organizational objectives.[4]

One can discern a similar phenomenon in the leadership structure of the CCP: A small group of party leaders is at the topmost echelon of the CCP party-state, whose relationship is largely informal and natural. A minimum of repetition and standardization, considerable discretion, and a relatively long decision cycle in a variable and fluid task environment characterize their work. Although the performance of their work could not be evaluated mechanically with precise measurements, the performance appraisal has to rely on peer group evaluation, often with diffuse criteria on an intersubjective basis over a long period of time.[5]

Political power is also likely to assume an informal form in the light of its evolutionary process. Power in China is not exercised in the context of a fully established political framework or governmental institution. Weber took for granted that the informal forms of political power did exist at the territorial level, for example, the charismatic and patrimonial ideal types in the early

2 Philip Selznick, "Leadership in administration," in Robert T. Golembiewski et al., eds. *Public Administration: Readings in Institutions, Processes, Behavior, Policy* (Chicago: Rand McNally College Publishing, 1976), pp. 563–575.
3 Henry Mintzberg, *Structure in Fives: Designing Effective Organizations* (Englewood Cliffs, NJ: Prentice-Hall, 1983), pp. 25–44.
4 Ibid., p. 38.
5 Frederick C. Teiwes, *Leadership, Legitimacy and Conflict in China*, (Armonk, NY: M. E. Sharpe, 1984), pp. 46–48.

stages of institutionalization.[6] In other words, the paradigm of formal politics should not be indiscriminately applicable to all forms of territorial dominance during the modern era. The paradigm should fare better in a fully routinized polity and in the realm of interactions that are normally repetitive, routine, and measurable.[7]

The People's Republic of China (PRC) has been established for about a half-century. The revolutionary tradition is still very much alive, exerting considerable influence on the conception of political leadership and its succession. First, the leadership role in the top echelons of the CCP is still shaped by the heroic self-conception of a combat-oriented and movement-oriented party. The term "charisma" is not entirely apt to characterize the CCP's top leadership, due to its excessive emphasis on the leadership qualities of the single leader. The top CCP leadership actually worked as a collective and demonstrated their extraordinary talents, contributions, and sacrifices in an intense struggle on a broad socioeconomic and political front. Therefore, the CCP central leadership can be taken as a charismatic collective led by one prominent individual that emerged in extreme distress. Such a view of a charismatic status group is useful to underscore the organizational culture of the power monopoly game and a highly skewed distribution of political power. Analogous to the case of the former Soviet system,[8] the calculus of power in China is concerned with gains and losses at the territorial level, rather than with incentives at the bureaucratic level or costs and benefits in the marketplace.

In addition, the informal structure of the central leadership team can be attributed to the situational imperatives of an "externally created party."[9] For instance, in its original design, the party branch (or party cell) was organized in a workplace or a residential unit. According to Chen Yun (head of the Organization Department of the Central Committee during the Yanan period), the party branch at the grassroots level was intended to conduct mass

---

6 H. H. Gerth and E. Wright Mills, trans. & ed. *From Max Weber: Essays in Sociology* (New York: Oxford University Press, 1946), pp. 51–55; S. N. Eienstadt, *Max Weber on Charisma Building* (Chicago and London: The University of Chicago Press, 1968), pp. 3–77.

7 Max Weber, *Economy and Society – An Outline of Interpretive Sociology* (ed. by Guenther Roth and Clauwittch) (New York: Beminster Press, 1968), pp. 956–1005.

8 Ken Jowitt, "Soviet neotraditionalism: The political corruption of a Leninist regime," *Soviet Studies*, 35:3 (July 1983), pp. 275–329.

9 Here the notion of "externally created party" refers broadly to the type of political party whose leaders are not represented and incorporated within the ruling circle, but it has to fight for a share of power from the periphery to the center. See Maurice Duverger, *Political Parties* (New York: John Wiley, 1962), pp. xxiii–xxxvii. In the capacity of the Head of the Organization Department of the Central Committee during the Sino-Japanese War period, Chen Yun repeatedly cautioned about the danger of penetration by opponents into the CCP's lower level organization. See Chen Yun, "Dang de zhibu" (The party branch) in Chen Yun, *Chen Yun wenxuan (Selected essays of Chen Yun 1926–1949)*, (Beijing: Renmin chubanshe, 1983), pp. 76–85.

mobilization and to maintain secrecy in a hostile and dangerous environment.[10] This tradition has persisted to the postrevolutionary period, as is well illustrated in Martin Whyte's study of a small group and Andrew G. Walder's analysis of party activities in the workplace.[11] In other words, the leadership role as well as other political functions (including mobilization, indoctrination, and political recruitment) at the top leadership level replicate the practices of the party branch at the grassroots level.

In the evolution of the CCP regime, power was gradually centralized in the hands of the leadership core for a variety of reasons, for example, the spirit of comradely solidarity. This centralization of power resulted inadvertently from the organizational imperatives of the struggle against political opponents. As suggested in Robert Michels' "iron law of oligarchy," the elite tend to gain advantages and to set themselves apart from the rank and file in the process of struggling for power. The relevant factors include competence and accumulated leadership skills, visibility and working relations, and the privileges and vested interests within and out of the organization.[12] In addition, the logic of the high concentration of power has to do with operational imperatives in a crisis situation, viz., unity, secrecy, effectiveness, and time constraints. In Tsou's view, this centralized leadership type emerged from a crisis situation, holding out the promise of extricating the party from the crisis and leading the movement to victory.[13] Mao proved a competent and effective decision maker in the three-man command team starting from the Zunyi Conference in 1935. His "charisma," which was inseparable from the central leadership team, developed only later, during protracted crises.

THE CCP'S SELF-CONCEPTION OF LEADERSHIP

There have been extensive discussions within China study circles on informal politics in China. However, there are basic definitional and methodological questions that are yet to be answered. For instance, How do patronage, factionalism, and "connections" (*guanxi*) differ from one another in conceptual terms? Does a faction necessarily consist of a network of interlocking

---

10 Chen Yun, "Dang de zhibu" ("The Party branch") in Chen Yun, *Chen Yun wenxuan* (*Selected essays of Chen Yun, 1926–1949*), (Beijing: Renmin chubanshe, 1983), pp. 79–83.
11 Martin Whyte, *Small Groups and Political Rituals in China* (Berkeley: University of California Press, 1974); Andrew G. Walder, *Communist Neo-traditionalism: Work and Authority in Chinese Industry* (Berkeley, Los Angeles, and London: University of California Press, 1986), pp. 85–122. Whyte's study of small groups in fact concerns largely regular meetings and activities at the party branch (or cell) level, which may be routine and ritualistic sometimes but not always. See also the chapter by Lu and Dittmer in this volume.
12 Robert Michels, *Political Parties* (New York: Dover Publications, 1959), pp. 21–80.
13 Tang Tsou, "Prolegomenon to the study of informal groups in CCP politics," *China Quarterly*, No. 65 (March 1976), p. 111.

patron–client relations, as is suggested by Andrew Nathan? Is patronage necessarily a derivative from the dependency inherent in a formal command relationship, as claimed by Andrew Walder in his study of the workplace? Many empirical and theoretical issues also have yet to be settled. For example, how does an observer identify and classify informal politics? Under what circumstances does informal politics tend to carry greater weight than its formal counterpart? How does informal politics find its expression in a disciplined Leninist Party such as the CCP? How is one form of informal politics related to others? We will not be able to discuss all of the relevant questions and issues above because of the complexity of the problem area as well as the limited length of this chapter. Nonetheless, for analytical purposes, let us identify some basic forms of informal politics together with their formal counterparts.

Scholars have taken note of the informal characteristics of the CCP's top echelon power structure, which is built on collective solidarity and led by a powerful, charismatic leader.[14] In such a structure, the inner kernel is deemed the "leadership core," often referring to one individual, such as Mao Zedong during 1935–1976, Hua Guofeng during 1977–1979, Deng Xiaoping during 1979–1989, and Jiang Zemin from 1989 to the present. The outer layer is termed "central leadership team" (*zhongyang lingdao banzi*), where consultations take place and decisions of routine nature are made. Furthermore, the CCP top leadership structure is well supported by its organizational culture: for example, a sense of collective solidarity and often intense involvement in "party life" in the basic level organizations, such as party cells/branches. At the central level, the "life meetings," which have an informal aura, often deal with serious political matters with profound implications.

However, the Chinese Communist party-state is an amalgam of both informal and formal elements, although the informal elements constitute the kernel of the power hierarchy. At the formal level, the top leadership structure builds on a Leninist style of a disciplined and militarized party as well as the explicit principle of "democratic centralism." Therefore, the "Mao-in-command model" that is based on a powerful personality tells only part of the story pertaining to the central leadership structure of the CCP. Another part should be the leadership core that is embedded in the collective solidarity of a revolutionary party. Such a structure could sustain powerful leadership and perpetuate its predominance even in those cases where a given incumbent is seen as losing competence to lead in the long process of routinization, for example, Mao in 1959–1976.

14 Frederick C. Teiwes, in his studies of CCP elite politics, emphatically suggests that Mao's dominant role be seen as the linchpin of party unity and rallying point of collective solidarity. See Frederick C. Teiwes, *Politics at Mao's Court: Gao Gang and Party Factionalism in the Early 1950s* (Armonk, NY: M. E. Sharpe, 1990), pp. 142–145; Teiwes (1984) (fn. 5), pp. 23–31, 62–76.

Given the CCP's political history, the formation of the central leadership team and the leadership core is a natural and organic process that can be traced back to a crisis situation as early as the Zunyi Conference in 1935 and marked by a growing centralizing tendency from 1940 onward.[15] In some other contexts, Mao's colleagues wanted to promote his personality cult for a variety of reasons, for example, Liu Shaoqi's effort to enhance the CCP's political image during the Yanan period or Lin Biao's attempt to make use of Mao's name during the Cultural Revolution. During the reform era, Deng made explicit reference to the leadership core for the first time, reiterating that in the party's fine tradition, a balance should be maintained between the role of the leadership core and the proper functions of collective leadership.[16]

While Deng did appreciate the merits of the "leadership core," he attacked the perverted forms of the centralized party leadership in terms of "paternalism, bureaucratism and life-tenure employment of leadership."[17] To put it another way, such a leadership structure has its intended and functional dimensions as well as its unintended dysfunctional consequences. The combination of the two dimensions (formal versus informal, functional versus dysfunctional) is reproduced in Table 7.1 with the four types. The formal-functional type is illustrated by the "democratic centralism," in which a decision is made by discussion, consultation, and consensus-making in a committee setting, operating via majority rule but respecting minority views; the decision is then normally executed by the party secretary and the apparatus, and it is binding to all members as a collectivity at the same level and below. Examples of the informal-functional type include the "leadership core" and the "central leadership team," both of which operate according to such norms as "collective leadership." This type of leadership represents a form of high concentration of power, but it is nevertheless regarded as "correct" conventionally. The formal-dysfunctional leadership style is seen in the cases of commandism, bureaucratism, and departmentalism that involve abuses of formal power. The informal-dysfunctional type is identified in the instances of personality cult, factionalism, and sectarianism.

In Table 7.1, the central leadership team, including its "core," is the most essential part of the CCP hierarchy. The "leadership core" is normally anchored on the topmost formal posts of the party, state, and military hierarchies. Understandably, in functional terms, the informal "leadership core"

---

15 Deng highlights the trend of concentration of power from 1940 onward. See Deng Xiaoping, "Guanyu xiugai dang de zhangcheng de baogao" (The report concerning the revision of the Party's charter), *Renmin shouce* (*The handbook of the people*), (Beijing: Dagongbao she, 1957), p. 30.

16 Deng Xiaoping, "Dang he guojia lingdao zhidu de gaige" (The reform of the leadership system of the Party and State), in Deng Xiaoping, *Deng Xiaoping wenxuan* (*Deng Xiaoping's selected essays*) (Beijing: Renmin Chubanshe, 1983), pp. 289–290.

17 Ibid., pp. 289–91.

Table 7.1. *Types of Top Leadership*

Consequences	Degree of institutionalization	
	Formal	Informal
Functional	Formal-functional type (e.g., democratic centralism)	Informal-functional type (e.g., central leadership team, including its "core")
Dysfunctional	Formal-dysfunctional type (e.g., commandism, bureaucratism, and departmentalism)	Informal-dysfunctional type (e.g., personality cult, patronage, factionalism, and sectarianism)

performs a powerful integrating function for the entire political structure and combines the informal structure with its formal counterpart. To highlight the importance of the central leadership team, Tsou Tang conceptualizes the party-state in terms of "concentric circles."[18] The circle has multiple layers, from the inner kernel of the "party center" to the peripheral "basic echelon organizations" (or party branch and "party cells," so to speak), from the party Secretary and "party group" (or *dang zu*) to the functional counterparts of the government, and from the CCP apparatus to the "mass organizations" and satellite organizations under the United Front Ministry and local bureaus.

Deng made explicit the so-called three-generational leadership groups, very likely to justify his prerogative to choose and install a new central leadership team and its core. In his view, the first generational leadership group of the CCP was formed after the Zunyi Conference in 1935 and included Mao Zedong, Liu Shaoqi, Zhou Enlai, and Zhu De with Ren Bishi, who joined it later. Chen Yun was included after the death of Ren (in the early 1950s). This group was formally incorporated into the Politburo Standing Committee of the CCP during the period of the Eighth Party Congress from 1956 onward. Lin Biao and Deng Xiaoping subsequently joined the group, which lasted until the beginning of the Cultural Revolution in 1966. Mao remained the core of the group throughout the Cultural Revolution during 1966–1976, in spite of the wholesale change of its other members.[19] The second generational leadership group was formed after the 3rd Plenum of the 11th Party Con-

18 Tang Tsou, *The Cultural Revolution and Post-Mao Reforms: A Historical Perspective* (Chicago: The University of Chicago Press, 1987), pp. 249, 266–267, 309–310, 317–319.
19 Deng (1993), p. 309.

gress in 1978. "I occupied a crucial place in the group," said Deng.[20] Subsequently, in his view, the party leadership remained stable and continuous throughout, regardless of the change of two leaders, that is, Hu Yaobang and Zhao Ziyang, during the period of the second-generational leadership group. Accordingly, he suggested that the new Politburo Standing Committee make its first task to defend this third-generational leadership group and its leadership core.[21] Nonetheless, as the leadership core, neither Mao nor Deng was "chosen" by anyone; and the criteria and procedure of selection have never been made explicit and discussed within the CCP, let alone by the citizens of the People's Republic.

LEADERSHIP SUCCESSION AND GERONTOCRATIC POLITICS

During the post-Mao era, there have been four attempts to transfer power, that is, from Hua Guofeng to Deng Xiaoping, from Deng to Hu Yaobang, from Deng to Zhao Ziyang, and from Deng to Jiang Zemin. The last three attempts represent deliberate endeavors to select, install, and build a "leadership core" and a central leadership team. They are taken as a process of group-oriented leadership succession. Through this group-oriented leadership succession, Deng Xiaoping meant to pass political leadership from one generational group to another.

When Deng gained his ascendancy in the early 1980s, he made his first attempt to arrange "group-oriented succession." His main task was to build a new central leadership team with Hu Yaobang acting as its "core." Why Hu, and how was he made the "leadership core"? Was it because of patronage or factional ties? What kind of politics was involved? To answer these questions, first note that Hu's rise to power was definitely facilitated by Deng's support. Moreover, Hu's position became untenable by the end of 1986, when Deng indicated the withdrawal of his backing. Hu's loyalty and deference to Deng could be derived from a formal relationship of subordination in the past; however, their patron–client relationship has been disputed by inside observers such as Ruan Ming. Besides, it was Hua rather than Deng who appointed Hu as the head of the Organization Department of the Central Committee in 1977 and subsequently vice president of the Central Party School; Hu took his own initiative in starting the debate on "practice as the criterion for truth" from which Deng benefited politically.[22]

20 Ibid., pp. 309–310.   21 Ibid., p. 310.
22 Ruan Ming, *Zhonggong renwulun (Chinese Communist figures)*, (Hong Kong: Global Publishing Co., 1993), pp. 64–65.

As a result of the rivalry between Hua Guafeng and Deng Xiaoping, the former was stripped of his posts of the premier of the State Council, party chairman, and chairman of the Central Military Commission (CMC). Subsequently, Hu Yaobang was appointed party chairman in 1981 and then, later on, secretary general on the abolition of the party chairman post in 1982. Zhao Ziyang was appointed premier of the State Council to divest another formal post from Hua. Meanwhile, Deng was appointed to the position of chairman of the Central Military Commission (CMC), the most substantial official post that he held, from 1981 to 1989.[23]

However, after the restructuring of the Central Committee and the abolition of party chairmanship in 1982, Deng's dominance was established not merely because of his post as chairman of the CMC; he instead started to exercise his power as the leadership core as the "collective representative of the Standing Committee of the Political Bureau," which was not a formal post. Lowell Dittmer's conception of "bases of power"[24] makes sense here because Deng installed himself as the "leadership core" within the central leadership team by relying on his "influential constituency." Here it is analytically important to identify the so-called influential constituency. In the case of the "Gang of Four," the focus of Dittmer's analysis, the "influential constituency" could refer to those disgruntled youth, those cadres who lacked scientific and technological literacy, and, perhaps, those politically marginalized strata. To examine elite politics in post-Mao China, however, the "influential constituency" was the corps of veteran revolutionaries who had built an extensive interpersonal network within the party, government, and the army in a long history of revolution and state-building processes. They gained strength during the reform era as soon as they were "liberated" through the "reversal of verdicts." Relative to his rivals, such as Hua Guofung, Deng had a natural advantage to reestablish himself politically because he was an insider and a prominent figure within the corps of revolutionaries. To put it another way, the corps of veteran revolutionaries played a crucial role in the process of leadership succession in the post-Mao era.

Hu was, of course, overshadowed by Deng, because in his capacity as secretary general Hu was merely given power to convene the meetings of the Politburo Standing Committee and other important committees, but his power was restricted to the mechanical parts of the policy process. Hu's exit, together with Zhao's, had actually been planned, but they took place sooner

---

23 Ruan Ming, *Deng Xiaoping diguo* (*The empire of Deng Xiaoping*) (Taipei: Shibao wenhua chuban qiye gongsi, 1995), pp. 120–123, 228–229. Gao Gao, *Hou wenge shi* (*History of Post-Cultural Revolution*) (Taipei: Lian jing chubanshiye gongsi, 1994), pp. 466–468.
24 Lowell Dittmer, "Bases of power in Chinese politics: A theory and analysis of the fall of the 'Gang of Four'," *World Politics*, No. 43 (1978), pp. 26–60.

than expected. Hu reached 70 years of age in 1985. After the 6th Plenum of the 12th Party Congress in 1986, Deng said to Hu,

> I shall retire fully, tendering resignation from all my [present] posts, and not even retaining the Chairmanship of the CMC. You should retire partly, taking my post of the Chairman of the CMC and finding a young person to fill [the post of] Secretary General. Zhao Ziyang [should] retire partly, keeping the post of State President, and giving the Premiership to someone else young. By doing so, we could persuade a batch of senior people to retire so as to promote the policy for more young cadres.[25]

Analysts have identified several factors about Hu's fall in 1987: first, his ambivalent attitude toward and sympathy with the liberalizing tendency within the party as well as student demonstrations; second, his violation of "collective leadership," for example, some policy initiatives taken without prior consultations within the Politburo Standing Committee; third, his cleavages with Zhao Ziyang at both the policy and political levels; and fourth, his political liability for being given the task to complete the process of retiring the whole cohort of veteran revolutionaries.

In his capacity as secretary general in 1982, Hu was on the forefront in restructuring the central leadership team from 1982 to 1986. His first effort concentrated on the further improvement of retirement benefits for veterans and created more posts for them through the establishment of the Central Advisory Committee, CC, CCP. Among others, these measures resulted in accelerating the retirement of veteran revolutionaries and other senior cadres from 1982 onward. Hu was also very active in promoting the idea of selection and cultivation of the "younger, more knowledgeable, more professional cadres" that were sponsored and pushed rigorously by both Deng Xiaoping and Chen Yun.[26] Moreover, Hu was responsible in concrete terms for promoting the idea of Deng and Chen on "three-generational groups" to enhance long-term political stability as well as the continuity and consistency of the retirement policy.[27] According to Hu, the "ladder shape structure" of the three-generational groups would facilitate a dynamic and orderly exit. In his words, "the second generational group today will become the first generational group tomorrow, and the third generational group today will become the second generational group tomorrow."[28]

25 Ibid., pp. 186–189.
26 Hu Yaobang, "Tuanjie fendou, zaizhan hongtu" (Unite and fight on, further fulfil the grand design), in Zhonggong zhongyang dangxiao, ed, *Shiyijie san zhongquanhui yilai zhongyao wenxian xuandu* (*The selected readings of the important documents since the 3rd plenum of 11th Party Congress*) (Beijing: Zhonggong zhongyang dangxiao chubanshe, 1988), pp. 914–915.
27 Zhang Chuantin, "Ganbu duiwu nianqinghua de zhengche Buhuibian" (No change for the policy of rejuvenation of cadres), *Liaowang Zhoukan (Lookout Weekly) (Overseas)* (June 1 1987), p. 3.
28 Ibid.

It is noteworthy that the "circulation of elite" was slow during the 12th Party Congress in September 1982; for example, about one-sixth of the members of the Central Committees were replaced. That is to say, 64 young and new members and alternate members out of 348 joined the Central Committee for the first time. Consequently, Hu was under tremendous pressure to engineer an even larger scale of retirement of top-level senior cadres for the 13th Party Congress for 1987. Hu was sandwiched between pressure from Deng and Chen on the one hand and considerable resistance from veteran revolutionaries on the other. After the 1st Plenum of the the 12th Party Congress was concluded in September 1982, Deng was not entirely satisfied with the pace of the transfer of power to junior cadres. He commented that if the problem could not be completely solved by the 12th Party Congress, it should be dealt with further in the 13th Party Congress, which was to be held in 1987.[29]

Hu accordingly proposed an even more ambitious plan for the "changing of the guards" in a meeting with senior cadres of the party and government in Sichuan Province on May 24, 1986: "[We] must make up our mind to solve the problem of younger cadres in the 13th Party Congress next year," said Hu. According to Hu, one-third of the members and alternate members of the Central Committee should be retired, coupled with [the promotion of] 110 to 120 new comrades. Among these 110 to 120 new comrades, 80 to 90 percent should be around 50 years old. He further remarked that "[we] should also have new Central Committee members between 35 and 40 years old."[30] Hu's talk must have sent shock waves throughout the country as its transcript was being circulated. Hu reaffirmed his position, moreover, when receiving the delegation of journalists from the *Wall Street Journal* in October 1986.[31]

With the heat of the retirement issue behind, Hu's cleavage with veteran revolutionaries found another manifestation in the controversy over democratization and liberalization in China, for example, the antispiritual pollution movement that began in 1983 and Hu's "ambiguous" position in the incorporation of antibourgeois liberalization into the "Resolution on the Guideline of Construction of Socialist Spiritual Civilization" at the 6th Plenum of the 12th Party Congress in September 1986. Their patience with Hu wore thinner than ever before in view of his inaction against the student demonstrations throughout the country at the end of 1986.

Veteran revolutionaries came together to put pressure on Hu to resign in

29 Zen Jianhui, "Xing lao jiao ti de li cheng bei" (The landmark of the exchange between senior and junior [cadres]), *Liaowang Zhoukan (Overseas)* (October 7, 1985), pp. 3–5; Yang Zhongmei, *Hu Yaobang Pingzhuan (The Biography of Hu Yaobang)* (Hong Kong: Benma chubanshe, 1989), pp. 216–217.
30 Ibid., p. 221.   31 Ibid.

an expanded meeting of the Political Bureau that was held on January 16, 1987.[32] Deng took the initiative to handle Hu's case personally, presumably to maintain better control over the course of events.[33] Hu was stripped of his post as secretary general and replaced by Zhao Ziyang; but in a spirit of tolerance and respect for Deng, Hu was allowed to retain memberships in both the Politburo and its Standing Committee.

Zhao did have good reasons for disagreeing with Hu with regard to their overlapping responsibilities and relevant policy issues (e.g., centralization versus decentralization, the pace of democratization, etc.). Furthermore, it is not precluded that Zhao might have wished to extend his tenure and to secure the upper hand in the 13th Party Congress and beyond. In fact, Hu's fall would not have been possible if he did not alienate veteran revolutionaries by trying his utmost to implement Deng's and Chen's policy of retiring veteran revolutionaries.

So far, "gerontocratic politics" has been employed in a general sense. However, in the conception of the top CCP leaders, the role of veteran revolutionaries was informal, but it was well defined in a series of policy talks by Deng and Chen from 1979 on. First, some of them would still stay on the "first front" and would be in charge of important policy matters. Moreover, they were assigned the task of selecting and grooming a new generation of "successors." In their expression, they had a job of "transfer of power, assistance to new appointees, and the provision of guidance." Although Deng underscored that the veteran revolutionaries should be cautious and not interfere with the work of newly promoted cadres, in practice it was difficult to refrain those senior leaders from interfering with the work of newly promoted cadres on the first front, considering the informal power of selection, training, and advice that was given to them.

THE GUARDIANS AND THE SUCCESSOR

Deng and Chen Yun proposed to proceed with a group-oriented leadership succession in two steps: first, selection on the basis of a personal and intimate knowledge of candidates; and second, a probationary procedure.[34] Such a process of selection and installation bears close resemblance to the recruitment procedure at the party branch level. Needless to say, the current "leadership core," together with the corps of veteran revolutionaries, should play a pivotal role in the process through which the new members of the central leadership team, especially at its "core," were selected and installed. Moreover, the probationary period serves an effective mechanism to allow

32 Ibid., p. 222.   33 Ibid., p. 224.   34 Ibid.

time to observe and weed out any candidates who may be found undesirable. Nonetheless, this probationary period created considerable ambiguity as well as tension in the division of labor between the former leadership core and his successor, as witnessed in the case of Hu and Zhao and perhaps even in the case of Jiang.

Being himself a gerontocrat, how did Deng handle gerontocratic politics while he was implementing his policy of group-oriented succession? Traces of evidence suggest that after Hu was gone in 1987, Deng intended to deal with the problem of political succession by himself as his trusted protégé, Bo Yibo, was asked to prepare the personnel matter together with other six team members in preparation for the 13th Party Congress to be convened in 1987.[35] In a very delicate process of bargaining Deng, Chen, and Li Xiannian agreed to have "half-retirement." That is, they all were to be retired from the Central Committee, the Political Bureau, and its Standing Committee, but each would retain a formal post within either the party or the state: Deng would retain the chairmanship of the CMC; Chen would still hold the directorship of the CAC; and Li Xiannian would keep the chairmanship of the National Political Consultative Conference. In the meantime, the other four senior leaders – Peng Zhen, Deng Yingchao, Xu Xiangqian, and Nie Rongzhen – promised to undergo "full retirement."[36]

Zhao Ziyang should have sustained a better chance than Hu Yaobang to succeed Deng Xiaoping as the leadership core for a variety of reasons. Zhao did not have to bear the political burden that Hu did in the formation and execution of a retirement policy for veteran revolutionaries. Nor was he insensitive and disrespectful in his working relationship with veteran revolutionaries. Additionally, in his platform of "neo-authoritarianism," Zhao's political concessions to the people were minimal: some measures of "transparency" and consultation (e.g., the citizens' right to be informed).[37] However, at Deng's request, Zhao devoted considerable time to the drafting of proposals for the reform of political institutions with some democratic tendency, the timing and implementation of which were controlled by Deng. Nonetheless, Zhao's fall was caused partly by his differences with some veteran revolutionaries over not only the crisis management of the June 4th inci-

---

35 Deng Xiaoping, "Gaoji ganbu yao daitou fayang dang de youian chuantong" (The high cadres should take lead to promote the Party's fine tradition), in Deng Xiaoping, *Deng Xiaoping wenxuan (dierchi)* (*Collected essays of Deng Xiaoping*, vol. 2), (Beijing: Renmin chubanshe, 1994), pp. 215–230; Chen Yun, "Tiba peiyang zhong qingnian ganbu shi dangwu zhiji" (The current priority should be the promotion and training of middle and young aged cadres), in Chen Yun, *Chen Yun Wenxuan (disanquan)* (*The collected essays of Chen Yun*, vol. 2) (Beijing: Renmin chubanshe, 1995), pp. 292–297.

36 Li Shangzhi, *Zhengtan Caifanglu* (*The memoir of journalistic investigation of politics*) (Jinan: Shandong renmin chubanshe, 1988), pp. 673–676; Chang Tianyu, "Laoren zhengzhi de weiji" (The crisis of gerontocratic politics), *Guangjiaojing yuekan* (*The Wideangle Monthly*) (July 1989), p. 18.

37 Chang, "The crisis of . . .," (fn. 38), p. 19–20; Li (1988), (fn. 38), pp. 673–675.

dent itself, but also the extent of political space that should be given to students.

On June 4th, much criticism was directed at Deng for his "intervention behind the scenes." This highlighted the ambiguity of the relationship between Deng as the former leadership core and his successor (either Hu, Zhao, or Jiang) during this probationary period. In the 1st Plenum of the 13th Party Congress 1987, Deng was given the role of "guardian" by the Central Committee and the "Party Center" (i.e., the Politburo Standing Committee) upon Zhao's recommendation to institutionalize Deng's position amid the political transition.[38] Zhao Ziyang again confirmed this during Gorbachev's visit to the PRC in May 1989. Nevertheless, Deng claimed subsequently that the arrangement of "guardian" should not be a precedent with reference to Jiang's case.[39] Accordingly, he did verbally decline the role, explaining that he would lend Jiang Zemin and his leadership team full support and autonomy to run the party and the government by themselves.[40] In reality, Deng was still involved in top-level politics from his full retirement in 1989 until 1994.

When commenting on the downfall of Hu and Zhao, Deng made explicit in September 1989 that "two secretaries general [meaning Hu and Zhao] did not hold up, not because they were not qualified when they were first elected. No error was committed when they were first elected [either]. Yet what happened later on was that [they] stumbled and committed a fundamental mistake with regard to the four cardinal principles, most essential of which are Party leadership and Socialism."[41] In other words, Deng was insistent on not giving up the monopoly over the political arena and not allowing any political space to new political forces emerging from the societal level – a policy-making view characterized as "winner takes all" by Professor Tang Tsou.[42]

Jiang was subsequently appointed to the chairmanship of the CMC, the secretary general of the Central Committee after the fall of Zhao in 1989, and in 1992 the president of the state after the retirement of General Yang Shangkun. The top CCP leadership did not announce the completion of the

38 Ruan (1995), pp. 221–224.
39 Zhang Mu, "Deng Xiaoping jinggao wupi 'shi san da', 'jianhu ren' fangshi buneng cheng zhidu," (Deng warns not to criticize the 13th Party Congress, the "guardian" arrangement should not be treated as a precedent), *Jingbao yuekan* (*The Mirror Monthly*) (January, 1990), pp. 49–51; "Zhao Ziyang wei chuli dongluan jinxin zibian quanwen" (The full text of self-defense by Zhao Ziyang on the handling of turmoil" in *Xinbao* (*Xin Daily*) (June 4, 1994), p. 10.
40 Deng Xiaoping, "Di sandai lingdao jiti de dangwuzhiji" (The urgent priority of the third generation leadership group) in Deng (1993), vol. 3, pp. 310–311.
41 Ibid., pp. 310–311.
42 Deng Xiaoping, "Women you xinxin ba Zhongguo de shiqing zuo de genghao" (We are confident to do better job with China's affairs), Deng (1995), vol. 3, p. 324.

"change of guards" from the second generational group to the third generational group until the 4th Plenum of the 14th Party Congress in September
1994.[43]

After his "full retirement" in 1989, Deng made several major moves to
clear the obstacles for Jiang to assume the leadership core. First, with his full
support, the CAC was abolished in the 14th Party Congress in 1992. During his presence, moreover, about one-third of new members were first elected to the Central Committee (CC, CCP) in the 13th Party Congress as
originally announced by Hu. With Deng's backing, the circulation of elites
did not slow down. For example, at the 14th Party Congress in 1992, 46.7
percent of the members of the CC were newly elected, and in the 15th Party
Congress in 1997, about 56 percent of the new members were first elected
to the CCP. Those members of an age of 55 or younger comprised 61 percent in 1992 and 63.5 in 1997. The percentage of CC members with a tertiary education reached 83.7 percent in the 1992 and 92.4 percent in 1997.[44]
By 1997, a majority of top-echelon Chinese leaders were junior to Jiang. Thus
Jiang faced no credible group of veteran revolutionaries who were in a position to challenge him, as had been in the case of Hua, Hu, and Zhao.

Second, Deng was involved in retiring General Yang Shangkun, the first
vice chairman of the CMC, and his half-bother, General Yang Baibing, vice-
chairman of the CMC and concurrently secretary of the CMC. The "clan of
General Yangs" was persuaded to step down in 1992, mainly because Deng
did not want any powerful military men in the way as power was being passed
to Jiang. In addition, Deng skillfully played down and set aside his policy
differences with the Yangs, for example, the nationalization of the PLA as
well as the matter of appointments.[45] Reflecting on the role of the People's
Liberation Army in the power succession, Deng said to Jiang: "The most
important item is to do military work well, and to ensure that no problem
will arise; when we [veteran revolutionaries] are not around, the whole situation could not be maintained stable if the military could not be maintained
stable; this is [our] experience for many years."[46] As a transitional measure,
in the 14th Party Congress in 1992, General Liu Huaqing and Zhang Zhen
were appointed to the posts of vice chairmen of the MAC to assist Jiang in
military affairs; in the 15th Party Congress in 1997, both were replaced by

43 Tang Tsou "The Tiananmen tragedy: The state-society relationship, choices, and mechanisms in his-
    torical perspective" in Brantly Womack, ed., *Contemporary Chinese Politics in Historical Perspective* (New
    York: Cambridge University Press, 1991), pp. 265–327.
44 Gao Xin, *Jiang Zemin de Muliao (Jiang Zemin's staff)* (Hong Kong: Mingjing chubanshe, 1996),
    pp. 141–142.
45 *Ta Kung Pao*, 19 October 1992, p. 2; *Ta kung Pao*, 19 September 1997, p. A1; *Apple Daily*, 19 Sep-
    tember 1997, p. A18.
46 Ren Huiwen, *Zhongnanhai Quanli Jiaojie Neimu (Inside Stories of China's Power Succession)* (Hong Kong:
    Pacific Century Research Institute, 1997), pp. 216–223.

Chi Haotian and Zhang Wannian, younger generals of Jiang's choice.[47] Jiang was able to consolidate his grip over the PLA by accelerating the "circulation of elite" of PLA representatives to the CC in 1997, that is, more than 75 percent of the forty-one military representatives were newly elected.[48] Besides, no PLA representative was elected to the Politburo Standing Committee, and only two PLA generals entered the Politburo.[49]

Third, Deng played a key role in the policy change toward the property-rights–centered reform of state-owned enterprises by calling for the establishment of a socialist market economy in his "inspection tour to the South" [nan xun]. In the meantime, he provided substantial support to Zhu Rongji to assume the post of the first vice premier of the State Council at the 14th Party Congress in 1992 to ensure the success of market-oriented reform.[50] It is apparent that leadership succession was more than the transfer of top formal posts to the successor in the case of Jiang.

CONCLUSION

In this chapter we have argued that, in the post-Mao era, the structure of the CCP's top leadership as well as its installation have been shaped through an informal and organic process under the strong influence of the CCP's conventions and practices of the revolutionary period. This informal process is secretive and not open to external influence, but it has been adapted to a new political setting during the 1980s and 1990s. With all of its weaknesses, this informal process has nonetheless been applied to the selection and installation of successors such as Hu Yaobang, Zhao Ziyang, and finally Jiang Zemin.

If Deng's observation with regard to the informal and organic growth of the "leadership core" is valid, his intervention to install and foster a new "core" is by no means "natural." Deng had to take the task of installing a new "leadership core" into his own hands, while lacking the formal mechanisms and established institutions to carry it out. For Deng, it was not sufficient to appoint the "core" to the topmost posts in the military, party, and state hierarchies; it was also necessary to ensure that the core so appointed was able to build a strong informal power base and to function effectively as the Paramount Leader. Among other possible explanations, Deng failed to transfer his power to Hu Yaobang and Zhao Ziyang because of gerontocratic politics at the informal level. That is to say, political succession was very difficult during the post-Mao era, when it coincided with the retirement of a massive cohort of veteran

47 Ibid., pp. 22–23.
48 Ibid.; South China Morning Post, 20 September 1997, p. 10.
49 Xin Pao, 20 September 1997, p. 20.
50 Apple Daily, 20 September 1997, p. A6.

revolutionaries who had enormous influence and were fully capable of challenging any new "leadership core." However, as a result of the learning process, Deng did play the game of "half-retirement and full retirement" to clear the obstacles for leadership succession after the fall of Hu Yaobang. Zhao was fully aware of the strength of the corps of veteran revolutionaries. Thus he made a conscientious effort to build up support for himself by being respectful to his "senior comrades" and consulting them from time to time. Even though Deng succeeded in retiring most of the veteran revolutionaries from their formal posts, he still had to lobby heavily on Jiang's behalf, not only within the party but also in the military establishment.

This chapter has highlighted the fluidity, variability, and nonroutine nature of elite politics. To put it another way, informal politics at the elite level is least amenable to the process of routinization. So far, age limits, educational qualifications, and professional competence have been introduced into the process of "circulation of the elite," but it has proven difficult to eliminate entirely the hard kernel of informal politics. With the low degree of institutionalization of the transfer of political power, however, it is questionable that Deng's successors could reproduce the historical environment that ensures the successful installation of a new "leadership core" in the next round. Expectedly in the Chinese case, leadership succession would be very costly, entailing potential instability, conflicts, and breakdowns.

PART III

CASE STUDIES IN CHINESE CORPORATISM

CHAPTER 8

ORGANIZATIONAL INVOLUTION AND SOCIOPOLITICAL REFORM IN CHINA: AN ANALYSIS OF THE WORK UNIT

LOWELL DITTMER AND LU XIAOBO

The *danwei*, an enclosed, multifunctional and self-sufficient entity, is the most basic collective unit in the Chinese political and social order. It finds its origins in the early administrative arrangements of the Red Army and the Soviets and wartime base areas, which were designed to be highly autarkic: Each military unit had responsibility for its own provisioning, training, discipline, propaganda, and morale.[1] Unit organization was then generalized across the country in an effort to restructure society in the context of the relatively complete socioeconomic disaster (e.g., industrial destruction, hyperinflation) that followed thirty years of invasion and civil war. Although the unit is the lowest tier of the executive, it is also a production unit and social community. In its political role, the *danwei* functions as a mechanism through which the state controls members of the cadre corps implementing its policies among the working populace. As an economic and communal entity, the *danwei* fulfills the welfare and social needs of its members. *Danwei* membership is inclusive, entailing entitlement to a potentially infinite range of goods and services, for example, housing, bonuses, transportation subsidies, medical care, recreation, and other rationed commodities.[2] The *danwei*'s omnifunctionality has led to a relationship of mutual dependency between the organization and its membership that is not unlike kinship.[3] Yet

1 Cf. Lu Feng, "Danwei: Yizhong teshu de shehui zuzhi xingshi" [The unit: A particular form of social organization], in *Zhongguo shehui kexue* [*Chinese social science*] (1989), pp. 72ff.
2 Inasmuch as the *danwei* was introduced in the context of systemic shortages, rationing was for a long time quite important: In the 1960s there were some 102 different ration cards being distributed in Beijing and 92 in Shanghai; in the 1970s there were still some 73 ration cards in common use nationwide. Han-lin Li, *Die Grundstruktur der chinesischen Gesellschaft: vom traditionellen Klansystem zur modernen Danwei-Organisation* (Opladen: Westdeutscher Verlag, 1991), pp. 114–115. Inasmuch as ration cards were only valid within the issuing unit, their use constituted an effective constraint on lateral mobility.
3 See Martin King Whyte and William L. Parish, *Urban Life in Contemporary China* (Chicago: University of Chicago Press, 1984), esp. Chaps. 1–4; Andrew Walder, *Communist Neo-Traditionalism: Work and Authority in Chinese Industry* (Berkeley: University of California Press, 1986); Jean Oi, *State and Peasant in Contemporary China: The Political Economy of Village Government* (Berkeley: University of California, 1989); and Mayfair Yang, "Between state and society: The construction of corporateness in a Chinese socialist factory," *Australian Journal of Chinese Affairs* 22 (July 1989), pp. 55ff.

the *danwei* is hardly a voluntary association; rather, it is a quasipermanent, quasiascriptive identity in almost the same sense as a nationality or native place.[4]

The *danwei* seems to have come to the attention of the West via the first wave of reporters to take residence in China after the Cultural Revolution, an experience that gave them the opportunity to experience (and report on) the social structure of the unit first hand,[5] only later becoming the object of social scientific analysis. In its early incarnation, the unit tended to be understood as an omnifunctional "cell" in a totalistic party-state that arranged and monitored every aspect of its members' lives, from marriage to family planning to the purchase of grain. In later studies, this conceptualization changed to reflect shifting perceptions of Deng's reform movement; thus, in the wake of the spontaneous protest demonstrations that swept China in the fall of 1986 and again in the spring of 1989 – in which many units participated *en bloc*, complete with identifying banners – the unit began to be interpreted less as an agent of control and more as a nongovernmental organization (NGO), a potentially autonomous antecedent of "civil society."[6]

What makes the humble *danwei* so attractive as a research focus is its universality (in the countryside, the basic units were communes, brigades, and teams). Albeit greatly varied in many different dimensions, to the extent that all units are analogous, which they may be assumed to be insofar as they bear the same administrative appellation and formal structure, the *danwei* may be regarded as a microcosm of Chinese social structure, making it an ideal place to delve into the relationship between public and private, between formal structure and informal *Gemeinschaft*, and many other issues. The purpose of this chapter, then, is to understand the nature and extrapolate the fate of the basic unit under the impact of reform and opening up. Our research is based on both documentary analysis and field work: We conducted a series of open-ended interviews in both a large metropolitan area (Shanghai) and a mid-sized city (Shijiazhuang) in the summer of 1993 and in 1994 with a sampling of respondents in state-owned enterprises (SOEs, or *quoying qiye*); government agencies (*xingzheng jiguan*); nonprofit, nonproduction units such as colleges

---

4 Thus it is expected and demanded that to spend a night at a hotel, to order airplane tickets, or to visit the office of another *danwei*, one must have documentary confirmation and an identification card from one's *danwei*. If involved in an accident or crime, one is first asked for confirmation of one's *danwei* membership. Li, *Grundstruktur*, p. 184.

5 See, for example, Ross Munro's series in the *Toronto Globe and Mail* in October 1977, also Fox Butterfield, *China: Alive in the Bitter Sea* (New York: Quadrangle Publications, 1982); Jay and Linda Matthews, *One Billion: A China Chronicle* (New York: Random House, 1983), and Yuichi Funabashi, *Neibu: One Report on China* (Tokyo: Asahi Shimbun, 1982, in Japanese).

6 See especially Corinna-Barbara Francis, *Paradoxes of Power and Dependence in the Chinese Workplace* (New York: Columbia University, unpub. Political Science Ph.D. Diss., 1993). In the post-Tiananmen crackdown, all units were required to conduct investigations and to report anyone who had taken part in the protests. The fact that most units conducted this work half-heartedly or not at all and protected their memberships has not discouraged this new view of the unit as a potential shield against repression.

or high schools (*shiye danwei*); units in Sino-foreign joint venture firms (JVs), as well as the looser associations of self-employed persons (*getihu*) and private entrepreneurs (*siying qiye*).[7] The chapter consists of three parts. The first part attempts to plot a basic structural-functional "map" of the *danwei*, particularly during the reform era. The second part investigates the impact of the unit on informal relationships within it. The third, theoretical section attempts to outline a theory of organizational change according to which the *danwei* is subject to countervailing "evolutionary" and "involutionary" tendencies and to project its likely future in the course of reform accordingly.

CHANGING FUNCTIONS OF THE DANWEI

The *danwei* is the functional equivalent of the extended family or clan (*zu*), whose elimination coincided with the *danwei*'s establishment in Chinese society. Like the clan, the *danwei* might be said to have both "paternal" (control) and "maternal" (welfare) functions. Indeed, the *danwei* served these functions with such systematic efficiency that its membership was typically locked into place by this system of needs. However, after some fifteen years of reform, particularly since reform moved into the cities after the (October 1984) 3rd Plenum of the 12th Central Committee (CC), the functions of the *danwei* have changed. Inasmuch as the *danwei* system came into being as a concomitant of central planning and comprehensive political control, to the extent that the market replaces the plan as a resource allocation mechanism and personnel mobility reduces the power of the work units over its members, the *danwei* loses its raison d'être. The changing functions of the work unit are thus our first concern.

The Control (Statist) Function

Traditionally, work units have a disposition of personnel dossiers (*dangan*), without which the employee could not transfer freely. Because of the lack of such mobility, employees of a unit, once assigned, usually live and work in the same unit for the rest of their lives. This created what has been called *danwei suoyouzhi* (unit ownership) – a work unit becomes the de facto owner of its membership. Unit ownership helped foster what Andrew Walder has called "organized dependency" and "principled particularism." Working and living in an enclosed social environment, socialized and constantly monitored in countless meetings of diverse types, people became hypersensitive about

---

7 By late 1997, the PRC had a total of 4.4 million work units [*danwei*] functioning as independent, legal entities (*duli faren*), of which 2.62 million were *qiye danwei*, 620,000 *shiye danwei*, and 40,000 "social organizations" [*shehui tuanti*]. CCTV "China News" broadcast, September 27, 1997.

conformity. The *danwei* is also the local agent of political movements: For some thirty years, the rule was that each unit assigned one work day per week to political activities (*huodong*), when unit members would study and discuss political materials and engage in criticism and self-criticism. In cases of deviance, the *danwei* could request self-examination, reassign a member to a less desirable job or housing allocation, or, in extreme cases, even evict one from the unit (in which case one would be remanded to a street committee).[8] The penetration of the Leninist state in urban society was thorough indeed.

In our study, we found that the statist political control function has tended to atrophy in the course of reform.[9] This can be illustrated by the case of a typical bureaucratic organization, a provincial government agency. This agency had some 160 staff members, about 60 percent of whom were cadres, and the rest supporting staff and workers. In any change in the political functions of the *danwei*, one would expect this type of government agency to be among the last to be affected. However, as an informant working in this agency put it, of the two major functions of the *danwei* – *kong* (control) and *bao* (welfare) – the control function has been most drastically reduced. He used his own case to demonstrate:

> There is increasing mobility of personnel, and *danwei* members dare to speak out. I was one of the active organizers of a demonstration by staff of this and several other government agencies in June 1989. Had I not taken part, I would have been promoted to a higher position. After June 1989, I was demoted. But since then, I have had a lot more "freedom" in that I can come to work whenever I want, or not even come to work, and the leaders cannot do anything about it. They now turn a blind eye to this. There are many other things they have to worry about, such as how to raise funds to build an apartment building for the members, also now the *jiguan* pays a certain amount of fees to the nearby middle school so that children of *jiguan* members can attend. Another example is the expanding car fleet. Nearly all the main chiefs of this unit have a car assigned to them.[10]

In enterprise units (*qiye danwei*), the control function is even weaker than in administrative or nonproduction units, as employees in this type of unit have more freedom to transfer or simply to quit, attracted by an increasingly dynamic private and quasiprivate sector where there is no *dangan* system. A joint venture employee in Shanghai reflected on how different this is from

---

8 Li, *Grundstruktur*, pp. 132–133, 178.

9 For concurrent findings, see Francis, *Paradoxes*; Brantly Womack's critique of Walder, "Transfigured community: New traditionalism and work unit socialism in China," also Walder's "Reply to Womack," *China Quarterly* 126 (June 1991), pp. 313–332 and 333–339, respectively.

10 Interview, Shijiazhuang, 1993.

the prereform era, when he would not have had the chance to quit his job teaching in a middle school (a typical *shiye danwei*) and land a job in a joint venture corporation by responding to an ad in a newspaper.[11] Even among SOEs, there are two parallel personnel systems in operation: Some SOEs still require a dossier to gain admission, while others do not. One informant working in a Shanghai SOE wanted to leave and was told to either remain with the unit or pay RMB 3,000 as compensation: Without compensation, the unit would not release her *dangan*. But she did not need a dossier for her new job, so she simply left.[12]

One of the reasons that the control and monitoring of party members by the CCP has become more lax is because of the greater personnel mobility made possible by the rapid growth (in east coast cities) of a nonstate-controlled industrial sector. An internal report found that among the 7,548 party members in a large state-owned mine, 75 had *tingxin liuzhi* (reserve position without pay) arrangements with the mine, which means that their party organization affiliation and activities were suspended. In the same unit, 69 party members had requested long-term leave for various reasons and the party organization had lost contact with them. The same investigation also found that when some employees who were party members were hired by other units, they left without transferring their party organization affiliation, partly because their new employers did not require it.[13]

In general, the power of work units to control their members has eroded since the reforms began. One may extrapolate that, with continuing market reforms, especially those related to the failing SOE sector, "*danwei* ownership" in the sense of personnel control will further attenuate. However, *danwei* ownership in its other sense, that is, the welfare function that provides comprehensive services to unit members, remains vital and may have even intensified.

The Welfare (Communal) Function

It has long been the case in China that certain public goods such as housing, primary education, public security, and health care were provided by work units rather than directly by the state. Moreover, during periods when consumer products and groceries were in constant shortage, work units were expected to compensate by purchasing or producing them for its members.[14]

---

11 Interview #D8, Shanghai, July 1993.   12 Ibid.
13 Xinhuashe, *Neibu Cankao* [internal reference], no. 97 (December 10, 1993).
14 For a detailed analysis, see Lu Xiaobo, *Organizational Involution and Official Defiance: A Study of Cadre Corruption in China, 1949–1993* (University of California at Berkeley, Political Science Department, Ph.D. Diss., 1994).

The consequence of such an arrangement has proved to be both a blessing and a curse for the system. As a buffer mechanism, work units helped to relieve the state of certain financial burdens when its resources were strapped. The state was able to maintain a very low unemployment rate in urban areas with the help of the *danwei* system, which absorbed a large number of workers. Even today, while the state sector has become less significant as a percentage of gross domestic production (GDP), its importance in employing the working population remains vital. In most large cities, SOEs are still the major employers.

Yet the reliance on the units for the provision of welfare has also placed a tremendous burden on the fiscal and administrative capabilities of the units.[15] A recent survey in the city of Xiamen disclosed that one-half (51 percent) of *danwei* cadres' activities were devoted to nonoccupational matters.[16] The burden is particularly onerous for large industrial and administrative units, where a large, if not majority proportion, of the operating budget and staff must be devoted to logistics and welfare. According to an official estimate by the State Commission on System Reform (*tigaiwei*), currently there are some 30 million SOE employees who are redundant and would have to be cut to make such enterprises efficient, comprising up to 50 percent of the workforce in some enterprises. Not only do they rely on their *danwei* for salaries, but more importantly for the provision of vital welfare benefits such as housing and health care. Many of these redundant employees are in the service units of the SOEs. For instance, in one large SOE, the Hubei Synthetic Fiber Corporation (HSFC), 12 percent of the 8,500 employees were working in service-related positions.[17] Redundant employees, lack of social security funds for aging employees, and the undertaking of service functions are three of what Chinese authorities call the four main "historical burdens" of SOE reform.[18] Hence, one of the main goals of industrial reform is to mitigate the welfare function of the units to enhance their efficiency and productivity. In the words of some Chinese managers and administrators, the goal is to transform the existing situation of "units running society" (*danwei ban shehui*) into one of "society serving units" (*shehui hua fuwu*).[19]

There are various ways of accomplishing this goal. One expedient way that became common in the 1990s is to operate *disan chanye* (tertiary industry). In this context SOEs were encouraged to spin off commercial branches specializing in trade or services. This amounts to setting up a separate division

15 *Banyuetan*, no. 8 (August 1994), p. 16.   16 Li, *Grundstruktur*, p. 141.
17 *Banyuetan*, no. 11 (November 1994), p. 12.
18 The other is enterprise debts and liabilities. See *Renmin ribao* [*People's Daily*] (overseas ed.), February 1, 1994 (hereinafter *RMRB*).
19 In China, "society" [*shehui*] is conceived as the "great public" realm beyond the work units.

that belongs to the factory, from which it may receive an office, furniture, and start-up capital, and is then authorized to engage in "business." For example, even Shanghai's BOMT (Bureau of Marine Transportation, an enormous "iron rice bowl") has been reorganized into a "consortium" or "group of companies" (*jituan gongsi*) that are subdivided into smaller, more specialized units. In an attempt to rationalize the division of labor, firms also subdivide into manufacturing and commercial units. A young worker in the No. 4 Electric Fan Factory in Shanghai noted that his firm now consisted of four distinct *danweis*:

> Now *danwei*s consist of [both] *chang*s and *gongsi*. A *chang* is engaged in production, a *gongsi* is engaged in sales. This is all to eliminate "all eating in the big pot" [*chi da guofan*]. Now more people have responsibility. Every *chang*, every *gongsi*, is relatively independent, each has its own salary scale. Each division corresponds to a different product.[20]

The personnel usually remain the same, with new assignments. Thus at least one function of the new units is to soak up surplus or underemployed labor, a problem that is notoriously endemic to China's large SOEs. In this model, the SOE provides some subsidies to the new entities in the beginning, but the new firms eventually become totally independent of their "parent." The aforementioned HSFC is among the SOEs that have successfully set up new corporate entities, including factories as well as trading companies. The new enterprises that HSFC helped to establish hired more than 700 former employees from HSFC and became profitable operations.[21] In one new, recently constructed harbor in Shanghai, the labor savings were significant – the number of workers was reduced from 2,000 to 600, of which one-half were seconded to *disan chanye* spinoff firms.[22] A tertiary enterprise is apparently authorized to engage in any sort of trade, even if it is completely unrelated to the factory (e.g., steel). In most cases there is however a tendency for the business interests of the tertiary enterprise to dovetail with those of the parent firm. Thus a publication house in Shanghai (Shanghai *dabao chubanshe*) spun off a calendar printing division, and a young female staff photographer related:

> We also have a tertiary industry, and it compensated for our bimonthly pictorial magazine [*huabao*], which incurred losses [*kui benle*]. Our tertiary sector produces calendars with girls' photos on them, and they make a profit. Thus the reform polcies really improved our lives [laughs]. Another [project] is to

---

20 Interview #D9, Shanghai, July 1993.   21 *Banyuetan*, no. 11, p. 12.
22 Interview #D15, Shanghai, July 1993.

have new entities provide the routine service functions that were once provided by the SOE itself.[23]

However, as indicated below, progress has been limited. Many SOEs and administrative units have faced difficulties in downsizing. Not many *disan chanye* are very successful in their businesses, and many still rely on subsidies from their parent companies.[24]

Even before the onset of reform, central planning in China had been much more fragmented and rudimentary than in the former USSR or the more advanced Eastern European socialist republics. Many welfare provisions were thus spun off and downloaded to work units at various levels. The work unit sphere, often termed the "small public" (*xiaogong*), had to service the needs of its members for such a long time that these units began to amass their own surpluses. Thus one big enterprise in Shanghai owns more than twenty buses just to convey its workforce to and from their factory jobs, being used only twice a day for less than two hours altogether (while public buses are extremely crowded).[25] Unlike the Soviet Union, where public housing in major cities was controlled and allocated by municipal housing authorities, public housing in China was in most cases built and allocated by work units. Work units, not the state, had property rights, even though it was the state that appropriated budgets (or at least subsidies) for housing construction. According to one statistical report, by the late 1980s over 80 percent of the housing in China was owned by work units.[26] Moreover, work units will evidently continue to dispose of some housing even after urban housing reform, which is aimed at the privatization of housing.

Contrary to early hopes that such reforms as "tertiary industry" would reduce the welfare functions of the *danwei* by providing more open, socially oriented rather than exclusive, community-oriented services, in some cases the welfare responsibilities of the *danwei* have actually been intensified. This may be attributed to a number of factors. First, as employees in SOEs grow older, many units must provide services that did not exist before, such as retirement homes, clinics, funeral homes, or new housing.[27] Inclusive service obligations are a major drain on the resources of many a money-losing SOE.

---

23 Interview #D8, Shanghai, July 1993.   24 See *Liaowang*, November 21, 1994, pp. 10–18.
25 Oral communication from a former Shanghai resident, based on observations made in 1992.
26 *Zhongguo chengshi jianzhu nianjian* [*Yearbook of urban construction in China*] (Beijing: Zhongguo jianzhu chubanshe, 1989).
27 Since 1978, direct state investment in urban housing has decreased dramatically. Work units have become the main investors in housing. They must raise funds themselves to finance residential projects. Housing built with "self-raised funds" by units counted for 60% of the new urban housing in the 1980s; in some cities, the proportion was as high as 80%. *Zhongguo chengshi*, p. 138.

Ironically, while there is pressure on the units to cut costs, there is parallel pressure on the SOEs to be economically self-sufficient (often meaning: download tasks to the unit). The case of a paper mill in Shijiazhuang illustrates these new developments: The mill, with some 2,000 employees, was a model enterprise in the mid-1980s for its successful *chengbao* (contracting out by individuals) to a purchasing agent of the factory. Yet after a few years of rare prosperity, the factory was once again facing enormous difficulties in the early 1990s. When asked why, the manager (who had seen both good times and bad), responded:

> Now the government advocates we "stop enterprises from running a small society" – enterprises should externalize the many services within the *danwei* organization they run and leave it to society to provide them. But there is no society yet, how can I stop running my own?

He admits that, to build a cordial manager–employee relationship, he went beyond implementing rules and following strict guidelines. He paid close attention to the daily life of his employees. The factory not only built apartment housing for employees and used involuntary funds raised by other units to build "public projects," it also regularly provided retirees with miscellaneous needed materials (e.g., lending factory cars to employees who needed them for weddings).[28]

Under the Maoist economic model, retirees and unemployed workers were either taken care of by the units or absorbed administratively; in some SOEs, over one-half of the personnel are retirees. Reform implied the externalization of these responsibilities. China began to experience serious bottlenecks in industrial reform, partly due to the lack of a safety net providing social welfare for retirees. One of the reasons why the 1993–1994 industrial reform of inefficient SOEs stalled is that units could not simply lay off people without an established social security system.[29] This poses a dilemma to the authorities, for the state sector has been losing money and its share of total GDP has been shrinking. To establish an efficient market economy and sustain long-term growth, the state sector must be reformed and downsized. This ranked high on the agenda of reforms introduced at the party's 15th Congress in September 1997, for example. On the other hand, the state sector continues to employ most of the working population, especially in large

28 Interview #L3, Shijiazhuang, December 1993.
29 Originally, China planned to take a major step in reforming the SOEs in January 1994. However, due to strong local resistance, the reforms have been slowed, seemingly stalled. See *New York Times*, June 18, 1995.

urban areas.[30] Too much downsizing would cause widespread discontent, likely aimed at the communist regime itself. Thus, as a long-time SOE reform watcher put it, "the state seems to have decided to keep pumping in *anding tuanjie fei* (funds to maintain stability and unity)" – subsidies to keep the SOEs afloat – to avoid social unrest.[31]

Second, many work units must provide funding for public projects that were previously funded by the state. This is a result of a new practice, "social fund-raising" (*shehui jizi*): Instead of relying on the state to provide funds for public projects (e.g., schools, public roads, the maintenance of public works), local governments are expected to raise funds themselves, and they then turn to local units to share the costs. The long-standing responsibilty to provide public goods has been exacerbated by the growing budgetary constraints on the state (which has incurred a substantial deficit for much of the reform period). Nonetheless, the unit is also under pressure to become economically self-sufficient. Of course, the norm of self-sufficiency (*zeli gengshen*) is hardly new, dating all the way back to Yanan, but in a market context it takes on a new meaning, shifting focus from collective solidarity to entrepreneurialism. This contributes to a reduction of the focus on control and greater reliance on economic incentives to motivate members. The legitimacy of the *danwei* leadership becomes tied to its performance in improving the livelihood of unit employees; to safeguard their positions, *danwei* leaders must do better at providing perquisites and services to members.

THE IMPACT OF REFORM ON HUMAN RELATIONS

One of the major concerns of our study is how the reform of the *danwei* system has affected human relations (*renji guanxi*) within and among work units.

Definitions

The informal norm of *danwei* interaction is *guanxi*. *Guanxi* refers to a personal, value-rational relationship based on one of several possible primordial

---

30 Despite the relative growth of the collective and private sectors in terms of their contributions to GDP, the proportion of the Chinese labor force employed by SOEs was 18% in 1978 and 18% in 1993, meaning that there were 35 million more Chinese working in SOEs in 1993 than in 1978. Moreover, SOEs accounted for 70% of the total industrial investment in 1993, an increase from 61% in 1989. Jeffrey D. Sachs and Wing Thye Woo, "Understanding China's economic performance," unpublished paper, Harvard University and University of California at Davis, January 1996, p. 8.

31 This comment was made by Su Ya, who studied and published a number of works on the SOEs, at a seminar at Columbia University in March 1995. Ms. Su pointed out that if the SOEs in Guangzhou were to begin downsizing and/or declaring bankruptcy today, there would be some 200,000 people unemployed, 150,000 without salaries, and half a million people receiving only a fraction of their salaries.

attributes.[32] Although often associated with corrupt transactions, *guanxi* are not deemed corrupt when they involve private parties. The use of *guanxi* to induce cadre complaisance however transcends the formal organizational role prescriptions sanctioned by the regime. "[The] connection is established to mutual advantage," an official newspaper editorialized, "people trying to establish such connections must have something to offer – power, money, or material objects – or they are not qualified to join the ranks."[33] Reform has had an impact on *guanxi* both within and between units. First, the former:

Intraunit relations. Economic reform has had a number of consequences on intraunit relations. First, the proliferation of new types of organizational entities (such as tertiary industries) has offered opportunities for long-standing intraunit connections to formalize their relationship profitably simply by persuading the authorities to provide the necessary authorization and resources:

> Three of our leaders got together to form a trading company, three old pals known as the iron triangle [*tie san jiao*], part of a *disan chanqiye.* . . . They just decided to do this – have some *guanxi* with the higher-ups. Can get assigned some ships for freight, etc. We use *hetong* now – if I leave work, I sign a contract. Not too formal, not a big change. If you sign, you get a position and salary.[34]

And the proliferation of quasiformal units has been quite remarkable – there are literally units within units:

> Another issue is *danwei zhong de danwei* [unit within the unit]. For instance, in our *jiguan*, the *mishu qu* [secretariat] runs its own copying service, newsletter editing office, runs a bookstore, also sells Chinese paintings. Nobody knows how much money each small unit [*danwei zhizhong you danwei*] makes. This is called *ge xian shentong* [everyone utilize their own advantages]. There is no clear stipulation or rule about this. Some of the income or revenue that these small units earn may be shared by the larger units. But you can be sure that it's a very small proportion.[35]

32 By "value-rational relationship" we mean one that is valued as an end in itself, rather than being limited to the achievement of some short-term transaction and thereafter disposable, like a paper towel. Of course such relationships also have a short-term utility, but they differ from instrumental relationships in the perceived need to preserve them beyond the immediate end in question. By "primordial" we mean ties formed relatively early in the life cycle, such as kinship, common geographic origin, the "old school tie," or some other bonding experience. See Lowell Dittmer, "Chinese informal politics," *The China Journal* (July 1995); and Dittmer and Yu-shan Wu, "The modernization of Chinese factionalism," *World Politics* 47: 4 (July 1995), pp. 467–495.
33 *Tianjin ribao* [*Tianjin Daily*], December 9, 1981.
34 Interview #D10, Shanghai, July 1993.
35 Interview #L1, Shijiazhuang, December 1993.

Although such arrangements are now formalized in the form of an "agreement" (*hetong*) or "contract" (*chengbao*), the discretionary, informal manner in which they are formed may arouse suspicion. This is perhaps particularly true when the resulting tertiary enterprise promptly prospers. As one SOE employee complained:

> Yes, corruption is very serious in China – everyone is engaged in business. I don't like *disan chanye*. Shanghai Magic Troupe runs a restaurant on *disan chanye*. It solves the unemployment problem, but corruption is very serious, because there is no superior organization to monitor it. Also no financial regularization – the accountant is appointed by the boss, and can keep two sets of books.[36]

The government cadre in Shijiazhuang confirmed that, in their zeal to raise capital and invest in new enterprises and otherwise realize their full entrepreneurial potential, the tertiary enterprises would take many shortcuts:

> Also, the "grey area" [*huise quyu*] has been expanding. In many cases, where the rules are not quite clear, people are very resourceful in getting around them. And sometimes, even if there are clear rules, units still try to do what they want. For example, *ji zi jian fang* (pulling together funds for housing), in this unit they ask individual personnel to put in a certain amount of money with an annual interest return of 30%, which is against the outside rules, but still, they did it.[37]

Second, there are some indications that competition and the growing differentiation of personal incomes made relations among *danwei* members "tense," at least in the beginning, when the gap between personal incomes became conspicuous. As one informant put it, "people are used to the situation where everyone ate from a big rice bowl (*chi daguofan*) and earned more or less the same." In work units, where the discrepancy among salaries and other incomes is substantial, people tend to maintain good relations with those who have similar incomes. Also contributing to intraunit tensions is the more open, less exclusive personal relations that have emerged with the possibilities of employee mobility and transunit connections. This is especially evident where a unit does not have a common living compound and people go their own ways after work.

Third, even in the most traditional SOEs, marketization and greater personal mobility have led to a decline of official control over unit membership, which has in turn led to a decrease in enthusiam for pursuing good *guanxi*

---

36 Interview #D14, Shanghai, August 1993.   37 Interview, Shijiazhuang, December 1993.

with *danwei* leaders. Several informants indicated that, so long as they had no interest in promotion to a political position (*sheng guan*), they saw no need to cultivate good *guanxi*. On the other hand, if someone wants to be promoted, especially but not exclusively to political positions, or wants a change of housing assignment, skill at cultivating connections (*shou wan*, or "hand play") could still be quite useful.

Fourth, in terms of whom one is most likely to pursue good *guanxi* with, our informants indicated that such connections are most highly valued with unit leaders and supervisers (*shangji*), less highly valued with colleagues and peers (*tongshi*), and least valued with subordinates (*xiaji*) – the circulation of flattery (*pai ma pi*) moves from bottom to top. This in itself represents no departure from the Maoist era, but some informants suggest, interestingly, the desirability of avoiding friendships within the unit. "One should not mix *guanxi*," opined some (not all) respondents. Real friends to whom one can bare one's innermost thoughts can only exist outside the unit, beyond the range of rumor networks or criticism and self-criticism sessions. This suggests, perhaps, an emerging differentiation of value-rational and purpose-rational connections.

Fifth, the coexistence of two kinds of ownership – public and private – has led an increasing number of people to opt to straddle the two (the so-called one family, two systems deal): One person works in a state sector unit where welfare and services (including health insurance, cheap housing, and child care) are provided (i.e., one "eats the royal grain" [*huang liang*]) while the spouse works in a private enterprise where salaries are higher and there are more opportunities for upward mobility. Housing remains one of the most contested provisions on which sometimes intense "connection pulling" (*la guanxi*) takes place among *danwei* members. The privatization of housing, which has already begun in some cities, may eventually ameliorate this situation, obviating the need for one family, two systems.

Finally, the growing significance of the *danwei* in the commercial supply of materiel and services has also given *danwei* leaders greater discretion over resource allocation. Cadres seem to batten disproportionately on reform, monopolizing not only economic resource flows, but also the stream of extra-unit information. As one Shanghai teacher notes:

> However, some leaders themselves got a better apartment [larger, better view, higher floor]. People in charge of assigning housing actively do their best to see to it that leaders get the best housing. If it's unified distribution by the government [*tongyi fenpei*], would the *danwei* leaders have gotten better housing? [N.B. This is a government unit.] Of course, if the housing were assigned by the government, there would still be *renqing* and *houmen* where people could use *guanxi*. But the *danwei* leaders would not have such an easy time. The main-

tenance and development of the *danwei suoyouzhi* really benefit the *danwei* leaders a great deal, so they are most active in preserving such a system.[38]

It is intriguing to note that the units in which members felt their units were doing well economically and were themselves generally satisfied with their place in the unit were those in which no one knew exactly how much money the unit leaders disposed of and how they dispensed it among the staff.

Guanxi is not only cultivated to optimize personal gain, it may also be used by organizations (e.g., work units, particularly *qiye danwei*) to achieve certain goals, economic and otherwise. The interest in promoting "tertiary industry" (commerce and services) amplifies the need to cultivate good *guanxi* with other units. As one factory supply and purchasing agent put it, "pulling strings" (*la guanxi*) "is vital and legitimate because while others do it for private purposes, I do it for public [*gong*] purposes, for our work unit. Leaders in my unit fully support me."[39] He made an interesting but suggestive observation on the thin line between a corrupt practice of *guanxi* and a noncorrupt, nonetheless immoral one: "I spent two years in prison for embezzlement. Still, the leaders of this unit wanted me because I have an uncle who is an official in a state timber mill and they need lumber. Now I have realized that only fools embezzle. They have to do it illicitly at the risk of breaching the law. Smart ones do it openly. Now I am living a luxurious life but do not have to pay for it. It is all covered under the category of socializing expenses, not embezzlement."[40]

Lin Yimin has noted this utilitarian aspect of *guanxi*, arguing that "effective *guanxi* networking with state agents was a necessary condition for the success of economic organizations in the 1980s."[41] One Shanghai informant cited the case of Huzhou City in Zhejiang province, where the workers protested to their leaders that they should not have so many banquets. In response, the leaders in fact cut down on their celebratory expenses. But paradoxically, the unit soon found that its business prosperity and income levels had nosedived. So the unit mandated its leaders to go ahead and have more feasts. However, *guanxi* may be becoming less important in the context of market reform because of the money factor: State agencies can be bought if the price is right. The cost varies with the status and bureaucratic leverage of the target:

> A teacher of a graduating class can probably get a lot of bribes, also the graduate office. But if you bribe the leader of BOMT, it costs much more, maybe 2,000 *yuan*. But it's worth it to get a good job.[42]

38 Interview, Shanghai, July 1993.   39 Interview #LT1, Tianjin, September 1992.   40 Ibid.
41 Lin Yimin, "*Guanxi*, the state, and inter-organizational stratification in post-Mao China," unpub. paper, University of California Center for Chinese Studies, Berkeley, 1992.
42 Interview #D10, Shanghai, August 1993.

In the market, one need no longer cultivate *guanxi* but must pay a variable sum of money. This is not to deny the utility of *guanxi*, which is still a cheaper and more effective way of getting through, all other conditions being equal. We also found no clear consensus on the impact of the market – while some say it makes *guanxi* obsolescent, others point out that cadres may be willing to exchange needed services or licenses for gifts or professions of endearment but not for cash. *Guanxi* is used not only for such tangible gains as a tax writeoff or an export license, but to gain influence. As one media report put it, "if you strain your relations [with a senior cadre] to the breaking point, he can . . . turn off the engine of your car and stall your movement. But he also can lubricate the engine well and make it go fast."[43] Or, as another report put it, "the official seal does not count so much as a good word put in by someone."[44]

"Familization" of the Danwei

One of the most noteworthy yet least discussed developments in postreform urban work units, especially state agencies and administrative organs, has to do with their "familization" (*chundai guanxi*). Whereas patron–clientelism[45] has existed throughout the history of the CCP, nepotism is a relatively new form of informal relations in the post-Mao period.[46] A public circular of the CCP Central Committee reveals the scope of the problem of *renren weiqin* (selecting people by familial or lineage ties) in the party's organizational work:

> There are some problems in our current work of cadre selection and appointment. The most salient ones include: (1) some leading cadre select cadres according to their own personal standards or to their own needs and interests, or out of feudal kinship values, violating the principles of the Party and dis-

---

43 *RMRB*, February 7, 1982.   44 *RMRB*, February 1, 1982.
45 See, for example, Oi, *State and Peasant*; and Walder, *Neo-Traditionalism*. A similar approach has been taken in the analysis of other Leninist and less developed systems; see, for example, S. N. Eisenstadt and R. Lemarchand, eds., *Political Clientelism, Patronage and Development* (London: Macmillan, 1982); Nobutaka Ike, *Japanese Politics: Patron-Client Democracy*, 2nd ed. (New York: Knopf, 1972); and Steffen W. Schmidt, *Friends, Followers and Factions: A Reader in Political Clientelism* (Berkeley: University of California Press, 1977).
46 In post-1949 China, the hierarchical status of personnel and units is very significant, because it is closely linked to the treatment and privileges that the person or unit may enjoy. The higher the rank, the better the treatment and the more the privilege. Rank in the official hierarchy entails not only salary scale, but also access to vital information, such as who can read what internal circular from which level of party or state organ. For example, when a CCP Central Committee document is issued, it has different levels of readership, reflecting the degree of confidentiality. The higher the rank of the *danwei*, the more information available; this prompts the *danwei* to seek a higher ranking. See Dittmer, "The politics of publicity in reform China," in Chin-Chuan Lee, ed., *China's Media, Media's China* (Boulder: Westview Press, 1994), pp. 89–113.

cipline of the organization; (2) some use *"zouhoumen"* [taking the back door] through various means to select or promote their own relatives and friends; (3) some abuse their office to engage in illicit exchanges; (4) some scramble hard to increase the rank and treatment [*daiyu*] of their units or sector [*xitong*], disregarding policies and regulations; (5) some comrades who are in charge of organizational work misperform their duty.[47]

Many cadres have people with direct family or lineage ties working in the same agency. Although most notorious in Western media with regard to favored children of high cadres, or "princelings," this is not an isolated phenomenon – it is found from the central ministries down to rice-roots level agencies, from military units to educational institutions. A popular satire illustrates its ubiquity: "Pop–son bureau, hubby–wife section, son pours water for dad, grandson drives for granny, spouses share an office desk" (*fuzi chu, fuqi ke, erzi daocha laodie he, sunzi dangsiji, yuanyang gongyong bangongzhuo*). In the Ministry of Justice, 20 percent of some 500 staff members have relatives in one way or another working in the same ministry.[48] Among the 850 personnel of the State Statistics Bureau, 15 percent (130 people) have kin relations within the bureau.[49] In the county government agencies in a remote northern province, 68 of 148 cadres who held important positions had relatives working in the same agencies, of whom 27 children worked with their parents, four couples shared the same office, and 23 people had cousins, uncles, brothers-in-law, or godchildren working in the same agencies.[50] In the same province, of the 84 cadres in a prefecture court, 17 were related in one way or another; one deputy chief-judge had his wife and daughter both working under one roof.[51] According to another investigation of 1,499 cadres and workers in seven urban *danwei*, there were 87 couples (2 county-level, 14 section-level, and 71 general staff): 141 people with parent–child ties, 26 siblings, and 85 with in-law relations working in the same unit. Whereas 25 families had three or more people working together, 79 people had relatives working in one of the seven units. This means that over one-half (56.7 percent) of the cadres and staff workers were related in one way or another.[52]

47 *RMRB*, February 2, 1986.
48 Xia Xin, "Huibi, weile qinglian" [Avoidance, for the sake of being clean and upright], in Liu Jialin and He Xian, *Huibi zhidu jiangxi* [*An analysis of the law of avoidance*] (Beijing: Zhongguo renshi chubanshe, 1990).
49 Cheng Ying, "Qianbaiwan ganbu mianlin dajingjian" (Hundreds of thousands of officials are facing streamlining), *Jiushi niandai* [*The nineties*], November 1992, pp. 31–33.
50 Yu Shaojun and Dai Guanxiong, "Guanyu danwei neibu ganbu qinshujuji zhuangkuang de diaocha" (An investigation on the internal conglomeration of relatives in work units), *Lilun xuekan* [*Journal of Theoretical Studies*] 5 (May 1986), pp. 22–26.
51 Yu and Dai, "Investigation."
52 This investigation was conducted by the *ganbu* division of the Yiyang Prefecture Personnel Bureau, Hunan Province, in 1989.

Another investigation reveals that "inbreeding" is not limited to administrative agencies: Of 14 SOEs investigated, the number of employees grew from 2,154 in 1983 to 4,006 in 1989, an 86 percent increase. During this six-year period, the number of employees who were related directly or indirectly increased 4.75 times – from 251 to 1,422! The percentage of related employees among total employees increased from 11.6 to 33 percent;[53] among these lineage relations, 92 percent were nuclear relatives (spouses, parent-children, and siblings). The most startling case is a local supply and marketing cooperative in Hunan province, where 302 of the 409 employees (75%) had some kind of familial relation.[54] Even in the supposedly most modern institution, the military, the problem exists. In a PLA air force division headquarters, eight out of twelve division-rank officers were either related to each other or to someone in the same division.[55] In local administrative agencies nationwide, it is estimated that 10 percent of all cadres have relatives working in the same agency and in some places as many as 30 percent.[56] Although there have been some local efforts to remedy the problem,[57] a nationwide regulation or law of avoidance has yet to become effective with the overall reform of the officialdom toward a "state public servant" system. The problem still haunts state agencies and other organizations: In a 1993 commentary, the PLA Daily revealed that the problem of "cadre inbreeding" is far from being solved, even in the military.[58]

Why has inbreeding become so pervasive? There are at least three reasons: (1) Under the state socialist system, incoming personnel usually expect their work unit to take care of the job assignment of their spouses as well. One relatively unusual arrangement is that discharged servicemen and their families were assigned jobs in a work unit and its adjuncts. This policy, made in the wake of the major military retrenchment of 1 million servicemen in the mid-1980s, was aimed at absorbing a large number of ex-military officers, many of whom were from rural areas and hence not as easily sundered from their families as urban professionals. (2) In the late 1970s, the practice of *dingti* (replacement of retired workers or cadres with their child[ren] or other

---

53 Yang Guan, "Qiye 'jiazu' xianxiang" (The phenomenon of "familization" in enterprises), *Shehui* [*Society*] 4 (April 1991), pp. 42–45.

54 Liu and He, *Huibi zhidu*.

55 Jin Bang, "Zhide yinqi renmen yanzhong zhuyi de weiti: Hebeisheng bufen shixian jiguan qinshuhua weiti diaocha" (A serious problem worth our attention: An investigation of familialization in some cities and counties of Hebei province), *Hebei shelian tongxun* [*Bulletin of the Hebei Social Science Association*], December 1986, pp. 44–46.

56 Li and He, *Huibi*.

57 For example, the authorities in Tongling City, Anhui Province, where 89% of the *ke* rank and 10% of the county rank officials had relatives in the same units, announced its decision to implement a system of avoidance in 1988. See Liu and He, *Huibi*, pp. 206–207.

58 *Jiefang junbao* [*People's Liberation Army Daily*] (hereinafter *JFJB*), May 4, 1993.

relatives) was officially sanctioned and became common,[59] as well as the policy of "internal recruitment" (*neizhao*) – hiring the children of enterprise or agency employees before searching outside.[60] The old personal network ties were thus transmitted from one generation to the next, further inbreeding human relations within the unit. (3) The need to rectify "historical" problems, notably consequences of the Cultural Revolution, is also involved. These include bringing together separated couples who had worked in different units,[61] returning educated urban youth who were sent to the countryside,[62] restoring agencies that were dismantled during the years of chaos, and rehabilitating "purged" cadres.

In a detailed study of the postrevolutionary elite in China, Lee noted one remarkable aspect: Despite ten years of chaos and purges, most cadres managed to regain their political power.[63] Indeed, many rehabilitated officials became ardent reformers. Yet the rehabilitation of cadres entailed reassigning those cadres to high-level posts, which was particularly difficult in the context of the "reform" emphasis on younger and better educated cadres. Intervention by family members into the decision involving job assignments further complicated cadre rehabilitation, particularly among cadres with posi-

---

59 Although it was a practice that preceded the Cultural Revolution, *dingti* only became fully legitimate at this time. With thousands of youth returned from the countryside and thousands more graduating from high schools, the government gave the green light to its implementation to reduce the pressure of urban unemployment. Indeed, as early as 1953, "the revised draft of the labor insurance regulations" introduced the idea of occupational inheritance. In the years that followed, many circulars and directives were issued on this matter, most notable of which is the number of restrictions and qualifications that the government placed on the practice of *dingti*. The policy seems to have been essentially reactive rather than active in the sense that most of the documents were replies by the central authorities to local or ministerial authorities on the matter. This has prompted some scholars to suggest that the regulations represent a codification of practices long established at the grass roots under local sanction. See Michel Korzec, *Occupational Inheritance in the People's Republic of China* (Amsterdam: University of Amsterdam, Department of South and Southeast Asian Studies, no. 57, 1985). On *dingti*, see also Gail Henderson, "Danwei: The Chinese Work Unit" (PhD Dissertation, University of Michigan, 1982), subsequently published as Gail Henderson and Myron Cohen, *The Chinese Hospital: A Socialist Work Unit* (New Haven: Yale University Press, 1984), p. 31, and Thomas B. Gold, "Back to the city: The return of Shanghai's educated youth," *China Quarterly* 84 (1981).
    What concerns us here, however, is not the practice itself but its consequences. As Korzec noted, the actual process of replacing retired workers or cadres was often plagued by irregularities and the use of *guanxi*.
60 The official endorsement of the practice of *dingti* began with State Council Circular no. 104, issued in June 1978, which stipulated that in the state-owned enterprises one child of a retired employee was allowed to "replace" the parent. It lasted until October 1986, when another State Council document invalidated the practice.
61 Due to tight restrictions on migration or the transfer from work units before the reforms, there were many married couples who worked in different places for years.
62 To absorb this large labor force and avoid unemployment, the government was pressed to allow practices such as *dingti* and *neizhao*. Each work unit was responsible to a certain degree for finding work for the children of its employees. One of the ways was the opening of "labor service companies." See Gold, "Back to the City," 1981.
63 See Hong Yung Lee, *From Revolutionary Cadres to Party Technocrats in Socialist China* (Berkeley: University of California Press, 1991).

tions above division chief (*chuzhang*). If family members (usually spouses) found the new job assignment undesirable, they might go to the party organization department, pulling old strings and exerting pressure on previous subordinates. A case cited by the CCP Central Organization Department is illustrative: During a *danwei* leadership shuffle in 1980, an old cadre expressed his intention to retire from his formal position and become an "advisor." The party committee of his unit accepted his request and prepared to select his successor. However, once news of his retirement reached his home, his decision was not welcomed by his family. The cadre changed his mind and declared to the party committee that his prior decision "does not count." His wife then proceeded to call each member of the committee, putting them under heavy pressure. Only after intervention from the higher level was agreement reached to confirm the original decision.[64]

DYNAMICS OF ORGANIZATIONAL CHANGE

How can we make sense of these developments at the basic level of the Chinese political and social hierarchy? We conceive of the *danwei* under reform as the product of dialectical cross-pressures: On the one hand, the historical legacy and structural constraints still exert a powerful impact on the internal and external relations of the *danwei*; on the other hand, it is a social structure that shows signs of disintegrating under the impact of marketization, loss of faith in the CCP and its legitimating doctrines, and the liberalization of the household registration regime. The *danwei* system no longer monopolizes *guanxi* as it once did, and there are now transunit *guanxi* – although they are still relatively rare and fraught with a sense of risk. There are signs that a new set of norms is emerging, according to which *xiangxia*, or vertical *guanxi*, are deemed at least mildly distasteful, "feudal," and corrupt while horizontal connections, often formalized in contractual terms, are considered efficient and progressive.

To better capture the nature of informal relations in the *danwei* system and to better understand their changes, we propose a model of organizational change consisting of two transformational options: *evolution* and *involution*. These are conceptual "ideal types" only; they are also meant to be "value-neutral." There are both structural and behavioral dimensions of each pattern, to wit:

Involutionary Organization (neotraditionalism): inward, closed, cellular structure; "soft" budget constraint; elaboration of existing modes of operation; informal, ritualistic, faction-prone

---

64 *Zugong tongxin* [*Bulletin of Organizational Work*] 190 (December 17, 1981).

Evolutionary   Organization (marketization): outward, open, flexible structure; "hard" budget constraint; adoption of new modes of operation; formal, procedural; rule-oriented

The evolutionary pattern corresponds roughly to the "modernization" paradigm that has informed Western theories of political development since Marx and Weber: It is conducive to rationalization, individualization, commercialization, and so forth. The involutionary pattern is somewhat more novel, necessitating a brief digression.

The concept of involution was borrowed from the anthropologist Alexander Goldenweiser by Clifford Geertz to characterize the Indonesian cultivation system set up in 1830 by then Governor-General Johannes van den Bosch to prop up the ailing finances of the Netherlands. It consisted of the extensive cultivation of cash crops (predominantly coffee) in a commercial, "swidden" sector on the one hand, and the intensive cultivation of rice and sugar in a subsistence "sawah" sector on the other. Whereas swidden agriculture was highly successful and remunerative, spreading rapidly throughout the outer islands, the sawahs had to absorb the surplus population from commercial agriculture and cultivate their limited land area with ever greater intensity and static technology. The sawahs thus became "involuted," that is, "having reached what would seem to be a definitive form, [they] nonetheless fail either to stabilize or transform themselves into a new pattern but rather continue to develop by becoming internally more complicated."[65] Involution is said to exhibit a "late Gothic" quality, with intricate tenure systems, complex labor arrangements, and an "increasing tenacity of basic pattern, internal elaboration and ornateness; technical hairsplitting, and unending virtuosity." While Geertz's initial formulations have subsequently come under criticism for their flawed explanations of how the pattern came about, for his characterization of involutionary social structure as "shared poverty," and other points, the essence of the involutionary pattern itself – functionally irrelevant internal elaboration in response to developmental blockage – seems to have survived intact.[66]

The concept of involution in this broad sense has recently been enlisted by Chinese historians to illuminate our understanding of Chinese rural economic

---

65 Clifford Geertz, *Agricultural Involution: The Process of Ecological Change in Indonesia* (Berkeley: University of California Press, 1963), here quoting Goldenweiser, "Loose ends of a theory on the individual pattern and involution in primitive society," in R. Lowie, ed., *Essays in Anthropology: Presented to A. L. Kroeber* (Berkeley: University of California Press, 1936), pp. 99–104.

66 Cf. R. E. Elson, *The Cultivation System and "Agricultural Involution"* (Monash University, Department of History, 1978). Elson acknowledges Geertz's critique of the system that the peasants remained "firmly entrenched in traditional patterns of production" (p. 11), while challenging the explanation of this stagnation – specifically, that sugarcane cultivation "fences off" the areas of intensive rice cultivation, thereby forcing peasants there into an involutionary pattern of intensive rice cultivation.

development and the Chinese state building process. They have adopted and amplified the concept to depict "technological involution," the central concern of Geertz, what the Potters call "sociological involution" and what Duara calls "political evolution." The former, as in the works of Philip Huang, is described as "involutionary growth (without labor productivity development)" of the Chinese rural economy lasting from prerevolutionary times up to the reform era. Chinese agriculture, Huang contends, had not yet broken out of its involutionary pattern even after years of radical collectivization.[67] Sociological involution, rather than depicting a discrepancy between the growth of production output and the development of productivity, has been applied to the analysis of the state–society relationship in both pre-1949 and post-1949 China.[68] Prasenjit Duara introduces the concept of "state involution" to describe a form of pathology in which state organizations expand not through the increasingly efficient use of existing inputs, "but through the replication, expansion, and elaboration of an inherited pattern of state–society relations."[69] Influenced by this perspective, some analysts of recent Chinese politics see a similar pattern of state penetration in local society not accompanied by a strengthening of central political integration.[70]

We use "organizational involution" in a more specific sense, to depict a possible pattern of development of a revolutionary organization facing the challenges of economic modernization. It is certainly worth hypothesizing that organizational involution implies social and political involution as well (e.g., such involutionary models as Dazhai did tend to minimize the importance of technology in their effort to dramatize human heroism), but we recognize that our present data can neither confirm nor falsify this. Organizational involution may be identified both structurally and behaviorally: Structural features include closed social cellularization containing one or more entrenched personalized networks; behavioral traits center around an elaboration of existing, often traditional, modes of action, predominantly *informal* relationships (e.g., factionalism, *guanxi*) and the proliferation of tacit rules (i.e., rules never formally codified but routinely practiced; e.g.,

67 Cf. Philip Huang, *The Peasant Economy and Social Change in North China* (Stanford: Stanford University Press, 1985), and *The Peasant Family and Rural Development in the Yangzi Delta, 1350–1988* (Stanford: Stanford University Press, 1990).
68 Sulamith and Jack Potter, *China's Peasants: The Anthropology of a Revolution* (New York: Cambridge University Press, 1990).
69 State involution occurs when the state increases tax revenues without expanding social infrastructure or services, resulting in diminished state legitimacy and galloping inflation precipitated by rising deficits. Parasenjit Duara, *Culture, Power and the State: Rural North China, 1900–1942* (Stanford: Stanford University Press, 1988); see also Helen F. Siu, *Agents and Victims in South China: Accomplices in Rural Revolution* (New Haven: Yale University Press, 1989), pp. 273–290.
70 Wang Shaoguang, *Failure of Charisma: The Cultural Revolution in Wuhan* (New York: Oxford University Press, 1995).

years of service to the *danwei* as a standard of seniority in welfare distribution). The relationship between structural and behavioral aspects of the model is reciprocal – structural arrangements confine the behavior of members, while informal rules and relations are an adaptive response to structural constraints.

The basic pattern of development of China's social/economic organizations from 1949 until the onset of reform in 1979 was involutionary. There are three main reasons for this: First, during the Communist revolution, dispersed, self-sufficient organizations were useful in helping the CCP and Red Army to survive. Freely adopting organizational techniques from China's rich legacy of secret societies and lacking financial support from the outside, dispersed guerrilla and party units turned inward to make the best use of their own resources and to shield themselves from hostile penetration. These victorious revolutionary bands became the legendary prototypes for the ideals of the basic unit even when such bonds were no longer functionally necessary.

Second, the *danwei*'s lack of formal autonomy in the administrative hierarchy led to evasive tactics by enterprise managers and unit directors, who had to get around policy guidelines and rules to fill production quotas and cultivate political bases. The formal structure of the Chinese administration is one of "vertically integrated systems" (*chuizhi xitong*), meaning that all important decisions must be made in Beijing; even the acquisition of fixed property worth as little as 100 yuan required specific approval from the relevant central ministry.[71] Thus even before the free market was legitimized, local cadres engaged in "second economy" activities to obtain goods and materials outside the central plan to overcome their dependence on the bureaucracy. The government never ceased fighting what it called "departmentalism" and "small public interests." Informal leadership in turn led to informal politics within the unit, nurturing a dense and complex network of *guanxi*[72] – a pattern that Naughton calls "insularity without autonomy."[73] A *danwei* typically harbored several latent cliques, each maneuvering for the acquisition of offices, housing, and other prized assets. Such informal modes

---

71 Zhou Taihe, ed., *Dangdai Zhongguo de Jingji Tizhi Gaige* [*Economic Reform in Contemporary China*] (Beijing: Chinese Social Science Publishing House, 1984), p. 84; as cited in Suisheng Zhao, "China's central-local relationship: A historical perspective," in Jia Hao and Lin Zhimin, eds., *Changing Central-Local Relations in China* (Boulder: Westview Press, 1994), pp. 19–34. The *danwei* was conceived to be autarkic but never independent, always part of a vertically structured system [*xitong*] in the "central and regional administration" [*tiaotiao kuaikuai*]. Every *danwei* is responsible only to its own system, having minimal relations with other units at the same level.

72 Dittmer and Lu, "Personal Politics," pp. 255–259.

73 Barry Naughton, "*Danwei*: The economic foundation of a unique institution," in Xiaobo Lu and Elizabeth Perry, eds., *Danwei: The Changing Chinese Work Place in Historical and Comparative Perspective* (Armonk, NY: M. E. Sharpe, 1998).

of operation became prevalent during later Maoism and have intensified in the course of reform.[74]

Third, the need to be a multifunctional entity with heavy social service responsibilities, plus soft-budget constraints and loose accounting practices, gave enterprise management an incentive to seek extrabudgetary revenues unknown to higher authorities. Fraudulently reporting profits and expenditures is not rare among SOEs, as units are always well advised to retain extra resources; this has given rise to the so-called small treasury (*xiao jinku*), or unit budget phenomenon. During periods of commodity shortage, units would try to get consumer goods through barter exchange or other routes to provide for their own employees. Enterprises would sometimes operate their own farms or exchange industrial items with peasants for food.[75]

The original impetus for the involutionary trend seems to have been the revolutionary experience, which established the values of communal solidarity and self-reliance, and this trend was then reinforced over the years as the regime cellularized Chinese society into units and relied on these cells as an administrative, redistributive, and socialization device. Thence the pattern has been: External shock (e.g., revolution) sets the organizational parameters, followed by involutionary development reinforcing those parameters. True, there were two subsequent external shocks in the form of the Great Leap Forward and the Cultural Revolution, but these only intensified the involutionary pattern by shaking up the administrative apparatus and turning the unit in on its own resources. Evolution was not an option in this ideologically charged political climate, and there were marked tendencies toward ritualization and factionalism.

The inauguration of reform in 1979 could thus count as the fourth seismic shock to the *danwei*, but its impact has been quite different from the three previous shocks. By decentralizing the bureaucratic apparatus and introducing the market, the reform program functioned to stimulate evolutionary tendencies. But due to the reformers' ambiguous attitude to their political legacy, repudiating the Cultural Revolution and the Great Leap while reaffirming the revolution and Mao Zedong Thought, the involutionary tendency has retained a tenuous but tenacious lease on life. Thus, on the one hand we find numerous indications of evolutionary progress, ranging from the complete dissolution of agricultural "units" (teams, brigades, and communes) to the "modernization" of industrial units by forcing them to support them-

74 For a detailed analysis, see Xiaobo Lu, *Organizational Involution and Official Deviance: A Study of Cadre Corruption in China, 1949–1953*, Ph.D. Dissertation, Political Science Department, University of California at Berkeley, 1994.

75 Xiaobo Lu, "Minor public economy: The revolutionary origins of the *Danwei*," in Lu and Perry, *Danwei*.

selves on the market through sales of service, commerce, or production capacity. On the other hand, the involutionary tendency is still quite widespread, in the form of passive resistance in many large SOEs, some of them operating in the black and winning awards for excellence but most of them running in the red. Yet the involutionary tendency is not necessarily defunct or even technologically Luddite. In the model village of Nanjie, in a backward region of central China, with its 30-foot white marble statue of Mao towering over living quarters housing 3,000 permanent inhabitants and 8,000 temporary workers, the village allegedly decided after 1986, when reforms had failed to lift it from poverty, to recollectivize agricultural land and establish township and village enterprises to absorb surplus manpower and capital. This crimeless village now boasts the biggest instant noodle factory in China, as well as plants producing beer, cakes, and packaging materials.[76]

Involution retains its inward-looking, communitarian focus, but without the egalitarian impact of ideology it has become increasingly particularistic, even nepotistic. As one study notes, the problem of nepotism actually began to appear in the late 1950s, but the party did not pay much attention, believing that the rising communist morality and consciousness would naturally lead people to subordinate their familial and kinship interests to those of the larger collective.[77] It is not that the party failed to realize that old family ties had not been permanently displaced by revolutionary "comradeship," but that its faith in internal transformation rather than external controls led to a frontal assault on residual elements in people's consciousness (as in the Socialist Education Campaign or the Cultural Revolution) at the expense of institutional regulations and rules as the critical mechanism to subdue them. As a recent analysis of the problem noted, cadre nepotism "has made rules and procedures nothing but shallow skeletons, obstructing scientific management . . . it also has further complicated personal relations. Routine and normal operation of intra-Party and intra-unit affairs cannot be carried out smoothly."[78] The upshot is that while more rational, impersonal forms – organizational streamlining, recruitment of capable people – have been imposed in several rounds of administrative reforms, internally developed personal networks have also grown. Typical involutionary tenacity is reflected in the popular saying: "They have their policy, but we have our countermeasures" (*shang you zhengce, xia you duice*). The result has been a lot of foot-dragging, an inability to make decisions, and ineffectiveness in sanctioning deviant organizational behavior.

Such an impasse is often attributed to the lack of a law of avoidance, which according to Chinese administrative historians actually originated in the tra-

---

76 See the account of James Miles, who visited the village, in his *The Legacy of Tiananmen: China in Disarray* (Ann Arbor: University of Michigan Press, 1996).

77 Liu and He, *Huibi*, pp. 50–51.   78 Liu and He, *Huibi*, p. 239.

ditional Chinese bureaucracy.[79] One tenet of this was to avoid appointing officials who were natives of the locality to which they were posted: locality
avoidance. Officials could thus be cut off from their ties to lineage relations,
who in China usually reside in the same locality. After the communist revolution, this practice, along with other types of avoidance (such as avoidance
of relatives in the same state agency), was discontinued.[80] However, at issue
is whether the administrative system – recruitment, promotion, assignment
– can be blamed solely for the incurrent problem, as many Chinese administrative reform advocates claim. In fact, there has been a de facto law of avoidance (posting nonnatives to key positions) since the late 1950s. In the
immediate post-Liberation period, many retired military veterans were put
into administrative posts throughout the country. In the South, northerners
who came south with the PLA during the final battles with the Nationalists
monopolized most of the high- and middle-level regional and provincial positions. The frictions between local cadres (accused of "mountaintopism") and
those from the North (who often did not speak the local dialect) became a
salient issue during the Hundred Flowers campaign.[81] There has been no lack
of cadre rotations and other antisectarian efforts in the history of the CCP.

Thus, due to the ambiguous current status of political reform, there is for
the first time in the PRC something like a free market for both evolutionary
and involutionary tendencies. Further research will be needed to determine
which factors lead a given unit to resolve this issue one way or the other, but
some preliminary hypotheses may be suggested.

First, our data lead us to posit a direct correlation between economic and
political reform within the unit; that is, those units most energetic in adopt-

79 The avoidance principle was first instituted in the Sui dynasty, prohibiting the appointment of local
   officials to offices that had jurisdiction over their native places and barring relatives of senior officials
   from becoming officials in the capital metropolitan area. These rules were reinforced in the Ming period and became more elaborate during the Qing. In the Qing central government organs, persons could
   not have relations in the same office, and in local governments leading officials could not employ close
   relatives. The offices of local officials must not be within 250 km of their place of origin. Sons of senior
   officials above the 3rd rank, viceroys, and grand coordinators could not be censors. Every three or five
   years officials would change offices and positions (to prevent the formation of powerful cliques). When
   officials retired, they were obliged to leave the capital and return to their native places. Zhengyuan
   Fu, *Autocratic Tradition and Chinese Politics* (New York: Cambridge University Press, 1993), pp. 83–84
   et passim.
80 Thus, by December 1981, 43% of the fifty-eight provincial leaders were either natives of the province
   of appointment or had spent most of their working lives there. Zhao, "China's Central-Local," p. 30.
81 In the Chinese context, "localism" refers to both factional collusion on the basis of local ties and the
   unwarranted pursuit of local political and economic interests. The former is a problem of organization, the latter a problem of policy. We use the term here in the first sense. It is worth noting that,
   while Beijing pursued decentralization in economic management during the Great Leap Forward, it
   also assailed (organizational) localism in some provinces, such as Guangdong. See Wang Kuang, "Fandui difangzhuyi" [Oppose localism], *Xuexi* [*Study*] 3 (1958), pp. 9–12; for a good retrospective case
   study, cf. Keith Forster, "Localism, central policy, and the provincial purges of 1957–1958: The case
   of Zhejiang," in Timothy Cheek and Tony Saich, eds., *New Perspectives on State Socialism in China*
   (Armonk, NY: M. E. Sharpe, 1997), pp. 191–234.

ing new economic reforms also tend to be most enterprising in adopting electoral reform for unit offices (i.e., more than one candidate per vacancy), meritocratic promotion and pay, and other noneconomic reforms; while those units least economically and politically innovative often tend to undergo structural decay: a general sense of alienation or "inner migration" among unit members; "complicated" or factionally entrenched intraunit *guanxi* networks; and a tendency to "moonlight" or even to break permanently with the unit. So far as "corruption" is concerned, the trend is not yet clear (one must also take into account different understandings of corruption – for example, many Chinese workers seem to feel that the equal distribution of bonuses or promotions based on seniority is more "fair" than distribution strictly according to merit), but we suspect that the two models will give rise to different *forms* of corruption, involution being more conducive to "traditional" corruption (nepotism, factionalism, *xiao jinku*) and evolution to more "modern" forms (bribery, tax evasion).

If economic and political reforms tend to be positively correlated, what causes both? While a number of factors are undoubtedly involved, including location (southern and eastern coasts) and central policy (external shocks), we find that those units with relatively brief or nondescript traditions and tenuous structures are more likely to embrace reform than those with entrenched structures and illustrious traditions. Most likely to be interested in reform are JVs and private enterprises, followed by *disan chanye* firms, township and village enterprises, and collectives. Exogenous variables remaining equal, large, old, prestigious units (such as Shanghai's BOMT) are not apt to be in the vanguard of either economic or political reform. This is because such units, like the Party Center itself, have a hallowed tradition to uphold (and a great many employees and other vested interests at risk).

What difference does it make for political life within the *danwei* whether a unit is pro- or antireform? Contrary to Lieberthal's hypothesis of an inverse relationship between the strength of formal and informal institutions (i.e., the stronger the formal structure the weaker the informal, and vice versa),[82] our preliminary findings are that the strong, traditional *danwei* are inclined to have well-articulated factions and a vigorous (but sometimes divisive) informal political life while the weak, almost nonexistant *danwei* found in (say) the JVs have relatively little factionalism or informal politics. Thus we would infer that the relationship between formal and informal structure is not inverse but positive, or "balance-of-power" (i.e., strong power arouses strong counterpower). The reasons for a positive correlation are not only struc-

---

82 Kenneth Lieberthal, *Governing China: From Revolution through Reform* (New York: W. W. Norton, 1995), Chap. 7.

tural; they also have to do with the fact that weaker units are most fully immersed in economic reform — and the impact of reform on the basic unit is essentially disintegrative, to wit:

(1) Exposure to the market economy has a rationalizing effect on all values, including *guanxi*. Loyalty (and other sentiments) tends to be recalculated in monetary terms, so that everything (and everyone) has its price — the future is discounted.

(2) The market is a great equalizer: as soon as a unit is put on the market and told to live on its profits, it begins to regard itself as a *gongsi*, that is, autonomous from the parent organization.[83] A member of the BOMT discussed the plans of that unit to get into direct competition with the COSCO, the corresponding national shipping company under the State Council. When asked whether the COSCO might not welcome such an intrusion, the response was, "We don't have to look at their face." Thus, BOMT branches have been set up in Thailand, with plans for additional branches in Japan and Singapore and eventually even the United States. "We have good *guanxi* with the marine administration," he explained. "So we have the right." The leader of a *qiye* (enterprise) explained the contractual arrangements his firm would make with a (county-level) factory manager, including provision for division of profits (*shangjiao liren*) and tax revenue, emphasizing his firm's autonomy:

It doesn't matter to which level you belong. The corporations are legal entities [*faren daibiao*]. So all the corporations are equal to one another, whether they belong to the Shanghai government or to the State. It's not like I am a township/village enterprise, you are an SOE, there is a hierarchical relationship between us — actually the relationship is equal. It's legal entity to legal entity.[84]

(3) At least among the middle classes in the southeastern seaboard cities, the influx of new and different types of units has entailed that *guanxi* become fungible. Of course, this has always been true in the sense that one could "loan" a valued connection to someone else, but now the connection itself is no longer a unique sine qua non — just get another contact, another stamp (*zhang*), another job.

(4) From the perspective of the central government, the fiscal advantage of reform is that the unit is cut off from fiscal dependency and put under the discipline of a "hard" budgetary constraint. Hard budget constraints, *ceteris paribus*, are conducive to evolution, soft budget constraints to involution. But of course there are many facets of "softness" — medical coverage, education (in "key" schools, at higher levels), access to internal (*neibu*) communication channels, an official car, even a special burial plot — all of which constitute vested interests against evolution.

---

83 Of course, this is all contingent on economic success, in the absence of which dependency continues.
84 Interview #D7, Pudong (Shanghai suburb), August 1993.

CONCLUSION

We view the *danwei* as the basic building block and organizational microcosm of the Chinese political system. Both structurally and in terms of membership behavior, it illustrates the pattern of organizational adaptation to broader currents of social change. After market forces were repressed and urban and rural communities were segregated in the 1950s, enterprises and noneconomic units *in*volved into enclosed, self-serving, and multifunctional organizations. Finally, in the course of some fifteen years of reform, *danweis* began *e*volving structurally. As the efficacy and viability of the *danwei* system was reduced by increasing personnel mobility, greater freedom to work outside the unit, and the influx of foreign private capital and management, the cellularization described by Vivienne Shue began to break down.[85] As noted, this evolutionary trend is not yet triumphant, but gradual and perhaps still reversible.

Informal political relations within the *danwei* are to some degree analogous to personal politics within the CCP Central Committee, or "Center," which has been studied much more intensively than any other unit due to its strategic decision-making power.[86] Both "units" have a relatively firmly bounded frame facilitating the development of internal solidarity, which is also promoted by intensive interaction in a system of meetings and internal communications, a relatively self-sufficient economic system, and restrictions on entry and exit. In both, although inner relations are relatively intensive, the external bounds are arbitrarily drawn and do not define political fraternity, which still consists of elective "factions" formed for self-protection and the pursuit of common interests. In both units informal politics is used to reinforce traditional leadership perquisites, including prestigious appointments and political base-building opportunities. Both units include residential families, facilitating the politicization of the family and the familization of the unit: The inbreeding now proliferating within the *danwei* was to some extent anticipated by the cases of Jiang Qing, Wang Guangmei, and Ye Qun, not to mention the generation of "princelings." In a sense, the compound at Zhongnanhai might be said to be the archetype and model for basic units throughout the country.

Yet there are also essential differences between the top and the bottom, and these differences have grown more pronounced in the course of reform.

85 Vivienne Shue, *The Reach of the State: Sketches of the Chinese Body Politic* (Stanford: Stanford University Press, 1988); cf. also Lowell Dittmer, *China's Continuous Revolution: The Post-Liberation Epoch, 1949–1981* (Berkeley: University of California Press, 1987), especially Chap. 3, "Structure and Its Critique."

86 The literature on the informal politics of the CCP elite is rich. A relatively comprehensive bibliography can be found in Lucian Pye, *The Dynamics of Chinese Politics* (Cambridge: Oelgeschlager, Gunn & Hain, 1981), pp. 267–276.

To begin with, although not everyone within the central elite loves one another, they are all there because they wish to be, which is not necessarily the case in the basic work units. This has to do with the fact that the Center is far more autonomous and self-sufficient than any other basic unit – indeed, it makes the rules that all of the others are obliged to follow. Such an elite institution has a self-conscious sense of tradition and *esprit de corps*: Though once shaken by the Cultural Revolution, it has since been restored in solemn rehabilitation ceremonies and vigorously defended against various perceived threats, giving it much greater ability to withstand the winds of change than the average SOE. Indeed, it is ironic that the leadership has been so sheltered from the reforms that it has unleashed – despite electoral reform and term limitations – that leading cadres have greater security of tenure under reform than at any time since the early 1950s.

The Center, as a *danwei*, remains quite definitely an involutionary unit par excellence. The basic units have been much more exposed to the effects of reform than the elite, about which they evince mixed feelings. On the one hand, there is ample evidence of shrewd, adaptive behavior, enabling some units to thrive. On the other hand, there are inevitable regrets: nostalgia about "equal distribution" (*tongyi fenpei*); misgivings about rampant corruption, inflation, unemployment, or loss of social security; a sense of anomie. Meanwhile, the CCP elite, sheltered from these unsettling dislocations, has tended to limit its experience of modernization to the vicarious realm – the mass media, internal media, and intelligence reports, their own more venturesome children.

Although Zhongnanhai and the unit of local petty entrepreneurs (*getihu*) are extreme cases, they are poles on a continuum, between which *danwei* of every variety are interspersed. As noted above, the biggest single determinant of a unit's evolutionary/involutionary propensity is budgetary. Those units with hard budget constraints are increasingly forced onto the market to compensate for budget shortfalls, and marketization forces evolution. This may be true even if those units are not production units: An increasing number of universities and research institutes, which are nonprofit units (*shiye danwei*), have turned to private donations and "lateral contributions" (say, from enterprises) to supplement revenues. Those units that have soft budget constraints and can rely comfortably on state budgets have no need for such expedients. Whether a unit has a hard or soft budget constraint is to a considerable extent hierarchically determined. Vertically, there are five hierarchical levels: central, administrative, provincial, municipal, district, and local (street/village/enterprise). Those highest in the hierarchy seem the least susceptible to evolutionary pressures. One might speculate that this has given rise to a certain gap in consciousness between the elite and the masses, as an economically cushioned leadership continues to venerate revolutionary socialist traditions (which have indeed served them well) while the working masses struggle to survive in an increaingly marketized, cutthroat environment.

In sum, reform has clearly brought with it a metastasis of informal connections of every type, for both legitimate and *sub rosa* (or outright corrupt) activities. Among the diverse contradictory tendencies we are most struck by the contrast between what we call the evolutionary and involutionary trends, either of which will logically entail major micropolitical changes in the long run. From the present perspective, the evolutionary trend seems prevalent, although an involutionary revitalization movement of some sort cannot be precluded. The question is whether the existing framework of the *danwei* will be sufficient to contain these two conflicting trends or whether it will instead go the way of the People's Commune, giving way to a new and more varied assortment of informal structures.

ACKNOWLEDGMENTS

The authors (listed alphabetically) are grateful to the Center for Chinese Studies at the University of California at Berkeley for research assistance, and to Professor Liu Xin for his perceptive comments. This chapter represents a theoretical reworking of empirical materials first presented in Lowell Dittmer and Lu Xiaobo, "Personal politics in the Chinese Danwei under reform," *Asian Survey* 36: 3 (March 1996), pp. 246–267.

CHAPTER 9

CLIENTAGE IN THE PRC'S NATIONAL DEFENSE RESEARCH AND DEVELOPMENT SECTOR

BENJAMIN C. OSTROV

This chapter will attempt to highlight the relationship between a certain type of informal group, that characterized by patron–client relations, and formal organization. While not wishing to rule out the possibility that such groups can find their origins in phenomena like common regional or generational origins, this study will explore the possibility that sometimes these groups may have their basis in formal organization. It will not provide a conclusive resolution to the question of the nature and primary activity of these groups. Instead, through a brief case study of politics within China's national defense science and technology research and development (R&D) sector up to and including the Cultural Revolution, a path for further investigation will be proposed.

Informal, in contradistinction to formal, politics concerns a process that occurs outside formal rules and among groups that cannot be considered formal organizations. The process is marked by a behind-the-scenes, hidden character, as opposed to public and open procedures such as the election of the president of the United States. The informal groups that are major actors in this form of politics have usually been classified as factions in Chinese studies. Andrew Nathan considers a faction to be a structure mobilized on the basis of clientelist ties to engage in politics and consisting of a few, rather than a great many, layers of personnel.[1] The clientelist tie at the heart of it is a "one-to-one rather than a corporate pattern of relationships between leaders (or subleaders) and followers." He also endorses the approach taken by William Whitson, who proposes that factionalism is rooted in loyalties and rivalries based on the five field armies of the pre-1954 military administrative system.[2]

---

1 Andrew J. Nathan, "A factionalism model for CCP politics," *China Quarterly* 53:38, (January/March 1973) pp. 40–41, 43, 47.
2 Nathan, "A factionalism model," p. 60; Whitson, "The field army in Chinese Communist military politics," *China Quarterly* 37:2 (January/March 1969), pp. 8–10, 21–26.

Whitson's discussion was part of a debate about the sources and nature of conflict within the PLA prior to and during the Cultural Revolution.[3] While in disagreement about the origins of such conflict and the basis of such groups – one author even denying them to be factions but referring to them as cross-factional interest groups[4] – most imply agreement that policy disputes were one of the main aims of conflict. In the case of the military, the dispute was between whether promoting professionalism or maintaining proper ideological character should be given priority. Another writer includes this dispute among a list of policy disputes – including "economic development models, the role of the Party . . . foreign policy . . . , and trade policy" – that have resulted in factionalism in the Chinese Communist Party since the late 1950s. Yet Copper also claims that factionalism has been "based on personalities [and] the concentration of leadership authority."[5]

The concept of faction as used by various analysts is confusing. As used by Nathan, faction denotes groupings of people tied by vertical linkages or patron–client networks. Meanwhile, commentators on the PLA use the term more loosely to include groupings united by horizontal as well as vertical ties. Whitson, for example, explores several other possibilities beyond his original field army thesis to account for the basis of factions, including common regional origin and common generational status.[6]

The recognition that groups linked vertically as well as horizontally are significant and need to be discussed has led Tang Tsou to avoid the use of the term "faction" altogether; instead, he favors the term "informal group."[7] In its attempt to clarify key concepts, however, this denotation overlooks another problem, confusion over objectives. Copper and other PLA analysts suggest that these groups are attempting to influence policy. Nathan, in contradistinction to those setting forth a "Mao-in-command" model for the period of the leader's ascendancy, also views factionalism as a policy-making model.[8] However, as Tsou indicates, the inconsistencies and reversals of policies that Nathan views as indications of factionalism were instead primarily "adjustments to changes in circumstance or the results of the per-

3 Harvey Nelsen, "Military forces in the cultural revolution," *China Quarterly* 51 (July/September 1972), p. 467; William L. Parish, Jr., "Factions in Chinese military politics," *China Quarterly* 56 (October/December 1973), pp. 667–699; and William Pang-yu Ting, "Coalitional behavior among the Chinese military elite: A nonrecursive, simultaneous equation and multiplicative causal model," *American Political Science Review* 73 (June 1979), pp. 478–493.
4 Ting, "Coalitional Behavior," pp. 478–493.
5 John F. Copper, "Recent troubles in China," *Asian Affairs* 14 (Spring 1987), p. 50.
6 William Whitson, *The Chinese High Command* (New York: Praeger, 1973), pp. 404–517.
7 Tang Tsou, "Prolegomenon to the study of informal groups in CCP politics," *China Quarterly* 65 (January 1976), pp. 98–114.
8 Nathan, "A factionalism model," pp. 34–35, 54.

ceived failure of a policy."[9] He views Mao and those closest to him as primarily responsible for setting most of the fundamental policies during his ascendancy while bargaining, co-opting, and compromising with others to retain power and achieve policy objectives. Indeed, Tsou suggests that this would normally be the case since "the struggle for power in the CCP has, during most of its history, resulted in the ascendancy of one group or coalition of groups."[10]

This would suggest that policy making could be explained primarily in terms of informal group conflicts only during periods when no one group or coalition has captured the formal organization and gained ascendancy, an example being the period between Mao's and Deng's leadership. Such a period, in the context of the history of the CCP, would be viewed as abnormal. Thus a question is raised: If informal groups are not primarily engaged in policy making, then in what are they primarily involved? The answer to this question is not simple because, as was shown earlier, the term "informal group" is a broad one that embraces groups of varying character, some defined by horizontal and others by vertical ties. Hypothetically, it is even possible that groups of each type can work together for a period for a common objective. Therefore, to avoid confusion, this discussion will be limited to groups characterized by vertical ties, which Nathan refers to as *clientelist*.

Nathan considers the tie at the core of the patron–client relationship to be a relationship characterized by the exchange of gifts and services between two people;[11] however, it is more than this. In her study of peasant–state relations in China, Jean Oi views the clientelist tie as a dyad that not only illuminates how elites mobilize masses but also how the nonelites can try to influence the policy implementation process in the direction of their interests.[12] This perspective, especially the attention given to the actions taken by nonelites, calls for looking "beyond the formal structures . . . of participation . . . to explore the less obvious . . . methods by which citizens pursue their interests. . . ."[13] The pursuit of interests by both parties to this tie in a behind-the-scenes

9 Tsou, "Prolegomenon," p. 104.
10 Tsou, "Prolegomenon," p. 108. Where the issue was more technical, like developing nuclear weapons, Mao would delegate authority to others to make policy. The only possibility for competition by groups to influence policy would be when the delegation of authority was not clear, for example, resulting in overlapping jurisdictions by two or more units in some policy arena. Such was the case with the Science and Technology Commission for National Defense and the National Defense Industry Office prior to the Cultural Revolution. Both had areas of responsibility in developing advanced, especially nuclear, weapons. See Benjamin C. Ostrov, *Conquering Resources* (Armonk, NY: M. E. Sharpe, 1991), pp. 31–39, and John Wilson Lewis and Xue Litai, *China Builds the Bomb* (Stanford: Stanford University Press, 1988), p. 127.
11 Nathan, "A factionalism model," p. 37.
12 Jean C. Oi, *State and Peasant in Contemporary China: The Political Economy of Village Government* (Berkeley and Los Angeles: University of California Press, 1989), p. 8.
13 Oi, *State and Peasant*, p. 7.

manner seems to lie at the heart of the concept of clientelism. Thus, mutual benefit largely acquired outside channels of formal organization is implied.[14]

The significance of informal, as opposed to formal, ties is clarified by the classicist E. Badian. As he explains in his study of the late Roman Republic, this relationship cannot come under the rubric of formal organization because it has a moral, not legal, basis. Therefore, clientage can be said to be, generally, a relationship that must rest on *mutual* trust and loyalty (*fides*). The client takes on a certain status (*officium*) that is subordinate to the patron. This status carries with it unspecified benefits (*beneficia*).[15] The client's status carries with it certain obligations to serve that the patron can call on, resulting in the mobilization of political support.[16] This was a central feature both of electoral politics and, in the first century B.C., the civil wars that racked Rome and destroyed the Republic.[17] In return, the client is entitled to benefits such as land, but above all, protection.

A crucial premise of this study is that the bond at the core of the patron–client relationship has longevity. Nathan does not rule this out but implies otherwise when claiming that the relationship "can be abrogated by either member at will."[18] However, Badian's emphasis on the moral, extralegal obligations incumbent on both parties in the relationship militates against such flexibility. He considers the bond "permanent (or at least long-term)."[19]

THE THESIS

The difference of opinion between Badian and Nathan need not mean that either is wrong. They are dealing with two highly distinct cultures. Certainly we would expect there to be a discrepancy between the two value systems. So while not ruling out the possibility that the patron–client relationship might be more fluid in contemporary China than in ancient Rome, the recognition that the relationship can persist over time is essential to this study. Indeed, the core hypothesis here is that clientelist ties can arise out of the

---

14 Oi, *State and Peasant*, pp. 134–135. Indeed, Oi notes that patrons, in particular production team leaders during the period of collectivization, derived authority from their ability to influence the distribution of rewards. This was done through the allocation of jobs, distribution of work points, cash, sideline work, welfare, etc. Team leaders in turn were dependent on the peasants' cooperation for a successful harvest to be achieved. See also p. 143.

15 E. Badian, *Foreign Clientelae (264–70 b.c.)* (London: Oxford University Press, 1958), pp. 5–10. The perspective on clientage developed in this book is very useful for the study of politics in general since it applies to many diverse situations. Badian applies it to both electoral politics as well as civil war in the Roman Republic.

16 Badian, *Foreign Clientelae*, pp. 10–51.

17 Badian, *Foreign Clientelae*, pp. 162–163, 192, 228–272, 289–290.

18 Nathan, "A factionalism model," p. 37.

19 Badian, *Foreign Clientelae*, p. 10.

hierarchical relationships in conventional bureaucratic organs or, in other words, formal organization. Years later, long after the individuals affected have left the organ in question, the clientelist tie will be reactivated, either by the patron or the client, should the need arise.

This thesis will be examined by focusing on the case of four individuals. Nie Rongzhen can be considered in the context of this study to have been a patron. Qian Xuesen, Wang Bingzhang, and Han Guang will be viewed as his clients. In the case under study here, clientelist ties will be assumed to have been formed by Nie with two of these individuals in the 1950s through two organizations that he headed, the Scientific Planning Commission (SPC) (*Kexue guihua weiyuanhui*) and the Aviation Industry Commission (AIC) (*Hangkong gongye weiyuanhui*). The third individual will be assumed to have formed clientelist ties with Nie based on a much earlier military association. Based on the preceding premises, it is reasonable to assume that these ties would have been reactivated during the Cultural Revolution by the patron (Nie) as well as his clients in an effort for political as well as material survival.

At this time, Nie Rongzhen was in charge of the Science and Technology Commission for National Defense. As shall be explained later, this organ — which was then in charge of all advanced weapons, especially nuclear weapons, and research and development — superseded the SPC and the AIC. The history of organizational development shared by these organs makes for the possibility of clientelist ties cutting across organizational boundaries that persist and can be activated even after the organizations in which these ties were formed had ceased to be.

FORMAL ORGANIZATION AND
THE BASIS OF CLIENTELIST TIES

Nie Rongzhen's ties went back furthest with Wang Bingzhang. In the late 1930s, after the war with Japan had begun, Nie was Deputy Commander of the 115th Division of the 8th Route Army. Wang served under him as warfare section chief. Following the end of this war, when the military was reorganized into the five field armies system, part of the 115th Division was absorbed into the 4th Field Army and part into the North China Field Army. Nie took command of the North China Field Army and Wang followed him, serving as a member of the Hebei-Shandong-Henan (*Ji-Lu-Yu*) military district command staff.[20]

20 *Zhonggong renming lu* [*Chinese Communist who's who*], 3rd ed. (Mucha, Taipei: Guoli zhengzhi daxue guoji guanxi yanjiu zhongxin, 1983), pp. 986, 5A; William Whitson, "The Field Army in Chinese Communist Military Politics," *China Quarterly*, no. 37 (January/March 1969), pp. 6, 8, 27.

Qian Xuesen's ties with Nie Rongzhen were established in national defense R&D organs. The AIC was established in April 1956 with Nie as chairman and Qian as one of its members. He and Nie had worked closely together before. Together with Zhou Enlai, they planned the establishment of the AIC to be a leading organ for the guided missile aviation scientific research field. Its purpose became the direction of the PLA's guided missile and airplane research work. Members of the unit took part in the military industrial side of the Twelve-Year Plan for research in the natural and social sciences, drafting plans for armaments development.[21]

This plan, also known as the National Plan for Long-Range Development of Science and Technology 1956–67, was called for at the same time as the SPC was set up.[22] The SPC was an all-inclusive agency charged with planning and administering all scientific research and development, both military and nonmilitary. It was established in 1956 to alleviate the administrative burden imposed on scientists by the Twelve-Year Plan.[23]

Nie Rongzhen and Han Guang were not among the original members of the unit. The change in membership that saw them enter the SPC was brought about by the organ's clarification of the Twelve-Year Plan into fifty-seven projects that were in turn reduced into twelve key points. Eight of these concerned science and technology necessary for strengthening China's military-related scientific capability.[24] What had been a heavy burden was complicated by an enhanced need for expertise. The organization "was unable

---

21 Huang Kecheng and Zhao Erlu served as vice-chairmen. Wang Shiquang, Wang Jing, An Dong, Liu Yalou, Li Qiang, and Qian Zhidao were members. An Dong was secretary-general. The effort to establish the AIC was undertaken in response to an initiative take by Qian Xuesen. In February 1956, Qian wrote *Jianli wo guo guofang hangkong gongye de yijianshu* [*An opinion on establishing our country's national defense aviation industry*]. It attracted attention from the highest authorities. Consequently, Zhou Enlai personally presided over a meeting of the Military Commission that decided to establish the unit. See Nie Rongzhen, *Nie Rongzhen huiyi lu* [*Nie Rongzhen's memoirs*], 3 vols. (Beijing: Jiefangjun chubanshe, 1984), vol. 3, pp. 774, 782–783, and the Ministry of Aviation Industry of the People's Republic of China, "Fenjin buxide Zhongguo hangkong gongye" [China's ceaselessly vigorously advancing aviation industry], in *Guanghui de chengjiu* [*Glorious achievements*], 2 vols. (Beijing: Renmin chubanshe, 1984), vol. 1, pp. 296–297.

22 Tong Dalin and Hu Ping, "Science and technology," in Guangyuan Yu, ed., *China's Socialist Modernization* (Beijing: Foreign Languages Press, 1984), p. 622.

23 Guo Moruo expected the program to be formulated within a month of the commission's establishment. See "Xiang kexue jishu jinjun" [Onward towards science and technology], *Renmin shouce*, 1957 [*People's handbook*, 1957], 2 vols. (Beijing: Dagongbaoshe, 1956), vol. 2, p. 575. Also see Xinhua (Hong Kong), English Service, March 15, 1956 and Mikhail A. Klochko, *Soviet Scientist in China*, trans. Andrew McAndrew (London: Hollis and Cater, 1964), p. 19.

24 Tong Dalin and Hu Ping, "Science and technology," p. 622; "Gongfei junshi kexue fazhan zhi yanjiu" [A study of military and scientific development in Mainland China], *Feiqing yanjiu* 4:8 (Taipei: Intelligence Bureau, Ministry of National Defense, August 1961), p. 115. (The journal cited here, *Feiqing yanjiu*, is an official source and is not to be confused with the journal of the same name published by Taipei's Zhonggong yanjiu zazhi she [Institute for the Study of Chinese Communist Problems]. The title of this nonofficial source was changed in 1969 to *Zhonggong yanjiu*.)

by itself to pursue the demands of actual work" (my translation), for which reasons, in June 1957, it underwent some modification.[25]

At the same time as this delineation of the SPC's duties, its staff was augmented from 35 to 106 members.[26] This vast expansion suggests an attempt to cope with an increased administrative burden on the SPC. It also implies an effort to enable the SPC to carry out the more specific tasks with which it had been charged. Such a notion is further supported by changes in the leadership of the commission that were made at the same time.

A number of staff changes at the leadership level reveal an effort to enhance the expertise of the unit. Of the new additions, three of the deputy general secretaries had scientific backgrounds. Li Qiang was an expert in communications electronics, Wu Heng was a geologist, and Yu Guangyuan was an economist. Furthermore, of the two leaders retained, Li Siguang was a geologist.[27] At this time, mid-1957, Nie Rongzhen became chairman and Han Guang became a member.[28]

FORMAL ORGANIZATION AND
THE DELIVERY OF *BENEFICIA*

Nie Rongzhen was in charge of the State Science and Technology Commission (STC) and the Science and Technology Commission for National Defense (NDSTC) by the time of the Cultural Revolution. The former had been established by a merger of the SPC and the National Technology Commission in November 1958.[29] It was a unit under the state council responsible for promoting and coordinating civilian-oriented R&D. The latter was established

---

25 Xinhua (Hong Kong), Chinese Service, June 13, 1957.

26 Ibid.; Fei Lung, p. 18.

27 For Li Siguang, see *Zhonggong renming lu*, 44A. For Li Qiang, see p. 222, Wu Heng, p. 360, and Yu Guangyuan, pp. 10–11 in *Zhonggong renming lu*.

28 Xinhua (Hong Kong), Chinese Service, June 13, 1957; *Zhonggong renming lu*, p. 952; *Renmin shouce*, 1957, vol. 1, p. 313. Prior to this change, Chen Yi had been chairman and Li Fuchun, Guo Moruo, Bo Yibo, and Li Siguang vice-chairmen. Zhang Jingfu had served as general secretary. Out of these individuals, only Guo Moruo and Li Siguang stayed on as vice-chairmen after June 1957. The replacements included Lin Feng, Huang Jing, and Yang Xiufeng as vice-chairmen. Fang Changjiang became general secretary and Li Qiang, Wu Heng, An Dong, Yu Guangyuan, Wang Shuntong, and Liu Daozheng became deputy general secretaries.

29 *Renmin ribao* (*RMRB*), June 2, 1959, p. 6. The National Technology Commission (Guojia jishu weiyuanhui) had been set up on May 12, 1956, only a few months after the establishment of the Scientific Planning Commission to take up some of the SPC's administrative burden. By this time the Twelve Year Plan had been formulated. Its mandate extended only to civilian-related sectors of production, preventing it from alleviating the main burden of the Scientific Planning Commission, which stemmed from military-related tasks. See Xinhua (Hong Kong), Chinese and English Services, May 13, 1956.

a month earlier through a merger of the AIC and Section 5 of the Ministry of Defense.[30]

Section 5 had been responsible for promoting cooperation between the AIC and the Equipment Planning Department (EPD) of the General Staff (*Zongcan Zhuangbei Jihuabu*) to coordinate research work for the army's entire armaments. The EPD, through an organ that it had established, the Equipment Scientific Research Section (ESRS) (*Zhuangbei keyanchu*), had been involved in planning the army's conventional weapons research work. Section 5, established in May 1958, therefore had been a brief, abortive effort to end the administrative separation between conventional and advanced weapons R&D administration.[31]

The NDSTC was the organization in charge of China's defense-related R&D, especially that concerning advanced weapons from 1958 into the 1970s.[32] Of these weapons, nuclear weapons were paramount. Prior to the 1970s it was a party unit directly responsible to the Central Committee's Military Commission.[33]

By the time of the Cultural Revolution, the NDSTC had been able to use the advantages that came with such a position to be directly organizing all of the experimental work at the Academy of Science, state organs concerned with metallurgy, chemical industry, machine industry, electronics, aviation, space-flight, armament, shipping, railways, education, and so forth across Qinghai, Gansu, Inner Mongolia, Xinjiang, Shanghai, Beijing, and twenty other cities,

30 Nie, *Nie Rongzhen huiyi lu*, vol. 3, p. 783, and Guo Qingshu, ed., *Zhongguo renmin jiefang jun lishi jianbian* [*A concise edition of the history of China's People's Liberation Army*] (Shenyang: Liaoning daxue chubanshe, 1985), p. 222.

31 Nie, *Nie Rongzhen huiyi lu*, vol. 3, p. 783. The ESRS had been under the leadership of Deputy Chief of the General Staff Zhang Aiping, who went on to become a vice-chairman of the newly formed NDSTC and, in 1975, its chairman. See also "Memorial Meeting Held for Chung Chih-ping," Xinhua (Peking), English Service, December 27, 1975, p. E1.

32 Nie, *Nie Rongzhen huiyi lu*, vol. 3, p. 783, and Guo Qingshu, p. 222.

33 Nie Rongzhen, "How China develops its nuclear weapons," *Beijing Review* 28 (April 29, 1985), p. 18; Huang Chenhsia, *Zhonggong junren zhi* [*Mao's generals*] (Hong Kong: Research Institute of Contemporary History, 1968), p. 697; Military Commission, Central Committee, Chinese Communist Party (1958), "Objectives of the development of nuclear weapons," cited by Warren Kuo, "A Study of Mao Tse-tung's Military Thought," *Issues and Studies* 9 (December 1972), pp. 18–19; *Feiqing nianbao*, 1967, (Taipei: Feiqing yanjiu zazhishe, May 1967), p. 750; Kang Ti [pseud.], "Zhonggong guofang keji fazhan xiankuang" [Defense science and technology development], *Zhonggong yanjiu* [Studies in Chinese communism] 11 (April 15, 1977), p. 81; Hsiang Chuan-shu, "Zhonggong de hezi zhengce" [Nuclear policy of Red China (3) – nuclear weapon development], *Zhonggong yanjiu* 13 (June 15, 1979), p. 134; "Guowuyuan guanyu tiqing shenyi jueding sheli guofang kexue jishu gongye weiyuanhui de yi'an" [Proposal by the State Council to submit the decision to establish the Commission in Charge of Science, Technology and Industry for National Defense for discussion] (August 16, 1982) and "Quanguo renmin daibiao dahui changwu weiyuanhui guanyu sheli guofang kexue jishu gongye weiyuanhui de jueyi" [Decision by the Standing Committee of the Natiuonal People's Congress on the establishment of the Commission in Charge of Science, Technology and Industry for National Defense] (passed on August 23, 1982), *Zhonghua renmin gongheguo guowuyuan gongbao* [Bulletin of the State Council of the People's Republic of China], nos. 1–21, 1982 (Beijing: Guowuyuan bangongting, 1983), p. 643; and Ostrov, *Conquering Resources*, pp. 62, 108–109.

provinces, and autonomous regions; and PLA ministries, commissions, and arms of the service. Altogether, by 1964, the NDSTC had reached the position of supervising over 1,000 science research organs, institutions of higher learning, and factories in the atomic bomb program.[34] The effort to create this vast network was fueled by the quest for resources, both personnel and equipment, necessary for the development of nuclear weapons.[35]

By this time, the NDSTC and Nie Rongzhen had also made many enemies in those units that the organ had taken over, especially some of the ministries of machine industry. Being such a powerful unit, the NDSTC was also a natural target for the Red Guards, some of whom worked in tandem with representatives of the ministries. The sharpest attacks came from a body called the September 16 Group. Its prime antagonist, as well as a defender of the NDSTC, was the September 15 (which after an internal struggle renamed itself the New September 15) Group. September 16 accused the New September 15 of being formed by "reactionaries" who had dominated September 15 until internal conflict led to the collapse of their position and their departure.[36]

---

34 Liu Jie, "Juyou Zhongguo tese de shehui zhuyi keji fazhan daolu de yige shengli" [A victory for the socialist path of developing science and technology with special Chinese characteristics], *Wenhui bao* (Shanghai) (November 1, 1985), p. 3.

35 Ostrov, *Conquering Resources*, pp. 25–37.

36 "Bo 'xin' jiuyiwu de 'rangquan' lun" [Refuting the 'New' September 15's 'yielding power' thesis], *Zaofan youli* (February 19, 1967), p. 4. The social composition of the members of these groups is not typical. The personnel in them worked in the national defense science and technology sector. Consequently, they had been given security clearance. Such clearance was limited mainly to people from the correct class and, more specifically, family background. Societal cleavage probably had far less to do with the conflict between September 16 and the New September 15 than organizational alliances. September 16, the NDSTC's antagonist, had several members of quite prominent lineage: Liu Shaoqi's son Liu Yunruo, Ye Ting's son Ye Zhengguang, Zhou Yang's daughter Zhou Mi, and one woman never mentioned in the attacks by the New September 15, Mao Zedong's daughter Li Min. See "Liu Shaoqi de yulinjun – 916 de zhenrong" [Liu Shaoqi's imperial guard – the line-up of September 16], *Feimingdi* (March 8, 1967), p. 4; "Zhanduan Liu Shaoqi shenjin qijibu de heizhao," *Feimingdi* (February 17, 1967), p. 3, translated as "Chop off Liu Shao-ch'i's claws in the Seventh Ministry of Machine-Building" in *Joint Publications Research Service Translations on Communist China: Political and Sociological* (JPRS) 397 (June 2, 1967), pp. 15–23; and "Paoda Nie Rongzhen – chedi jiekai kewei jiguan jieji douzheng gaizi," *916 Tongxun* (August 1968), p. 1, translated as "Bombard Nieh Jung-chen and completely lift the lid of class struggle off organs of Scientific and Technological Commission" in *Survey of China Mainland Press* (SCMP) 4236 (August 12, 1968), p. 1. The translator incorrectly refers to Li Min as Mao's niece. For evidence of their real relationship to him, see Roxanne Witke, *Comrade Chiang Ching* (Boston: Little, Brown, 1977), pp. 165–166. In interviews, Jiang Qing also informed Witke that Li Min had studied natural science. Furthermore, on page 368, Witke reports that Jiang informed her that she had made Li a leader of the NDSTC. Jiang Qing then notes that Li Min got into trouble during the Cultural Revolution but is quite disingenuous about the reason. She says that Li, "by association, was . . . held responsible for mistakes which she [Jiang] had made." While noting that Li Min was a member of September 16, Jiang Qing fails to mention that Li and this group launched the most hostile attack against Nie Rongzhen of all. (See the item mentioned above from *916 Tongxun.*) She instead defends herself against charges that she had attacked Nie. I have found no evidence of any such attack nor any such charges.

In his memoirs of two trips as an adviser to China, *Soviet Scientist in China*, pp. 34–36, Mikhail A. Klochko, a chemist who later defected to Canada, reports on a meeting that he had in 1958

September 16 was allied with the National Defense Industry Office (NDIO) and the Seventh Ministry of Machine Industry (7MMI). The NDIO, having been in charge of advanced weapons production, had come into conflict over resources with the NDSTC and lost out prior to the Cultural Revolution.[37] The 7MMI was responsible for manufacturing delivery systems (missiles and planes) for nuclear warheads.[38] It accused the New September 15 of protecting Wang Bingzhang, the chairman of the 7MMI, at the order of Nie Rongzhen.[39] Such an accusation implies a link between the New September 15, the NDSTC, and Wang Bingzhang. The existence of this alliance is demonstrated by a few significant events. Nie Rongzhen did try to protect Wang Bingzhang. Although he could not prevent Wang from being attacked and purged, he did manage to rescue Wang from September 16. On May 7, 1967, after having been under the control of the various competing Red Guard groups connected with the 7MMI for nearly four months, Wang Bingzhang suddenly disappeared. The New September 15 reported that he had been hospitalized. September 16 charged that Nie Rongzhen was behind this move.[40] Such was likely to have been the case because, when Wang reassumed an official position in October 1968, it was as a vice-chairman of the NDSTC.[41]

The New September 15 in turn accused September 16 and the "reactionary" leaders of the NDIO and Seventh Ministry of Machine Industry (7MMI) of forming a counterrevolutionary faction, the "Red Army Fighting Team" (*Hongjun zhandou dui*).[42] Apparently, September 16 formed the armed

with a son of Liu Shaoqi. He implies that this person agreed with his view that excessive political education and campaigns were interfering with scientific research, stating that this individual complained that "we spend more time at meetings and conferences than at our jobs." Klochko notes that this individual worked in the Institute of Physics and states that at that time the institute was doing work in nuclear physics. Klochko never mentions this person's full name. If it is Liu Yunruo, then, even allowing for the possibility that one may radically change his views over eight years, it would be reasonable to doubt the sincerity of his "revolutionary" ideals and character as did the New September 15.

37 "Quanguo renmin daibiao dahui changwu weiyuanhui guanyu sheli guofang kexue jishu gongye weiyuanhui de jueyi," p. 643; "Zhonggong zhongyang gongzuo xiaozu [Guanyu Luo Ruiqing cuowu wenti] de baogao," in *Zhonggong nianbao, 1970* (*Yearbook of Chinese Communism*, 1970), 2 vols. (Taipei: Zhonggong yanjiu zazhishe, 1970), vol. 2, chap. 7, p. 17; "Speech by Premier Chou En-lai at Interview with Some Representatives of the Scientific and Technological Commission for National Defense, the Congress of Students, the Military Control Committees, the Revolutionary Mass Organizations of the Seventh Ministry of Machine Building, and the Academia Sinica," *Tsu-liao Chuan-chi,* in *Selections from China Mainland Magazines* (SCMM), no. 631 (October 21, 1968), pp. 19–20; and Ostrov, *Conquering Resources*, pp. 32–38.
38 Zhong Mu [pseud.] "Zhonggong keji zuzhi yi qi huodong xiankuang," [Science and technology organs and events], *Zhonggong yanjiu* 12 (November 15, 1978), pp. 100–101, and Kang Ti, p. 83.
39 "Women wei shenma yao paohong Nie Rongzhen tongzhi," *Zaofan youli* (May 28, 1967), p. 2, translated as "Why we bombard Comrade Nieh Jung-chen," in SCMP, no. 4003 (August 17, 1967), pp. 6–10. In the translation appearing in SCMP, see pp. 8–9.
40 "Women wei shenma yao paohong Nie Rongzhen tongzhi," p. 2. In the SCMP translation, see p. 8.
41 *Zhonggong renming lu*, p. 5A.
42 "Gantong emo zheng tianxia, buxiang bawang rang banfen" [Dare to struggle with the demon for the world, do not give in half way to the tyrant], *Feimingdi* (February 24, 1967), p. 3. In this issue, the

force of this faction. For example, according to the New September 15, September 16 invaded PLA headquarters in Beijing on behalf of the NDIO, presumably to obtain weapons.[43]

The ability of Nie Rongzhen to protect Wang Bingzhang did not rest on Nie's influence alone. Zhou Enlai supported Wang Bingzhang. Indeed, he also defended Nie Rongzhen and the NDSTC against attack and presumably supported Nie's effort on behalf of Wang.[44]

This suggests that patrons, such as Nie Rongzhen, can themselves be clients of somebody even higher. The benefit that they can derive from this superior personage can be translated into aid given to those below them.

Nie Rongzhen can be said to have been a client of Zhou Enlai. At least from the 1950s until Zhou's death in 1976, Nie at various times served directly under Zhou. For example, besides working under Zhou Enlai when establishing the AIC, Nie also served under him in a fifteen-man special commission designed to directly supervise the establishment of nuclear weapons and industry.[45]

Nie Rongzhen had other occasions during the Cultural Revolution to actualize his clientelist tie to Zhou Enlai. By April 1967, he had already lost control of the State Science and Technology Commission to a revolutionary committee directed by a cadre from science and technology bureaucratic circles named Zhang Ben.[46] Subsequently, when threatened with the loss of control of both the 7MMI and the NDSTC itself, Nie turned to Zhou for help.

As with other organs during the Cultural Revolution, a "three-in-one alliance" had been called for to establish a revolutionary or, in this case,

"reactionary leaders" included Wang Bingzhang, but in the following issue, on March 8, his name was dropped from the list. See "Liu Shaoqi de yulinjun – 916 de zhenrong," p. 4.

43 "Jianjue yu xin jiuyiwu lianhe qilai" [Resolutely stand up and unite with the New September 15], *Feimingdi* (February 24, 1967), p. 3. This raid occurred long before such seizures received, temporarily, official sanction. In July 1967, the Central Committee issued a "Directive concerning the arming of revolutionary leftists" endorsing such arms seizures. However, due to the increased chaos and violence that resulted as rival groups fought over the military supplies, this directive was superseded by another one on September 5. The "Order of the CCP Central Committee, the State Council, the CCPCC Military Commission, and the CCPCC Cultural Revolution Group concerning the prohibition of the seizure of arms, equipment, and other military supplies from the PLA" prohibited further seizures of arms and called for the return to the PLA of all those already seized. See *Classified Chinese Communist Documents: A Selection*, (Mucha, Taipei: Institute of International Relations, National Chengchi University, 1978), pp. 644, 663–665.

44 "Speech by Premier Chou," pp. 2, 4, 17, 19, 25.

45 Ministry of Nuclear Industry of the People's Republic of China, "Wo guo hegongye de chuangjian yu fazhan" [The founding and development of our nation's nuclear industry], in *Guanghui de chengjiu*, 1984, vol. 1, p. 284, and Liu Jie, "Juyou Zhongguo tese de shehui zhuyi keji fazhan daolu de yige shengli" [A victory for the socialist path of developing science and technology with special Chinese characteristics], *Wenhui bao* (Shanghai) (November 1, 1985), p. 3.

46 See "Jingen Mao Zedong sixiang, xue yidian yong yidian" [Closely follow Mao Zedong thought, learn a bit then use a bit], *Keji zhanbao* (June 9, 1967), pp. 6, 8, and *Who's Who in Communist China*, 2 vols. (Kowloon, Hong Kong: Union Research Institute, 1969), vol. 1, p. 41.

"preparatory" committee. This alliance could take two forms. One is a combination of PLA representatives, representatives of those cadres who had not been purged, and representatives of revolutionary mass organizations. The last element of the combination provided an avenue for nonmilitary, nonofficial individuals like Red Guards to gain a share in power, at least in theory. The other form that such combinations might take is a union of old, middle-aged, and young cadres.[47]

Nie tried to turn the establishment of such a committee to the NDSTC's advantage. Instead of losing power or having their power reduced, he and the others who controlled the commission saw the formation of this committee as a way to reinforce their domination of those units already subordinate to the NDSTC. In late February 1968, the commission organized elections to set up a new preparatory committee. The committee's members were to represent all of the units within the NDSTC orbit. However, these representatives were not to be freely elected; a provision was attached, stipulating that only those who agreed that it was necessary "to support the correct leadership of the Party Committee of the Scientific and Technological Commission for National Defense with Vice Chairman Nieh as the core" would be elected. Nie Rongzhen was probably responsible for the addition of this provision. However, when it became clear that the top leaders (represented by Zhou Enlai) frowned on this move, four members of the Standing Committee of the Party Committee of the NDSTC, Luo Shunchu, Cai Shunli, Liu Huaqing, and Zhang Chenhuan, took the blame. They claimed that they did not report their action to Nie Rongzhen.[48] However, considering that Nie Rongzhen was the head of the Standing Committee, it is hard to believe that he was unaware of the addition of this stipulation to the election procedure. This appears to be a case of clients serving their patron by offering to take the blame for what, due to the shifting rules of the game during the Cultural Revolution, had become a wrongful act.

The consequence of the provision stipulating how the preparatory committee should be elected was that a disproportionate number of supporters of Nie Rongzhen and the NDSTC became members of this committee. In the case of the 7MMI, more members of the New September 15 were "elected" to the preparatory committee than the vote warranted. The NDSTC, with the aid of the military control committees at the various units,

---

47 Zhou Enlai, speaking of these types of revolutionary alliances, recognized some overlap between the two. As he put it, "military representatives and revolutionary cadres are probably all old and middle-aged, while representatives of revolutionary mass organizations are mostly young. But this is still a combination of old, middle, and young. It is merely another 'three-way combination.'" See "Zhou zongli de jianghua," *Keji zhanbao* (June 2, 1967), p. 4, or the translation "Premier Chou's Speech" in SCMP, no. 4011 (August 29, 1967), p. 5.   48 "Speech by Premier Chou," p. 1.

accomplished this by simply designating its preferred candidate as the winner, regardless of the outcome of the vote.[49]

The election failed to stabilize conditions within the organizations under the NDSTC; instead, it provoked more conflict, leading to intervention by the top leaders. On April 4, the order prohibiting those who failed to support Nie Rongzhen and the NDSTC from being elected was abrogated, thereby nullifying the elections that had already taken place.[50]

On April 20, 1968, Zhou Enlai held a meeting with representatives of the NDSTC and the organizations within its domain to get to the bottom of the problems affecting the commission and its subordinate units. The result was a compromise. Nie Rongzhen remained in charge of the NDSTC. However, the unit had to surrender control of many large factories to the NDIO because they were considered unnecessary for research.[51] These were probably the Nanyuan missile factories.[52]

Nie Rongzhen was also able to protect Qian Xuesen, who, in turn, extended this protection downward to cover most of his subordinates. The nuclear weapons program had two divisions, one concerned with the warhead and the other with missiles. Qian Xuesen headed the missile division while Qian Sanqiang ran the warhead section.[53] Qian Xuesen was the only scientist in the nuclear weapons program who had previously been in the AIC. Qian Sanqiang did not have the connections that he had. The result was that Nie Rongzhen brought Qian Xuesen into the NDSTC and made him a vice chairman of the unit.[54]

Qian Xuesen was able to extend the protection he enjoyed down to almost all of the rest of the members of the missile division. Only one of its members, Guo Yonghuai, was purged while nearly the entire warhead division, including its leader, suffered this fate.[55]

49 "Speech by Premier Chou," pp. 5–6, 8.   50 "Speech by Premier Chou," p. 1.
51 Zhou Enlai noted other reasons for reducing the NDSTC jurisdiction as well. He thought that there were too many personnel under its control, implying that excessive personnel under one organizational roof constrains efficiency in research and development. Zhou also thought that the NDSTC was ill equipped to handle the problem of mass serial production faced by large factories. See "Speech by Premier Chou," pp. 19–20.
52 Richard J. Latham, conversation with author in Hong Kong, November 23, 1987.
53 Chu-yuan Cheng, *Scientific and Engineering Manpower in Communist China, 1949–1963* (Washington, DC: National Science Foundation, U.S. Government Printing Office, 1965), pp. 238–240.
54 Nie, *Nie Rongzhen huiyi lu*, vol. 3, p. 783. Qian Xuesen's position as vice-chairman of the NDSTC is noted in *China Directory, 1979* (in Chinese, English, and Japanese) (Tokyo: Radiopress, 1978), p. 313; *Zhonggong renming lu*, p. 942; and *Zhonggong nianbao, 1969* (Taipei: Zhonggong yanjiu zazhishe, 1969), vol. 2, chap. 9, p. 160. Even after the NDSTC ceased to exist, Qian Xuesen remained within the national defense science and technology bureaucratic orbit. By April 1984, he had become a vice-chairman of the commission in charge of science, technology, and industry for national defense. (This unit had been formed from an amalgamation of three units, including the NDSTC and NDIO in 1982.) See *China Directory, 1985* (in Chinese, English, and Japanese) (Tokyo: Radiopress, 1984), pp. 164–165.
55 Qian Sanqiang's purge is noted in *Keji zhanbao*, September 1968, cited in *Xianggang shibao* (Hong Kong), September 7, 1968, p. 3; *Jinri dalu banyuekan* (Taipei), December 1, 1968, pp. 17–18; and *Hongqi tong-*

In the case of Han Guang, the result was very different. As vice chairman of the Science and Technology Commission, he was the main casualty of struggle there.[56] Apparently, he was in charge of the day-to-day management of the commission. Nie Rongzhen suggested as much when, during his own self-criticism, he stated that Han Guang failed to report many things to him. By way of blaming his deputy, Nie was able to deflect attack from himself onto Han.[57]

CONCLUSION

The choice of individuals to focus this study on was not purely arbitrary; instead, it was dictated by what information was available. Of course, this can skew the outcome. However, no predetermined outcome was targeted. Indeed, were this not the case, Han Guang would not have been included in this study. The inclusion of his case, though, does indicate problems.

Contrary to expectations, clients were not always helped by patrons, as the case of Han Guang shows. There are three ways to explain this. One is that the informal rules underlying patron–client relations in China are different than those in ancient Rome. Consequently, either party can instantly abrogate the relationship when it no longer serves his purpose.

Another explanation is more significant because it draws attention to the methodological uncertainty at the core of this approach. Perhaps Nie Rongzhen and Han Guang did not have a patron–client relationship. It is

xun, no. 1, mid-June 1968, translated in "Letters from Peking," SCMP, no. 4210 (July 3, 1968), p. 17. For Qian's deputy, Wang Ganchang, see *Keji zhanbao,* September 1968, cited in *Xianggang shibao* (Hong Kong), September 7, 1968, p. 3, and *Jinri dalu banyuekan* (Taipei), December 1, 1968, pp. 17–18. For the rest in the warhead division, see Ostrov, "The impact of the cultural revolution on the nuclear weapons program of communist China," *Issues and Studies* 19 (July 1983), pp. 42–45.

Guo Yunghuai was not only purged but killed. He is listed among a roster of purged scientists in *Keji zhanbao,* September 1968, which is cited in the issues of *Xianggang shibao* and *Jinri dalu banyuekan* mentioned above. Besides this information, what makes it reasonably certain that Guo was purged is the unusual obituary he received in *Renmin ribao* on December 13, 1968, p. 4. It was remarkably brief, considering that as [deputy director of the Institute of Mechanics, Guo] was one of the men most responsible for . . . China's development of delivery systems for nuclear weapons. Also unusual is the part of the obituary saying that [Guo] had made a contribution (not a "great" contribution) to scientific and technical work. Finally, there is the statement concerning the manner of his death: [Guo] "was sacrificed" as a result of an "unfortunate incident." This incident was probably a fatal encounter with Red Guards.

See Ostrov, pp. 45–46.

56 "Jingen Mao Zedong sixiang, xue yidian yong yidian," *Keji zhanbao* (June 9, 1967), pp. 6, 8.
57 "Nie fuzongli de jianghua," *Keji zhanbao* (June 2, 1967), p. 3, translated as "Vice Premier Nieh's Speech" in SCMP, no. 4011 (August 29, 1967), p. 9. For Han Guang's position prior to his purge, see "Chedi qingsuan Han Guang fandang zongpai jituan fandui zhongyang, pohuai wenhua da geming de daotian zuixing" [Thoroughly liquidate the Han Guang anti-party sectarian clique opposing the Party Central Committee and destroy the crimes of the Great Cultural Revolution that stink to the heavens] *Keji zhanbao* (March 1, 1967), p. 3.

very tenuous to assume an affective bond between two people who happen at some point to work together. It is also questionable to impute a cause (patron–client relationship) from an effect (mutual support). Even in the cases of Wang Bingzhang and Qian Xuesen, there may not have been a clientelist tie with Nie Rongzhen. The only way to remove the uncertainty and do justice to this approach would be to hold in-depth interviews with the parties involved (or those close to them) or to have access to memoirs that are more personal and revealing than those of Nie Rongzhen.

Finally, one may account for the case of Han Guang by considering the essence of the clientelist tie, trust, not to be absolute but a matter of degree, depending on a number of factors, such as the usefulness of the individual concerned to the other party to the relationship. Such a consideration presents a conceptual difficulty because, according to the perspective developed here, parties enter into such a relationship primarily for reasons other than utilitarian calculation. It may be that the nature of the relationship can change over time.

Most of the cases encountered in this study show that the investigation of patron–client relationships can provide useful insight into organizational behavior and policy implementation. However, as the case of Han Guang shows, one must proceed with caution.

If the use of a patron–client relations perspective is a valid approach to examine politics, significant insights become available. The use of formal organization by those prominent in it to provide benefit to others outside can be better understood. This approach also suggests that there can be a close relationship between formal organization and informal groups such that the boundary between them becomes blurred. When Nie Rongzhen used his position to rescue clients and bring them into his organ, the relationship between them was no longer simply patron–client; they were all in the same formal organization and subject to its values and rules.

The most significant insight to be drawn from this approach concerns the acquisition of resources by organizations. In a patron–client relationship, benefits flow both upward and downward. Not only does the client derive benefits, such as protection, but the patron derives them as well. The patron may head an organization charged with certain goals. However, administrative deficiencies may deny it the resources needed to achieve these goals. Only the patron's relationship to clients in other organs may allow the patron's organization to procure the resources that it needs. The patron, with the aid of his clients, may even expand his organization to incorporate others or at least dominate them, thereby providing him the necessary resources. Therefore, a focus on clientelist ties can show that, contrary to expectations by Max Weber, the patrimonial authority they provide can lead to successful administration in situations where rational-legal authority is inadequate.[58]

The NDSTC itself is a case in point. By the criteria that are usually put forth by analysts of public administration, efficiency, and effectiveness, it appears to have been a success. The main task assigned to the commission in 1958 was to develop the atomic bomb within ten years. It did so in six. Only three years later, it launched its first successful test of the hydrogen bomb.[59] The time required to go from one accomplishment to the next was less than that for any other nuclear power.

However, appearances can be deceiving. There are numerous indicators that obstacles to coordination such as restrictions on resources and jurisdictional limitations – problems that can impede the efficiency and effectiveness of organizations – as well as severe harassment during the Cultural Revolution, hampered the operation of the NDSTC.[60]

First, there are the comments of the second and final director of the NDSTC, Zhang Aiping, to the effect that, prior to the creation of the Commission in Charge of Science, Technology, and Industry for National Defense, the organ that replaced and succeeded the NDSTC in 1982, there had been too much "decentralism" among the units involved in military science and technology. He also criticized the prevalence of the attitude of "each doing things in his own way." Such problems, Zhang noted, would be obstacles to the achievement of the unity necessary for accomplishing great tasks. These comments suggest the existence of tensions between the NDSTC and NDIO that interfered with policy implementation.[61] The establishment of a fifteen-person special commission by the Central Committee in November 1962 to supervise these two units suggests that the conflict between them was a long-standing one.[62] That policy implementation should have suffered is entirely plausible.

58 The limitations of the Weberian paradigm of bureaucracy and the manner in which traditional authority relationships can compensate for them to bring about administrative ends are explored by Suzanne H. Rudolph and Lloyd I. Rudolph in "Authority and power in bureaucratic and patrimonial administration: A revisionist interpretation of Weber on bureaucracy," *World Politics* 31 (January 1979), pp. 195–227.
59 Ostrov, *Conquering Resources*, pp. 5, 36, 91.
60 Much of the following discussion on the limitations to efficiency and effectiveness is taken from *Conquering Resources*, p. 91.
61 "Zhang Aiping yaoqiu tongyi zuzhi guofang keji guofang gongye liliang [Zhang Aiping demands unified organization of national defense science and technology and national defense industry capability]," *Renmin ribao* (March 1983), p. 3, and "Zhang Aiping speaks on defense modernization," Xinhua (Beijing), Chinese Service, February 28, 1983. In *Foreign Broadcast Information Service Daily Report on China* (FBIS), no. 42 (March 2, 1983), p. K5.
62 "Zhongguo yanzhi yuanzidan, qidan heqianting zhi mi" [The mystery of China's development of the atomic bomb, hydrogen bomb and nuclear-powered submarine], *Liaowang* (overseas edition) (June 15, 1987), p. 6; "Wo guo hegongye de chuangjian yu fazhan" in *Guanghui de chengjiu*, vol. 1, p. 284; and Liu Jie, p. 3. This unit gradually ceased to function and then disappeared during the Cultural Revolution.

There are many indications that it did suffer during the Cultural Revolution. After a previously successful H-bomb test, China launched a second attempt on December 24, 1967. While the first explosion on June 17, 1967 produced a three-megaton yield, the second was under twenty kilotons. This test was never officially announced. Another test did not take place until December 27, 1968. This one, China's eighth test explosion, successfully reached a three-megaton yield. However, it was not until the eleventh test, on October 14, 1970, that this level was surpassed.[63]

The problems cited above strongly suggest that, during the Cultural Revolution, at least, the nuclear weapons program did suffer.[64] Official statements released from Beijing following the fall of the Gang of Four clearly support the contention that the nuclear weapons program was hampered.

One explanation for the failure of China's second hydrogen bomb test is that only the initial fission cycle in the process was completed and no fusion cycle occurred. In other words, only the atomic bomb trigger of the thermonuclear device exploded, not the H-bomb itself.[65] These difficulties were probably related to the purge of scientists involved in designing the warhead itself, not the missile.[66] According to one report,

> whoever wanted to develop guided missiles and nuclear weapons would be attacked through the allegation that if satellites flew in the sky, the red flag would surely fall to the ground.[67]

This statement, in the context of the wave of condemnation of the Gang of Four following their downfall, might, by itself, remain doubtful. However, taken in conjunction with more recent reports of such setbacks during

63 *Zhonggong nianbao*, 1971 (Taipei: Zhonggong yanjiu zazhishe, 1971), chap. 2, p. 74, and Leo Yueh-yun Liu, *China as a Nuclear Power in World Politics* (New York: Taplinger Publishing Company, 1972), pp. 35–36.
64 For information on the destructive impact of the Cultural Revolution on research, education, personnel, and the efforts to establish production concerned with developing a nuclear capacity, see Li Jue et al., eds., *Dangdai Zhongguo de hegongye [Contemporary China's nuclear industry]*, Dangdai Zhongguo [Contemporary China] Series (Beijing: Zhongguo shehui kexue chubanshe, 1987), pp. 74–78.
65 Liu, *China as a Nuclear Power in World Politics*, p. 37.
66 Ostrov, "The Impact of the Cultural Revolution on the nuclear weapons program of Communist China," *Issues and Studies* 19 (July 1983), pp. 47–49.
67 Chanchiang (Zhanjiang) Military Subdistrict, "Handgun surely defeats sharp arrow," Peking Domestic Service, April 10, 1977, translated as "Peking radio stresses importance of improved weapons" in FBIS, no. 71 (April 13, 1977), p. E5. See also Theoretical Group of the National Defense Scientific and Technological Commission, "Integration of 'millet plus rifles' with modernization – Criticizing the crimes of the Gang of Four in undermining modernization of national defense," Peking Domestic Service, January 20, 1978, translated as "National defense scientific commission stresses modernization" in FBIS, no. 15 (January 23, 1978), pp. E1–E3, and Atomic Energy Research Institute, "Atomic energy research should serve both military and civilian purposes and make more contributions to the four modernizations," Peking Domestic Service, March 29, 1978, translated as "Atomic Energy Institute calls for increased research" in FBIS, no. 63 (March 31, 1978), pp. E11–E12.

the Cultural Revolution, the above-mentioned weapons testing difficulties, and the purge of scientists, it appears to be reliable.[68]

Furthermore, what success the nuclear weapons program had (which, despite the above comments, was considerable) can be attributed in large part to access to information outside of China. Chinese scientists became aware of the advantages of uranium 238 over plutonium as the fissionable material for the atomic bomb, and of implosion over the gun barrel method as the means of detonating it, from a study of foreign documents.[69] A considerable portion of the scientists involved also had excellent overseas training and experience. The director of the scientists working on the missiles, Qian Xuesen, and others trained and worked in the United States. Qian Sanqiang, the head of those working on the warhead, and his wife, He Zehui, trained and worked in France. Others got their training in Britain and prewar Germany.[70] This overseas experience, together with benefitting from being aware of break-throughs that the Americans and Russians had made in their programs, was probably, in large part, responsible for the speed with which China developed first an atomic and then a hydrogen bomb.

The gist of the discussion above is that, despite apparent success, the NDSTC was an inefficient, if not ineffective, implementer of policy. The success of the atomic weapons program is attributable to factors other than the formal organizational capacity of the NDSTC. The growth that the unit underwent might make one think that it must have been an able policy implementer. However, in light of the discussion above, a more valid inter-pretation would be that such growth reflected a deficiency on the part of the organization. Indeed, if growth can be seen as a search for crucial resources, it is then an attempt to remedy an organizational defect.

That the NDSTC reached the achievements that it did can be attributed more to informal, personal factors than those concerned with formal organi-zation. Consequently, patron–client networks can compensate for adminis-trative deficiencies in policy implementation. However, this is a subject for discussion elsewhere.

A NOTE ON RED GUARD SOURCES

This chapter makes use of a number of *Red Guard* newspaper documents found in the original Chinese text. They come from Red Guard Publications

68 Li Jue, pp. 74–78.
69 Li Jue, pp. 42–43, 68–70, 264, 266.
70 William L. Ryan and Sam Summerlin, *The China Cloud* (Boston: Little, Brown, 1967), pp. 28–31, 43–50, 64–67, 77–81, 160–163, and Cheng, *Scientific and Engineering Manpower in Communist China, 1949–1963* (Washington, DC: National Science Foundation, U.S. Government Printing Office, 1965), pp. 234–240.

(20 volumes), Washington, D.C.: Center for Chinese Research Materials, Association of Research Libraries, 1975. The *Red Guard* newspapers cited are listed below, followed by the English translation of their names and their sources of publication:

916 tongxun [*Bulletin* of September 16] (Guangzhou Middle Schools Red Guard Congress and September 16 Corps of Huanghuagang Middle School)

Zaofan youli [*To Rebel Is Justified*] (September 16 Revolutionary Rebel Corps of the Seventh Ministry of Machine Industry in Beijing)

Feimingdi [*Flying Whistling Arrow*] (New September 15 Revolutionary Rebel Headquarters of the Seventh Ministry of Machine Industry in Beijing)

Keji zhanbao [*Science and Technology Fighters' News*] (Revolutionary Rebels of the State Science and Technology System)

PART IV

ASIAN AUTHORITARIANISM ON THE CHINESE PERIPHERY

CHAPTER 10

NORTH KOREAN INFORMAL POLITICS

SAMUEL S. KIM

The concept of "informal politics," refurbishing previous work on informal power, informal institutions, and informal economy, has recently witnessed rejuvenation in East Asian comparative politics in general and Chinese politics in particular. Yet despite its obvious relevance, informal politics has largely remained *terra incognita* in the study of North Korean politics. The prevailing assumption was that, given North Korea's inaccessibility and the paucity of data, we are not able to peer into the "black box" of Pyongyang's informal politics. Moreover, if socialism has mono-organizational tendencies, the North Korean political system is mono-organizational to a fault.[1] To the extent that factional strife is deemed coterminous with informal politics, the concept thus seemed a poor "fit" for the study of contemporary North Korean politics.

Yet the informal dimension has always remained an integral part of North Korean politics, albeit in shifting form. This has more to do with the unsettled nature of the politics of a divided Korea than with traditional political culture. The division of the nation in 1945 set in motion a politics of competitive legitimation and delegitimation as each Korea, starting from an identical cultural and historical baseline, began pursuing separate paths in a parallel state-building and legitimacy-seeking process underwritten by the two competing superpowers. This was the beginning of a legitimacy *cum* identity challenge that a divided Korea would have to cope with for years. The sources of this abiding challenge have remained more or less the same for both Koreas: (1) leadership and succession crises from within (legitimacy

1 T. H. Rigby, "Introduction: Political legitimacy, Weber and communist mono-organizational systems," in T. H. Rigby and Ferenc Feher, eds., *Political Legitimation in Communist States* (New York: St. Martin's Press, 1982), pp. 12–16. Scalapino and Lee argue that the political system in North Korea is "monocracy," not totalitarianism, which "is inescapably dependent upon an individual personality, his strengths and weaknesses – and, above all, his reach. Totalitarianism in its 'ideal' form is organizational, impersonal, and wholly dependent upon institutional operations." See Robert A. Scalapino and Chong-sik Lee, *Communism in Korea*, 2 vols. (Berkeley: University of California Press, 1972), pp. 784–785.

challenge); (2) continuing threat, real or perceived, from the other Korea (national identity challenge); and (3) twin security dilemmas of allied entrapment or abandonment in the international arena (security challenge). Both formal and informal politics in North Korea pivot around these three distinct but mutually interdependent spheres – domestic, international, and inter-Korean.

INFORMAL POLITICS CONCEIVED AND APPLIED

As formulated in the introductory and concluding chapters of the present volume, the concept of informal politics proceeds from the premise that what we see at the official level is not necessarily what we get. Only by defining the formal and the informal as two separate but related domains and comparing the changing dynamics of the relationship can we arrive at a fuller understanding of how politics actually gets done – to wit, as Haruhiro Fukui expands Lasswell's classical definition of politics in the Introduction, "who gets what, when, how, and at whose expense." The relationship between formal and informal politics is one of functional interdependence, mutually enhancing at best and mutually corrupting at worst; as Dittmer aptly points out, informal politics is ensconced in the middle of a continuum from overt formalization to covert corruption. It is important to point out in this connection that the concept has little to do with the state/society paradigm, which in the North Korean case commands little if any heuristic value.[2] In traditional Korea as well, political disputes were concentrated in the vortex of court politics in Seoul, never having the chance to arise in an absent "civil society."

The leadership/succession challenge is the most important variable involved in parsing the *Gestalt* of informal politics in North Korea. As in China and South Korea, the paramount leaders (Park Chung Hee, Mao Zedong, and Deng Xiaoping) exercise such unique authority that factional strife and debate among informal groups have had rather marginal and tangential effects. It is in the absence of such a paramount leader, such as at the height of a succession crisis, that informal politics tends to rise or can be held hostage to elite factional strife. During the present heyday of the supreme

2 For a cogent analysis along this line, see James Cotton, "Civil society in the political transition of North Korea: The limitations of the East European model," *Korea & World Affairs* 16:2 (Summer 1992), pp. 319–337. To cite another example, in a major multiauthored book on state and society in contemporary Korea, we find only one chapter by Bruce Cumings who says a lot about the North Korean state – as "the corporate state," as "the leader as core of the state," and so on – but virtually nothing about "civil society," presumably meaning that there is no civil society to talk about. See Bruce Cumings, "The corporate state in North Korea," in Hagen Koo, ed., *State and Society in Contemporary Korea* (Ithaca: Cornell University Press, 1993), pp. 197–230.

suryong (gr. leader system) based on dynastic perpetation of strongman Rule, [handwritten annotation]

leadership, factional strife remains quiescent or goes underground, even as informal politics shifts gears toward embracing policy issues. Indeed, the single greatest challenge stimulating North Korea's informal politics over the years may be seen as the progressive development and dynastic perpetuation of a strongman rule known as the *suryong* (great leader) system.

The methodological problem of plumbing the actual workings of informal politics in the absence of empirical information and data is serious but not insurmountable. To begin with, an archival-documentary approach, even if it were possible, is not without its own problems, as the concentration on documents alone can easily foster a kind of document blindness that obscures the discrepancies between official rhetoric and political reality. Obsessed with the imperative of secrecy and strategic deception in the planning of a surprise attack against the South in June 1950, for instance, North Korea's top leadership subjected its own administrative and military apparatuses to a strong dosage of deception. "Even secret Central Committee documents that were seized by UN forces when they captured Pyongyang made absolutely no mention of the forthcoming invasion."[3] Yoo Sung Chill, one-time head of the North Korean Army's Operations Directorate, predicted to an interviewer in the early 1990s, "Even after Kim Il Sung dies, you won't be able to find any legal document about an [the] attack."[4]

Since we are unable to observe Pyongyang's informal politics directly, we can only draw causal inferences from the manifest outcomes plus whatever other materials come to hand, including defectors' accounts.[5] We may hypostatize what informal decisions would have been necessary for given observable political outcomes to have occurred. There is no point in trying to probe elite motives, perceptions, and norms unless these are linked to manifest con-

3 John Merrill, *Korea: The Peninsula Origins of the War* (Newark, DE: University of Delaware Press, 1989), p. 176.

4 Sergei N. Goncharov, John W. Lewis, and Xue Litai, *Uncertain Partners: Stalin, Mao and the Korean War* (Stanford: Stanford University Press, 1993), p. 150.

5 The single greatest information gold mine about North Korea's informal politics and decision-making process is Hwang Jang-yop, North Korea's chief ideologue and theoretician of Juche ideology and the highest-ranking party leader yet to defect to South Korea in April 1997 via China and the Philippines. As of late 1998, several letters of his written in late 1996 and early 1997 plus a number of articles and a series of long interviews have already been published in *Chosun Ilbo* (Seoul), February 13, 1997, pp. 3–4; June 15, 1998; "Hwang Jang-yop bimil p'ail" [Hwang Jang yop secret file], special edition of *Wolgan Chosun [Monthly Korea]* (April 1998); *Sindong-a [New East Asia]* (July 1998), pp. 328–345; and "Running against history: Defector sees Kim's regime as increasingly brittle," *Far Eastern Economic Review* (October 15, 1998), pp. 30, 32. In mid-1998, Hwang's postdefection book, *North Korea's Truth and Falsehood*, was "published" as a secret internal document by the Unification Policy Research Institute, and the main points of the book were published in *Wolgan Chosun* (August 1998), pp. 111–124. In early 1999, Hwang Jang-yop's memoir was published as *Nanun yoksa ui chinri rul patta (I witnessed historical truth)* (Seoul: Hanul, 1999). In addition, a text of Kim Jong Il's secret speech delivered on December 7, 1996, at the Kimilsung University was published in *Chosun Ilbo*, (March, 1997) and *Wolgan Chosun* (April 1997), pp. 306–317 – hereafter cited as "Kim Jong Il's Secret Speech" – giving rare insight into North Korean informal politics.

sequences: In politics as in law, what really matters is manifest behavior. As Alexander Wendt argues in rebutting structural realism in international relations theory, "agents and structures are produced or reproduced by what actors *do*."[6]

We postulate that the important decisions of informal politics will eventually be expressed in constitutional form (either a new constitution or amendments to the extant constitution), in the restructuring of the formal authority structures, in appointments to top government and party positions – particularly the Central Committee of the Workers' Party of Korea (WPK), the Politburo, and its standing committee (Presidium since 1980) – and in major ideological doctrines or policy pronouncements. Given the centrality of the ruling WPK, any change in the formal party hierarchy (even the pecking order in newly published pictures of leading political figures at important state events) can tell a lot about what had already happened in informal politics. Any radical shift in policy or ideology – either domestic or international – indicates that there is firm leadership or a new consensus in Pyongyang's informal politics, as only a paramount leader would be able to overcome the vested bureaucratic interests resisting such change (e.g., Kim Il Sung's decision to accept Jimmy Carter's proposal in mid-June 1994 for a North–South summit and to dismantle its nuclear weapons program in exchange for a light-water reactor, leading to the historic U.S.–DPRK Agreed Framework four months later).

Informal politics is by no means fixed on one issue area but may vary across issue areas and over time, subject to the long-term underlying and short-term proximate causes. A short list of the former in the North Korean case include: (1) traditional factional strife for power – what Gregory Henderson called "Korea's chief hereditary disease," referring to "the unlimited atomized competition for the highest posts";[7] (2) the long tradition of relatively weak and restrained central monarchical power;[8] and (3) cultural aversion to the rule of law and the correspondingly inadequate institutionalization of the formal rules of the game. The proximate causes refer to crises requiring a quick response unencumbered by formal rules and structures. Even in democracy, a crisis, especially a national security crisis, provides an alibi for extraconstitutional response, permitting informal politics to rise through back doors.[9]

6 Alexander Wendt, "Collective identity formation and the international state," *American Political Science Review* 88:2 (June 1994), p. 390; emphasis in original.
7 Gregory Henderson, *Korea: The Politics of the Vortex* (Cambridge, MA: Harvard University Press, 1968), p. 360.
8 For this weak state thesis in traditional Korean politics, see Palais, *Politics and Policy in Traditional Korea* (Cambridge, MA: Harvard University Press, 1975).
9 Tellingly, participants in American informal politics during the Cuban missile crisis numbered less than a dozen, approximating the number of key participants in the Soviet Politburo. See Robert F. Kennedy, *Thirteen Days: A Memoir of the Cuban Missile Crisis* (New York: W. W. Norton, 1971).

Despite the obvious normative problem, informal politics can play a variety of positive roles, such as providing flexibility in decision making or opening up channels of communication to permit small groups of experts to submit new ideas or policy proposals directly to the upper echelons, giving the leadership fresh options. This type of informal politics has been crucial to the progress of reform in post-Mao China.[10] Whether it can succeed in the DPRK remains to be seen.

The style of informal politics in North Korea is personalistic and charismatic, with personal loyalty to and intimate ties with the Great Leader serving as the glue holding together the inner nucleus of power. Indeed, Kim Il Sung has been touted as "the sun of the nation"[11] and "the highest brain of the living socio-political entity and represents the life of the community. . . . He is to the people exactly as the brain is to human activity."[12] The nerve center of informal politics in Pyongyang has remained, at least since 1972, the *suryong* system, involving a small number of participants enjoying the Great Leader's highest degree of confidence because the stakes are so high, personal loyalty and judgments so crucial, and secrecy of informal deliberations so imperative. We can sketch a continuum of informal power in terms of proximity to the Great Leader. Put differently, access to the Great Leader that one cannot enjoy without personal closeness, loyalty, and trust – and what can constitute greater personal closeness and trust than a father–son relationship in Confucian culture? – is nine-tenths of informal power.

But to develop a conceptual synthesis about North Korean politics, we need to relate informal politics to formal politics. One of the ways to construct such a continuum is to bring the agent/structure nexus back in – that is, to accept the formal structure as first defining the parameters of informal politics – providing "both feeding trough and temple for the practice of informal politics," as Dittmer suggests in the concluding chapter, and later redefining those parameters by the outcomes of informal politics. Such a process-oriented definition seems more suitable at this early stage of analysis. Another possibility is to adopt a diachronic perspective, asking whether North Korea's informal politics has a life cycle similar to the Eriksonian stages in the mutation of personal identity. That is the approach adopted here, viewing informal politics as a response to stage-specific threats to – and opportunities for – elite goals in the context of North Korea's political

10 Joseph Fewsmith, "Institutions, informal politics, and political transition in China," *Asian Survey*, 36:3 (March 1996), pp. 230–245.

11 Tellingly, the official three-volume hagiography of Kim Il Sung by Baik Bong, published in Korean, English, and several other languages, is entitled, *The Sun of the Nation: Marshall Kim Il Sung*. See Baik Bong, *Minjok ui taeyang: Kim Il-song changkun* [*The sun of the nation: Marshall Kim Il Sung*], 3 vols. (n.p.: Inmun kwahaksa, 1969–1971).

12 Kim Jong Il's statement as cited in *Vantage Point* 12:2 (February 1989), pp. 2–3.

development. A life cycle of informal politics can be schematically delineated as follows:

Long-term Underlying Causes + Short-term Proximate Causes → Formal Institutional Setting → Onset of Informal Politics → Tactics Employed and Ends Pursued → Manifest Structural, Normative and Policy Outcomes

THREE DEVELOPMENTAL CYCLES

For analytical convenience, the life span of North Korean informal politics may be divided into roughly three major cycles. In the first consolidation cycle, from 1945 to 1972, informal politics mutated through a series of alternating strategies – from national united-front coalition (short-lived) to party coalition to party uniformity – in the gradual but steady process of eliminating all rivals for the establishment of a strongman rule – the *suryong* system – in North Korea. In the second cycle, from 1973 to 1993, informal politics was consumed in the preparation of the father-to-son succession. In the third system crisis cycle, from 1994 to the present (early 1999), informal politics has encountered the daunting challenge of coping with deepening chasms between the formal and the informal as unofficial spheres in ideology, state, economy, and culture have grown unabated, undermining the official spheres of the North Korean political system.

The long-term underlying and short-term immediate catalysts of informal politics in North Korea were fragmentation, division, and factionalism. Contrary to the popular notion that depicts Yi Korea (1392–1910) as highly centralized and very strong, and that Kim Il Sung's centralizing power drive was thus culturally determined, the traditional Korean state was relatively weak because the formal centralized autocratic structure was a facade that obscured more than revealed the reality of aristocratic power. As James Palais put it, "The weakness of royal prestige and authority was characteristic of Korean states since the formation of the earliest kingdoms."[13]

The picture of fratricidal factionalism emerging from the formative years (1918–1925) of the Korean communist movement provides a preview of many troubled years ahead. More than anything else, the factional strife reflected and effected other problems, such as the nature and structure of group relations in Korean culture; the dispersed, self-contained character of overseas bases; the diverse and often divisive influences of Soviet, Chinese, and Japanese communists; the morale-weakening effects of continuous failure; the narrow base of recruitment; the shortage of funds; the constant

---

13 Palais, *Politics and Policy*, p. 11.

change in the organization and leadership; the lack of training in the basic ideological discipline of Marxism-Leninism; the tactical and strategic blunders, the efficiency of the Japanese police; and the indecision, ineptitude, and ignorance of the Comintern.[14]

THE FIRST CYCLE (1945–1972)

The initial post-Liberation political landscape of North Korea was one of political fragmentation and institutional void, with at least five major political groups contending for power. These can be identified on the basis of several separate but overlapping criteria, such as geographical origins and territorial power bases (Soviet, Yan'an, Manchurian or Kapsan, North Korean and South Korean), international connections (Soviet, Chinese communist), and, after 1948, functional and institutional power bases (party, military, state bureaucracy, etc.): (1) the domestic noncommunist nationalists led by Cho Man-sik – the most respected noncommunist leader in North Korea during the short interim period between Liberation and the arrival of the Russians on August 24, 1945; (2) the domestic communist group, most numerous and most of them aligned with Pak Hon-yong but with their divided operations in the South and the North (a major strategic blunder); (3) the Yan'an group of returned revolutionaries from China; (4) the Soviet-Korean group, composed of Soviet-Koreans who returned home with Soviet military forces; and (5) the partisan group – also known as the Kapsan group – made up of Kim Il Sung's own guerrilla fighters in Manchuria.

During the Soviet occupation period (1945–1948), Pyongyang's informal politics *faute de mieux* represented nearly the sum total of North Korean politics. Under Soviet support the informal politics of everyday life was largely devoted to building the Soviet-style party, military, and governmental infrastructures needed for the founding of the WPK (August 28–30, 1946), the Korean People's Army (KPA, February 8, 1948), and the DPRK (September 9, 1948). Soviet Major General Romanenko's office in Pyongyang served as "the nerve center of Soviet authority" and the trellis from which contending factional groups, especially the Soviet-Korean and Kim Il Sung's partisan groups, exerted their influence.[15] One thing seems clear enough – that Kim Il Sung could not possibly rise in informal politics as *primus inter pares* without Soviet support. The first constitution of the DPRK (1948) that formalized the outcome of informal politics of the occupation period was patterned after the Soviet (Stalin) Constitution, and even after the Soviet occupation

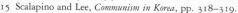

14 Scalapino and Lee, *Communism in Korea*, chap. 2, pp. 66–136, and Dae-Sook Suh, *The Korean Communist Movement 1918–1948* (Princeton: Princeton University Press, 1967).
15 Scalapino and Lee, *Communism in Korea*, pp. 318–319.

army withdrew from North Korea a large number of Soviet advisors remained to assist Kim Il Sung.[16]

There is no easy or simple answer to the question as to why Moscow picked Kim Il Sung as the Soviet man in Pyongyang in the critical first stage of the first cycle of informal politics. Perhaps one basic factor might well have to do with a Soviet determination to pick a man without a past factional entanglement. Kim Il Sung was one of a few communists who not only escaped Japanese arrest but also avoided getting himself trapped in the old factional strife. Kim Il Sung, in his early thirties during the Soviet occupation period, was too young to have been deeply entangled in and contaminated by the factional feuds of the past.[17] Without minimizing the decisiveness of Soviet influence in the rise of Kim Il Sung, Gavin McCormack argues that Kim Il Sung "was also the choice for leader of both the Korean and Chinese guerrillas, and he had the priceless asset of a nationwide reputation as resistance fighter and patriot."[18] That Kim Il Sung could speak a little Russian and that he was perceived as a man of swift action, according to Hwang Jang-yop, helped a lot as well.[19] From a Soviet perspective, then, Kim Il Sung seemed well suited for rising above the fray to build a broad-based communist coalition. Whatever the real reasons, Soviet support and backing was *sine qua non* for Kim Il Sung's ascent.

Emerging from a fractured and muddied political scene in the Soviet occupation period, Kim Il Sung has demonstrated the resilience, resourcefulness, tenacity, and absolute opportunism of a formidable guerrilla fighter turned into a superb politician with a Machiavellian/Stalinist sense of timing and sensitivity to the changing correlation of domestic and external political forces. His masterful maneuver to control the agenda of informal politics and gradually and methodically smash all rival political groups evolved through several stages in the completion of the first consolidation cycle, which lasted two and a half decades. During the Soviet occupation period the domestic noncommunist nationalist group was quickly reduced to impotence through assassination, arrest, and disappearance, never having a chance to get off first base. Still, the dominant feature of informal politics right up to the eve of the Korean War was united-front coalition building.

16 It has recently come to light that, for more than two years during the Korean War, American and Soviet air forces had actually fought against each other over North Korea and part of northeastern China without the rest of the world knowing about it. See Jon Halliday, "A secret war," *Far Eastern Economic Review* (April 22, 1993), pp. 32–36.

17 Scalapino and Lee, *Communism in Korea*, p. 326. For a similar argument, see also Suh, *The Korean Communist Movement*, p. 26; Gavan McCormack, "Kim country: Hard times in North Korea," *New Left Review* 198 (March–April 1993), pp. 22–23, and Wada Haruki, *Kim Il-sŏng kwa Manchu hanil chŏnchaeng* [*Kim Il Sung and the Manchurian Resistance War against Japan*], trans. Yi Chong-sok (Seoul: Ch'angchak kwapi pyongsa, 1992).

18 McCormack, "Kim country," p. 24.   19 *Chosun Ilbo* (Internet version), June 15, 1998.

The Korean War – or rather its unsuccessful conclusion – presented the gravest peril to the survival of the DPRK and the greatest challenge yet to Kim's leadership. More than anything else, North Korea's infamous June 1950 surprise attack against South Korea was primarily the function of Kim's "magnificent obsession" to settle once and for all the problem of national unification by force of arms. The idea of initiating the war came directly from Kim Il Sung, who "began lobbying for a Soviet-backed invasion of the South as early as March 1949. He proposed it, fought for it and with a Soviet army battle plan to guide him, executed it. The invasion of June 25, 1950, was preplanned, blessed, and directly assisted by Stalin and his generals, and reluctantly backed by Mao at Stalin's insistence."[20] However, as documents from the Soviet archives and interviews with high-ranking DPRK émigrés have subsequently revealed, Kim Il Sung and his top advisors launched the attack based on the serious miscalculation that such a military unification could be accomplished in less than a month.[21] The Korean War turned out to be a national unification war that Kim Il Sung started but could not finish, nor could he even bring about an armistice by himself.

The war brought about a decisive shift in the overall balance of Soviet and Chinese forces influencing North Korean informal politics. The Soviet army that had successfully maneuvered Kim Il Sung into power failed to return while the Chinese "volunteers" intervened in October 1950 to rescue the fledgling socialist regime on the verge of collapse and stayed on until 1958, marking the end of the Soviet domination and the beginning of Chinese influence. And yet, remarkably, Kim turned the multiple dangers of the Korean War into opportunities to smash one by one all potential rivals and challengers. The serendipity factor cannot be ignored here. Once the Korean War became globalized, involving many countries and the United Nations, Kim had to deal only with his domestic rivals.

Having gained breathing space from the internationalization of the Korean War, Kim Il Sung proved to be a master politician of informal politics in the consolidation of absolute power in the 1950s and 1960s. He first turned against the domestic communist group (converting his own strategic miscalculations and blunders into those of the domestic communist group), then turned against the Soviet-Korean group, taking advantage of the absence

---

20 Sergei N. Goncharov, John W. Lewis, and Xue Litai, *Uncertain Partners: Stalin, Mao and the Korean War* (Stanford: Stanford University Press, 1993), p. 213. This is the best account to date of Kim's methodical planning, lobbying, and execution of the war, one that shatters the revisionist interpretation beyond repair.

21 Goncharov, Lewis, and Xue, *Uncertain Partners*, pp. 136–137, 154–155; Kathryn Weathersby, "Soviet aims in Korea and the origins of the Korean War, 1945–1950", *Cold War International History Project Working Paper* 8 (1993), pp. 24–26; and Hakjoon Kim, "Russian foreign ministry documents on the origins of the Korean War," *Korea and World Affairs* 20:2 (Summer 1996), pp. 248–271.

of Soviet military presence in North Korea, and finally turned against the Yan'an group. In a decade-long guerrilla-style informal campaign, Kim prevailed especially after the withdrawal of the Soviet troops from the North in 1948, not because of Soviet support, but *in spite of* Soviet and Chinese intervention, by raising the costs of allied intervention and by projecting great-power intervention and factionalism as cause and effect of *sadae-jui* (serving the great or "flunkeyism" in Pyongyang's political vocabulary), a traditional disease in Korean foreign-policy thinking that led to a loss of national independence (*Juche*). By the Fourth Party Congress (WPK-IV), held in September 1961, traces of all rival groups save the partisan group had disappeared, as was made evident in the restructuring of the formal authority hierarchy of the Central Committee and the top twenty party leaders and for the first time complete evacuation of allied troops from North Korea.

The rise of partisan hegemony at WPK-IV set the stage for another wave of purges – this time directed against Kim Il Sung's own partisan generals. Taking advantage of their prominence in the reconstituted party hierarchy, the partisan generals moved quickly in initiating a crucial change of policy under the banner of "arms on the one hand and hammer and sickle on the other" at the fifth plenum of the Central Committee, held December 10–14, 1962. In actuality, this guns-and-butter policy was overlaid by four basic policy goals: arming the entire populace; fortifying the entire country; training every soldier to become cadre; and modernizing military weapons and equipment. Such an emphasis on the military buildup in the 1960s raised the prominence of the partisan generals too high for Kim Il Sung's comfort. The overzealous generals were domineering in informal politics, issuing directives on nonmilitary affairs. Against this backdrop, in 1969 Kim Il Sung moved quietly and swiftly in purging the top twelve partisan generals, including Ho Pong-hak, Kim Kwang-hyop, Kim Ch'ang-bong, Choe Gwang, Yi Yong-ho, and Sok San. Oh Chin-u survived the purge to later become the defense minister and stayed on as defense minister and a member of the Political Committee (Presidium) right up to his death in February 1995. Apparently, the partisan generals were purged via removal and disappearance, not execution, subject to recall (as with Choe Gwang), and there was no official announcement of their fall.[22] From 1966 to 1970, Kim Il Sung purged six of eleven members of the Politburo and seven of ten party secretaries.

The first long consolidation cycle of informal politics came to a successful conclusion in late 1972 with the enactment of a new socialist constitution replacing the first (Stalinist) constitution of 1948. Informal politics took the

---

22 For details on the rise and fall of the partisan generals, see Suh, *Kim Il Sung*, pp. 211–223, 238–248.

form of classical factional power politics. Kim Il Sung's masterful struggle to control and eventually wipe out the fratricidal factionalism of competing leadership groups with non-Communist nationalist, Soviet, Chinese, indigenous, and even his own partisan (Kapsan) connections – and to consolidate his personal power and to superimpose his vision of national identity – lasted more than two and a half decades. As if to emulate the tactics in Sun Zi's *Art of War* (e.g., subduing the enemy without fighting, attacking the enemy where he is unprepared, waiting until the enemy reveals weaknesses and vulnerabilities, and so on), Kim Il Sung always picked one "enemy" group at a time, never scattering his shots. If the WPK-IV marked the triumph of the partisan group, WPK-V signaled its disappearance and the emergence of a new group of relatively unknown leaders who were not partisans themselves but partisan-trained technocrats and Kim Il Sung's relatives (e.g., Kim Il Sung's younger brother, Kim Yong-ju; Kim Il Sung's wife, Kim Song-ae; and such others as Pak Song-chol, Yang Hyong-sop, and Ho Tam, all reported to be related to Kim Il Sung).

Indeed, the 1972 Constitution can be said to have successfully embodied the ideological, structural, and policy outcomes of the first cycle of informal politics. First, the 1972 Constitution signaled the resolution of a national identity crisis by proclaiming the *Juche* idea as a "creative application of Marxism-Leninism to the conditions of our country" (Article 4) and the transformation of the DPRK into an independent (*Juche*) state. Although Kim Il Sung made his first reference to the term *juche* in his speech to party propaganda and agitation workers on December 28, 1955, it was the socialist split, not the socialist solidarity, in the communist world in the 1960s that energized the progressive development and codification of *Juche* ideology; it was through Kim Il Sung's alternating feuds with Soviet revisionism and Chinese dogmatism in the 1960s that he was able, and to a certain extent forced, to find his way clear to seeking Korean national identity. Tellingly, Kim Il Sung began to call himself *suryong* at the height of the cult of personality in China, when the Chinese Red Guards hurled all kinds of personal insults (e.g., "a revisionist swine who lived like an emperor of bygone days"). The *suryong* system emerged as Pyongyang was trying to outdo Beijing in the game of the cult of personality with its own list of hagiographical prefixes, calling Kim Il Sung "the great leader, the great suryong, peerless patriot, national hero, ever victorious iron-willed brilliant commander, an outstanding leader of the international communist movement, an ingenious thinker, the sun of the nation, the red sun of the oppressed people of the world, the greatest leader of our time," and on and on.[23]

23 Suh, *Kim Il Sung*, p. 316.

As well, the new constitution seemed tailor-made enough for the *suryong* system by not only creating an all-powerful office of presidency (*chusok*), but also by stipulating that the highest leadership organ of the state – the Central People's Committee (CPC) – was to consist of members elected by the Supreme People's Assembly on recommendation by the president of the republic. For formal politics the shift of emphasis from the party to the state was palpable. The restructured partisan group – Kim Il Sung's extended political family, as it were – now made up more than 80 percent of the Central Committee of WPK-V. While avoiding such massive disruptions as Mao's Cultural Revolution, Kim Il Sung nonetheless kept the upper echelons of the WPK in constant turnover so as to prevent the rise of any coalition and to ensure that no faction stayed in the upper leadership echelons long enough to constitute itself as an actual or potential opposition. An extremely high turnover rate of the membership of the Central Committee from one party congress to the next – approximately 60–70 percent – was an integral part of Kim Il Sung's divide-and-conquer strategy in the consolidation and codification of the *suryong* system from which stemmed all political blessings and punishments.

The Second Cycle (1973–1993)

The formalization of the *suryong* system had hardly begun when Pyongyang shifted its gears toward the political succession of a second kind, setting in motion another long cycle of informal politics. The political logic of a first-ever hereditary succession in the communist world, at least for Kim Il Sung, was perhaps plain enough. By the end of the first cycle, the basic core group supporting Kim Il Sung's protracted struggle to eliminate all rival factions – actual or perceived – had begun to disintegrate due to natural attrition, purges of the partisan generals, and an extremely high turnover rate of the top leadership echelons. The unity of the partisan group, his mainstay in winning and sustaining political power, was no longer necessary or even viable for Kim. While many partisan-trained loyalists and technocrats were brought in to take up the slack, Kim Il Sung's "continuing revolution" – to wit, to carry out the *suryong* system from generation to generation – still required a new generation of leaders, all loyal and all close to the Great Leader. The beginning of the North–South dialogue in 1972 in the wake of Sino-American rapprochement required formal presidential politics – hence the creation of an office of presidency in the new socialist constitution. Thus, the logic of domestic and external challenges required a shift of power from the party to the state in formal politics. In informal political terms, there was no significant shift because of overlapping memberships of top leaders in the party, the state (government), and the military.

The second cycle of informal politics had been predominantly concerned with the gradual preparation of the father-to-son succession. Not surprisingly, legitimation remained the Achilles heel. In the wake of Kim Il Sung's death, the DPRK government and official media could not even get their numbers act together. "*Thirty years* have passed since the dear leader Comrade Kim Jong Il began to direct Party work," we are told, "in political, economic, cultural and military fields."[24] And yet, the North Korean chief negotiator, Vice Foreign Minister Kang Sok-ju, reassured the inquiring Western journalists in Geneva in mid-August 1994 that "Our dear leader comrade Kim Jong Il has been overseeing the overall affairs of our country – political, military, economic and foreign affairs . . . for as long as 20 years."[25]

In fact, this long succession process took some twenty years, and it may be divided into roughly three stages. In the first stage, from February 1973 [when the Political Committee of the Politburo decided to accept Kim Jong Il's idea of the Three-Revolution Team Movement (*Samdae hyongmyong sojo undong*) – regarded by many as the North Korean equivalent of the Cultural Revolution] or perhaps more accurately from February 1974 (when he was elected a member of the Politburo of the Central Committee and the crucial decision was apparently made to make him the sole heir to Kim Il Sung)[26] to October 1980, North Korea was engaged in covert politics with elliptic references to the "party center," even as official spokesmen vehemently denied that such a feudal practice as hereditary succession was possible under socialism. In any case, it was Kim Il Sung's decision, presumably made without the advice and consent of his top advisors but pro forma endorsed by the Political Committee of the Politburo in a secret session. In the second stage, from October 1980 to May 1990, the succession/legitimation politics came out in the open with the accompanying cult of personality of the "Dear Leader" and the publication of Kim Jong Il's writings – no fewer than three books (one running to two volumes) on the life and exploits of Kim Jong Suk (Kim Jong Il's mother and Kim Il Sung's first wife). At the WPK-VI in October 1980, Kim Jong Il was formally appointed to the most powerful organ of the North Korean political system, Presidium of the Politburo, then consisting of five members, securing by 1984 the second highest ranking in the party hierarchy. In the third and final stage, from 1990 to 1993, Kim Jong Il assumed power over the military with one military promotion after another.

24 "Thirty years of guidance," *The Pyongyang Times*, June 18, 1994, p. 1; emphasis added. See also editorial, *Rodong sinmun*, June 19, 1995, p. 1.
25 Cited in *New York Times*, August 14, 1994, p. 18; emphasis added.
26 A full-page advertisement, "Kim Jong Il Emerges as the Lodestar for Sailing the 21ˢᵗ Century," appeared in the *New York Times* of December 16, 1997, p. A21, stating among other things that Kim Jong Il became "the sole heir to President Kim Il Sung" in February 1974.

Apparently, Kim Il Sung defined the parameters of Kim Jong Il's leadership in informal politics – that the Dear Leader should take command over the political, ideological, and administrative restructuring of the ruling party as well as the military restructuring, just as the Great Leader himself had done during the first long cycle, while still retaining the triple crowns of formal authority as president of the republic, secretary general of the WPK, and the supreme commander of the KPA for formal politics, especially in foreign affairs. Kim Il Sung's actual role in the second cycle was perhaps that of a final arbiter rather than that of actual decision maker. Kim Il Sung, who was in his early sixties, was too old to get himself involved in informal politics and too concerned about capturing leadership in Third World global politics in the 1970s.

It seems evident that there was such a division of responsibility between the Great Leader and the Dear Leader in the second succession cycle. For Kim Il Sung, apparently, foreign affairs still remained too important a challenge to be entrusted to his successor-designate. That the Great Leader completely dominated the official conduct of foreign affairs – and that the Dear Leader had no foreign policy experience of any kind to speak of – has been made evident in a posthumous account. In the course of conducting "energetic foreign policy for the cause of independence, peace, and friendship," we are told, President Kim Il Sung met and conversed with about 70,000 foreigners – including 230 heads of state and government – from 136 countries in his lifetime. In June 1994 alone, he met and had an hour-long conversation with former U.S. President Jimmy Carter and energetically worked with delegations and high-ranking officials of different countries on nearly twenty occasions.[27]

The manifest outcomes of the second succession cycle can be seen in three areas: party restructuring; the emergence of a military-industrial complex; and Kimilsungism. The second cycle did not experience a series of purges as in the first cycle. Still, though, as rumors of a succession struggle spread in the mid-1970s, Kim Jong Il managed to bring down a few more partisans in the process. From the mid-1970s, a number of top party leaders began to disappear from important public functions: Kim Tong-gyu (the third highest ranking party member), Kim Chung-nin (member of the Political Committee and party secretary), Yang Hyong-sop, and Yi Yong-mu. By WPK-VI in 1980, however, it was clear that the Great Leader and Dear Leader prevailed by purging all opposition to the father-to-son succession.[28] Kim Il Sung's partisan faction increased its representation from 90 percent in 1970 to 100 percent in 1980 in the top twenty leadership positions of the Central

---

27 FBIS-EAS, December 7, 1994, p. 30.   28 See Suh, *Kim Il Sung*, pp. 280–281.

Committee of the WPK, even as Kim Jong Il received triple-crown promotions – secretary of the party's Secretariat right after his father, the fourth
highest ranking member of the Politburo (and advanced to the second highest ranking member in 1984), and the third highest ranking member of the
Military Commission of the party behind his father and General Oh Jin-u.
The ten-member Secretariat of the party that manages the party's daily work
was packed with Kim Jong Il's supporters. Thus the WPK-VI marked a
major step in formalizing the hereditary succession. Unlike his father, Kim
Jong Il managed to avoid purging anyone in the upper echelons of the party
hierarchy. During the period 1980–1994, while Kim Jong Il was exercising
full control over personnel affairs, six (out of nineteen) Politburo members
died and six were transferred to other posts, but no purge took place.[29]

More significantly, the second cycle of informal politics spawned nepotism,
with many of Kim Il Sung's relatives recruited into the top leadership echelons. Starting in 1958, all North Koreans have been classified into three main
classes (the core class, the wavering class, and the hostile class) and fifty-one
group categories based on the following attributes and criteria: (1) the intensity of their loyalty to Kim Il Sung and Kim Jong Il; (2) family background,
going back to great-grandparents to determine their proletarian lineage; and
(3) birthplace origins – whether in the North or South – to determine if their
loyalty is firm or vulnerable. The three main classes were divided into the
core class with twelve groups (about 5 million or one-fourth of the entire
population), the wavering class with eighteen subgroups (over one-half the
population), and the hostile class with twenty-one subgroups (about 4 million or 20 percent of the population). The core of the core class was further
divided into three subclasses: (1) members of Kim Il Sung's extended family; (2) high-ranking party and government leaders; and (3) top elites' followers or loyalists and the descendants of deceased revolutionaries or war
heroes.[30]

By the end of the second cycle, five main groups constituted an extended
and restructured Kim Il Sung and Kim Jong Il support group: (1) a few
remaining Kim Il Sung's elder partisan comrades-in-arms showing absolute
loyalty to the father–son succession – for example, Oh Jin-u (defense minister until late February 1995, when he died), Pak Song-chol (vice president),
Li Ul-sol (head of the Secret Service), Choe Gwang (defense minister since
October 1995, who died in February 1997); (2) Kim Il Sung's relatives; (3)

29 Yu Suk-ryol, "Changes in power positions of North Korean leaders and Pyongyang's policy trends,"
   Vantage Point 20:1 (January 1997), p. 37.
30 Richard Kagan, Matthew Oh, and David Weissbrodt for the Minnesota Lawyers International Human
   Rights Committee and Asia Watch, *Human Rights in the Democratic People's Republic of Korea (North
   Korea)* (Washington, DC: Asia Watch, 1988), pp. 34–40.

partisan-trained technocrats or offspring of first-generation partisans; (4) Kim Jong Il's schoolmates (from the Mangyongdae Revolutionary School and Kimilsung University); and (5) Three-Revolution Squad Movement members whom Kim Jong Il recruited to serve as his advance guards (numbering about 46,000). A screening system was set up at party offices of all levels to review and eliminate all of those from the core class who were prone to oppose the hereditary succession as a way of building a solid political infrastructure for the father-to-son succession process. By the end of 1993, relatives of Kim Il Sung in top leadership positions numbered about twenty.[31]

As a result, the North Korean political system has been dominated and controlled to an almost unique extent by the Kim Il Sung family, with far-reaching consequences for informal politics. Indeed, the extraconstitutional signature of North Korea's national identity is Kim Il Sung's extended family: North Korea as "the Kim country" or as "the corporate state" or "a family state" or "the leader as core of the state."[32] The constitution of the DPRK – as amended on April 9, 1992 and officially published on November 26, 1992 – still makes no reference to the Kim family state as such, let alone socialist dynastic succession, except to say that "revolutionary fighters, families of revolutionary and patriotic martyrs, depends of People's Army personnel and disabled veterans enjoy the special protection of state and society" (Article 75). Despite the intensive preparation for the first-ever socialist dynastic succession, the national identity-cum-legitimation crisis remained unresolved at the end of the second cycle of informal politics.

Another noticeable outcome can be seen in the rise of a military-industrial complex. As early as 1972, Scalapino and Lee characterized North Korea as "probably the most highly militarized society in the world today" as the country of fewer than 14 million inhabitants at the time had over 400,000 men in its regular armed forces.[33] By 1993, North Korea's military manpower had grown to 1.2 million, the world's fifth largest armed forces after China, Russia, the United States, and India; and at 53.0 troops per 1,000 population, it also has the world's highest troop-to-population ratio. Measured in terms of defense spending as a percentage of the GDP, North Korea, with its defense expenditure estimated at 25.2 percent of its GDP, became the world's third largest defense spender (after Bosnia and Angola).[34] When its 1.2 mil-

---

31 Hyun-Joon Chon, "Structure of the power elite of North Korea," *Korean Journal of National Unification*, special ed. (1994), pp. 7, 9–12.
32 McCormack, "Kim country," and Cumings, "The corporate state in North Korea."
33 Scalapino and Lee, *Communism in Korea*, p. 919.
34 See "Defense technology survey," *Economist* (London) (June 10, 1995), p. 7. In 1996, North Korea's GNP was about $20 billion and its defense expenditure about $5.4 billion, or 27% of the GNP. See *The Military Balance 1997/98* (London: International Institute for Strategic Studies, 1997), p. 183.

lion active military personnel are combined with a total of 5.9 million in
active reserve, security, and paramilitary forces, a whopping 29 percent of the
population make up a swollen garrison state. While the security challenge
from the South was a contributing factor, the main cause was largely political. Indeed, the father–son succession and a new wave of rapid militarization
developed in tandem in a mutually complementary way. In his rise to power
during the second cycle, Kim Jong Il was forced to circumvent the formal
authority structures, spawning parallel institutions through which to discipline party members who were resistant to the father–son succession process.
The military may well have been strengthened and expanded beyond any reasonable national defense requirements for that purpose.

All the same, for Kim Il Sung, as it was for Mao, political power could only
grow from the barrel of guns. By 1990, Kim Il Sung was ready to take a second major step in the father–son succession preparation process with a series
of military promotions – first vice chair of the National Defense Commission
in May 1990, supreme commander of the Korean People's Army (KPA) in
December 1991, the rank of marshal in April 1992, and chairman of the
National Defense Commission (NDC) in April 1993. It is worth noting in this
connection that Kim Jong Il's appointment as the supreme commander of the
KPA in December 1991 was in direct contravention of the extant socialist constitution of 1972 (Article 93), which stipulates that the president of the republic is ipso facto the supreme commander of all of the armed forces and the
chairman of the National Defense Commission. Ex post facto, this constitutional contravention was fixed up in April 1992, when the SPA made a
partial revision of the constitution to provide a legal basis for the 1991
appointment of Kim Jong Il as supreme commander of the armed forces by
removing the military from the command of the president. Still, North
Korea's official media failed to state how or why the constitution was amended,
except to say: "Part of the constitution was revised or supplemented in a way
to reflect the ideologies and theories newly presented by Comrade Kim Il Sung
and the Party since the adoption (in 1972) of the socialist constitution as well
as the achievements attained by our people in their revolution and construction which were led wisely by the Party and the Great Leader."[35] On the eve
of his passing, the Great Leader still retained his top party and state
posts, while the Dear Leader had two top military positions, chairman of the
National Defense Commission and supreme commander of the KPA.

Part of Kim Jong Il's claim to be a fitting successor derived from the notion
that he was uniquely blessed and groomed by the Great Leader himself to
carry the revolution to new heights. At WPK-VI in October 1980, Kim Il

---

35 Quoted in *Vantage Point* 15:4 (April 1992), p. 25.

Sung first raised leadership succession as the fundamental question decisive to the destiny of the party and the revolution – as any socialist revolution would take more than one generation to complete – and then "solved" the problem by putting forward a theory for the inheritance of the revolution, one that would ensure wise leadership from generation to generation. After all, who would be better suited for this role than the leader's filial son? With such a blessing, Kim Jong Il made a head start as the preeminent "theorist" of Juche ideology. As early as February 19, 1974, for example, it is alleged that the Dear Leader had coined the term "Kimilsungism" in an effort to elevate the Juche ideology to a level equal to that of Marxism-Leninism. It is not surprising that the great bulk of his published works has to do with ideological issues in the progressive development, refinement, and codification of Kimilsungism.[36] The project of publishing Kim Jong Il's works has become an integral part of building the political and ideological foundation for the father–son succession. In the 1992 revision of the constitution, the definition of Juche as "a creative application of Marxism-Leninism to the conditions of our country" (Article 4) was extinguished. *Juche* ideology became "the guiding principle of its actions" in the revised constitution (Article 3). Thus, a trinity of father, son, and *Juche* constituted the ideological foundation of North Korean theocracy.

The Third Cycle (1994–1999)

North Korean informal politics seemed to have been forced to gravitate toward another cycle without having successfully completed the second succession cycle. The sudden death of Kim Il Sung on July 8, 1994 may be accepted as having set in motion the third cycle of informal politics. Indeed, this epochal event was pronounced to the world as nothing less than "the greatest loss that our nation has suffered in its five-thousand-year history."[37] The passing of the Great Leader so suddenly at a critical juncture of North Korea's political life seemed like a great tornado violently sweeping through the entire Korean peninsula and throwing everything asunder. For at least the next four years and two months, from July 1994 to September 1998, Kim Il Sung's death became the starting point for the redefinition of North Korean politics, both formal and informal.

Still, the proximate cause for the third cycle of informal politics is a widening and deepening systemic crisis. From the mid-1980s, internal contradic-

36 For a content analysis of Kim Jong Il's published works, see the Research Institute for National Unification (RINU), *The Advent of Kim Jong-il Regime in North Korea and Prospects for Its Policy Direction*, Series no. 1, Policy Studies Report (Seoul: RINU, 1994).
37 See UN Doc. GAOR, A/49/PV.19 (5 October 1994), p. 5.

tions and external disasters (e.g., Gorbachev's decision to recognize and establish full diplomatic relations with Seoul and German reunification by absorption in 1990, the demise of the Soviet Union and the collapse of communism at its epicenter in 1991, Beijing's decision to adopt a two-Koreas policy in 1992) have been dogging one after another. But the sudden death of the Great Leader, a demigod in North Korean theocracy, has had the immediate effect of suspending Pyongyang's formal politics. As in the first phase of the first cycle in 1945–1948, informal politics became nearly the sum total of North Korean politics during the third cycle. Faced with an unprecedented systemic crisis, the ends of informal politics became clear enough: survival.

The onset of such a crisis has further deepened the structural contradictions within the system. Harry Eckstein once advanced a theory of "congruence," according to which unless the various levels of state and society are organized in a mutually congruent way, strain and dissonance – symmetry-breaking – will ensue with system-destabilizing consequences.[38] Indeed, systemic incongruence has been growing unchecked since the mid-1980s, as Pyongyang has encountered staggering economic problems at home and serious diplomatic and political setbacks abroad. Moreover, North Korea's economic development and international standing are closely keyed to the extent to which the government can establish a congruence between its domestic and foreign policies. Due to a high degree of systemic rigidity (maladaptability), however, North Korea has almost lost the unification game by lagging so far behind the South in practically all relevant dimensions of polity.[39]

As a result, the "balance-of-power" relationship between formal and informal politics during the third systemic crisis cycle has been skewed to an unprecedented extent in favor of the latter. The North Korean political system experienced the rapid expansion of an unofficial sphere at the expense of an official sphere in all four subsystems – political, ideological, economic, and cultural – accelerating the symmetry-breaking and dissonance-expanding processes. The feedback and coupling effects of adverse external events have facilitated a vicious circle – the more the duality in each subsystem, the more the systemic incongruence; the more systemic incongruence, the greater the symmetry-breaking between the ideological and economic subsystems.[40]

38 Harry Eckstein, *The Natural History of Congruence Theory* (Denver: Graduate School of International Studies Monograph, University of Denver, 1980). See also Harry Eckstein, *Division and Cohesion in Democracy: A Study of Norway* (Princeton: Princeton University Press, 1966), pp. 234–253.
39 See Samuel S. Kim, "The impact of the division of Korea on South Korean politics: The challenge of competitive legitimation," in *Korean Democracy Toward a New Horizon*, 5th International Conference on Korean Politics, July 20–21, 1995 (Seoul: Korean Political Science Association, 1995), pp. 57–90.
40 See Sung Chull Kim, "Development of systemic dissonance in North Korea," *Korean Journal of National Unification* 5 (1996), pp. 83–109.

Nowhere is the symmetry-breaking process between the ideological and economic subsystems more starkly manifest than in the rise and spread of the informal (black market) economy. With the introduction of the Joint Venture Law and the consumer goods production drive in the 1980s came the second economy fueled by an inflow of foreign currency, especially U.S. dollars. With foreign currency as the informal but real money substituting for the formal money (won) and lubricating the informal black market economy came deviant bureaucratic behavior. According to recent North Korean defectors, it has already become common practice for people to offer bribes for a travel permit, admission to a hospital, or when they encounter interrogation by security agents while traveling by train. A structural crisis of an unreformed command economy, with critical shortages of food, energy, and foreign currency reinforcing and compounding one another, has led factories to operate at 30 percent or even lower capacity in recent years due to an acute shortage of energy, raw materials, and spare parts, forcing more and more black markets to crop up all over the country, especially along DPRK–PRC border areas.

Indeed, the formal economy seems to have already passed the point of no recovery, and it is the informal substitution economy that has created some breathing space – a kind of neo-Darwinian private marketplace for the survival of the fittest. Self-help unilateralism of all kinds and at all levels of the state (e.g., bartering, smuggling, stealing, bribing, and even defecting by bribery) defined the informal dimension of the so-called *juche*-based political economy. The amount of consumer goods (daily necessities) rationed through the formal state supply network constitutes no more than 10–20 percent of total consumer goods in circulation; consequently, black market prices are 3–50 times higher than state prices. Another measure of the extent to which the informal economy has expanded is the wide gap between the official and unofficial (black market) exchange rate of the North Korean won to the U.S. dollar. At a current black market rate of Won 170–180:$1 (as of late 1996) rather than the official rate of Won 2.15:$1, most North Korean salaries are worth less than a dollar a month.[41] At the end of 1996, the black market price of rice was 1,239 times as much as the official price set by the government.[42]

If formal politics is punctuated by formal institutional decay, informal politics seems to be working overtime on an ad hoc emergency basis – a kind

41 Seung-Yul Oh, "Assessment of the North Korean economy," in Tae Hwan Ok and Gerrit W. Gong, eds., *Change and Challenge on the Korean Peninsula: Past, Present and Future* (Seoul: Research Institute for National Unification, 1996), pp. 1–17; "Cover story: Darkness at noon," *Far Eastern Economic Review* (October 10, 1996), pp. 26–33; and Economist Intelligence Unit (London), *Country Report: South Korea/North Korea*, 4th quarter 1996, p. 47.

42 Korean Broadcasting Station (KBS)-I Television Network in Korean, as transmitted by WNYC channel 25 in New York, December 1, 1996.

of extraconstitutional crisis management center. The extent of decay in formal politics, or the extent to which informal politics surged to fill in self-created lacunae in the reach of formal politics, can be seen in the Workers' Party of Korea and the Supreme People's Assembly. It is a remarkable testimonial to the importance of informal politics that the North Korean party-state has not convened its party congress for eighteen years, not since WPK-VI in October 1980, despite the stipulations of the party charter that "the highest organ of the party is the party congress" and "the party congress is convened once every five years by the party Central Committee" (Article 21).[43] For three years and three months (between July 1994 and October 1997), the party remained, formally, headless and the membership of the most powerful organ in the North Korean political system – the Presidium of the Politburo – steadily declined from five in 1980 (Kim Il Sung, Kim Il, Oh Jin-u, Kim Jong Il, and Li Jong-ok) to three in March 1984 (Kim Il Sung, Kim Jong Il, and Oh Jin-u) to two in July 1994, with the death of Kim Il Sung (Kim Jong Il and Oh Jin-u), and to one in February 1995, with the death of Oh Jin-u (Kim Jong Il).

As of late 1998 there has been no report of any meeting of the Central Committee or the Politburo in the first four years or more of the post–Kim Il Sung era despite the requirement of the party charter that "the party Central Committee shall convene a plenary meeting of its own at least once every six months" and "the Political Bureau of the party Central Committee shall meet at least once every month" (Articles 24–25). From April 1994 to early September 1998, North Korea has also failed to hold any session of the Supreme People's Assembly to discuss and approve the state budget or to deal with other critical issues. Although the five-year term of office for the 9th SPA expired in April 1995, as of July 1998 North Korea failed to hold elections for the 10th SPA until July 1998. There have been no reports or announcements that Kim Jong Il has called in or presided over any meeting of military leaders, that of party leaders, or any cabinet session despite the repeated claim that the Dear Leader is in charge of the party, the government, and the military. Even the much awaited "election" of the party charter requirement that "the plenary meeting of the party Central Committee . . . elects the general secretary, secretaries and members of the Political Bureau and its Presidium" (Article 24).

That appointments to the highest state and party positions, especially secretary general of the ruling WPK (until October 8, 1997), have been frozen for more than three years after the death of President Kim Il Sung produced

---

43 For the full text of the Charter of the Workers' Party of Korea, see Sung Chul Yang, *The North and South Korean Political Systems: A Comparative Analysis* (Boulder: Westview Press, 1994), Appendix 4, pp. 905–931.

some abnormal consequences for the official management of foreign affairs. Receiving and presenting diplomatic credentials was entrusted to the dead President Kim Il Sung and/or Vice President Li Jong-ok.[44] *The Central Yearbook 1995* published by the North Korean Central News Agency (KCNA) in December 1995 still featured Kim Il Sung, who died sixteen months earlier as chairman of the Military Committee, while giving no names of its members. That the Supreme People's Assembly, "the highest organ of power in the Democratic People's Republic of Korea" (Article 87 of the Constitution) has not held a single session for more than four years means no officially announced government budgets for 1995, 1996, 1997, and 1998. For three years in a row, the annual New Year Address (for 1995, 1996, and 1997) was given not by the president of the republic, as in the Kim Il Sung era, but in the form of a joint editorial of the official organs of the WPK (*Rodong Sinmun*), the Korean People's Army (*Joson Inmingun*), and the Socialist Youth League (*Chongyon Joni*). Even after Kim Jong Il's succession to the top party post, the 1998 New Year Address was still presented in the form of a joint editorial of the *Rodong Sinmun* and *Josen Inmingun*, but with the newly renamed Kim Il Sung Socialist Youth League disappearing from the joint editorial.

During the third systemic crisis cycle, Kim Jong Il has "ruled" the country from behind the scenes in his dual military capacity as the supreme commander of the armed forces and the chairman of the NDC. In an apparent effort to demonstrate his formal control over both the state council and the military, for instance, Kim Jong Il promulgated the Fifty-First Order of the Supreme Commander of the Armed Forces in November 1994, ordering not only the military, which is under his control, but also the government – the Administrative Council, supposed to be headed by the president of the republic – to complete the construction of a bridge and a tunnel in Pyongyang within eleven months. On the occasion of the 50th anniversary of the WPK in October 1995, Kim Jong Il made use of his military position again by declaring the Sixty-Fifth Order of the Supreme Commander of the Armed Forces, which appointed Chief of General Staff Choe Gwang as defense minister and reshuffled some high-ranking military personnel. In addition, as supreme commander and chairman of the NDC, Kim Jong Il reviewed troops and received a report from newly appointed Defense Minister Choe Gwang. The exercise of power through military positions is abnormal, because the

---

44 On November 16, 1995, for example, the KCNA reported that the new Gabonese Ambassador to the DPRK, Joseph Obiang Ndoutoume, presented his credentials to Vice President Li Chong-ok at the Mansudae Assembly Hall. However, on June 5, 1995, the new North Korean ambassador to Cambodia presented his credentials issued in the name of "President Kim Il Sung" to Prince Norodom Sihanouk. The South Korean Yonhap News Agency also reported on June 10, 1995 that Pyongyang's new ambassadors to five other countries around that time also carried credentials issued in the name of Kim Il Sung.

Constitution (as amended in 1992) provides no provisions for such an exercise of power by the supreme commander of the armed forces. Without formally declaring martial law, the country was governed by General Kim Jong Il.

The formal trellis of informal politics remains an increasingly parasitic and dysfunctional *suryong* system, as the Cult and the Plan are mutually conflictive and corrupting.[45] According to Hwang Jang-yop, the politics of everyday life "is filled with praising the leader and pledging loyalty from morning until night."[46] It has become mandatory for newlyweds to make their marriage vows before one of some 33,000 Kim Il Sung statues scattered throughout the country. An inordinate amount of state resources and expenditures has gone to the militarization as well as the idolization of the *suryong* system. Although hundreds of thousands of people starved to death in 1995, the Kim Jong Il government managed to spend US$890 million on expanding the Kumsusan Memorial Place (where Kim Il Sung's body is laid).[47] More recently, Kim Jong Il has formally ordered several "monumental" projects, including an eight-kilometer (five-mile) boulevard leading to the Kumsusan Memorial Place.

In a speech delivered at a secret meeting of party officials at Kimilsung University on December 7, 1996, Kim Jong Il spoke directly in his "command and control" leadership style. On the one hand, he warned that the current food crisis if not quickly alleviated may lead the people to rise up against their leadership as they did in late 1945 in the northern city of Sinuiju. On the other hand, Kim Jong Il deferred the responsibility of the current food crisis to party cadres. He opted not to get involved in economic matters so as to be able to spend more time on the military, the strengthening of which was said to be more important than anything else in today's complex situation. "The Great Leader (Kim Il Sung) advised me again and again not to get myself involved in economic matters so as not to deprive me of the time and energy needed for the more important military matters."[48] What was made clear in the secret speech was his determination to make the military happy and well-fed as the backbone of the country's political and social stability as well as the core support group for his leadership.

The style of informal politics in the third cycle appears to be very ad hoc, vertical, secretive, and personalized, with Kim Jong Il calling the shots. It seems evident that Kim Jong Il has shown a penchant for a behind-the-scenes leadership, preferring informal connections and channels to formal party and

45 McCormack, "Kim country," pp. 35–36.
46 Hwang's letter dated 3 January 1997 as published in *Chosun Ilbo*, February 13, 1997, p. 3.
47 *Chosun Ilbo* (Internet version), June 15, 1998.
48 *Wolgan Chosun* (April 1997), pp. 306–317, especially p. 309.

government organs and channels in formulating or developing policy. According to Hwang Jang-yop, there has never been any official meeting or conference of any kind since Kim Il Sung died in mid-1994, even as Kim Jong Il carried out everything in secret: "He does everything secretly, behind closed doors, together with a handful of his closest advisers."[49]

And yet he is said to be using both formal and informal channels as a way of maintaining his overall control over a one-man system of rule. Kim Jong Il is said to be maintaining a dual system of control and reporting with an official channel and an unofficial channel comprised of his in-laws and close associates so that the two can check each other while vying to demonstrate loyalty to the Dear Leader. In the conduct of foreign relations, for instance, 80 percent of instructions are said to be flowing from Kim Jong Il to First Vice Foreign Minister Kang Sok-ju (North Korea's chief negotiator in the US–DPRK nuclear negotiations in 1993–1994), with Foreign Minister Kim Yong Nam formally in charge but informally a puppet.[50]

Kim Jong Il's style of informal politics is one of maintaining a system of checks and balances by distributing important positions among all age and functional groups as well as periodic readjustment of the ranking order of the various groups. As the military is the only group that could make or break the regime, Kim Jong Il seems to be employing a balance-of-power game controlling this group through multiple political surveillance and reshuffling mechanisms. After Defense Minister Oh Jin U died in February 1995, Kim Jong Il accelerated this system of checks and balances through frequent military promotions and reshuffling as a way of maintaining leader absolutism.

As of early 1997, this core military security group, consisting of such high-ranking military officers as Choe Gwang (defense minister), Kim Gwang Jin (deputy defense minister), Paek Hak Rin (public security minister), and Li Ul Sol (head of the Secret Service), was playing a leading role in national and regime security matters. Oddly enough, Hwang's defection on February 12, 1997 was quickly followed by a succession of mysterious and almost synchronized deaths of senior leaders – Choe Gwang at 78 (February 21, 1997) and Kim Gwang Jin at 68 (February 27, 1997), and the retirement of Prime Minister Kang Song San. North Korea, which had almost no major purging or reshuffling of top leaders in the thirty-one months since the death of Kim Il Sung in July 1994, "lost" four senior leaders within fifteen days, spawning conspiracy theories and drawing international attention to the shape of authority structures to come. In fact, the first three years of the post–Kim Il Sung era witnessed the death of about fifty influential figures, including Oh

49 *Chosun Ilbo*, June 15, 1998, and *Far Eastern Economic Review* (October 15, 1998), p. 30.
50 *Tong-A Ilbo* (Seoul), February 14, 1996, p. 5.

Jin U (armed forces minister), Kim Bong Ryul (deputy armed forces minister), Li Hwa Sun (deputy director of the Party Organization and Guidance Department), Kang Hi Won (deputy premier), Pak Jung Kook (deputy armed forces minister), Choe Gwang, and Kim Gwang Jin.[51]

This growing mortuary table has made a generational shift in the power hierarchy well-nigh inevitable. Indeed, on the occasion of Kim Il Sung's 85th birthday, on April 15, 1997, Kim Jong Il promoted 123 generals. This marked the fifth military reshuffle executed by Kim Jong Il since assuming the office of supreme commander in December 1991, boosting North Korea's top brass with roughly 797 promotions, excluding the latest ones and bringing the total tally of generals to 1,220 (compared to about 500 generals in South Korea). Although the first-generation revolutionary leaders still stand out, formally, in high party, government, and military positions, a generational shift began to take place in late 1996.

This inner circle of informal politics, which holds the greatest power and exercises the greatest influence, has already become dominated by leaders in their early fifties, including Kim Jong Il's relatives, except Kim Yong Ju (Kim Il Sung's younger brother and Kim Jong Il's uncle) and Kim Pyong Il (Kim Jong Il's younger stepbrother), the bereaved family of the first-generation leaders, and Kim Jong Il's schoolmates of Kimilsung University. According to an article based on extensive interviews with North Korean elite defectors that was published in Mal (a South Korean dissident monthly), ten leaders, five from the party and five from the military, make up the inner circle of real power in North Korean informal politics. It has also been revealed that Kim Jong Il makes major policies and decisions through a "twenty-man group" – an informal advisory organization consisting of close and loyal party, government, and military aides – rather than through the formal party and government channels. It was through this informal organization, according to a senior official of the intelligence authorities in Seoul, that Kim Jong Il was trying to maintain stability in his ruling system while at the same time playing them off against each other: "Kim Jong Il invites the members of the private organization all together two to three times a week, is briefed by them with up-to-date information, and receives advice and suggestions for his policymaking."[52]

One name that appears on almost everybody's list, including Hwang Jang-yop's, is Chang Song Taek, first deputy director of the Organization and Guidance of the WPK Central Committee and Kim Jong Il's brother-in-law, the husband of Kim Jong Il's only blood sister (Kim Kyong Hui), who is

51 Chung Kyu-sup, "A reshuffle in the power hierarchy under Kim Jong-il's leadership, and an analytic study on its stability," Vantage Point 20:7 (July 1997), pp. 36–44.
52 Chungang Ilbo, September 20, 1997, p. 2.

regarded as Kim Jong Il's "right-hand man" and as such the real power-holder among power-holders. According to Ko Yong-hwan, who defected to South Korea in 1991 while serving as first secretary at the North Korean Embassy in the Congo, "Chang Song-taek is North Korea's number three man after Kim Il-song and Kim Chong-il." Ko also quoted Kim Jong Il as saying to Chang Song Taek, "You are the only one I can trust and rely on."[53] Hwang Jang-yop concurs with this assessment.[54]

On September 5, 1998, more than four years after Kim Il Sung died, "the highest organ of power in the Democratic People's Republic of Korea" (Article 87) held the first session of the 10th SPA to consider and pass only three items on the agenda: (1) amendment and supplement to the constitution (1992); (2) election of the chairman of the NDC; and (3) election for the state leadership organs. In some respects, the new constitution – 7 chapters and 166 articles – reflects and formalizes the important decisions and practices of Kim Jong Il's leadership style and informal politics during the third cycle. First, unlike the 1992 constitution, the new constitution has a preamble that codifies the signature identity of the DPRK as a theocratic Kim Il Sung state – that Kim Il Sung is "the founder of the DPRK and socialist Korea," that he is "the sun of the nation," that he is "the eternal President of the Republic," and that the DPRK Socialist Constitution is the Kim Il Sung constitution. As if all of this weren't enough, Kim Jong Il failed to deliver any policy or inaugural speech, allowing instead a replay of Kim Il Sung's speech delivered at the first plenary session of the 9th SPA on May 24, 1990! This eight-year-old speech, entitled "Let Us Bring the Advantages of Socialism in Our Country into Full Play," was touted as "highly important guidelines which give a comprehensive exposition of the basic mission and duty of the government of the DPRK" in the Kim Jong Il era.[55] In this way the presidential system was "abolished" so that Kim Il Sung could be "resurrected" as "the eternal President of the Republic" while at the same time making it possible for Kim Jong Il to continue to practice his behind-the-scenes leadership style without ceremonial duties and formal accountability. Even the reelection of Kim Jong Il as chairman of the NDC of the DPRK, although nominally proposed by Kim Yong Nam, was legitimized by the Father, as his election was "initiated and recommended by the great Kim Il Sung, the eternal leader of the Korean people in his lifetime."[56] The first session of the

53 Quoted in Sin Chun-yong, "Top 10 power elite of the successor Leader Kim Chong-il Era," *Mal* (Seoul) (August 1997) in FBIS-EAS-97-252, September 9, 1997 (Internet version).
54 *Hangyore* (Seoul) (October 9, 1997), p. 7; see also Ch'oe Yong-chae, "The real power holders in North Korea are the young reform-oriented faction," *Sisa Journal* (Seoul) (July 24, 1997), in FBIS-EAS-97-204, July 23, 1997 (Internet version).
55 Korean Central News Agency (KCNA), September 5, 1998 (Internet version).
56 Ibid.

10th SPA was said to be "an epochal occasion in firmly defending and exalt-ing the *nature of our republic as the state of President Kim Il Sung.*"[57]

Second, to a significant extent the new Kim Il Sung constitution formalizes the progressive shift of power from the state to the party to the military (NDC) that has already taken place during the third cycle by abolishing the office of presidency, the Central People's Committee, and the standing committee of the SPA, and by setting up a seventeen-member SPA Presidium consisting of elderly and largely powerless revolutionaries. The President of the SPA Presidium – former Foreign Minister Kim Yong Nam – comes closest to being a "head of state" as the president's authority and duties concerning diplomatic affairs have been transferred to the SPA presidium and its president: "The President of the SPA Presidium represents the State and receives credentials and letters of recall of diplomatic representatives accredited by a foreign state" (Article 111). The Kim Il Sung constitution has also abolished the Administration Council to be replaced by the newly instituted cabinet. If President Kim Yong Nam of the SPA Presidium *represents* the state in foreign affairs, the premier (Hong Song Nam) *represents* the government (Article 120) in the management of the economy. Despite the substantial reshuffling of two-thirds of the state leadership organs – more than 60 percent of the 687 SPA deputies (members) were replaced in the latest election, compared with 31 percent in the election of April 1990 for the 9th SPA, and 24 out of 31 cabinet ministers were newly appointed – the Kim Il Sung constitution makes Kim Jong Il in practice, if not in theory, the de facto head of state by making the chairman of the NDC the nerve center of a crisis management garrison state. The SPA is still "the highest organ of State power in the DPRK" (Article 87), and the NDC is still "accountable to the SPA" (Article 105). Yet the ink on the new constitution was hardly dry before it was "amended" by SPA Presidium President Kim Yong Nam, who declared: "The NDC chairmanship is the highest post of the state" and controls all of the political, military and economic capabilities of the republic.[58] The logic of separating power and control from responsibility and accountability, and military and ideological control from economic matters – as already made manifest in Kim Jong Il's secret speech that was alluded to earlier – seems simple enough: North Korea needs such a crisis management military government capable of system maintenance and regime survival.

Third, the Kim Il Sung constitution formally acknowledges the existence of the informal economy by expanding the range of those "social cooperative

---

57 KCNA, September 7, 1998; emphasis added (Internet version).
58 KCNA, September 5, 1998.

organizations" that can possess such property as land, agricultural machinery, ships, and medium- to small-sized factories and enterprises (Article 22)
by encouraging "institutions, enterprises or associations" to establish and
operate "equity and contractual joint venture enterprises with corporations
or individuals of foreign countries within a special economic zone" (Article
37) and by granting the citizens freedom to reside in and travel to any place
(Article 75), among others. All the same, Pyongyang has reaffirmed that *juche*
will remain the backbone of the political economy: "It is a foolish daydream
to try to revive the economy by introducing foreign capital, not relying on
one's own strength. . . . We will set ourselves against all the attempts to
induce us to join an 'integrated' world. We have nothing to 'reform' and
'open'."[59]

If the formal politics of everyday life remained chock full of trumpery about
the omnipotence of *juche* ideology as the motive force "leading our country
toward the strongest position in the world," the policy means employed in
the service of system maintenance during the third cycle, right up to the first
session of the 10th SPA in early September 1998, were almost entirely tactical in nature. Apparently, there is no consensus on how best to pursue survival strategies, as is made evident in the Janus faces of its foreign policy
behavior. There is little evidence that any serious system-reforming approach
has been in the works. Whether judged by manifest policy pronouncements,
multilateral participatory behavior in the United Nations, or bilateral negotiating behavior with the United States, Japan, and South Korea, the third
systemic crisis cycle of informal politics has shown some adaptive, situation-
specific learning, especially in connection with seeking UN humanitarian aid,
but virtually no cognitive/normative learning to speak of.[60] That is,
Pyongyang has been responding to its deepening systemic crisis in a variety
of situation-specific, tactical ways.

The most obvious policy outcome of the third cycle is a more vigorous promotion of the Rajin–Sonbong Free Economic and Trade Zone (RSFETZ).
Apparently influenced by and modeled on post-Mao China's four special economic zones (SEZs) in Shenzhen, Shantou, Xiamen, and Zhuhai, Pyongyang
adopted the RSFETZ in late 1991. In September 1993, Kim Il Sung reportedly told a visiting Chinese delegation that he admired China "for having
achieved brilliant reforms and openness" while continuing simultaneously to

59 *Rodong Sinmun* (Pyongyang), September 9, 1998.
60 For further analysis, see Samuel S. Kim, "PukMi hyopsang kwa Pukhan ui chunryak" [DPRK–US
   negotiations and North Korea's strategy] in Kwak Tae-hwan, ed., *Pukhan ui Hyopsang Chunryak kwa
   Nam Pukhan Kwangkye* [*North Korea's negotiating strategy and South-North relations*] (Seoul: Institute of
   Far Eastern Studies, Kyungnam University, 1997), pp. 163–186, and "North Korea and the United
   Nations," in *International Journal of Korean Studies* 1:1 (Spring 1997), pp. 77–105.

build socialism with Chinese characteristics" and that the Chinese experience should become "an encouraging factor to us Koreans."[61] With the assistance of the UNIDO, Pyongyang sponsored the Rajin–Sonbong Zone International-al Business and Investment Forum, which was held September 13–15, 1996 as a way of attracting more foreign direct investment (FDI) into the RSFETZ.[62] It also was the catalyst for some more changes in the new Kim Il Sung constitution.

Is this not evidence enough of Pyongyang's system-reforming approach? However, a simple reality check suggests that the RSFETZ is no more than a select and controlled opening and that post-Kim Il Sung North Korea is no post-Mao China. The initial conditions of post-Mao China do not apply to and are not readily reproducible in post-Kim Il Sung North Korea. First, there is an important difference in global geopolitical timing. Post-Mao China's reform and opening came about during the heyday of the second Cold War, when anti-Soviet China enjoyed and exercised its maximum triangular leverage, as was made evident by Beijing's easy entry into the World Bank and IMF in May 1980. Second, unlike post-Mao China, post-Kim Il Sung North Korea does not have rich and enterprising overseas Koreans to gener-ate the kind and amount (about 80%) of FDI that post-Mao China had attracted. The closest functional equivalent of North Korea's "overseas Korean entrepreneurs" is ethnic pro-Pyongyang Koreans in Japan associated with the *Chosen Soren*, whose membership and remittances to North Korea have registered rapid and dramatic declines in recent years (from $US476 million in the peak year of 1990 to about $US47 million in 1997).[63] Also, post-Mao China in 1978–1979 had no foreign debts to speak of, and North Korea's foreign debts are estimated at about $US 10–11 billion, with one of the highest country risk ratings in the world. Third, the propitious initial social and economic conditions that enabled post-Mao reformers to launch reform in the agricultural sector to free up and channel surplus farm labor into the emerging nonstate or semiprivate light-manufacturing and service sectors do not exist in heavily industrialized North Korea. Moreover, North Korea's reform and opening Chinese style would still have to compete with China, Vietnam, and other Southeast Asian countries in the global market-place, while at the same time being handicapped by its own high wages mea-sured in terms of low productivity, poor infrastructure, unstable energy

61 *North Korean News*, no. 702 (September 27, 1993), p. 5.
62 See James Cotton, "The Rajin-Sonbong free trade zone experiment: North Korea in pursuit of new international linkages," in Samuel S. Kim, ed., *North Korean Foreign Relations in the Post-Cold War Era* (Hong Kong and New York: Oxford University Press, 1998), pp. 212–234.
63 Shim Jae Hoon, "Disillusioned donors," *Far Eastern Economic Review* (December 4, 1997), pp. 28–30.

supply, a dismally low international credit rating, geographic isolation, ideological and bureaucratic constraints, and an uncertain future of the post–Kim Il Sung system.

That extensive reform and restructuring are required to avert system collapse seems beyond doubt. Lacking his father's charisma, authority, and power, Kim Jong Il would have to shift decisively from charismatic or revolutionary legitimation to performance-based legitimation. Yet in none of his writings has Kim Jong Il expressed anything positive about reform and restructuring. To the contrary, he has argued that it was the "collusion between the imperialists and counterrevolutionary forces" and the "penetration of imperialist ideology and culture" (i.e., *perestroika* and *glasnost*), that had accelerated the demise of the socialist world.[64] He is reported to have said on more than one occasion, "Are you waiting for me to initiate changes? You will not live to see me doing anything of the sort."

 Kim Jong Il faces here a systemic catch-22 dilemma – to save the *juche* system requires deconstructing important parts of it. It also requires considerable opening to and help from its capitalist southern rival. And yet a departure from the ideological continuity of the *juche* system that the Great Leader Kim Il Sung created, developed, and passed on to his son is viewed not as a necessity for survival but an ultimate betrayal of *raison d'état*. In short, to ask North Korea to follow the system-reforming trajectory is to ask North Korea to change its national identity, to be like South Korea. Herein, apparently, lies the logic of a highly selective and controlled opening without any reform and restructuring. Indeed, with Pyongyang alternately rattling its saber and tin cup, it is now all too clear that a *juche*-centered national policy can no longer cope with the most pressing issues of legitimacy, national identity, and economic well-being.[65]

CONCLUSION

Taken together, the preceding analysis leads to several clear conclusions. First, North Korean informal politics can be usefully defined in dialectical terms as having mutated through three types of cycles – the consolidation cycle, the succession cycle, and the systemic crisis management cycle – and as having responded to three types of challenges – the leadership/succession chal-

---

64 Samuel S. Kim, "North Korea in 1994: Brinkmanship, breakdown and breakthrough," *Asian Survey* 35:1 (January 1995), pp. 13–27.

65 Because of more than five years of severe food shortages and a total breakdown of the public health system, an entire generation of children under seven years old suffer from stunted growth physically and are mentally impaired, a new study by international aid groups has found. See Elizabeth Rosenthal, "In North Korean hunger, legacy is stunted children," *New York Times* (December 10, 1998), pp. A1, A14.

lenge, the national identity challenge, and the survival challenge. Still, the leadership/succession challenge has remained the greatest single factor shaping North Korean informal politics over the years. To an extraordinary extent the first cycle of informal politics was a triumph made manifest in the enactment of the socialist constitution embodying *juche* identity and the *suryong* system. At the end of the first cycle, the chasm between formal and informal politics – between formal authority and actual power – was bridged and dysfunctional factionalism eradicated from the body politic. The second cycle, although not as successful as the first, still has gone a long way in setting the stage for the first-ever socialist hereditary succession. Paradoxically, the leadership success and the succession strife of the first two cycles have planted seeds of internal contradictions, spawning a systemic crisis that the third cycle of informal politics has to deal with. The protracted struggle of North Korean informal politics can be summed up as having moved from leadership triumph to a hereditary succession struggle to systemic crisis.

Second, despite its changing saliency, scope, and intensity, the informal dimension has remained an integral part of North Korean politics. As long as the system does not provide the formal rules of play for "who gets what, how and why," the struggle for political power and plenty gets pushed into the informal behind-the-curtain domains. Even at the end of the first cycle, when the formal and the informal became virtually coterminous, the 1972 constitution, especially Article 75, on a four-year term for the SPA and the president of the DPRK, was more honored in the breach than in compliance. What was made formal and legal in the constitution may be considered trivial compared to what was informally practiced. All of the provisions of the state constitution and the party charter become irrelevant if they come into conflict with the momentary whims and caprices of the Great Leader.

Third, the defining and differentiating feature of North Korean informal politics is the deified role of the Great Leader. No modern state or modern political leader has come as close to saying "L'état, c'est moi" and in equating "moi" with the ruling family. The image of the Kim Il Sung family and the image of what Wada Haruki of Tokyo University calls a "Guerrilla Unit State" (*Yugekitai Kokka no Genzai*)[66] operate symbolically and substantively in both formal and informal politics. Paradoxically, the strength of the leadership cult in wiping out rooted factionalism is gradually proving to be its own weakness. The leadership cult is "command politics" since all great ideas and policy initiatives are reserved to the omnipotent Great Leader. The leadership cult in contemporary North Korea is different from the cults of Mao or Stalin not

---

66 Wada Haruki, *Kita Chosen: Yugekitai Kokka no genzai* (North Korea: The Guerrilla Unit state) (Tokyo: Iwanami shoten, 1998).

only in its persistence, intensity, and grandiosity, but also in the stress on the "blood vein for the continuation of the revolution" from generation to generation. To put it differently, the North Korean political system does not primarily work as a set of parallel vertical institutions (army, party, state) but as a system of power radiating outward from the "core" (*haeksim*) – Kim Jong Il – with one's political position depending on one's informal and especially familial relationship with the Great Leader. At the symbolic level, the whole nation is portrayed as the "Kim family state," reminiscent of, for example, prewar Japan. In the wake of the official succession to the top party post, Kim Jong Il has been extolled as "the great father" of a big, harmonious family-state. This does not mean that factions have completely disappeared from informal politics; it means instead that the sizes and shapes of factional groupings have been blurred and overlaid by the Kim family-state, with any factional group waiting for the opportune moment to arise. As matters stand now, the kinds of flexibility and maneuverability stemming from the emergence of epistemic (policy) communities in post-Mao Chinese informal politics are not readily detectable in post–Kim Il Sung informal politics.

Finally, the family-state that Kim Il Sung has built and passed on to the Dear Leader is actually a weak, if not yet collapsing, state in which formal ideology, formal politics, formal economy, and formal culture no longer work. It is a failing state that cannot provide for even the most basic human needs without an external life-support system. This means that informal politics would have to work overtime to get things done. As matters stand, the *suryŏng* system of a one-man dictatorship and theocratic fundamentalism is not prepared for a crucial "what-if" question – what if Kim Jong Il were to die suddenly? As well, the *suryong* system has yet to show any convincing ideology and strategy of reform and opening to the capitalist world system that escapes capture or corruption by the market. For the most obvious question – whether informal politics can rise to the challenge of averting system collapse – the jury is still out.

ACKNOWLEDGMENTS

I am grateful to Lowell Dittmer, Charles Armstrong, and Andrew Nathan for their helpful comments and suggestions on an early version of this chapter.

CHAPTER 11

INFORMAL POLITICS IN VIETNAM[1]

DOUGLAS PIKE

The Vietnamese tend to have a rather singular regard for politics, formal and informal alike. Their perceptions can be traced back through the centuries to various historical experiences and social traumas, many of them of searing quality. These formative forces shape individual Vietnamese' outlook on life's struggles, the proper response to society's challenges, as well as general political behavior. The resultant clutch of attitudes is marked by a deep distrust of politics in general and a cynicism about political leadership. All this, taken as a whole, forms the bedrock of today's Vietnamese political culture. It must be taken into account when studying Vietnamese politics. One simply cannot understand today's political scene without such consideration.[2]

---

1 Material for this chapter is drawn from the holdings in the Indochina Archive, now at Texas Tech University, chiefly from Unit Seven: DRV/SRV – Politics, Social Organization (about 5,000 pages). Also consulted: "Informal Politics in East Asia," special edition of *Asian Survey* March 1996 (introduction by Robert Scalapino). Included are "Institutions, Informal Politics and Political Transition in China" by Joseph Fewsmith; "Personal Politics in the Chinese Danwei Under Reform" by Lowell Dittmer and Lu Xiabao; and "General Reflections on Informal Politics in East Asia" by Tun-jen Cheng and Brantly Womak. The author is particularly indebted to Lucian Pye's *Asian Power and Politics: The Cultural Dimension of Authority* (Harvard Univ. Press, 1985), especially Chapter 8, "Forms of Aggressive Confucianism." For general background on the subject, consult the works of William Duiker, William Turley, Stephen B. Young, Thai Quang Trung (*Collective Leadership and Factionalism: An Essay on Ho Chi Minh Legacy*, ISEAS, Singapore); Huynh Kim Khanh, Lewis Stern, Nguyen Van Canh, Neil Jamison, Carlyle Thayer, and Robert Turner. Also see the author's chapter on Vietnamese leadership in Raymond Taras, ed., *Leadership Change in Communist States* (Unwin Hyman Publishers, 1989); and his *History of Vietnamese Communism* (Hoover Institution Press, 1978). The author's forthcoming work is titled *Leadership in Vietnam: Past, Present and Future.*

2 To the best of my knowledge, there is no full-scale book-length study of informal politics in Vietnam and only a limited literature of local politics. Such monographs and journal literature that do exist are microstudies, of a single village or at most of a single province. And of course it is difficult if not dangerous to extrapolate from these to reach generalized, societywide conclusions about the subject. Michigan State University academics under Wesley Fishel did some Mekong Delta village studies in the early 1960s, but these can now only be treated as historical studies. In northern Vietnam, that is, the former DRV, research by outside academics was not possible, even for Soviet scholars. Hanoi academics today say that there was little such study done by themselves during the wartime years, and that what was done was largely confined to ethnic minorities in the Highlands. Today, while it is difficult to obtain cooperation, it is possible to do local politics research in Vietnam.

Of the many factors of influence, four have been singled out here for discussion as being of overriding importance: (a) lingering traditionalism; (b) clandestinism in political and social organization; (c) weak political institutions; and (d) a special kind of political divisiveness.[3]

LINGERING TRADITIONALISM

Vietnam today remains deceptively traditional.[4] The basic sociopolitical unit is the village. In the cities and towns can be found the transitional and modern Vietnamese, the movers of society. The 5,121 villages, where two-thirds of the population lives, remain bastions of traditionalism.

As in like societies, this traditionalism is characterized by a tyranny of custom; an overriding spirit of noninnovation; and acceptance, even defense, of hierarchy. The parochial villager is concerned with the particularistic but seldom with the universalistic. Outsiders from modern societies find it all but impossible to grasp the primordial quality of the village; they can only dimly appreciate what life is like for a youth who grows up in a world without strangers, where he knows everyone and is related by blood to most.[5]

Life in traditional days was marked by great continuity. Things went on, decade after decade, with virtually unchanged political thinking, each generation behaving as the one that preceded it. The economy was agrarian and homogenous. The state took on little of what has come to be called the socialization process, educating and bringing the young into society as trained, useful members; this was left to the family, and as a result family–state relations were highly compatible. Demands from the royal court in Hue were low: taxes to be paid, group-labor supplied for road-building and public works, and young men furnished in time of war or invasion. That was about all, and the villagers lived out their lives without much governmental interference. The emperor's authority stops at the village bamboo hedge, runs an ancient Vietnamese proverb. Political goals and values thus were those of the elitist ruling aristocracy. Standards, such as justice, were elite standards. This

---

3 Conceptualization of the socio-anthropological triad of social divisions employed here is the standard one, i.e., traditional societies, transitional societies, and modern societies; the distinguishing determinant is the communication-of-ideas matrix and attitudes toward social change and progress.

4 Serving as an additional bond is the small size of the original Vietnamese tribal groupings. There are less than ninety Vietnamese family names; about 40% of all Vietnamese are named Nguyen.

5 The Cao Dai was founded in 1919 by one Ngo Van Chieu, ostensibly as a new religious movement seeking to merge all of the world's major religions. Not until 1931, French Sureté records have since revealed, did the French become aware that this new religious movement was also a nationalist, anti-French organization. The Cao Dai in the 1920s did not advocate militant opposition against the French, as did other nationalist organizations, and hence it did not force itself on the attention of the authorities. Even so, it seems surprising to an outsider that 10% of the people of a colonized nation could belong to an anticolonial organization without the colon themselves being aware of it.

was not altered significantly under the French except to impose the goals and values of the French colon, the new elite.

The village, where still today some 80 percent of all Vietnamese live, was itself a mutual protection association comprising various groups, guilds, and religious organizations. These could own property, perform charitable and social welfare work, maintain granaries against years of famine, and in general serve villagers in a paternalistic if somewhat authoritarian manner. Every village had an emergency relief organization (*nghia tuong*). The mutual-aid society (*hoi tu cap*) existed for some specific purposes, the most common being organizing funerals and burials; others managed weddings, helped in home-building, did repairs after a typhoon, or celebrated *Tet* (the lunar new year). The village guild (*hoi bach nghe*) was made up of craftsmen, many of whom did apprenticeships in China, who set standards of craftsmanship in much the same manner as the guilds in feudal Europe. Associations of wrestlers, boatmen, or devotees of cock fighting were also considered *hoi bach nghe*. Other groups preserved literary traditions, protected the interests of the elderly, or acted as what would today be called a mutual-fund investment club, not unlike the Chinese *hui*. The elderly women's Buddhist association (*hoi chua ba*) was open to women over fifty and sometimes to widows in their forties who were supported by their children and thus free to devote themselves to the matter of their salvation.

Thus Vietnam has a long tradition of associational interest groups, the stuff of informal politics. Unfortunately, however, these are not well suited for participation in modern politics, even assuming that eventually a system of political pluralism will develop in Vietnam, the product of the present trend toward a market economy. The larger and more prominent of these organizations – such as the militant religious cults Cao Dai and Hoa Hao (the former a syncretic sect with its own church and pope, the latter a Buddhist revival society) – when examined closely are seen to be secular-based as much as they are sacred-based. They attend to all of the interests of their members, from cradle to grave. Their scope is unlimited, not specifically defined. They are self-contained rather than externally oriented. They make a total claim on the loyalty of their members. Rather than an individual belonging to several overlapping self-interest groups, he is pressured to belong to a single traditional one. But multiplicity of organizational membership is the virtue in a modern society.

The traditional village–court relationship created two more or less separate political arenas. The village political world was self-contained, with little upward movement. It is true that the mandarin administrative system, modeled after that of Imperial China, provided a certain amount of political mobility based on merit. A youth could enter the world of court politics, but entry was based on written examinations that could be passed only if a youth schooled himself for years in the Confucian classics. It could not be done without tutelage. Occasionally, a village would collectively finance the education of a particularly bright boy. Hopefully, years of study would culminate with his passing his examinations and becoming a mandarin. Obviously, this system meant that only a few could be chosen. Concepts of the system, although not the system itself, were preserved by the French colonialists in those rather rare cases where they did not reserve the prerogatives of government to their own people. In some ways, the recruitment and promotion of Vietnam Communist Party members and cadres is based on the same elitist principle, although one of the worst sins of a cadre is termed "mandarinism," that is, imperious and arrogant behavior.

Lingering traditionalism remains a heritage, an influence, and a problem. It manifests itself as villager disinterest in national affairs and impeding national consensus with respect to basic social and political goals. It works against the development of a single national political arena and tends to continue the separation of capital politics from village politics. It impairs mobilization for universal political participation.

The village environment in which Vietnamese informal politics operates is the kinship system, which is the bedrock of the entire social system. Loyalty, especially to family, is a primary virtue, a reflection of the Confucian ethic of *hieu*, or filial piety. The central social institution in traditional Vietnam was the household (*nha or gia*), which was also the basic political unit. It, rather than the individual, was the tax base (*nong ho*). The household, rather than the individual, was counted in a census. It assumed responsibility for a child's rearing and education. It was a collective work group forming a single economic unit – "one fire, one lamp," as a Vietnamese proverb describes it. The household was the place of worship, and the law never meddled in its internal affairs.

Such is the heritage of today's domain of informal politics in Vietnam. It remains as a cement holding together a social structure based on a broad nationalistic spirit and a sense of identity that is beyond ideology. Its roots are Confucianism, Taoism, and indigenous syncretic religions; also, Western philosophic thinking such as Rousseau, Jefferson, and French Personalism; and of course Marxism-Leninism. However, it should be noted that Marxism-Leninism had a difficult time establishing itself in Vietnamese thinking. It went against the cultural grain (it is exceedingly difficult to convince the Vietnamese to accept the materialist dogma that nothing is inherently unknowable). While Leninist ideas on political organization, mobilization, and motivation were useful, Marxism proved ineffectual as a sociopolitical problem solver. Marxism did, and still does in some Vietnamese minds, fill a psychological need. Vietnamese ideological writings on the subject are to be taken seriously. Unlike fascist propaganda, they present a worldview and a kind of truth, providing that one accepts certain key definitions of terms.

CLANDESTINISM

The practice of clandestinism in Vietnamese politics is more than a penchant for covert political activity or for politicking out of the limelight, which exists everywhere. It is also greater than the secret-society syndrome found throughout Confucian Asia. Rather, it is a form of political behavior that is deeply ingrained in the Vietnamese personality. In part it is the device for dealing with the foreign occupier: the Chinese for 900 years, the French colons, and today's foreign visitors of all stripes.

However, its basis is more fundamental. It rests on the assumption that society consists of a host of dangerous conflicting social forces with which only an enigmatic organization and its secret "in-ness" can cope. Power has always been something to be fought for, to be seized, and clung to exclusively. No emperor ever willingly shared it, nor do the present rulers.

To make it through life, the Vietnamese believe, one must establish a network (Americans would term this contacts) to cope with problems and challenges and to open doors of opportunity. Such bilateral relationships are existential and situational in that they can be altered to fit specific solutions. They have about them a mystic quality; they are a psychic support system that can run from cradle to grave (and perhaps beyond).

This sustenance is manifested through the strongest of all social groups (except the nuclear family), namely, the patrilineal lineage called the *ho*, which consists of all of one's descendants back through the male to one's great-great-grandfather. In most cases, the *ho* is a fairly large body of blood-related persons sharing a strong sense of identity. The *ho* itself gave rise to the "protective association" concept, similar to the *tong* in Chinese communities in the United States. Out of this concept grew the whole host of protective social organizations noted earlier. Encountering these groups, the French suspected them and sought to suppress them, which gave further impetus to clandestinism. It is understandable that these organizations would become covert under French suppression and thus contribute to the development of the spirit of clandestinism in politics. However, such was also the case even earlier, due to the low-grade but persistent struggle that went on between the Hue court and the village, the former oriented toward Confucianism and the latter toward Buddhism. Buddhism suffered recurrently at the hands of both the Chinese and the Hue court, through official encouragement of Confucianism and through outright repression. This tended to make religion semicovert, although in the village it was not so much underground as unobtrusive. The French subjected Buddhism to various official restrictions and controls, which tended to move it in the direction of nationalistic clandestinism. Buddhism, as practiced in Vietnam today, still carries many of the characteristics of this clandestinism, unlike the practice of the religion elsewhere in Asia.

Under the French, who for all practical purposes outlawed participational politics in Indochina, clandestinism reached a level, an art form even, that was probably unequalled anywhere in the world, even in fifteenth-century Italy under the Medici/Borgia families. Vietnam became a labyrinth of intrigue. To the French any political activity, certainly clandestine activity, represented a challenge to authority requiring stern countermeasures.

Even before the French, however, no legitimate political system existed to link the village with the court. Politics did go on in the village, but only within the confines of the bamboo hedge. And of course there was court politics in Hue, but there was little linkage between the two. In actuality, the three political institutions were the emperor and his court, the village with its Council of Elders, and the *ho*. No side directly faced the other two, and there were never confrontations or even competition among the three elements. Politics in Hue was the politics of a hierarchal structure, by insiders only. Village politics was semisocial, for the rule in the village had no power base – the court being decisive. Only by fact of isolation did the village have autonomy. There was no sense of "our political rights." Within the village and within the *ho*, hierarchy was all-powerful. Such politics as did exist was the politics of status, the test being who has the status. This made political affairs a personalized matter, the politics of entourage. Challenge was not seen as healthy loyal opposition, but a personal affront to the leader himself.

For several hundred years, then, there gradually developed in Vietnam what can be called a code of clandestinism in politics – a host of unwritten rules, imperatives, mores, and customs that became a tradition that still dominates today's political activity.

Many clandestine organizations grew out of the need for mutual protection and sought to serve various mutually self-supporting social, political, spiritual, and political purposes. Vietnam's famed esoteric sect, the Cao Dai,[6] is a classic example. Clandestine organizations are of two parts: an overt element known to the world and a covert one known only to insiders. This is not a case of erecting a "front" or a fraudulent facade. The overt element is vital and authentic; the Cao Dai and Hoa Hao were religious movements and not simply religious facades.

---

6 Anatoli Sokolov, a Russian scholar on Vietnam at the Institute of Oriental Studies, combed through Moscow archives and assembled a list of eighty-five aliases employed by Ho in the course of his life. See Anatoli Sokolov, ed., *Traditional Vietnam* (Moscow: Center for Vietnamese Studies, 1993).

Leaders of clandestine organizations must possess special virtues, and their leadership has its own value system. The proclaimed leader of an organization almost never is the real power-holder, although he may be quite influential within the group. If one is clever and penetrates this organization, one finds behind the ostensible leader another figure, apparently the true power-holder. Only later is one able to discover that the second figure was in effect put there for the world to discover and that behind him there is a third figure (or fourth or fifth) who wields maximum power. One finds that, like an onion, once it is peeled nothing is left. Worse, the system is in a state of constant mutation. New power-holders arise with new relationships and new alliances that outdate the old.

The ideal leader in this political arena is one who can best stage-manage his organization's public image. He should be sly, paternalistic, skilled at intrigue, a master of the deceptive move, and both a dramatist and a magician. At the same time, he must also be one who reciprocates loyalty, protects his followers, and achieves for them whatever goals they seek: power, status, money. Above all, the good leader is highly effective in the world in which he moves.

The model leader in Vietnam, of course, is the man whom the world calls Ho Chi Minh. We know little about this man, and probably much of what we do know is wrong. Of no other major world leader can it be said that his whereabouts for nearly a decade, the 1930s, are unknown. Some scholars maintain that the original Ho Chi Minh, or Nguyen Ai Quoc, as he was then known, died in a Hong Kong prison in 1932 (his obituary was carried in the British Communist Party newspaper, *Daily Worker*, on August 11, 1932) and his place taken by another Vietnamese who assumed the name. Ho Chi Minh lived under many aliases,[7] some of them apparently chosen lightly (puns in Chinese and French, for instance). Throughout his life Ho did nothing to clear up uncertainties about his past, pleading with one insistent French scholar, "You must allow an old man to have a little mystery." But in the best tradition of clandestinism in politics, he behaved as a good leader must: forever tossing sand in the eyes of the world.

Just as there is a model leader, so there is a model follower. He keeps in step with the movement's policy. He never takes an irrevocable position, never makes a final commitment. Proselytizing is common and little opprobrium

---

7 A methodological complication in tracing the historical influences here is encountered in the fact that we are dealing with a single political entity that was until quite recently two separate entities. Under the French there were three distinct Vietnams. After partition in 1954 there were two: the Democratic Republic of Vietnam (DRV), or North Vietnam; and the Government of the Republic of Vietnam (GVN), or South Vietnam. Each had its own government, economic institutions, and educational system. There were two sets of local/informal politics and hence two sets of elites with separate elite goals and values.

attaches to changing sides, providing that one observes a decent interval. Loyalty may be a virtue, but consistency is not. Hence there is not the strong quisling stigma in Vietnam as in some societies. Most Vietnamese of middle age or older have been on all sides of most political issues.

INSTITUTIONAL WEAKNESS

The third characteristic of informal politics in Vietnam – which also extends to the central government organization – is infrastructural weakness. Past governmental organizations were highly exclusive. There was a narrow system of recruitment, and those in control tended to recruit from their own group. Administration tended to be a subculture of its own. Politics had a glory, a grandeur; it was an expressive and affective way of life. Politics was not regarded as a means of carrying out a program or the painful solving of problems, and much of this attitude carries over today. The Vietnamese bureaucrat tends to see himself not in a job, but in a role. He is system- rather than program-oriented and tends to regard government as an avenue to success, the means of getting society's rewards. That this spirit is also alive and well in party politics was vividly demonstrated during the Vietnam Communist Party's (VCP's) Eighth Congress (June–July 1996). The congress did not convene to debate and approve new policies and programs, but to exchange moral exhortations. Orations by the leaders were matched by delegate responses from the floor. Stress was on consensus, unity, and harmony. The test of congress's success was how well the party faithful were mobilized to serve as a corrective or substitute for the existing institutional weakness.

Since 1975, the Socialist Republic of Vietnam (SRV) has, in fact, not been run by a socialist government, as its formal name would suggest, but by the Vietnam Communist Party. Without strong institutions of government, no sound legal base has developed. There is no firm sense of the concept of the rule of law. Government is by party whim, rather than by codified rule. This is now beginning to change in a significant way. Since 1991, the National Assembly has come into its own and the beginnings made for the development of a sound legal base that will allow the creation of a strong governmental system. But nothing is more difficult than putting together, where it has never existed before, a rational, technically efficient, and attractive government. And nothing is easier, either deliberately or inadvertently, than to throw it off track.

The most serious institutional weakness – the product of lingering traditionalism and clandestinism in politics – has to do with the use of the franchise in making political decisions, particularly in informal politics. Most Vietnamese, if candid, will tell you that they are skeptical of the idea that the best way to divide political power is to have people go into a little room and drop pieces of paper in a box. This is not, they explain, the way it has been done in Vietnam. In early Vietnam, the franchise was nonexistent. The village Council of Elders, while "democratic," was also co-optative. When a vacancy was to be filled, there usually was an unspoken consensus in the village as to the best candidate, and this normally was respected by the council. Should there be two equally eligible candidates, an "understanding" would be reached among the two and the council, such as an agreement that the person not chosen would fill the next vacancy. The Vietnamese consider there to be something un-Vietnamese about the stark win-lose, all-or-nothing Western electoral system. It ignores the imperative of group harmony, tears a society apart, and drives the losers to desperate measures because they have gotten nothing; with the Vietnamese manner of division of political power, through "private arrangements," the loser gets something. Harmony is preserved.

DIVISIVENESS

The final Vietnamese heritage with which we are concerned in informal politics is the force of divisiveness – geographic and social. Without question, the Vietnamese have enormous ethnolinguistic unity. They have managed to maintain it over centuries of Chinese military and political Sinicization pressures – the Vietnamese would say assimilation. So impressive has this unity been, so successful have the Vietnamese been in maintaining their identity, that the reality of Vietnam as a badly divided society is obscured.

The chief division is a deeply ingrained sense of geographic regionalism, with all that implies. Regional differences stem from a host of historical and geographic influences. Its roots are the Long March to the South, something akin to the American westward or frontier movement. Beginning in the tenth century A.D., the Vietnamese began pushing out from the Red River Delta in a movement that continued steadily over an 800-year period and ultimately covered a distance of some 1,500 miles. It ended with the arrival of the Vietnamese in the far south, the Camau peninsula, which they reached in the eighteenth century, shortly before the arrival of the French. En route, the Vietnamese destroyed the already decadent Cham empire and were in the process of disassembling the Khmer empire, present-day Cambodia, when the French arrived to halt the effort.

As was the case in the American frontier movement, this migration produced a type of individual who was somewhat different in mental makeup from the Vietnamese left behind, first in the Red River Delta area of the North and later in the center, the imperial court area around Hue. They were pioneer souls – adventurous, risk-taking, and perhaps hardier – differing sharply from their more sophisticated cousins who stayed behind in Hanoi and the more tradition-minded cousins who remained in Hue. The seeds of regionalism were planted.

Subsequent events tended to fix or entrench this regionalism. Vietnam underwent political division unceasingly for several hundred years. In the 1600s, after the secession period, it was divided into halves. During the reign of the Tay Son brothers (1788–1802), it was divided into thirds. In 1802, it was united by Emperor Gia Long, only to be divided into thirds again by the French. It became divided into halves during the Viet Minh war, a division that became firmer as a result of the 1954 Geneva Conference. Formal unification came in 1976 as a result of Hanoi's victory in war.[8]

Religion – especially when regarded as an intellectual thought system with secular importance – is second to geographic regionalism in Vietnamese political divisiveness.

The Vietnamese, unlike the Hindus, are not a passionately religious people, preoccupied with a spiritual quest. They concern themselves less with the hereafter than with the proper conduct of affairs and attainment of happiness in the here and now. The foundations of the Vietnamese social system rest not on revealed religion, but on ethics. The idea of God, which has enkindled so much of Western literature, art, and music, does not permeate Vietnamese arts, which instead are inspired primarily by a reverence for nature and natural life. The Vietnamese, indeed, are not very specific about God. There are no great apostles in Vietnamese history, no martyrs, no saviors, and few who could even be called religious leaders. The most venerated personage in the traditional Vietnamese community was not the priest, but the scholar, or man of learning. Even today, the religion of the common people, especially in the remoter villages, is characterized by superstition, animism, and the worship of local spirits passed down from the dawn of history.

Within this complex blend of creed, there rises two soaring pillars of thought: Confucianism and Buddhism.

Confucianism in Vietnam can be, and is, many things. It is essentially an ethical system defining relationships – a whole matrix of them – in an ideal moral order. The heart of the arrangement is the relationship within the family, but also included are those beyond such ruler-ruled relationships. In each case, mandates and legal-type structures are imposed.

It is difficult to determine the saliency of Confucian thought in Vietnam today and easy to exaggerate its influence. Evidence of its presence is encoun-

8 Pye, op. cit., chap. 8, says that the "aggressive form of Confucianism" is found in Vietnam, which he describes as "little dragon, bigger hegemonist."

tered everywhere – in law, education, art, social practice, and political behavior – yet one can never be sure whether this is imitation Chinese or stems from a prototype Vietnamese "purity," as many Vietnamese intellectuals maintain. The Vietnamese resent the contention that their society is but a pale carbon copy of China. Some of their scholars devote their lives to historical research seeking to prove that much of China's "civilization" actually originated in Vietnam. One encounters Vietnamese military who assert that Maoist guerrilla war tactics were learned from the Vietnamese, arguing that the Chinese as a "nation of farmers" could never have invented revolutionary guerrilla war. It is a moot point. Is the current Vietnamese leadership's lust for power indigenous or, as Pye suggests, an example of "aggressive Confucianism"?[9]

It does seem clear that much of Confucius was adapted by the Vietnamese, modifying and adjusting his thoughts according to need – fixing the weaknesses when required, exploiting the strengths in an appropriate manner, and always allowing room for pre-Confucian indigenous ways. It also seems clear that the Confucian heritage in Vietnam today is a respect for hierarchy, an appreciation of order, high regard for moral respectability, respect for the propriety of paternalistic authority, and the legitimacy of a corresponding dependency. How much of this is directly attributable to Confucian influence and how much of it is indigenous is not a matter that will ever be settled to the satisfaction of all.

Buddhism has the appurtenances of a formalized religion: a priesthood, prayer, a pantheon of gods in human form, and use of images. Central to all is the Law of Karma, the belief in reincarnation to a better or worse life depending on one's behavior in this one. Wisdom lies in the suppression of desires, which are the root of all human suffering. The ultimate reward is Nirvana, to become one with the universe.

Of the two great schools of Buddhism in Asia, the most common in Vietnam is the Great Vehicle or Big Wheel Buddhism. Little Wheel, which holds that Buddha was a teacher and not a god, is found mainly in Sri Lanka, Myanmar, and Cambodia. Big Wheel Buddhism has deified the Buddha and added many other gods who personify qualities or desires as well as Bodhisattvas who are humans who have qualified for divine rank.

Buddhism in Vietnam tends to be amorphous, even confused; its creed is more formless than elsewhere. The faithful are united in the belief that the Buddha is a sort of presiding deity, but beneath this there is room for varied doctrines such as ancestor veneration and simple animism.

---

9 The metaphoric description of formal and informal politics employed elsewhere in this volume of a green and viney trellis (formal, the trellis; informal, the vines) seems appropriate for Vietnam. Lowell Dittmer uses the biological metaphor of muscular (informal) and skeletal (formal).

Undergirding these two dominant religions are other forces of faith: Taoism, Christianity, and Islam, as well as more primitive folk beliefs – the expression of religious feelings through the worship of one's departed ancestors and a great reverence for mountains, rivers, and the soil. Here, attitudes toward gods is rather casual, like the early Greeks. Gods and spirits – especially under a Taoist influence – can be promoted, demoted, cursed, and punished. The emperor could do this, or his appointed representatives, who would make a dough figure, leave it in the sun to dry, and then pound it to pieces.

This combination of veneration for nature and down-to-earth regard for the deities endows the Vietnamese religion with color and pageantry. It also imparts to their many festivals an exuberance and gaiety that are characteristic of few other faiths on earth.

The final contributor of present-day divisiveness in Vietnam is a weak communicational matrix. This has to do with mass communication, word-of-mouth communication of ideas, and education. It is slowly being overcome – the party has done a good deal to erect systems for communication of ideological thought, but not much else. Chiefly, the problem is overcoming heritage. In early Vietnam, except within the village, there was little public communication. Life was parochial, elementary. People were ignorant of the world. Communication within the village was person-to-person. From the outside world there came, if anything at all, only a few rumors, tales by itinerant peddlers or traveling monks, and perhaps some court gossip. The emperor saw no need to keep the people informed. This was extended by the French so as to prevent consensus from developing. The French had a vested interest in keeping the country fragmented. They did this by controlling the channels of communication and sitting on their crosslines. They pitted one social or political group against another by using various rewards and punishments. French encouragement of the religious sects to become virtual enclave governments is an example of this policy of divisiveness. The French negotiated directly with such sects and regional groups but always tried to prevent them – or even villages – from getting together.

The present rulers in Vietnam are now wrestling with what can be called the dilemma of communication of ideas. They must have control of the media – all the modern technology of satellite relays, facsimile and photocopy machines, cellular phones, electronic mail, and so on. But how to control, and limit, content? The communication matrix could well prove to be the destroyer of their present political system. The party has yet to resolve the dilemma.

INFORMAL POLITICS

We now turn to an examination of the chief subject at hand – informal politics.

First a brief overview of Vietnamese political science in general. Political power is held in high regard in Vietnam, whether it is indigenous, an emulation of Confucian power concepts, the result of assimilating French imperial culture, or the influence of Stalinist political thought. It has created a sense of Vietnamese superiority and a self-confidence that allow its military forces to accomplish the unbelievable on the battlefield. It is a praetorian culture whose mystic slogan is struggle, forever struggle (*dau tranh*). Said one of its more perceptive novelists: "We have always lived in an armed camp." In political behavior, *dau tranh* makes status more important than achievement. As was noted above, power is employed as much for the inherent drama involved as for some political payoff or achievement without a meaningful reward. Such was the case with victory in 939, ending a millennium of Chinese control; with the victory over French colonialism in 1954; and with Hanoi's victory in 1975. In each instance, the drama of victory was more important than the proffering of new opportunities at home and abroad. At best there was some psychic reward for the elite, but these victories brought misery if not disaster for the society. It was seen by outsiders as snatching defeat out of the jaws of victory.

Vietnamese informal politics, as the term is used here, is defined as a set of interpersonal activities stemming from a tacitly accepted, but largely unenunciated, matrix of political attitudes existing outside the framework of legal government, constitutions, bureaucratic constructs, and similar institutions (the latter being the domain of formal politics). Informal politics reflects, but is distinct from, the general political culture, just as power-holders differ from other members of the society and are so recognized by them.

As an intellectual construct, the differentiation of formal from informal politics is alien to Vietnamese political thought, or at the very least is regarded as an imported, suspect idea. Indeed, there is in Vietnam little sense of politics and political behavior as distinct from society and social behavior, or for that matter of a political system apart from the general social order.

In examining Vietnamese political organization, the major methodological difficulty encountered has to do with structural size, that is, what place does magnitude occupy in distinguishing formal from informal: Does informal mean small and formal large? At what point in development does a faction become a political party?[10]

---

10 It should not be lost on us that the term "faction" is from the Latin *factio*, meaning the impresario who organized the Roman chariot races. Perhaps it is possible to arrange these forms along a continuum – i.e., faction, network, cluster, clique, entourage, "gang," old-boy network, etc. – but how useful this would be is questionable, to say nothing of how difficult it would be. In Vietnam it is possible to arrange factionalism horizontally as well as vertically, that is, factionalism at the Politburo level vs. factionalism in the military or on the state farm. Again, this would require a great deal of research and might not prove to be worth the effort.

Most Vietnamese, when asked about political discussions in the home when they were young, would say either that such matters were discussed by their parents but usually in terms of family interest – for instance, could the family benefit by becoming involved in some political activity? – or they would say that their parents were too busy to think much about politics. Indeed, some seem puzzled by the idea of political behavior as something separate from social behavior in general. Nor is the concept of two political entities – one formal, one informal – encountered in the literature of the field. To the extent that there is such an awareness, it is vague, with no agreement on precise meanings.

While there is no universal acceptance among Vietnamese political scientists of the proper translation of informal politics, probably the most suitable term is *chinh-tri ngoai chinh-truong* (lit., politics outside/beyond the political arena); another rendition would be *chinh tri phong khach* (lit., living room politics) or political groups in discussion in a private or less public forum. Vietnamese dictionaries carry the term *chinh thuc*, which is applicable to our interest here, that is, as a formal, legal, from an authentic source, or a pronouncement; in context, it conveys the notion of legitimacy. Adding the negative *khong* (not), as suggested by some, makes it *khong chinh thuc*, or not official (which is not exactly the same as informal). Also applicable is *Khong theo thu tuc quy dinh*, meaning to not follow rules or procedures; this is probably the term that Hanoi intellectuals would be most likely to use for informal politics. Even so, it does not convey the full flavor of the English.

Linguistic difficulty is one of several problems that are encountered in attempting to research informal politics in Vietnam. Beyond semantics there is the stark fact that little serious academic research has been conducted on the political process in general and virtually nothing on the dynamics of leadership. This means that, for practical purposes, the political culture of Vietnam remains an unexplored land. What is done currently is superficial. For instance, Hanoi bureaucracy is frequently described as "dense," but why or in what ways goes unexplained. Corruption is excoriated by all, including Politburo members, but its nature and extent never go beyond the anecdotal.

Recently, Hanoi intellectuals hesitatingly and tentatively have begun to address in a generalized way what can loosely be termed "informal politics." This literature, found almost entirely in party theoretical journals, is written – to a fault, actually – not to offend party conservative ideologues; indeed, its most remarkable aspect is that it is published at all. As with all political writing in Vietnam, various code words are employed. What is involved, it is explained, is the implementation of people's rights. This takes two systemic forms: representative democracy, which more or less equates with controls at the center by the party, and direct democracy in the villages. Together, these are the people's rights of ownership and embody both political institutions and the rights themselves. Discussion carefully intermixes informal politics and local politics, and it just as carefully avoids distinguishing one from the other.

An example of this literature is "Achieving Direct Democracy in the Rural Areas," by Bui Ngoc Trinh, a leading party intellectual, in *Tap Chi Cong San* (No. 19, October 1997, pp. 226–230). Trinh, as are others who are dealing with this genre, is maddeningly vague on key concepts, which was done deliberately in the name of self-protection. Hence, there is no clear image of politics, informal or local. However, from Trinh's and other articles on the general subject, two points emerge. First, local politics/informal politics have acquired status and legitimacy and are now acknowledged by the leadership as institutions. Second, informal politics still cannot be regarded as entirely legitimate. It carries the taint of bourgeois sentiment and, more importantly, by its very nature is largely beyond party controls.

FACTIONS

The central institution in Vietnamese informal politics is the faction, defined here as a small united group within the larger political construct that exists to serve its members, usually on a self-interest partisan basis, and occupies a domain between fully structured political institutions (such as the party and the Fatherland Front) and the leaderless political particularism (or anarchy, i.e., absence of structure) at the rice-roots level. It can be thought of as a political way of life. In Vietnam, factional politics resembles, and in some ways differs from, the factionalism of other Sinitic political systems. The system probably owes something to the French colonial experience, when dozens if not hundreds of political organizations developed, which the French chose to term "political tendencies." The Vietnamese faction is less than a party and greater than a clique. It is best thought of as a political combine.[11]

The most evident factions in Vietnam are found at the upper reaches of the party – at the Politburo and Central Committee levels – and to some extent at the provincial People's Party Committee level. They can also be

---

11 Report by Le Thi, director of the SRV Research Center for Family and Women, Hanoi, cited in "Family values challenges in 'Doi Moi' Era" by An Khang in *Vietnam Investment Review* (Oct. 13–Nov. 1, 1995). The Vietnamese household is large by world standards: 4.8 persons; 60% of the households are two generations, 30% are three generations or more. The divorce rate is low, about 1.9%. See also the interview with SRV Minister Phan Ngoc Tuong (chief of the Vietnamese Communist Party's Government Organization and Cadre Department) by Ha Thanh Son in Thoi Bao Kinh Te Saigon, Ho Chi Minh City, Aug. 31–Sept. 6, 1995, *FBIS Daily Report*: East Asia, Sept. 26, 1995.

found, with varying degrees of significance, within the armed forces, the National Assembly, the SRV Foreign Ministry, among party intellectuals, and in the economic institutions. In each venue factionalism is a murky, intrigue-filled, constantly shifting world. Politics is difficult to track, even by those on the inside. Nothing is ever neat and clear, and seldom is anything concluded. Officially, factionalism is proscribed. It exists but is denied. The infighting that goes on endlessly is described by the slang term *bung di* (faction bashing). Nowhere in the Vietnamese political scene are the dynamics of the politics of clandestinism more evident. No political position is irrevocable, no commitment ever total. Factions are relatively durable, but none is permanent; rather, they are forever splintering and reforming as circumstances dictate. By comparison with Japan and Taiwan, Vietnam factions seem quite primitive; they seem less personalized than in China. An unwritten law dictates that factional competition is not to be conducted in the name of personality, as are the politics of entourage in Southeast Asia. Orientation toward individual ego is considered bourgeois politics. Competition must be issue-oriented, factional infighting in the name of some substantive problem, policy, or course of action – for example, China policy, joining ASEAN, domestic social controls, economic sector reorganization, and so on. In the past this infighting was highly ideological; but this no longer seems to be the case, since ideology no longer has the character of cement holding a faction together. However, ideology remains as a lubricant, helping the faction machinery run smoothly.

All in all, over the years the system has served the Politburo well. Rule is collective; there is not even a *primus inter pares* in Hanoi, and Politburo decisions must be consensual. Factionalism allows the leadership more political control and greater latitude in action than most other ruling groups enjoy. It keeps the system porous. Its weakness, existing as it does as a self-contained apparat, is isolation from the general political scene. As advantageous as it may be for the ruling elite, it is detrimental for the society because it permits public debate to be manipulated and policy criticism to be dissipated. Public discontent is absorbed or shunted off, denying the system the redemptive benefits of criticism. It is highly resented by Vietnamese intellectuals.

INFORMAL POLITICS

As practiced in Vietnam today, the world of informal politics can be summed up as follows: The perception of formal versus informal politics draws on a legalistic heritage that always pits the few of the bureaucracy against the many of the rank and file. In any confrontation, the former is strong and its weapon is manipulation, while the latter is weak and its weapon is evasion.

The relationship may be yin-yang, but in the final analysis it comes down to who knows whom. Such may be only virtual reality, but it is what most Vietnamese believe. The relationship between informal and formal politics is complex and symbiotic; it is probably not fruitful to attempt to draw a line between where one ends and the other begins.

Formal–informal politics in Vietnam can be characterized as being institution versus individual. While governance over the centuries has been by formal directive, there has always been a weak tradition of rule of law. The fact is that today the law in Vietnam is what the party says it is at the moment, just as it was what the French colon said it was and, before that, what the emperor said it was.

There is no discernible one-on-one competition between formal and informal politics, probably because of the Confucian influence that abhors stark confrontation. Formal politics is artful management, informal politics skillful illusion. Political power often amounts to what you can get away with, and the Vietnamese place a great premium on such cleverness. It is better to achieve a political goal through complex maneuvers that few can follow than through straightforward action. Open decisions openly arrived at are not only the wrong way to get things done, they also are no fun.

Informal politics is based on hierarchy, as in China. It rests less on rights and privileges and more on obligations and responsibilities. It is a function of social and personal associations shored up by philosophic and religious beliefs. Its character stems from concepts of class; hence it is antiegalitarian. Allegiance by the individual within informal politics is an extension of attitudes toward clan and family. Often it is as spiritual as it is political, what the Buddhists term "the spirit of oneness."

The venue of informal politics remains the family, which, in true Confucian fashion, is still the all-important institution of the society. In traditional Vietnam and throughout the French period, the family was both the basic social and economic unit. With the coming of collectivization, the family as an economic unit was officially replaced by the cooperative, commune, state farm, or state-owned production enterprise. How much reality there was in this restructuring is difficult to determine, since available data are suspect. In any event, in 1989 the family began to reassume its economic role. Today, some 80 percent of all of Vietnam's 14 million households derive their livelihood from family businesses.

The system works because of general, and at least tacit, agreement – by both ruler and ruled, by both party and nonparty members – of the need to prevent instability (*bat an* and *bat on*) in Vietnam's political scene. Intellectual dissent over the present political methods – and it is considerable – is found both within and outside the party. Nonparty people assert that they must have a voice in policy decision making if stability is to be maintained and Vietnam is not to experience the chaos of 1989 in the USSR and Eastern Europe. Within the party, dissent turns on the contention that the present ruling system is anachronistic, that it no longer meets the needs of modern governmental administration, especially in the economic sector. Both dissenters stand for political pluralism, which will legitimize criticism of the system. This is a simmering political condition. At this writing, no one can be sure of the direction that it will take.

The important beneficial changes that have come in Vietnam since 1989, with the introduction of *doi moi* (renovation), are largely due to developments within the informal politics arena. The common perception of outsiders is that, in about 1990, the stagnant economic system suddenly took off in a seemingly effortless manner. How could this be explained? Nothing had eventuated at the Politburo level to account for it. Later it became evident that *doi moi* developed from the bottom up and was not mandated from above, as would be expected in a command economy. Since the end of the war, forces of change have been fermenting at the rice-roots level, establishing the preconditions for economic takeoff. It is a case in which the thinking of the general population (in and out of the party) was ahead of the leadership.[12]

The role of informal politics is shaped from one generation to the next by some major social trauma, that is, each generation in every society undergoes a formative experience that forms its existential outlook.[13] In Vietnam, these social traumas have been (1) the Viet Minh era (over age 60): liberation (anti-colonialism); (2) the Vietnam War era (age 30–60): unification (North), survival (South); and (3) the post–Vietnam War era (under 30): dashed expectations and continued spirit of revolutionary change (North), "breaking the (social) machine" and "never again" attitude (South), and postwar failure (both North and South).

Unlike much of Asia, where politics attracts the young, in Vietnam both formal and informal politics belong to the middle-aged. Young Vietnamese either say that they are too busy to devote time to politics, or that they are disdainful or bored by the process, or that the elderly monopolize political power. Some youths appear to be fearful of getting involved.

---

12 For a detailed discussion of the thesis that *doi moi* in Vietnam was a rice-roots phenomenon and not something mandated from the top, as might be expected in a command economy, see Adam Fforde and Stefan de Vylder, *From Plan to Market: The Economic Transition in Vietnam* (Westview Press, 1996). The thesis answers better than any other explanation the question: How did it happen that after 15 years of stagnation, Vietnam in 1989, suddenly and seemingly so effortlessly, took off in economic development? The answer is, it came from the bottom up.

13 U.S. examples: 1930s economic depression; World War II; the Cold War; Woodstock/cultural revolution, etc.

LEADERSHIP

This final section offers a few observations about political leadership in Vietnam that are applicable more or less equally to informal and formal politics.

Vietnam today has a weak social consensus, defined as agreement on three things: (1) What does the society stand for (how are we distinguishable from other societies)? (2) Where or what do we want the society to go or become (what is our social vision)? and (3) By what manner should we achieve this (what political decision-making mechanism do we want)? True political stability can come to Vietnam only with consensus on these three questions. No one is sure how to achieve social consensus. We do know that it begins with the leaders; it can never develop without good leadership.

The dilemma of rule in Vietnam is that the leadership must claim power and assert legitimacy, but under the present structure it can never be sure how much support it can expect or whom it can trust. There is the pretense to power – it may actually exist – but it does not rest on a reliable base. Political ambiguity and questionable legitimacy are ever present. Hence, all opposition becomes, by fiat, immoral and cannot be tolerated. At the same time, the leadership must prove its superiority to substantiate its right to rule. Such is the dilemma. It is also the leadership's defining challenge in establishing a governance system that will harness the power of informal politics.

Since its inception in 1945, the Hanoi Politburo has consistently failed to recognize its dilemma. Its rule from the end of the Vietnam War until 1979, with the advent of *doi moi* (for which it can claim little credit), has been a history of failed leadership. Wartime leadership, which made few serious mistakes in serving the cause, seldom did anything right after the war. It confronted China and eventually triggered a border war. It invaded Cambodia in an unsuccessful attempt to solve the Pol Pot problem. It drove its southern middle class into the sea and its Chinese ethnic minority in the north back into China. It savaged the southern domestic trade system without having a ready replacement. It mandated an economic self-reliance policy for Vietnam at a time when the entire world was moving toward economic interdependency. Yet through it all the Politburo leaders insisted that they were not the problem. In speeches and writings they would attribute Vietnam's problems and difficulties to a near endless list of culprits: counter-revolutionaries at home and revanchists abroad, China's cold/hot war against Vietnam, American imperialism, rapacious world capitalism, and lazy and incompetent party cadres. Everyone and everything were to blame, except the leadership. Because this assessment of the cause of their difficulties was

wrong, so were their prescriptions – chiefly security alerts, endless governmental reorganization, semipurges of middle-ranking party cadres, and constant moral exhortation.

Leadership legitimacy in Vietnam involves, first of all, power, but it also
involves the proper mindset by the leadership; this means moral and social
compacts having to do with propriety and exemplary conduct and legitimate
hierarchy in political life. One's formal position is extremely important in all
political spheres in Vietnam – the party, the state, the Fatherland Front, the
military. It is what confers status. Possessing status does not necessarily imply
political influence, but no influence exists in its absence.

Since 1989 there has been a tacit acknowledgment by at least some
members of the Hanoi leadership that the Politburo is, if not the problem, the
major impediment – particularly to improving the economy. As this is being
written, there are indications from Hanoi that the leadership problem is at last
being faced squarely. The Eighth Congress announced significant changes in
the Politburo and Central Committee, and by the end of 1997 more than one-
half of the ministerial-level state leadership had changed as well.

CONCLUSION

The basic strength, or perhaps the better word is *recommendation*, of our
methodology here in attempting to define informal politics is found in the
oft-quoted maxim: All Politics Is Local. The fact that in reference to Vietnam not a great deal is known (or set down) about our subject, certainly when
measured by the literature, should serve as an academic inducement.

The operative question in Vietnam today – and perhaps this extends to the
other Confucian systems – is how and in what ways will economic and political change affect the conduct of informal politics? Since the reform effort
began in earnest in 1989, the Vietnamese leadership has managed to keep
economics separate from politics, making whatever economic policy change
is deemed necessary (that does not carry undue risk) but making no significant political change whatsoever. How long can this line be held? As the one
immutable law of history is the law of change, it is inevitable that the present construct will end. Future political activity at various levels may become
stronger, or possibly weaker; change can be for good or ill. We are left with
trying to determine when change will come and what direction it will take.

Throughout 1997, it became increasingly evident that the long-standing
sociopolitical compartmentalization in Vietnam – state versus party, economics versus politics – had begun to degrade. Indications were seen on all
sides: open dissidence by farmers in the northern highlands and Mekong
Delta; the restive youth; complaints (and departures) by foreign joint-

venture entrepreneurs; more assertiveness by religionists, both Catholic and Buddhist; new and legitimate claims by the professional military; a steady infusion of foreign thought with the ever-spreading communications revolution; the end of the Cold War, with its search for some new geopolitical construct for the Pacific Basin; the ever-growing demands imposed by international economic interdependence; and the opportunities in the rise of regionalism in Southeast Asia. And beneath it all, the growth in influence and structure of Vietnamese informal politics.

The elite of Vietnam – those 10 percent or so who make things happen or not happen – are no fools. They recognize the situation that they face in managing a polity in economic and political flux, much of it the result of outside forces and largely beyond their control – indeed, even beyond their understanding. There are among them few who could be labeled conservative ideologues, that is, those who resist all calls for change. They were once in the majority, but now the consensus is on the need for change. Disputation now is over how much risk to take in effecting change without losing social control.

This may not strike one as much of an advancement, this recognition by the elites and their leaders that they face a situation that they neither fully understand nor can control, but compared to the thinking in the first two postwar decades, when leaders did hardly anything right and blamed all but themselves for what was wrong, the current perceptions represent a great leap forward. For as Socrates told us: Not to know, and to know that you know not, is the beginning of wisdom.

CONCLUSION:
EAST ASIAN INFORMAL POLITICS IN
COMPARATIVE PERSPECTIVE

LOWELL DITTMER

As our survey clearly shows, informal politics remains a prominent, pervasive feature of political life throughout contemporary East Asia. We have contended, however, that whereas "bringing the state back in" has made a major contribution toward conceptualizing the political economy of rapid growth in the region, it does not really take us very far toward understanding how politics actually gets done – perhaps anywhere, but certainly not in East Asia.[1] The "state," as in the "state–society" paradigm, is a concept that is far too homogeneous and monolithic, too static and rigid to capture the infinite variety of cross-cutting relationships that we find to be characteristic of informal politics. If the "state," conventionally defined, is too narrowly gauged, "society" is too broad and indiscriminate. The concept of "political culture" encompasses our interests, as is fruitfully realized within this volume by C. F. Yang, who shows how the normative dimension of informal politics in particular is inseparable from its cultural-linguistic dimension; or by Douglas Pike's evocative account of the impact of "lingering traditionalism" on Vietnamese politics. Yet the concerns of "political culture" also go well beyond informal politics – including, for example, theories of transhistorical versus psychocultural origin, or the relations between public symbolism and psychological motives, and other unresolved methodological controversies that need not detain us here. The analysis of "civil society," which was greatly stimulated by the collapse of communist regimes in Eastern Europe, seems initially more promising as a conceptual bridge to span the hiatus beween state and society. But the concept has in its most recent incarnation been too exclusively identified with a "public" realm (consisting of "voluntary associations," "interest groups," the market, an autonomous mass media) that is

---

[1] See Haruhiro Fukui's Introduction to this volume. See also Peter B. Evans, D. Rueschemeyer, and Theda Skocpol, eds., *Bringing the State Back In* (New York: Cambridge University Press, 1985); also, Paul Cammack, *Bringing the State Back In: A Polemic* (Manchester, England: Department of Government, 1987).

sharply differentiated from and opposed to the "state" to be particularly useful in East Asian cultures, which (as Fukui notes in the Introduction to this volume) are typically characterized by compromise formulations (blanket terminology, euphemism, etc.) emphasizing "fusion" rather than sharp contraposition. Investigations of civil society in the China case, for example, have typically been so preoccupied with whether various social groupings are truly distinct from the state that they neglect to analyze how such "infrapolitics" is actually conducted.[2] One troubling ramification of this preoccupation is that the term's usage is implicitly teleological, presuming a necessary (if not sufficient) relationship between civil society and democracy.[3] Kim thus finds very little use for civil society or state–society relations in dealing with informal politics in the DPRK, for example.

Thus we abandon this conceptual minefield and introduce instead the relatively new vocabulary of informal politics, a terminology that draws on previous work on informal economics and informal institutions.[4] We submit that this hitherto neglected approach is an indispensable key to a realistic understanding of East Asian politics.[5] Just as a failure to take into account the informal economic sector can lead to inaccurate estimates of a nation's GDP, the neglect of informal politics can lead to a serious misunderstanding of political realities in the East Asian Pacific region.

How may informal politics be most usefully defined? Although it is obviously a form of politics that is not formal, we require a definition that is not the mere obverse or residual of another definition.[6] That is mere question begging; nothing can be predicated about a variable unless it is clearly distinguished from other variables to which it might possibly have a causal relationship. Unlike, however, the SNTV (the single nontransferrable vote within

2 E.g., cf. William T. Rowe, "The public sphere in modern China: A review article" and the other articles collected in *Modern China* 16:3 (1990), pp. 309–329; also, David Strand, " 'Civil society' and 'public sphere' in modern China: A perspective on popular movements in Beijing 1919/1989," *Problems of Communism* 39:3 (1990), pp. 1–19; and Richard Madsen, "The public sphere, civil society and moral community," *Modern China* 19:2 (April 1993), pp. 183–198.

3 Cf. Nancy L. Rosenblum, "Civil societies: Liberalism and the moral uses of pluralism," *Social Research* 61:3 (Fall 1994), pp. 539–563; also, Jean L. Cohen and Andrew Arato, *Civil Society and Political Theory* (Cambridge, MA: MIT Press, 1992).

4 This literature is quite rich; cf. Alejandro Portes, Manuel Castello, and L. A. Benton, eds., *The Informal Economy* (Baltimore: Johns Hopkins University Press, 1989); Claus Offe and Rolf Heinze, *Beyond Employment: Time, Work and the Informal Economy* (Philadelphia: Temple University Press, 1992); the symposium on the informal sector in *Yale Law Review* 103:8 (June 1994); Darryl G. Waldron, "Informal finance and the East Asian economic 'miracle,' " *Multinational Business Review* 3:2 (Fall 1995), pp. 46–55; *inter al.*

5 See, however, Carl H. Lande, *Friends, Factions and Parties: The Structure of Philippine Politics* (New Haven: Yale University Southeast Asian monograph series, no. 6, 1965); also, Steffen W. Schmidt, James C. Scott, Carl Lande, and Laura Guasti, eds., *Friends, Followers, and Factions: A Reader in Political Clientelism* (Berkeley: University of California Press, 1977).

6 See above, "Informal Politics among the Chinese Communist Elite" see also Lowell Dittmer and Yushan Wu, "The modernization of factionalism in Chinese politics," *World Politics* (July 1995).

a medium-sized electoral district, which characterized Japanese elections
during much of the postwar era and has now been adopted in Taiwan), informal politics is systemically pervasive and not easy to isolate empirically. We
must perforce draw analytical distinctions to clarify its relationship
to other relevant variables. According to our definition, "informal politics" is
a more narrowly specified subset of political culture: narrow not necessarily
because it is empirically localized – although hitherto chiefly focused on
the elite, it may also include grassroots activists, as illustrated by Fukui and
Fukai's previous work on local electoral machines,[7] or by the Dittmer and Lu
study of work units – but because it is more analytically precise. It does not
encompass the public, symbolic dimension of political culture, for example,
but is rather exclusively concerned with the implicit, sometimes forgotten or
even concealed realm of politics. This means that the informal is widely confused with the "arbitrary, unfair, or corrupt." Yet we would draw a distinction between the two. Informal politics is not "authoritative," as Fukui makes
clear, because it is nonlegitimate and because it transcends the public, political realm that is its raison d'être.

To speak more precisely, informal politics consists of *the use of nonlegitimate
means* (albeit not necessarily illegal) *to pursue public ends*. Thus it is conceptu-
ally sandwiched between "formal politics" on the one hand and "corruption"
on the other. Formal politics consists of the use of legitimate means to pursue legitimate public ends: Easton's "authoritative allocation of values." Corruption consists of using *illegitimate* (i.e., at least immoral, possibly illegal)
means to pursue *private* ends, thereby constituting a violation of the "public
interest," or "trust." "Illegitimate means" may include either *expedients*, ranging from the merely shady to the downright nefarious (coup d'état, assassination), or *relationships*, which also vary from mere unofficial (*houtai*, or
"backstage") channels to criminal connections (as in the LDP's 1992 Sagawa
Kyubin scandal). *Informal politics*, like corruption, may involve the use of illegitimate means, but only to pursue *legitimate public ends* – power, "pork," or
policy. As Count Cavour is said to have remarked, "What rascals we would
be if we were doing all this for ourselves!" Several cases in this study confirm
the distinction that we draw between corruption and informal politics: Former ROK Democatic Liberal Presidents Chun Doo Hwan and Roh Tae Wu,
like LDP faction boss Shin Kanemaru before them, when caught with large
hordes of unexplainable cash in their possession, claimed that this was being
held for partisan rather than personal use – which would presumably have
justified their stash had the claim been credited, although it was not. As an

---

7 Haruhiro Fukui and Shigeko N. Fukai, "Pork barrel politics, networks, and local economic development in contemporary Japan," *Asian Survey* 36:3 (March 1996), pp. 268–287.

anonymous respondent in the Dittmer and Lu study observed, as a freelancer he had been criminally prosecuted for the type of work that he was now conducting with impunity on behalf of his work unit.

Although the table below risks drawing too sharp a distinction beween variables that are actually poles of a continuum, it may clarify the logical relationships.

| | Ends | |
Means	Public	Private
Legitimate	Formal politics	Partisanship
Nonlegitimate	Informal politics	Corruption, conspiracy

Definitions of course mark only the bare beginnings of analysis. The purpose of this anthology has been to bring together studies of analogous phenomena in a set of relevantly comparable political systems to compare and contrast how these variables relate to one another empirically, permitting us to move from definitions and speculative hypotheses to empirically grounded generalizations. Moving beyond this "core" definition of informal politics, the surrounding layers of our definitional onion can then be fleshed out on the basis of this comparative empirical data. How is informal politics distinguished from and yet related to formal politics? What is the exact nature of the tactics and relationships that comprise illegitimate (or at least extralegitimate) means? To what ends can informal means be applied, and where can they not be deployed without impugning those means? Finally, what has been the impact of political and economic development on informal relations?

In answer to these questions we have brought together in this volume studies of China, Japan, Korea, Vietnam, and Taiwan, all of which are part of the same Confucian cultural ecumene, with its denigration of formal legal institutions and its emphasis on cultivating a personal moral example and a public morality based on reciprocity. In all of them there is a marked gap between public rectitude and a semiprivate practical "backstage," leaving ample latitude for informal politics to achieve what cannot be trusted to occur according to morm, or "principle." All have hierarchical political traditions, giving the leader the symbolic resources to amplify his formal powers considerably (none has much experience with female leadership). And in all of them, despite considerable variation in their stages of modernization, informal politics remains vigorous. There are also, of course, significant differences. Despite the common emphasis on patrilineal kinship structures, the Japanese *ie* seems to have made more copious use of fictive kinship, within a geographically and functionally circumscribed "frame," or *ba*, than the more dispersed and reticulated Sinitic *jia*.[8] With the dawning of the modern era in the late nineteenth century and the somewhat agonizing induction of these systems into the race for modernization and national self-realization, our cases diverge considerably in their political and economic developmental trajectories, even to the extent of having engaged one another in warfare and colonization. But even here there are underlying similarities: All four cases have at one time or another in the modern era fallen victim to large-scale national disaster – war, revolution, economic turmoil, nuclear holocaust. Since then, they have all (albeit in staggered sequence) rebounded to launch highly successful economic modernization drives.

In trying to discover a common causal nexus behind the analogous patterning of informal politics in East Asia, we might hence consider the past, or "tradition," to be the common independent variable. Yet this is a past that after a broadly shared cultural legacy is characterized by diverging national paths to modernization. Among the most significant distinctions among them is in their different responses to the incursion of the West and its inherent modernization imperative: Whereas China, Vietnam, and North Korea experienced a violent revolution that resulted in a concerted attempt to socialize the means of production and make a transition to communist utopia, the other cases did not (indeed, Taiwan in a sense owes its separate existence to its rejection of this option). This attempted revolutionary transformation was accompanied by the imposition of a comprehensive Leninist organizational and ideological monocracy. With the rise of the Cold War, Japan on the other hand adapted a form of constitutional democracy imposed by its conqueror to its bureaucratic tradition, while its former colonies adopted nationalist developmental dictatorships. While both systems then pursued economic modernization within their respective political frameworks, economic entrpreneurship in the socialist dictatorships remained much more tightly controlled by the state apparatus than in Japan or even in Taiwan or South Korea. The Chinese party-state (and its socialist clients, the DRV and DPRK) still bases political legitimacy on a secularized form of divine right derived from Marxist doctrine, according to which the leadership boasts a historically ordained mission *cum* "leading role" (nonetheless mimicking the accoutrements of popular sovereignty in its formal structure and parliamentary apparatus), while the systems that underwent democratic transformation transferred legitimacy to the political marketplace: electoral systems, national parliaments, public opinion polls, mass protests, and the like. The democratizing systems, during their much longer experience with secularized, performance-based legitimacy, have had to open themselves to plebiscitary discipline.

8 See Chie Nakane, *Japanese Society* (Berkeley: University of California Press, 1970).

From this we emerge with two crucial distinctions: one of economic development, which stratifies our cases into three tiers – developed (Japan), newly industrialized (Taiwan, South Korea), and developing (China, Vietnam, North Korea); and one of political structures, which cleaves them into autocratic and democratic. As it happens (or perhaps not so coincidentally), the relatively industrialized systems are all democratic or democratizing, while the less developed systems are all autocratic. As we shall see, this overlapping political and economic cleavage has had considerable impact on informal politics. Political and economic development tends to strip informal politics of its clandestine character, for example, and to encourage its institutionalization, legalization, and commercialization.

The relationship between informal and formal politics, most analysts agree, is one of functional interdependence, that of musculature to a skeleton or a vine to a trellis.[9] Formal politics serves two functions for informal politics: spiritual and mundane. On the one hand, the formal hierarchy supplies the offices, status, and perquisites of power that political actors seek. But informal groupings do not merely plunder the hierarchy for these ends, but also use it to confer legitimacy on the policies that they enact, not only for themselves but on behalf of mass constituencies, perhaps even (if coincidentally) the "public" at large. Thus formal politics is both a "feeding trough" and a "temple" for the practice of informal politics. Because formal politics is typically well structured, it often lends its form to those informal actors pursuing their ends within it. Yet informal politics does not precisely replicate the structure that it occupies. Whereas the formal apparatus has both vertical and horizontal dimensions (*tiaotiao* and *kuaikuai*, in the Chinese parlance), the informal structure seems to be essentially vertical in the Asian systems we analyze, often with multiple executives, legislatures, and overlapping bureaucracies, for example, usually culminating in a single chief. And, as Fewsmith notes, whereas informal politics in the West tends to be a cover for collusion, in Asia it is often conflictual and divisive.[10]

The relationship between formal and informal is not only functionally complementary but interpenetrating and empirically fluid. Faction chiefs may attempt to take advantage of their power of appointment to transform a formal bureaucratic base into an informal factional network, either by befriending colleagues and subordinates or by restaffing the organization with their "own" people, resulting, if successful, in an "independent kingdom" (*duli wangguo*). Peng Zhen seems to have been a classic success story before

9 Cf. Andrew Nathan, "A factionalism model for CCP politics," *China Quarterly* 53 (January–March 1973), pp. 34–66; and Tun-jen Cheng and Brantly Womack, "General reflections on informal politics in East Asia," *Asian Survey* 36:3 (March 1996), pp. 320–337.
10 Joseph Fewsmith, "Formal Structures, Informal Politics, and Political Change in China," this volume.

his career was interrupted by the Cultural Revolution, creating such a tight structure in Beijing that Mao complained that he "could not stick a pin in"; in the reform era, Hu Yaobang in his heyday achieved pervasive organizational reach via strategic appointments of his "Youth League faction" (*qingnian tuan*).[11] In South Korea in the late 1980s, as in Japan on the fragmentation of the LDP in 1993 or in Taiwan upon the legitimation of first a nonparty opposition (*dangwai*) and then independent parties, the early parties were direct outgrowths of personal factions (e.g., Kim Dae Jung's Cholla-based Pyongmindang, the New Party in Japan and in Taiwan). The institutionalization of parties in South Korea remains at this writing so tenuous that party structure tends to attenuate upon the electoral defeat of its leader. The logic of the electoral system tends to militate in favor of plausibly victorious coalitions — resulting not necessarily in majority parties, but at least in loose coalitions of factions that may then realign in the light of electoral outcomes.

Formal and informal politics are, however, in some respects mutually exclusive. Factional activity and apparent strength tend to vary inversely with the power of the formal leadership, for example. Thus Chon notes in the South Korean case that Park's strong executive leadership temporarily precluded factional activity, as Kim confirms in the case of Kim Il Sung in the DPRK.[12] Similarly, Cheng and Chou detect a proliferation of factionalism only with the end of strongman rule in Taiwan.[13] Factional activity in Japan also tends to intensify when formal routines are disrupted, for example, during electoral campaigns and "succession struggles" (i.e., the selection of a new prime minister and cabinet). In China, too, factional activity remained relatively quiescent during the heydays of both Mao Zedong and Deng Xiaoping; only when the formal apparatus was held in check (as during the Cultural Revolution) or when supreme leadership was perceived to be at stake during struggles for succession (which tend to pervade the last years of the leader's tenure),[14] did factional activity intensify. (Factions do not disappear during periods of strong leadership; they go underground.) Thus, although formal and informal power are mutually interdependent, there may also be a fixed-sum, balance-of-power relationship between the two.

---

11 Hu Yaobang had long chaired the Chinese Youth League in the 1950s and as chief of the CC's Organization Bureau (1978–1982); then, as CCP General Secretary (1982–1987), he was in a position to promote his proteges.

12 Chon, "Election Process," *op cit.*; Samuel Kim, "North Korean informal politics."

13 Cheng and Chou, "Legislative Factions," *op cit.*

14 The struggle for succession is a vague and elastic phase that may also be used by the leader as a device to facilitate his rule by creating invidious distinctions among his colleagues that may then be manipulated. In the latter sense, the last seventeen years of Mao's life were a protracted premortem succession crisis, triggered by his announced intention to step down and groom a successor, whose identity he kept changing his mind about; Deng's premortem succession crisis lasted from 1986 through at least 1989, when he stepped down from all formal positions, or perhaps even 1995, when he became physically incapacitated. See the chapter by Peter Lee in this volume.

An indispensable component of any attempt to plumb the informal political universe is the *leader*. Leadership is where all of the most significant
factional networks converge. Empirically, leadership consists of one person
(the "supreme," "paramount leader," or "core"), hitherto exclusively male,
who surrounds himself with an entourage of like-minded advisors. The relationship between the core and his entourage is a delicate balance between
collective leadership and *primus inter pares* that may vary from case to case:
Deng Xiaoping seemed more comfortable with collective leadership than
Mao Zedong, for example, and the Vietnamese seem to operate it more
smoothly than the Chinese or North Koreans. The core need not be the chief
executive officer of the formal hierarchy, as both Kakuei Tanaka and Deng
Xiaoping have demonstrated. Yet the interdependency of formal and informal networks, of power and legitimacy, is such that there is usually some
intersection, even if one or two places removed: Thus the "sitting committee" of gerontocrats who coordinated the response to the Tiananmen demon-
strators from behind the scenes were all Politburo "alumni" with
patron–client links to the nominal superordinates who replaced them, like
the *genro* many years before them who supervised the Meiji restoration.

As Suisheng Zhao has noted, the ambit for informal freedom of maneuver
tends to vary hierarchically; thus, "revolutionary veterans" (*geming yuanlao*)
have great informal discretion, due to a wide range of lateral and vertical connections and high prestige, whereas middle- and lower level cadres tend to
have more limited political options, based on more narrowly defined bureaucratic roles.[15] The supreme or paramount leader is distinguished from
faction chiefs in that he has the greatest informal ambit of all. This is not
unrelated to the fact that the core leader is typically not committed to a
specific political faction but rather rules by balancing one faction against
another. This balancing process may in the more bitterly contested cases
result in building a coalition among a majority of faction leaders to ostracise
or "purge" a dissident minority, thereby reinforcing discipline and leadership authority. Inherent in such tactics is also the risk, if overused, of
creating an opposition prepared to resort to equally extreme measures to
survive politically – as Khrushchev discovered in 1964, or as Mao found
out in the case of Lin Biao. A leader is also expected to mobilize and lead
public opinion. Thus the rules for becoming leader, which include assem-
bling a large and powerful factional following but normally have little to do
with public opinion, are not identical to the rules for leading. This may be
one reason that Tanaka, although an extraordinarily resourceful and power-

15 Cf. Suisheng Zhao, "The structure of authority and decision-making: A theoretical framework," in
   Carol Lee Hamrin and S. Zhao, eds., *Decision-Making in Deng's China: Perspectives from Insiders* (Armonk,
   NY: M. E. Sharpe, 1995), pp. 233–245.

ful faction chief, had a relatively brief and disappointing tenure as prime minister.

The basic informal group unit is the "faction," a relatively small, face-to-face, monocratically organized action group. In its most generic sense, the term includes patron–client associations, conspiratorial cliques, ideological compadres – any group lacking formal standing. A faction does not usually coincide precisely with a formal department or bureau; although it may include many members of a bureau, that bureau will typically also include unaffiliated cadres or even members of rival factions, and the faction typically "spills over" the bureau. Nor does the faction typically coincide with the political party, which is driven by the strategic logic of minimal coalitions to embrace as many factions as possible. Informal politics may also, however, transcend face-to-face groupings, albeit at the price of a drop in efficacy. Spanning geographical and bureaucratic gaps, embracing multiple dispersed factions, sometimes even claiming a mass constituency (yet still linked by personal connections, sometimes electronically augmented by such media as the telephone, FAX, and e-mail) is the "network." Networks have been even less thoroughly investigated than factions, but they seem to operate on the basis of a loosely knit set of shared interests and attitudes. Both factions and networks have grown rampant throughout democratizing Asia and, although officially prohibited in the Asian dictatorships, operate less conspicuously there as well (e.g., the mass youth networks of the Cultural Revolution, Democracy Wall, or Tiananmen protests).

Within the broad category of informal politics a relatively large proportion of our accumulated knowledge concerns the formation and activities of factions. In the case of China this is sometimes ascribed to the lack of parties or other formalized alternatives (given the CCP's monopolization of organizational activity), but the fact that factions have retained their political significance in other East Asian systems with high per-capita incomes and autonomous multiparty systems (which, in the case of Japan, have operated effectively for more than half a century) demonstrates the inadequacy of such arguments. Moreover, factions in all of our cases are broadly homologous in structure and function. They are all organized on a bimodal, patron–client basis, in which the clients are vested with career security by a politician whom they in turn support in the political arena. Yet beneath this overarching kinship there are also important distinctions among types of factions.

First, they range from highly institutionalized groupings to completely uninstitutionalized cliques. Whether this difference is inherent in different cultural organizational propensities or simply an artifact of cultural variance in the level of official tolerance for informal organization is not entirely clear. In any event, Japanese factions are the most institutionalized and PRC factions the least, with Taiwan and South Korea occupying intermediate positions. Factional rosters of Japanese Diet members are listed in parliamentary gazettes, and factional strength can be objectively measured in the public media after each election or realignment.[16] North Korean and Chinese factions are in contrast not only uninstitutionalized but expressly forbidden, as a result of which they are invisible except during crises or purges. In the cases of Taiwan and South Korea, factions have, since their transition to democracy, either been transformed into parties or become more visible groupings within existing parties.

Second, factions vary in what we might call their "structural embeddedness." The predominant trend in these systems has been toward highly embedded systems dominated by professional bureaucrats, but in each case there are significant exceptions. In the Japanese, South Korean, and Taiwanese cases, electoral politicians have emerged to challenge bureaucratic veterans and/or military professionals. In China the mass campaign has traditionally served as an avenue of upward mobility for the zealous amateur; leaders may also pluck "favorites" out of the ranks to perform special tasks that are aversive to established officials. The "expanded meeting" is another informal expedient devised to permit the inclusion of nonembedded faction members at the discretion of the convener. Certainly, Chinese informal politics has grown more structurally embedded in the wake of institutionalization efforts since the death of Mao, however.

The factionalism literature is much more replete with discussions of the macropolitical behavior of the faction (e.g., interfactional competition) than with its micropolitical organization. Here Fukui's and Fukai's contribution is particularly valuable, demonstrating through a series of careful case studies exactly how the Japanese *koenkai*, and above them the electoral *keiretsu* (coalitions of *koenkai*), are organized and operated.[17] The internal organization seems to be roughly that of spokes in a wheel, with the patron at the hub nurturing face-to-face relations with each client; similarly, the prefectural *koenkai* are arranged in a hub-and-spoke fashion around a Diet member's *keiretsu*. South Korean *huwonhoi* and *sajojics* (see syllabus) appear to be similarly organized, with established local notables claiming long-term suzerainty over regional domains that are relatively exclusive and display a high degree of solidarity. Our picture of the Chinese situation is still fragmentary due to high information costs, but it suggests a quite different and

---

16 T. J. Cheng and Brantly Womack, "Conclusions," in *Asian Survey* (March 1996).
17 In addition to their chapter in this volume, see "The political economy of electoral Keiretsu: Cases and interpretations," unpublished paper presented at the Annual Meeting of the Association for Asian Studies, Boston, March 23–27, 1994; and "Campaigning for the Japanese Diet," in Bernard Grofman, Sung-Chull Lee, Edwin Winckler, and Brian Woodall, eds., *Elections and Campaigning in Japan, Korea, and Taiwan: Toward a Theory of Embedded Institutions* (forthcoming).

more complex pattern. There are to be sure instances of discrete spoke-and-hub clusters, such as Lin Biao's 571 clique (where security placed constraints on wide interorganizational extension). But these are deviant cases; more typically, Chinese factional organization (in both Taiwan and the PRC) appears to be extended, nonexclusive, and opportunistically ramified. We now know for example that membership in mainland Chinese "bourgeois democratic parties" overlaps with CCP membership, particularly at the highest leadership levels. Cheng and Chou note that Taiwan factions are "soft," lacking internal discipline and having multiple or overlapping memberships. Although this remains to be more firmly established empirically, it would appear that cadres claim membership in as many different *guanxi* (connection) networks as feasible (e.g., military bureaucrats may have had service in several different Field Armies) and then "pull" (*la*) a connection or network as the need arises. In the case of factional cleavage, a cadre may thus have multiple options, rather than a simple zero-sum choice of loyalty or betrayal. Much more work will be needed for us to be able to sketch a comprehensive sociometric diagram of Chinese factional organization.

Upending Lord Salisbury's dictum that politics is not concerned with permanent friends or enemies but only with permanent interests, the typical East Asian politician finds that interests or policies shift while factional affiliations tend to endure. The "glue" that holds the faction together is personal loyalty, rather than the short-term instrumental relations of the marketplace or the allegiance to a position in a functional division of labor or hierarchy. The patron reciprocates that loyalty by assuring the client's occupational security and career interests.[18] The resulting "connection" (*guanxi*) tends to be traced to some pre- or extrapolitical tie or *guanxihu* – kinship, common place of origin, "old school tie," the sort of "imprinting" experience that has fused veterans of PLA Field Armies long after they were demobilized after Liberation – that we might refer to cross-culturally as a *primary bond*. Albeit informal, and hence lacking constitutional or legal sanction, these tend to be culturally patterned to such an extent that there is honor (and dishonor) among thieves, so to speak. A primary bond is not *sine qua non*; if not based on primary bonds, a functional grouping, tested by shared adversity, becomes sentimentalized over time (the more of which passes, *ceteris paribus*, the stronger the bond). Thus, despite the lack of primary bonds, an affinity may develop on the basis of valued formal relationships in the same organization, as Ostrov shows in the long-term, hidden, vertical patron–client bonds that he finds between Nie Rongzhen, Qian Xuesen, Wang Bingzhang, and Han

---

18 See Robert Kaufman, "The patron-client concept and macro-politics: Prospects and problems," *Comparative Studies in Society and History* 16:3 (L974), pp. 284–308.

Guang.[19] Similarly, the "petroleum faction" that represented the interests of energy and heavy industry until its disbandment in 1980 traces its origins back to its opening the Daqing oilfield in 1963. This seems to be true even in the case of Japan, where the patron–client relationship has been most formalized: There is a personal loyalty transcending salary, explaining why *koenkai* or electoral *keiretsu* members do not more frequently switch patrons with the tides of electoral fortune, like American political consultants. The dietman's local constituency also tends to be loyal – certainly more so than would be warranted by the price of the tea parties and tours organized by the *koenkai*.

This is not to say that such loyalties are exclusively personal, as in the traditional Hindu institution of suttee, according to which a spouse may have no independent existence after the death of her spouse. Factional membership is in fact, within certain limits, fungible. The Japanese *koenkai* may be bequeathed from politician *pere* to politican *fils*, to other relatives, and even "loaned" to allied politicians,[20] just as the Chinese "radical reform" grouping migrated successively from Hu Yaobang to Zhao Ziyang to Zhu Rongji (albeit not without defections). It seems that the limit to factional fungibility is the veto power of the abandoned patron. "With you in charge, I am at ease," Mao's blessing to Hua Guofeng, is the clearest instance of an informal bequest, but failing such an explicit benediction (impossible posthumously) an apparent convergence of programmatic missions may suffice to validate a claimed line of descent. If approval is withheld by the original patron, on the other hand, a switch can misfire no matter how complementary the policy programs, as witnessed by Chen Boda's ill-fated switch from Mao (and Jiang Qing) to Lin Biao. Once the transfer has been transacted (i.e., the original patron dies), its survival of course depends on the ability of the new patron to find resources to maintain and possibly extend the network. As in a family inheritance, there may also be a posthumous division of the estate among rival claimants (*fenjia*), as Liu Shaoqi's legacy seems to have been divided between Deng Xiaoping and Chen Yun.[21]

In all of these systems, informal politics provides a temporary respite from law and administrative regulations (which in any case tend to be weaker, thanks to the anti-litigious Confucian heritage) and opens a way to bridge formal boundaries, making it possible to get things done that might otherwise be impossible or at least far more complex.[22] Informal politics is very pragmatic; it

---

19 Benjamin C. Ostrov, "Formal organization and the birth of clientage in the People's Republic of China: The national defense research and development sector," *supra*, ch. 9.

20 Fukui and Fukai, "Political economy of electoral Keiretsu," Ibid., pp. 12–13.

21 The likelihood of such a divided inheritance may be higher in Sinitic cultures, which lack strict primogeniture rules, than in Japan, which has such a rule. This issue will require further research.

22 The clearest case is the achievement of the group centered around the Chinese NDSTC, paralleling the achievement of the (also informally organized) U.S. Manhattan Project. Ostrov, "Clientage," pp. 221–222.

is concerned with doing what can be done through an expanded repertoire of tactics. The Achilles' heel of informal politics is clearly legitimacy. In terms of the legitimacy of political ends, we may posit a four-tier hierarchy, with ideal interests (e.g., principles, lines, platforms) ranked at the top, followed by bureaucratic interests (turf, budget share, policy), followed by career security, with personal self-interest ranking at the bottom (in practice, these are not sharply differentiated or mutually exclusive). In most of these systems, the formal governmental apparatus tends to monopolize the top tier, demanding participation in formal political institutions and adherence to formal procedural requirements in exchange for legitimation. This price may be demanded because of the public sanctity and seeming permanence thereby officially conferred. Thus there is a ceaseless struggle to climb the ladder of legitimacy and claim the legitimacy of formal office, publicity, and procedural legality. Descending the ladder of legitimacy, one moves simultaneously from the formal to the informal realm. In the capitalist democracies, state fundraising has been formalized in elaborate tax codes and administrative hierarchies, for example, whereas party budgets, being managed by informal groups, are typically more casual, even marginally corrupt, in both their debits and credits.

In all East Asian democracies, elaborate informal arrangements are made to make it possible for supporters to funnel money to their political patrons without infracting formal rules, such as the "assumed name" system of campaign financing in South Korea[23] (recently illegalized) or the gift of appreciable stock options or real estate in both South Korea and Japan. In Japan, a successful politician needs not one but two *koenkai*, or personal machines: one in the capital, to raise money from large corporations, and one in the district, to spend money and render services to local constituents. In South Korea, contributions to the party can sometimes offset tax liabilities or buy off an imminent audit.[24] The fundraising issue has been a sensitive one in Taiwan politics mainly for the opposition parties (notably the Democratic Progressive Party), due to the munificent resources bequeathed to the KMT from the era of bureaucratic capitalism, which lend it an enormous advantage over its impecunious rivals; the KMT is, on the other hand, more vulnerable to scandal for improper political expenditures (e.g., vote-buying).[25] Despite its lack of a popular electoral

---

23 Chon, "Election process," p. 72. Koreans were permitted to hold assets (e.g., in a bank) under another name, making it difficult to trace the real owner of the asset. This is used to hide assets accumulated illegally, to avoid taxes, or to hold the majority share of public-held corporations for management control. Kim Young Sam successfully targeted the assumed name system in his August 1993 campaign reform, precipitating an 8% drop in the stock market index.

24 Chon, "Election process," *supra*, pp. 71–72.

25 See Tun-jen Cheng and Tein-cheng Chou, "Legislative factions in Taiwan: A preliminary analysis," *supra*, pp. 58–59. "Money politics" is certainly a focal point in recent local factional politics, with some concern lest it move up to the provincial/municipal or even the national level (personal communication from Peter Lee).

market, the issue of political budget control has also become problematic for the CCP, which permitted among its reforms the devolution of responsibility for enterprises not only to subordinate departments or government levels but even in some cases to individual cadres (or members of their families), who could then put their access to government commodity flows and administrative prices to commercial advantage. At least this was the case until the late 1980s, when the suspension of such activities by cadres or their families pushed them from the realm of the informal to that of the corrupt, resulting inter alia in the 1995 scandal that brought down Beijing Mayor Chen Xitong (the line between cadre and government property even yet remains blurred, and the suspension has since been lifted).

In all of these systems, even those in which informal politics is given relatively wide latitude, the light of publicity tends to alter the rules of the game. Although one might expect the threat of public exposure to be peculiar to modern democracies, China's Cultural Revolution and its June 1989 protests demonstrate that this is not entirely true. We may thus distinguish between routine informal politics, conducted in a confidential, businesslike manner, and crisis politics, caught in the limelight of public scrutiny. The former would include, for example, the Japanese Diet member's procurement of public works projects and other "pork" for his/her constituency or the selection of a new cabinet by faction leaders following an election. Crisis politics differs from routine pork barrel in at least two ways: First, there is an escalation from conventional to extraordinary political goals; and, second, there is a mobilization of outside constituences, either due to the defection of dissident members from the informal circle to mobilize additional support or because outside media penetrate elite circles and expose the issue. The escalation of goals results in trivial disputes becoming divisive ideological issues. The PRC's most celebrated crisis was precipitated by Mao's desire to launch a "cultural revolution," which was greeted with such well-contained enthusiasm by his colleagues that Mao himself defected to mobilize the Red Guards to target those who opposed him, raising this formerly unexciting issue to the level of principle. Some of the other cleavages that then emerged were truly trivial, such as the latent rivalry between leading cadres' spouses. Japan's factions have maintained tighter discipline and scandals and hence await penetration by outside media, although one may surmise that such excesses as Tanaka's unprecedented amassing of informal power helped precipitate the 1976 Lockheed scandal (after which he nonetheless managed to expand his faction, or *gundan*, by some 50 percent and pick the next two prime ministers).

Due to the monopolization of the legitimate policy process by the formal apparatus, the purpose of routine informal politics tends to be limited to the acquisition of power, "pork," and patronage – although politicians caught in the glare of crisis politics may need to rationalize their case in loftier rhetoric. One Japanese *koenkai* or electoral *keiretsu* is not easily disinguishable from another in terms of policy or ideology. If a political patron changes his or her tack on policy, the faction shifts with him or her as a matter of course; there is no known instance of a faction member resigning or switching patrons as a matter of "principle" after, say, a defining vote. With the important proviso that it is organized on a personal rather than an impersonal basis, the faction is as cohesive and stable as the party; if a faction chief changes parties, his/her *koenkai* comes in tow. The major Japanese factions antedated the 1955 establishment of the LDP as separate parties (viz., the prewar Seiyukai and Minseito) and again in the 1993 party realignment, when Ozawa, Hosokawa, and other faction leaders split from the LDP, their factions formed the core of the new miniparties. In Vietnam, Pike writes that Confucian inhibitions on political egoism make for factions that are clandestine, amorphous, impersonal, and issue-oriented,[26] while in China the stress on ideology as the basis for legitimation has led to a stronger emphasis on ideological differences among factions.[27] Yet despite our very limited knowledge about the range of issues explored in the "black box" of intraelite policy discussions, there is reason to doubt to what extent policy or ideology constitutes the actual basis of factional alignments:[28] (1) Ideological or policy "line" differences are seldom visible until after a faction is purged and scapegoated; (2) instead of defending the alleged differences ("standing on principle"), the losing faction leader typically denies any breach and professes loyalty to the party and its leaders; (3) after the conflict is resolved, most members of the defeated faction, sometimes including former leaders, will usually be reabsorbed into the leadership (e.g., just as Deng Xiaoping recovered from his 1976 purge by reuniting with the victors the following year, Hu Qili survived Zhao Ziyang's purge in 1989, albeit in a reduced position). In sum, a policy "line" seems to be neither a necessary nor a sufficient condition for a faction: There may be policy lines without factional organization, and there may be factions without "lines."

This is by no means to say that factional organization has no impact on the policy process. First, as noted above, during crisis politics factions may

---

26 Douglas Pike, "Informal Politics in Vietnam," pp. 283–284.

27 Strictly speaking, a factional grouping with a distinct policy or ideological orientation is referred to as a "line" and is regarded as more reprehensible than a simple faction. Thus, in the revolutionary era the "ten great line struggles" triggered sweeping purges and went into the literature as defining moments in the evolution of Marxism-Leninism Mao Zedong thought.

28 Deng Xiaoping has emphatically denied that the Cultural Revolution involved a "line struggle" between the "proletarian revolutionary headquarters/line/road" led by Mao and the "bourgeois reactionary line" (etc.) led by Liu and Deng or even that the purge of Gao Gang and Rao Shushi involved "line" differences. While Deng's testimony on his own case may involve a conflict of interest, his comments on Gao–Rao must be taken seriously, as he played a key role in their purge.

raise issues to a higher level of public awareness, resulting in important policy shifts or factional realignments. Factional purges may be used as an effective pedagogic and mobilizational device regardless of whether the victims
in fact backed the policies for which they are being blamed, as Mao clearly
demonstrated in both theory and practice. Factions may also be used to concert support for specific policies, either because assigned to do so or to advance
their own interests; for example, Yasheng Huang shows how local leaders
manage to steer investments into projects designed to enhance the prestige
of their locality and then bask in the reflected glory.[29] If a patron thereby
wins a promotion based on this type of trophy achievement, the assumption
is that the entire entourage will benefit. Ostrov shows how the patron–client
network assembled by Nie Rongzhen fruitfully cooperated in the achievement of one of the sterling achievements of Chinese technology – the unexpectedly swift creation of nuclear weapons – and were ultimately rewarded.
Moreover, a compatible policy "line" position may provide suitable cover for
posthumous factional mergers. In the democratic systems, too, a compatible
policy orientation helps to rationalize broad factional realignments, as in the
1955 settlement that led to the formation of the Japanese Socialist Party in
mid-October and then fused the Liberal and Democratic parties into the LDP
in mid-November. The other side of the coin is that ideological or policy contradictions may lead to factional splits, as in the polarization between the
dominant United Caucus Clique (UCC) and the "liberal" CC Clique (CCC)
in the Kuomintang faction of Taiwan's Legislative Yuan,[30] or the cleavage
between KMT mainstream and antimainstream factions over the issue of
China policy in Taiwan's March 1996 presidential election, or the secession
of the Taiwan Independence Party (TIP) from the DPP the following year
over essentially the same issue.

CONCLUSION

From our comparison of cases stemming from a shared Confucian cultural
background and diverging into an array of industrialized, newly industrialized, and less developed democracies and dictatorships, we may certainly infer
that economic modernization does not necessarily result in the complete
rationalization or formalization of informal politics. Nor does democratization and the legalization of opposition parties eliminate factionalism. Informal politics remains alive and well in each of these systems – rumors of its

29 Cf. Yasheng Huang, "Bureaucratic incentives and behavior in China during the reform era," unpub-
    lished parer presented at conference on Informal Politics in East Asia, Chinese University of Hong
    Kong, August 17–18, 1992.
30 Cheng and Chou, "Legislative factions," *op cit.*

demise in the course of modernization are premature. It seems to be most salient at the margins or lacunae of the formal system, surging during systemic crises (e.g., the Cultural Revolution), succession struggle, or intraparty conflict. Informal politics specializes in the nonauthoritative production and distribution of political values that are in such short supply that they are not readily accessible via markets or formally licensed political rationing, short-circuiting clogged procedural channels via sentiment, connections, and "gifts." By thus "filling in the cracks," informal politics reveals and bridges shortcomings in the formal system; by basing itself on prepolitical ties and sentiments and the allocation of apolitical incentives, it broadens and deepens the political realm. At the heart of informal politics is power, and legitimacy is its Achilles' heel, but it can provide a sort of nonideological substitute for legitimacy based purely on getting things done, "black cat or white cat."

What of the future? There have been basically two different formal responses to the perceived threat of informal politics: suppression and marketization. Both pose a serious challenge, the former by driving it from public view through prohibition and shaming, and the latter by replacing long-term primary bonds with monetarily purchasable services. Although these are pure types that are in practice mixed, generally speaking we may say that the moralistic solution was preferred by Park Chung Yee, Mao Zedong, and Chiang Kai-shek, while marketization has been the option of choice in postwar Japan, post-Mao China, South Korea since Chun Doo Hwan, and post-Chiang Taiwan. The overall trend, which is clearly visible even though our cases are staggered in their development, is from suppression to marketization. The response of informal politics to suppression has been to go underground and operate more discreetly; the response to the market, in those systems in which markets have been most fully fledged, is "money politics." Early returns from reform China suggest that the costs of marketization may include at least a short-term upsurge in corruption – money politics without ballots.

Yet closer consideration of Japan, the East Asian system with the longest cumulative experience with both economic and political markets, suggests that informal politics may survive money politics as it survived suppression – by adapting. In a sense, one might say that markets are neutral, simply providing an objective currency to index the value of political loyalty. But in an insidious way, putting a price on loyalty also subverts its intrinsic meaning and personal specificity by making it freely exchangeable. The resulting tendency has been to "reduce" political markets to their monetary equivalents (making money markets the most "basic") and to bid up the price of a now elusive loyalty (*qua* votes) when competition and uncertainty drive up the demand for them. A discount on tour fares, small tea parties – hardly munificent bribes – but on a mass scale the cost of such services adds up: Japan's elections have become the most expensive in the world, with Taiwan's and South Korea's only slightly behind (in per-capita terms). The competitive demand for constituency support, however, also inflates the bargaining leverage of the client or voter in the transaction. Voters may use the threat of disloyalty to enhance their claims to "pork" or other benefits, particularly in closely contested elections. Thus, while all of the East Asian systems have informal politics and factional politics at the elite level, only in the democracies has it become fully rationalized and systematized at the mass level, with full-time professional local machines (*koenkai* and *keiretsu* in Japan, *huwonhoi* and *sajojics* in South Korea, *houyuanhui* in Taiwan) to raise funds and expend them for constituency services.

By comparing this phased array of cases as if they were predictable stages in a developmental sequence, it becomes possible hypothetically to extrapolate the future of informal politics, at least within the East Asian cultural ecumene. Economic and political marketization seems to imply the following changes.

First, there is a shift from implicit and conspiratorial to more open and public informal activity. The CCP still officially denies the existence of factions within its ranks, the KMT no longer bothers to deny it, while in Japan they have reached their highest level of visibility with the exact identity of faction chiefs and their entourage a matter of common knowledge. Greater visibility has led to greater explicitness in media analyses of factional maneuvers and their chances for success, hence indirectly to greater subtlety and sophistication in informal strategy and tactics. Although the basic raison d'-étre of informal politics remains power and pork, the bright glare of publicity has made "crisis politics" an apt vehicle for periodic watershed issue cleavages and policy realignments.

Second, with greater public visibility the faction has become more institutionalized, capable, for example, of withstanding the death of its chief. Whereas the survival of the South Korean party still hangs on the electoral fortunes of its chief standard bearer and Mao's designated successor proved unable to cash in his deathbed endorsement, Japanese factions routinely pass intact from generation to generation. Greater institutionalization entails a more fully ramified network, extending from national to local levels. The logical outcome of the process of factional institutionalization is formal parties, although this also depends on electoral viability and a no doubt lengthy fermentation period.

Third, there appears to be a shift from passionate, consummatory factional disputes resulting in violence or even death to progressively more civil means of settling differences. China has made visible progress from the suicide of Gao Gang and the imprisonment of Rao Shushi in the 1950s and the violent deaths of Liu Shaoqi and Lin Biao in the Cultural Revolution to the 1980 trial (however flawed as a juridical showpiece) of the "Gang of Four" and the mere demotion of Hua Guofeng to a low-ranking seat on the Central Committee or the retirement of Zhao Ziyang to the golf course. The fact that the Japanese Diet once also witnessed violent outbursts among its members may be an encouraging precedent for the still volatile National Assembly in Taiwan. A concomitant of this "civilization" of the political arena, one may hope, will be a shift from predominantly "dysfunctional" to predominantly "functional" informal politics.[31]

31 Cf. Peter Lee, "Informal politics of leadership succession in post-revolutionary China," *supra*, pp. 171–172.

GLOSSARY

Bao 报 [reciprocity]: The principles of *bao* in Chinese traditional culture govern relations among morally cultivated people and prescribe general rules applicable to all social interactions.

Chaebol: The large, family-owned industrial conglomerates in South Korea, similar to the prewar Japanese *zaibatsu*, that produce the major proportion of the nation's industrial output.

COSTIND: The PRC Commission in Charge of Science, Technology, and Industry for National Defense [*Guofang Kexue Jishu Gongye Weiyuanhui* 国防科学技术工业委员会, often abbreviated *Guofang Kehui* 国防科会], formed by the 1982 merger of the former NDIO and NDSTC (q.v.) with the Science and Technology Armaments Commission [*Kexue Jishu Zhuangbei Weiyuanhui* 科学技术装备委员会], this unit of the State Council is responsible to the premier and the Central Military Commission.

Danwei 单位 [unit]: The basic unit of society in the PRC, originally consisting of the former agricultural communes in the countryside and of various production enterprises [*qiye danwei* 企业单位] and nonproduction organizations [*shiye danwei* 实业单位], including schools, hospitals, and other nonprofit enterprises) in urban areas. These multifunctional organs provided comprehensive welfare needs and used a comprehensive set of personnel files [*dangan* 档案] to monitor their members, thereby exerting *danwei suoyouzhi* 单位所有制, or unit proprietary rights.

Dingti 顶替 [take the place of]: Former PRC employment rule whereby a retiring official or urban industrial worker could select his or her own replacement upon retirement, resulting in a hereditary job/office transfer. Though no longer legal, *dingti* has sometimes been replaced by the practice of inside recruitment [*neizhao* 内找, or internal search].

"Double" election: The 252 members of the upper house of Japan's bicameral parliament, the House of Councillors, serve a fixed six-year term, while the 500 members of the lower house, or House of Representatives (Diet), may serve a full term of four years. The Diet, however, may be dissolved by the cabinet virtually any time and is frequently dissolved at a time when an upper house election is upcoming, so that elections of both houses are held at once. A double election tends to have a higher voter turnout, which in turn tends to give an advantage to the Liberal Democratic Party, supported by mostly passive voters.

Enqing 恩情 [feeling of indebtedness]: In Chinese political culture this is the appropriate emotion [*qing* 情] governing patron–client relations, as the patron provides protection [*bao* 报] and favors [*en* 恩] to the client, who reciprocates with loyalty [*zhong* 忠] and gratitude.

Gong 公 [public]: The concept of the public in Chinese political culture wins even more moral approbation than in the West and is assumed to conflict with its antonym, private [*si* 私]; thus the *dawo* 大我 [big self], or in Confucianism the *junzi* 君子 [gentleman], identifies with the interests of the larger collectivity, whereas the *xiaowo* 小我 [small self] or *xiaoren* 小人 [small person, commoner] is exclusively preoccupied with individual self-interest [*li* 利].

Guanxi 关系 [connections]: Personal relationships, which although originally based on such "contact points" [*gongtongdian* 共同点] as marriage [*qundai guanxi* 裙带关系, or apron-string connections], old school ties, or shared bonding experiences, may also be "pulled" [i.e., *la guanxi* 拉关系] for utilitarian ends, such as political career advancement or business advantage. One's network of *guanxi* is referred to as a *guanxiwang* 关系网 [connection net].

Guohui Gongneng Gaige Hui 国会公能改革会 [Congressional Reform Coalition, or CRC]: This KMT legislative faction in Taiwan, most active in the 1989–1992 session, was comprised mostly of freshman legislators deliberately insulating themselves from factional conflict at the party center in order better to focus on legislation.

Heiretsu-sei: Literally a parallel system, the term refers to the Japanese Diet election system introduced in 1994 that combined a single-member district and a proportional representation system. The numbers of members elected under the respective systems were 300 and 200, making the two systems roughly "parallel," instead of one dominanting the other.

Huiguan 会馆 Chinese guild hall (literally "clubhouse"), usually owned by a trade or provincial association.

Jianshe Yanjiu Hui 建设研究会 [Constructive Policy Research Club, or CPRC]: KMT legislative faction, most active in the 1986–1989 and 1989–1992 sessions, composed mainly of legislators in need of renewing their terms. This faction was most forthcoming in working with senior legislators elected in 1947–1948.

Jisi hui 集思会 [Wisdom Coalition]: KMT legislative faction, most active in the 1989–1992 session, mainly composed of native Taiwanese legislators. It supported the mainstream leadership faction, but it failed to regenerate itself in the 1992 election. Many members of this now-defunct faction ascended to high positions in the party headquarters.

Jongchinhoi: Organization formed by large South Korean clans to promote their political interests.

Koenkai: Known as *koenkai* in Japan, *houyuanhui* in Taiwan, and *huwonhoi* in South Korea, this literally means a group to support someone, i.e., any group formed to support a particular candidate, specifically to win an election. Some consist of donors who help by making periodic contributions to a candidate's campaign coffer, but most consist of local constituents who help by committing their own votes to and soliciting other votes for the candidate. As a rule, the candidate's relatives and friends constitute his or her *koenkai*'s core membership.

Li 礼 [rites or propriety], not to be confused with *li* 利, self-interest: One of the cardinal Confucian virtues, the practice of proper ritual was thought necessary for moral behavior, also to be accompanied by the appropriate emotion 情 [*qing*]; together, propriety and right emotion constitute *renqing* 人情, "human feeling."

Nanxun 南巡 [Southern Voyage]: Historically associated with the Chinese winter migration to warmer climes, this term refers to Deng Xiaoping's trip to south China to rally support for rapid reform and economic growth in the winter of 1992.

NDIO: National Defense Industry Office [*Guofang Gongye Bangongshi* 国防工业办公室, often abbreviated *Guofang Gongban* 国防工办]: Unit of the Chinese State Council formally responsible for overseeing advanced weapons production, the NDIO came into being in the early 1960s and lasted until 1982.

NDSTC: Science and Technology Commission for National Defense [*Guofang Kexue Jishu Weiyuanhui* 国防科学技术委员会]: This unit, which existed from 1958 to 1982, was formally responsible for advanced weapons research and development, and oversaw the original development of the atomic and hydrogen bombs. The administrative distinctions between the NDSTC and the NDIO became blurred in the first half of the 1960s, and it subsequently also engaged in overseeing advanced weapons production. The NDSTC was originally a party unit under the Central Military Commission, but by the mid-1970s it had become a unit of the PLA proper.

Quanli 权力 [authority]: (Formal) political authority, which in PRC politics depends upon those colleagues or subordinates who can be expected in the event of conflict to support shared bureaucratic interests (unless intimidated by the stakes involved).

Sajojic: Private organization formed and funded by powerful South Korean politicians to defend and expand their power bases; larger, more formalized and better financed than the *huwonhoi*.

Shili 势力 [power]: Informal influence or power, which in PRC politics is usually realized through mobilization of an informal support network of trusted political associates.

Single Nontransferrable Vote (SNTV): An electoral system otherwise uncommon in national-level elections, in which each district elects more than one member of a legislature, while each voter has only one ballot to cast for a particular candidate and, if the candidate loses, that ballot may not be transferred to another candidate. More than 40 percent (104 of 252) of the members of Japan's upper house and nearly 80 percent (128 of 164) of those of Taiwan's legislative *yuan* are currently elected under such rules (though in Taiwan's case the districts are somewhat larger: 7–16 members vs. 3–5 in Japanese Diet elections), as were all members of the postwar Japanese Diet until 1993 and of Taiwan's legislature until 1992.

"Soft" factions: Factions that lack powerful leaders, permit overlapping and multiple memberships, practice and tolerate predatory recruitment of members, and cannot impose discipline and sanctions against uncooperative faction members.

Sungo Gwali Wiwonhoi: A government regulatory committee formed in the Republic of Korea to oversee all aspects of the electoral process.

Wenhua Geming Xiaozu 文化革命小组 [Cultural Revolution Small Group, or CRSG]: A quasi-formal group of radical literati and political activists, led by Mao's wife, Jiang Qing, and his former secretary Chen Boda, who led the radical forces during the opening phase of the Cultural Revolution (1966–1969), when the Red Guards had the most untrammeled freedom of maneuver and expression.

Xiao Jinku 小金库 [Small treasury]: An informal financial reserve sometimes kept by Chinese unit leaderships, the contents of which may be kept of the books made available for tax accounting.

Xin Guomindang Lianxian 新国民党联线 [New KMT Alliance, or NKA]: Most active in the 1989–1992 and 1992–1995 sessions, this KMT legislative faction consisted mainly of mainlander legislators and sided with the nonmainstream contingent of the KMT leadership. Most members bolted the party to form the core of the New Party in the summer of 1993.

Zhengzhi Jichu 政治基础 [Political base]: A prerequisite for survival in PRC inner-party politics, a political base consists of both a bureaucratic politician's mobilizable formal subordinates and colleagues and his or her informal network of connections [*guanxiwang*]. The support of base members depends on the chief's official stature and reputation for protecting/rewarding loyal followers.

Zhong 忠 [loyalty]: The Confucian concept of loyalty was absolute and usually personal, as in *sizhong* 私忠 [personal loyalty to the leader], though it could also be defined more abstractly, as in the notion of *gongzhong* 公忠 [loyalty to the public interest].

Zijiren 自己人 [literally, "self-persons"]: Members of a Chinese inner circle, consisting typically of a patron's close personal confidants (who may or may not be formal employees) and of course excluding *wairen* 外人, or outsiders.

INDEX

post-Weberian literature, 107
PR. *See* proportional representation
practice as the criterion for truth (China),
 174
Prasenjit Duara, 205
PRC. *See* People's Republic of China
pre-1973 Israel, 45
pre-1993 Japan, 45
pre-Andrew Jackson era, 43
prefectural *koenkai*, 299
Premier Hau Pei-tsun, 56, 60, 64
Premier of the State Council, 174, 181
premortem struggles, 132
premortem succession, 165
pre-Qin feudal era, 88
prereform era, 189
President Chun Doo Hwan, 73, 74
President Kim Young, 67, 68, 76, 78
President Lee, 55, 56, 60, 64, 65
president Lee Teng-hui, 55
President Park Chung Hee, 69, 70, 71, 74
President Roh, 67, 70, 71, 74, 76
presidential election, 69, 72, 74, 75, 76,
 79
presidential electoral college, 46
President Chun Doo Whan, 67, 71
Presidium, 240, 246, 249, 257, 263
primary bond, 300
primus inter pares, 297
princelings' party, 122, 200, 212
principled particularism, 187
private entrepreneurs, 187
professionalism, 216
proportional representation, 30, 35, 36, 38,
 42
psychocultural foundation, 86
psychocultural insecurity, 114
psychocultural security drives, 110
purge in 1989, 304; *see also* Tiananmen
purpose-rational relationships, 116, 136
Pye, Lucian, 110, 111, 114, 136, 279, 270,
 271
Pyongmindang, 296
Pyongyang, 237, 239, 240, 241, 243, 244,
 246, 247, 248, 255, 258, 259, 264,
 265, 266

Qian Qichen, 125
Qian Sanqiang, 227, 232

Qian Xuesen, 219, 220, 227, 228, 229,
 232, 300
Qiao Shi, 111, 114, 125, 128, 135
Qin Dynasty, 88, 94
qing (emotion or affect), 91, 100, 101
Qinghai, 222
qingnian tuan (Youth League faction), 296
qinxin (private and close confidants, 96, 97,
 98
Qiu Huizuo, 128
qiye (enterprise), 188, 198, 211
quanli (official power), 116

R&D, 215, 220, 221
radical reform, 301
Radio Fukushima, 25
raison d'être, 292, 307
Rajin-Sonbong Free Economic and Trade
 Zone, 264
Rajin-Sonbong Zone International Business
 and Investment Forum, 265
Rao Shushi, 109, 132
Red Army, 185, 206
 Fighting Team, 224
Red Guards, 109, 111, 133, 222, 223, 226,
 303
reform era, 166, 171, 175
Regulatory Agency for Elections, 69, 77, 80
Ren Bishi, 173
renji guanxi (human relations), 194
Renovation Club, 55, 47
Renqing (human emotion), 98
renren weiqin (selecting people by familial or
 lineage), 199
Republic of China, 87
Resolution on the Guideline of
 Construction of Socialist Spiritual
 Civilization (China), 177
retirement ordinance, 54
retirement policy, 176, 179
Returned Students, 112, 134
 leadership, 112
reversal of verdicts, 175
revolutionary veterans (China), 297
Rodong Sinmun, 258
Roh Tae Woo, 67, 70, 74, 76
Roh Tae Wu, 292
ROK (Republic of Korea), 292
Roman Republic, 218